THE MACARTHUR NEW TESTAMENT COMMENTARY

REVELATION 1-11

John MacArthur, Jr.

MOODY PRESS/CHICAGO

ISBN: 0-8024-0773-0

1 3 5 7 9 10 8 6 4 2

Printed in the United States of America

To my mother, Irene MacArthur,
who this year joined the chorus of heavenly worshipers.

Contents

Preface

It continues to be a rewarding, divine communion for me to preach expositionally through the New Testament. My goal is always to have deep fellowship with the Lord in the understanding of His Word and out of that experience to explain to His people what a passage means. In the words of Nehemiah 8:8, I strive "to give the sense" of it so they may truly hear God speak and, in so doing, may respond to Him.

Obviously, God's people need to understand Him, which demands knowing His Word of truth (2 Tim. 2:15) and allowing that Word to dwell in them richly (Col. 3:16). The dominant thrust of my ministry, therefore, is to help make God's living Word alive to His people. It is a refreshing adventure.

This New Testament commentary series reflects this objective of explaining and applying Scripture. Some commentaries are primarily linguistic, others are mostly theological, and some are mainly homiletical. This one is basically explanatory, or expository. It is not linguistically technical but deals with linguistics when that seems helpful to proper interpretation. It is not theologically expansive but focuses on the major doctrines in each text and how they relate to the whole of Scripture. It is not primarily homiletical, although each unit of thought is generally treated as one chapter, with a clear outline and logical flow of thought.

Most truths are illustrated and applied with other Scripture. After establishing the context of a passage, I have tried to follow closely the writer's
development and reasoning.

My prayer is that each reader will fully understand what the Holy
Spirit is saying through this part of His Word, so that His revelation may
lodge in the mind of believers and bring greater obedience and faithfulness—to the glory of our great God.

Introduction

The late British prime minister Winston Churchill once described the former Soviet Union as "a riddle wrapped in a mystery inside an enigma." Many Christians view the book of Revelation in much the same way. Bewildered by its mystifying symbolism and striking imagery, many believers (including some pastors, who never preach through Revelation) avoid serious study of the book. Even John Calvin, the greatest commentator of the Reformation, who wrote commentaries on the other books, did not attempt to write a commentary on Revelation. Such shortsightedness deprives believers of the blessings the book promises to those who diligently read it (1:3; 22:7).

Those who ignore Revelation deprive themselves of a rich treasure of divine truth. Revelation takes a high view of God's inspired Word. It claims divine inspiration for itself (1:2), and it has been estimated that 278 of its 404 verses allude to the inspired Old Testament Scriptures. Revelation reveals God the Father in all His glory and majesty, describing Him as holy (4:8), true (6:10), omnipotent (4:11), wise (7:12), sovereign (4:11), and eternal (4:10). Revelation details the depths of man's depravity. Despite experiencing the final outpouring of God's devastating wrath and judgment on sinful mankind, people will nevertheless harden their hearts (like Pharaoh before them; 1 Sam. 6:6) and refuse to repent (9:20–21; 16:9, 11). Scripture contains no clearer summation of the doctrine of redemption than that of Revelation 1:5, which declares that "Jesus Christ … loves us and released us from our sins by His blood." The ministry of angels also figures prominently in Revelation, which contains one out of every four references to angels in Scripture. Revelation warns the church of the dangers of sin and compromise with the world (chaps. 2–3), and teaches it how to properly worship God (chaps. 4–5).

Some who study Revelation do so seeking evidence to support their own (often bizarre or sensational) eschatological views. But they miss the point. Revelation *is* a rich source of truth about eschatology; in fact, it contains more details about the end times than any other book of the Bible. Revelation portrays Christ's ultimate triumph over Satan, depicts the final political setup of the world system, and describes the career of the most powerful dictator in human history, the final Antichrist. It also mentions the Rapture of the church (3:10), and describes the seven-year time of Tribulation, including the three and one-half years of the Great Tribulation (7:14; cf. Matt. 24:21), the second coming of Christ, the climactic battle of human history (Armageddon), the thousand-year earthly kingdom of Jesus Christ, the final judgment of unrepentant sinners (the Great White Throne judgment), and the final state of the wicked in hell (the lake of fire) and the redeemed in the new heaven and new earth.

But the book of Revelation is preeminently the "Revelation of Jesus Christ" (1:1). It describes Him by many titles, including "the faithful witness" (1:5); "the firstborn of the dead" (1:5); "the ruler of the kings of the earth" (1:5); "the Alpha and the Omega" (1:8; 21:6); "the first and the last" (1:17); "the living One" (1:18); "the One who holds the seven stars in His right hand, the One who walks among the seven golden lampstands" (2:1); "the One who has the sharp two-edged sword" (2:12); "the Son of God" (2:18); the One "who has eyes like a flame of fire, and … feet … like burnished bronze" (2:18); the One "who has the seven Spirits of God and the seven stars" (3:1); the One "who is holy, who is true" (3:7); the holder of "the key of David, who opens and no one will shut, and who shuts and no one opens" (3:7); "the Amen, the faithful and true Witness" (3:14); "the Beginning of the creation of God" (3:14); "the Lion that is from the tribe of Judah" (5:5); "the Root of David" (5:5); the Lamb of God (e.g., 5:6; 6:1; 7:9–10; 8:1; 12:11; 13:8; 14:1; 15:3; 17:14; 19:7; 21:9; 22:1); the "Lord, holy and true" (6:10); the One who "is called Faithful and True" (19:11); "The Word of God" (19:13); the "King of kings, and Lord of lords" (19:16); Christ (Messiah), ruling on earth with His glorified saints (20:6); and "Jesus … the root and the descendant of David, the bright morning star" (22:16).

Revelation also affirms the full deity of Jesus Christ. He possesses the attributes and prerogatives of God, including sovereignty (1:5), eternity (1:17–18), the right to judge men (19:11) and to decide who lives and who dies (1:18; 2:23). He also receives worship (5:13) and rules from God's throne (22:1, 3). Finally, Revelation affirms His equality of essence with God the Father by applying Old Testament passages that describe God to Jesus Christ (cf. Deut. 10:17 with 19:16; Prov. 3:12 with 3:19; Dan. 7:9 with 1:14; Isa. 44:6 with 1:17; also cf. 1:8 with 22:12–13).

Far from being the mysterious, incomprehensible book many imagine it to be, Revelation's purpose is to reveal truth, not to obscure it. That fact is evident in its title, "The Revelation of Jesus Christ" (1:1), primarily in His second coming glory. *Apokalupsis* ("Revelation") could be translated "an uncovering," "an unveiling," or "a disclosure." It is used in the New Testament to speak of revealing spiritual truth (Rom. 16:25; Gal. 1:12; Eph. 1:17; 3:3), the manifestation of the sons of God (Rom. 8:19), and of Christ's manifestation at both His first (Luke 2:32) and second (2 Thess. 1:7; 1 Pet. 1:7) comings. In each case, *apokalupsis* describes something (or someone) that was formerly hidden, but now becomes visible. Revelation unveils truths about Jesus Christ, and makes clear features of prophetic truth only hinted at in the Old Testament and other New Testament books. This clarity is often obscured by a rejection of the principles of literal interpretation in favor of an allegorical or spiritualizing hermeneutical method. Such approaches attempt to place Revelation's account in the past and present rather than the future. But once the plain meaning of the text is denied, an interpreter is left to his own imagination, and the truths of this book are lost in a maze of human inventions void of authenticity. See the further discussion of this matter under *Interpretation* below.

AUTHOR

Four times in Revelation the author identifies himself as John (1:1, 4, 9; 22:8). The early church unanimously (until the third century) affirmed that he was John the son of Zebedee, one of the twelve apostles and author of the fourth gospel and the epistles of John.

Writing early in the second century (possibly as early as A.D. 135) Justin Martyr declared, "There was a certain man with us, whose name was John, one of the apostles of Christ, who prophesied, by a revelation that was made to him, that those who believed in our Christ would dwell a thousand years in Jerusalem; and that thereafter the general, and, in short, the eternal resurrection and judgment of all men would likewise take place" (*Dialogue with Trypho,* chap. 81). Since Justin lived for a time in Ephesus, one of the seven churches to which Revelation was addressed, his testimony is especially significant.

Dating from about the same time as Justin (c. A.D. 100–150) is the Gnostic writing known as the *Apocryphon of John*. That document cites Revelation 1:19 and attributes it to John the brother of James and son of Zebedee (Robert H. Mounce, *The Book of Revelation*, The New International Commentary on the New Testament [Grand Rapids: Eerdmans, 1977], 28).

Another second-century affirmation that the apostle John penned Revelation comes from Irenaeus, who introduced a string of quotations from Revelation with the statement "John also, the Lord's disciple, when beholding the sacerdotal and glorious advent of His kingdom, says in the Apocalypse" (*Against Heresies*, 4.20.11). Later in that same work he added, "And if any one will devote a close attention to those things which are stated by the prophets with regard to the time of the end, and those which John the disciple of the Lord saw in the Apocalypse, he will find that the nations are to receive the same plagues universally, as Egypt then did particularly" (*Against Heresies*, 4.30.4). Irenaeus's testimony is valuable because he was a native of Smyrna, another of the seven churches to whom John addressed Revelation. Also, as a boy Irenaeus had been a disciple of Polycarp, who in turn had been a disciple of the apostle John.

Also writing in the second century, Clement of Alexandria noted that it was John the apostle who had been in exile on Patmos (*Who Is the Rich Man That Shall Be Saved?*, 42). Obviously, it was the John who had been exiled to Patmos who penned Revelation (1:9).

Writing late in the second century or early in the third century, Tertullian declared, "But we do confess that a kingdom is promised to us upon the earth, although before heaven, only in another state of existence; inasmuch as it will be after the resurrection for a thousand years in the divinely-built city of Jerusalem, 'let down from heaven,' which the apostle also calls 'our mother from above;' [cf. Gal. 4:26]...This both Ezekiel had knowledge of and the Apostle John beheld [cf. Rev. 21:2]" (*Against Marcion*, 3.24).

Other early testimony to the apostle John's authorship of Revelation comes from Origen (*De Principiis*, 1.2.10; cf. 1.2.7), Hippolytus (*Treatise on Christ and Antichrist*, 36), and Victorinus, author of a third-century commentary on Revelation (in his comments on Rev. 10:3).

Such strong, early, and consistent testimony to the apostle John's authorship affirms the book's internal claims (1:1, 4, 9; 22:8) and cannot easily be set aside. The testimony of Justin and Irenaeus is especially significant, since they lived in Ephesus and Smyrna when some of Revelation's original readers would still have been alive. That the church could have been mistaken about who wrote Revelation virtually from the time it was written is inconceivable.

It was not until the second half of the third century that Dionysius, the bishop (overseer, pastor) of the church in Alexandria, seriously questioned John the apostle's authorship of Revelation. Concerned that some were teaching that there will be a literal earthly millennium (which he rejected), Dionysius attempted to discredit that teaching by denying that John wrote Revelation. (Since Dionysius accepted Revelation as inspired and part of the canon of Scripture, it is not clear what he hoped to gain by denying that the apostle John was its author.) His arguments against apostolic authorship rested primarily on the difference in style and vocabulary between the gospel of John and the Johannine epistles (which Dionysius believed John the apostle to have written) and Revelation. Those arguments are the same ones used today by those who deny that the apostle John wrote Revelation (see the discussion of this point below). As to who did write Revelation, Dionysius could only speculate that there were two Johns in Ephesus when Revelation was written. All that he could offer in support of that hypothesis, however, was the hearsay evidence that "they say that there are two monuments [tombs] at Ephesus, and that each bears the name of John" (cited in Eusebius, *Ecclesiastical History,* 7.25). Donald Guthrie comments:

> Dionysius' alternative suggestion does not inspire confidence, for his "second John" has remarkably flimsy testimony to his existence. It is strange that such a scholar as Dionysius should give credence to a traveller's tale about the two tombs of John in Ephesus without entertaining the possibility that the rival tomb may be due to some local opportunist, after the pattern of the extraordinary multiplication of relics in subsequent history. In any case, Dionysius' inference that there may have been two Johns is an interpretation of the tale which seems to have been drawn out by his critical dilemma. If John the apostle was not the writer there must have been two Johns at Ephesus and the tale could, therefore, be made to do service in support. In this Dionysius foreshadowed, as a man born before his due time, those modern schools of criticism which have peopled early Christian history with a whole army of unknown writers, whose works attained as great a prominence as their authors obtained obscurity. (*New Testament Introduction,* rev. ed. [Downers Grove, Ill: InterVarsity, 1990], 934–35)

Seizing on Dionysius's theory that a John other than the apostle wrote Revelation, the church historian Eusebius put forth the thesis that Revelation was actually written by a "John the Elder" (*Ecclesiastical History,* 3.39). The existence of that shadowy figure rests entirely on a much-disputed statement attributed by Eusebius to Papias, who, like Polycarp, was a disciple of the apostle John. Eusebius quotes Papias as saying, "If, then, anyone who had attended on the elders came, I asked minutely after their sayings,—what Andrew or Peter said, or what was said by Philip, or by Thomas, or by James, or by John, or by Matthew, or by any other of the Lord's disciples: which things Aristion and the presbyter [elder] John, the disciples of the Lord, say" (*Exposition of the Oracles of the Lord,* 1).

It is doubtful, however, that Papias had two different Johns in mind. He mentions John again with Aristion because they were still alive (as the present tense verb "say" indicates). He repeats the word "presbyter" before naming John again to show that he is referring to the John he had previously described as one of the elders [presbyters]. R.C.H. Lenski notes:

> At the second mention of John, Papias carefully repeats the term, "*the presbyter* John," to show beyond question that he has in mind the John listed among the seven whom he has just called "the presbyters"; for if in this second instance he had written only "John," the reader might take this to be a different John from the one mentioned in the list of seven termed "the presbyters." Papias makes certain that we think of the same man when "the presbyter John is mentioned," one of the seven presbyters he has just named. (*The Interpretation of St. John's Revelation* [Minneapolis: Augsburg, 1943], 9)

Even if it could be proven that Papias spoke of two Johns, that would not prove that "John the Elder" wrote Revelation. It is unlikely that two such prominent men named John lived at Ephesus at the same time. Beyond all that speculation, the writer of Revelation simply identifies himself as "John," implying that he was so well-known to his readers that no further identification was necessary. Nor is it likely that the church was mistaken virtually from the time Revelation was written as to its author. Justin Martyr and Irenaeus, as noted above, were in a position to have known some of Revelation's original readers, making such a case of mistaken identity extremely improbable.

The differences in style between Revelation and John's other inspired writings noted by Dionysius still form the main line of argument for those who deny that the apostle wrote Revelation. While those differences do exist, because the nature of the material is so different, they are not significant enough to prove that the apostle John could not have written Revelation. Some of those differences can also, as noted above, be explained by the different literary style of Revelation. And it is also possible that John used an amanuensis (secretary) when he wrote the gospel and the epistles (as Paul did; Rom. 16:22)—something he could not have done while writing Revelation in exile on Patmos.

Despite the differences, there are striking parallels between Revelation and the apostle John's other writings. Only the gospel of John and Revelation refer to Christ as the Word (John 1:1; Rev. 19:13). Revelation frequently describes Christ as the Lamb—a title elsewhere given to Him only in John's gospel. Both the gospel of John and Revelation refer to Jesus as a witness (John 5:31–32; Rev. 1:5). Revelation 1:7 and John 19:37 quote Zechariah 12:10 differently from the Septuagint (the Greek translation of the Old Testament) but in agreement with each other. (For further examples of the similarities between Revelation and John's other writings, see Robert L. Thomas, *Revelation 1–7, An Exegetical Commentary* [Chicago: Moody, 1992], 11ff.; Henry Barclay Swete, *Commentary on Revelation* [Reprint, Grand Rapids: Kregel, 1977], cxxvi–cxxx; Leon Morris, *The Revelation of St. John,* The Tyndale New Testament Commentaries [Grand Rapids: Eerdmans, 1969], 30.) Commenting on the similarities between Revelation and John's other writings, Guthrie writes, "It should be noted, incidentally, that in spite of linguistic and grammatical differences the Apocalypse has a closer affinity to the Greek of the other Johannine books than to any other New Testament books" (*New Testament Introduction,* 940).

The arguments of some ancient and modern critics notwithstanding, the traditional view that the apostle John was the John identified as the inspired author of Revelation best fits the evidence. The strong testimony of the church almost from the time Revelation was written, the similarities between Revelation and John's other writings, the absence of any credible alternative author, and the improbability that two prominent men named John lived at the same time in Ephesus argue convincingly for apostolic authorship.

The circumstances under which John wrote Revelation are discussed in chapter 3 of this volume. The seven churches, to which the apostle addressed the book, are described in detail in chapters 4–10.

DATE

Two main alternatives have been proposed for the date of Revelation: during either the reign of Nero (c. A.D. 68), or that of Domitian (c. A.D. 96). The earlier date is held primarily by some who adopt the preterist interpretation of Revelation (see *Interpretation* below). It is based largely on questionable exegesis of several passages in the book and attempts to relegate its prophetic fulfillment entirely to the period before the destruction of Jerusalem in A.D. 70. Those who hold to the early date see in Jerusalem's destruction the prophesied second coming of Jesus Christ in its first phase. External evidence for the earlier (Neronian) date is almost nonexistent.

On the other hand, the view that the apostle John penned Revelation near the end of Domitian's reign was widely held in the early church. The second-century church father Irenaeus wrote, "We will not, however, incur the risk of pronouncing positively as to the name of Antichrist; for if it were necessary that his name should be distinctly revealed in this present time, it would have been announced by him who beheld the apocalyptic vision [the book of Revelation]. For that was seen no very long time since, but almost in our day, towards the end of Domitian's reign" (*Against Heresies,* 5.30.3). The church fathers Clement of Alexandria, Origen, Victorinus, Eusebius, and Jerome also affirm that Revelation was written during Domitian's reign (cf. Mounce, *Revelation,* 32; Swete, *Commentary on Revelation,* xcix–c). The testimony of the early church that Revelation was written during Domitian's reign is difficult to explain if it was actually written during Nero's reign.

Revelation was written during a time when the church was undergoing persecution. John had been exiled to Patmos, at least one believer had already suffered martyrdom (2:13), and more persecution loomed on the horizon (2:10). The extent of the persecution under Domitian appears to have been more widespread than that under Nero, which was largely confined to the city of Rome. Thus, the persecution of Christians referred to in Revelation fits better with a date during Domitian's reign.

The condition of the seven churches to whom John addressed Revelation also argues for the later date. As seen in Ephesians, Colossians, and 1 and 2 Timothy, those churches were spiritually healthy as of the mid-sixties, when Paul last ministered in that region. But by the time Revelation was written, those churches had suffered serious spiritual decline. Ephesus had left its first love, and most of the rest had been infiltrated by false doctrine and sin. Such a decline would have taken longer than the brief period between the end of Paul's ministry in Asia Minor and the end of Nero's reign. In a similar vein, some have argued that the lack of any mention of Paul in the letters to the seven churches implies an interval of at least a generation between his death and the writing of Revelation (Guthrie, *New Testament Introduction,* 954 n. 1).

Paul nowhere mentions the heretical sect known as the Nicolaitans that plagued the churches at Ephesus and Pergamum (2:6, 15). But by the time of Revelation the sect had become so notorious that John could simply name it; the Nicolaitans were evidently so well-known to his readers that no description was necessary. That again implies a long time gap between the time of Paul and the time Revelation was written.

Laodicea, one of the seven churches, was devastated by an earthquake about A.D. 60. For the rest of Nero's reign, the city was involved in reconstruction, and could hardly be considered "rich . . . wealthy" and having "need of nothing" (3:17). A date during Domitian's reign would allow time for Laodicea to regain its wealth.

There is evidence that the church at Smyrna was not founded until after Paul's death (about A.D. 67 [Guthrie, *New Testament Introduction*, 954]). It could hardly have begun, grown to maturity, and declined in the brief interval between the apostle's death and the end of Nero's reign at about the same time.

A final reason for preferring the late (A.D. 95–96) date for Revelation is the timing of John's arrival in Asia Minor. According to tradition, John did not leave Palestine for Asia Minor until the time of the Jewish revolt against Rome (A.D. 66–70). Placing the writing of Revelation during Nero's reign would not allow sufficient time for John's ministry to have reached the point where the Romans would have felt the need to exile him (Thomas, *Revelation 1–7*, 22). G. R. Beasley-Murray notes that

> John's banishment as a Christian preacher . . . reflects a policy of active hostility on the part of the state towards the Church. It cannot be shown that such legal measures were taken by the state against Christians prior to the later years of Domitian. The Revelation reflects a situation in which the cult of the emperor was a contemporary force and was bidding to become world-wide. Nero's persecution had nothing to do with this issue. (*The Book of Revelation*, The New Century Bible [London: Oliphants, 1974], 38)

The weight of the evidence clearly favors a date for the writing of Revelation in the mid-nineties, near the end of Domitian's reign. This is critically important, because it eliminates the possibility that the prophecies in Revelation were fulfilled in the destruction of Jerusalem in A.D. 70.

INTERPRETATION

Revelation's picturesque images, mysterious symbols, and apocalyptic language make it one of the most challenging books in Scripture to interpret. There are four main interpretative approaches to the book.

The *preterist* approach views Revelation not as future, predictive prophecy, but as a historical record of events in the first-century Roman Empire. The preterist view thus ignores the book's own claims to be a prophecy (1:3; 22:7, 10, 18–19). Nor were all the events predicted and depicted in Revelation fulfilled in the first century. The second coming of Christ described in chapter 19 obviously is yet to occur. But the preterist view requires that one see the words about Christ's second coming as fulfilled in the destruction of the temple in A.D. 70, even though He did not appear on that occasion. Nor is there any persecution in the first century that fits the description of the horrific events depicted in chapters 6–19.

The *historicist* approach finds in Revelation a record of the sweep of church history from apostolic times until the present. Historicist interpreters often resort to allegorizing the text in order to find in it the various historical events they believe it depicts (e.g., the fall of Rome to the barbarians, the rise of the Roman Catholic Church, the advent of Islam, even the French Revolution). Not surprisingly, such a subjective, arbitrary, and whimsical approach has given rise to a myriad of conflicting interpretations of the actual historical events in Revelation. Like the preterist approach, the historicist view ignores Revelation's own claims to be a prophecy. It also robs the book of any meaning for those first-century believers to whom it was addressed. And it removes the interpretation of Revelation from the realm of literal, historical hermeneutics, leaving it at the mercy of the allegorical and spiritualized meanings invented by each would-be interpreter.

The *idealist* approach sees depicted in Revelation the timeless struggle between good and evil that is played out in every age. According to this view Revelation is neither a historical record nor a predictive prophecy. Like the first two views, the idealist view ignores Revelation's claims to be a prophecy. It also, if carried to its logical conclusion, severs Revelation from any connection with actual historical events. The book is thus reduced to a collection of myths designed to convey spiritual truth.

The *futurist* approach sees in chapters 4–22 predictions of people and events yet to come in the future. Only this approach allows Revelation to be interpreted following the same literal, grammatical-historical hermeneutical method by which non-prophetic portions of Scripture are interpreted. As previously noted, proponents of the other three approaches are frequently forced to resort to allegorizing or spiritualizing the text to sustain their interpretations. The futurist approach, in contrast to the other three, does full justice to Revelation's claim to be a prophecy. The futurist approach is often criticized as robbing Revelation of any meaning for those to whom it was written, since it views much of the book as describing events in the distant future. In reply John F. Walvoord notes:

> Much of the prophecy of the Bible deals with the distant future, including the Old Testament promises of the coming Messiah, the prophecies of Daniel concerning the future world empires, the body of truth relating to the coming kingdom on earth as well as countless other prophecies. If the events of chapters 4 through 19 are future, even from our viewpoint today, they teach the blessed truth of the ultimate supremacy of God and the triumph of righteousness. The immediate application of distant events is familiar in Scripture, as for instance II Peter 3:10–12, which speaks of the ultimate dissolution of the earth; nevertheless the

> succeeding passage makes an immediate application: "Wherefore, beloved, seeing that ye look for such things, be diligent . . ." (II Peter 3:14). (*The Revelation of Jesus Christ* [Chicago: Moody, 1966], 22)

Anything other than the futurist approach leaves the meaning of the book to human ingenuity and opinion. The futurist approach takes the book's meaning as God gave it. In studying Revelation, we will take this straightforward view and accept what the text says. It is nearly impossible to consider all the interpretive options offered by people holding the other three views, so we will not try to work through that maze of options. Rather, we will take the book as it comes in the normal fashion of language.

OUTLINE

I. The Things Which You Have Seen (1:1–20)

    A. The Prologue (1:1–8)
    B. The Vision of the Glorified Christ (1:9–18)
    C. John's Commission to Write (1:19–20)

II. The Things Which Are (2:1–3:22)

    A. The Letter to the Church at Ephesus (2:1–7)
    B. The Letter to the Church at Smyrna (2:8–11)
    C. The Letter to the Church at Pergamum (2:12–17)
    D. The Letter to the Church at Thyatira (2:18–29)
    E. The Letter to the Church at Sardis (3:1–6)
    F. The Letter to the Church at Philadelphia (3:7–13)
    G. The Letter to the Church at Laodicea (3:14–22)

III. The Things Which Will Take Place After This (4:1–22:21)

    A. Worship Before God's Heavenly Throne (4:1–5:14)
    B. The Tribulation (6:1–18:24)
    C. The Second Coming of the Lord Jesus Christ (19:1–21)
    D. The Millennium (20:1–10)
    E. The Great White Throne Judgment (20:11–15)
    F. The Eternal State (21:1–22:21)

Back to
the Future
(Revelation 1:1–6)

The Revelation of Jesus Christ, which God gave Him to show to His bond-servants, the things which must soon take place; and He sent and communicated it by His angel to His bond-servant John, who testified to the word of God and to the testimony of Jesus Christ, even to all that he saw. Blessed is he who reads and those who hear the words of the prophecy, and heed the things which are written in it; for the time is near. John to the seven churches that are in Asia: Grace to you and peace, from Him who is and who was and who is to come, and from the seven Spirits who are before His throne, and from Jesus Christ, the faithful witness, the firstborn of the dead, and the ruler of the kings of the earth. To Him who loves us and released us from our sins by His blood— and He has made us to be a kingdom, priests to His God and Father—to Him be the glory and the dominion forever and ever. Amen. (1:1–6)

Many people are fascinated, even obsessed with the future. They faithfully read their horoscopes, seek out Tarot card readers, have their palms read, feed on futuristic science fiction material, or call one of the many "psychic hot lines" advertised on TV. Some people delve more deeply into the occult, seeking out mediums (as did King Saul), futilely and sinfully attempting to obtain information about what is to come by "consult[ing] the dead on behalf of the living" (Isa. 8:19). The dead cannot, of course, respond to such efforts at contact, but demons do, masquerading as the dead and propagating lies.

All such attempts to discern the future, however, are in vain. There is only One who knows and declares the future: God (Isa. 44:7; 45:21; 46:9–10). Only in Scripture can truth about the future be found. The Old Testament prophets, particularly Isaiah, Ezekiel, Daniel, and Zechariah, provide glimpses of the future. So did our Lord in His Olivet Discourse, along with Peter and Paul in their inspired writings. But the book of Revelation provides the most detailed look into the future in all of Scripture. The fitting capstone of God's revelation to man in the Bible, the book of Revelation unveils the future history of the world, all the way to history's climax in the return of Christ and the setting up of His glorious earthly and eternal kingdom.

By way of introduction, John lists eleven characteristics of this marvelous book: its essential nature, central theme, divine source, human recipients, prophetic character, supernatural delivery, human author, promised blessing, compelling urgency, Trinitarian benediction, and exalted doxology.

ITS ESSENTIAL NATURE

The Revelation (1:1a)

These two words are essential to understanding this book. Many people are confused by the book of Revelation, viewing it as a mysterious, bizarre, indecipherable mystery. But nothing could be further from the truth. Far from *hiding* the truth, the book of Revelation *reveals* it. This is the last chapter in God's story of redemption. It tells how it all ends. As the account of the Creation in the beginning was not vague or obscure, but clear, so God has given a detailed and lucid record of the ending. It is unthinkable to believe that God would speak with precision and clarity from Genesis to Jude, and then when it comes to the end abandon all precision and clarity. Yet, many theologians today think Revelation is not the precise record of the end in spite of what it says. They also are convinced that its mysteries are so vague that the end is left in confusion. As we shall see in this commentary, this is a serious error that strips the saga of redemption of its climax as given by God.

Apokalupsis (**Revelation**) appears eighteen times in the New Testament, always, when used of a person, with the meaning "to become visible." In Luke 2:32, Simeon praised God for the infant Jesus, describing Him as "a Light of revelation to the Gentiles, and the glory of Your people Israel." Simeon exulted that the Messiah had been made visible to men. Paul spoke in Romans 8:19 of the manifest transformation of believers in glory as "the revealing of the sons of God." Both Paul (1 Cor. 1:7) and Peter (1 Pet. 1:7) used *apokalupsis* to refer to the revelation of Christ at His second coming.

The book of Revelation contains truths that had been concealed, but have now been revealed. Though it nowhere directly quotes the Old Testament, 278 of its 404 verses refer or allude to Old Testament prophetic truth, and it amplifies what was only initially suggested in the Old Testament.

The Apocalypse reveals a great many divine truths. It warns the church of the danger of sin and instructs it about the need for holiness. It reveals the strength Christ and believers have to overcome Satan. It reveals the glory and majesty of God and depicts the reverent worship that constantly attends His throne. The book of Revelation reveals the end of human history, including the final political setup of the world, the career of Antichrist, and the climactic Battle of Armageddon. It reveals the coming glory of Christ's earthly reign during the millennial kingdom, the Great White Throne judgment, and depicts the eternal bliss of the new heaven and the new earth. It reveals the ultimate victory of Jesus Christ over all human and demonic opposition. The book of Revelation describes the ultimate defeat of Satan and sin, and the final state of the wicked (eternal torment in hell) and the righteous (eternal joy in heaven). In short, it is a front-page story of the future of the world written by someone who has seen it all.

But supremely, overarching all those features, the book of Revelation reveals the majesty and glory of the Lord Jesus Christ. It describes in detail the events associated with His second coming, revealing His glory that will one day blaze forth as strikingly and unmistakably as lightning flashing in a darkened sky (Matt. 24:27).

ITS CENTRAL THEME

of Jesus Christ, (1:1b)

While all Scripture is revelation from God (2 Tim. 3:16), in a unique way the book of Revelation is *the* revelation—the revelation of Jesus Christ. While this book is certainly revelation *from* Jesus Christ (cf. 22:16), it is also the revelation *about* Him. The other New Testament uses of the phrase *apokalupsis Iēsou Christou* (**Revelation of Jesus Christ**) suggest that John's statement in this verse is best understood in the sense of revelation about Jesus Christ (cf. 1 Cor. 1:7; Gal. 1:12; 2 Thess. 1:7; 1 Pet. 1:7). The Gospels are also about Jesus Christ, but present Him in His first coming in humiliation; the book of Revelation presents Him in His second coming in exaltation. Every vision and description of Him in Revelation is one of majesty, power, and glory.

Christ's unveiling begins in 1:5–20, where He is revealed in His ascended majesty. Those verses also provide a preview of His second coming glory. In chapters 2 and 3, as exalted Lord of the church, He reproves and encourages His church. Finally, chapters 4–22 provide a detailed look at His second coming; the establishing of His millennial kingdom, during which He will personally reign on earth; and the ushering in of the eternal state.

W. A. Criswell, long-time pastor of the First Baptist Church of Dallas, gave the following explanation as to why Christ must yet be revealed in glory:

> The first time our Lord came into this world, He came in the veil of our flesh. His deity was covered over with His manhood. His Godhead was hidden by His humanity. Just once in a while did His deity shine through, as on the Mount of Transfiguration, or as in His miraculous works. But most of the time the glory, the majesty, the deity, the wonder and the marvel of the Son of God, the second person of the Holy Trinity, were veiled. These attributes were covered over in flesh, in our humanity. He was born in a stable. He grew up in poverty. He knew what it was to hunger and to thirst. He was buffeted and beaten and bruised. He was crucified and raised up as a felon before the scoffing gaze of the whole earth. The last time that this world saw Jesus was when it saw Him hanging in shame, misery and anguish upon the cross. He later appeared to a few of His believing disciples, but the last time that this unbelieving world ever saw Jesus was when it saw Him die as a malefactor, as a criminal, crucified on a Roman cross. That was a part of the plan of God, a part of the immeasurable, illimitable grace and love of our Lord. "By His stripes we are healed."

> But then is that all the world is ever to see of our Saviour—dying in shame on a cross? No! It is also a part of the plan of God that some day this unbelieving, this blaspheming, this godless world shall see the Son of God in His full character, in glory, in majesty, in the full-orbed wonder and marvel of His Godhead. Then all men shall look upon Him as He really is. They shall see Him holding in His hands the title-deed to the Universe, holding in His hands the authority of all creation in the universe above us, in the universe around us, and in the universe beneath us; holding this world and its destiny in His pierced and loving hands. (*Expository Sermons on Revelation* [Grand Rapids: Zondervan, 1969], 1:16–17)

Even a cursory glance through the book of Revelation reveals that Jesus Christ is its main theme. He is "the faithful witness" (1:5); "the firstborn of the dead" (1:5); "the ruler of the kings of the earth" (1:5); "the Alpha and the Omega" (1:8; 21:6); the one "who is and who was and who is to come" (1:8); "the Almighty" (1:8); "the first and the last" (1:17); "the living One" (1:18); "the One who holds the seven stars in His right hand, the One who walks among the seven golden lampstands" (2:1); "the One who has the sharp two-edged sword" (2:12); "the Son of God" (2:18); the One "who has eyes like a flame of fire, and . . . feet . . . like burnished bronze" (2:18); the One "who has the seven Spirits of God and the seven stars" (3:1); the One "who is holy, who is true" (3:7); the holder of "the key of David, who opens and no one will shut, and who shuts and no one opens" (3:7); "the Amen, the faithful and true Witness" (3:14); "the Beginning of the creation of God" (3:14); "the Lion that is from the tribe of Judah" (5:5); "the Root of David" (5:5); the Lamb of God (e.g., 5:6; 6:1; 7:9–10; 8:1; 12:11; 13:8; 14:1; 15:3; 17:14; 19:7; 21:9; 22:1); the "Lord, holy and true" (6:10); the One who "is called Faithful and True" (19:11); "The Word of God" (19:13); the "King of kings, and Lord of lords" (19:16); Christ (Messiah), ruling on earth with His glorified saints (20:6); and "Jesus . . . the root and the descendant of David, the bright morning star" (22:16). The book of Revelation reveals the majesty and glory of the Lord Jesus Christ in song, poetry, symbolism, and prophecy. In it the heavens are opened and its readers see, as did Stephen (Acts 7:56), visions of the risen, glorified Son of God.

Its Divine Source

which God gave Him (1:1c)

In what sense is the book of Revelation a gift from the Father to Jesus Christ? Some interpret the phrase **which God gave Him** in connection with Jesus' words in Mark 13:32: "But of that day or hour no one knows, not even the angels in heaven, nor the Son, but the Father alone." In the humiliation of His incarnation, when He "emptied Himself, taking the form of a bond-servant" (Phil. 2:7), Jesus restricted the independent use of His divine attributes. In the book of Revelation, those holding this view argue, the Father finally gave Jesus the information He lacked in His incarnation and humiliation.

There are two insurmountable difficulties with that view, however. The most obvious one is that the book of Revelation nowhere gives the day or hour of Christ's return. Thus, it does not contain the very information the Father was supposedly revealing to the Son. Further, the glorified, ascended Son resumed the full use of His divine attributes more than half a century before the book of Revelation was written. Being fully God and omniscient, He had no need for anyone to give Him any information.

In reality, the book of Revelation is the Father's gift to the Son in a far deeper, more marvelous sense. As a reward for His perfect, humble, faithful, holy service, the Father promised to exalt the Son. Paul explains,

> Christ Jesus, . . . although He existed in the form of God, did not regard equality with God a thing to be grasped, but emptied Himself, taking the form of a bond-servant, and being made in the likeness of men. Being found in appearance as a man, He humbled Himself by becoming obedient to the point of death, even death on a cross. Therefore also God highly exalted Him, and bestowed on Him the name which is above every name, so that at the name of Jesus every knee will bow, of those who are in heaven and on earth and under the earth, and that every tongue will confess that Jesus Christ is Lord, to the glory of God the Father. (Phil. 2:5–11)

Christ's exaltation, promised in the last three verses (9–11) of that passage, is described in detail in the book of Revelation. It thus contains the full disclosure of the glory that will be Christ's at His return—His ultimate reward from the Father for His faithfulness during His humiliation. The first token of the Father's pleasure with the obedient Son was His resurrection; the second was His ascension; the third was the sending of the Holy Spirit; and the last was the gift of the book of Revelation, which promises and reveals the glory that will be Christ's at His second coming.

The book of Revelation, then, details the Son's inheritance from the Father. Unlike most human wills, however, this document can be read because it is not a sealed, private document. But not everyone has the privilege of understanding it, only those to whom God unveils it by His Spirit.

Its Human Recipients

to show to His bond-servants, (1:1*d*)

To further exalt and glorify His Son, the Father has graciously granted to a special group of people the privilege of understanding the truths found in this book. John describes those people as **His** [Christ's] **bond-servants.** *Doulois* (**bond-servants**) literally means "slaves" (cf. Matt. 22:8; Mark 13:34). The *doulos* (bond-servant), however, was a special type of slave—one who served out of love and devotion to his master. Exodus 21:5–6 describes such slaves: "But if the slave plainly says, 'I love my master, my wife and my children; I will not go out as a free man,' then his master shall bring him to God, then he shall bring him to the door or the doorpost. And his master shall pierce his ear with an awl; and he shall serve him permanently."

This is why unbelievers find the book of Revelation incomprehensible; it was not intended for them. It was given by the Father to the Son to **show** to those who willingly serve Him. Those who refuse to acknowledge Jesus Christ as Lord cannot expect to comprehend this book. "A natural man," explains Paul, "does not accept the things of the Spirit of God, for they are foolishness to him; and he cannot understand them, because they are spiritually appraised" (1 Cor. 2:14). To His disciples, when on earth, Jesus said, "To you it has been granted to know the mysteries of the kingdom of heaven, but to them it has not been granted. . . . Therefore I speak to them in parables; because while seeing they do not see, and while hearing they do not hear, nor do they understand" (Matt. 13:11, 13). Unbelievers couldn't grasp what Jesus meant when He was teaching about present spiritual realities. Neither can they grasp the future realities. Divine truth is hidden from the worldly-wise. The unbelieving skeptic finds in the book of Revelation nothing but chaos and confusion. But to the loving, willing **bond-servants** of Jesus Christ, this book is the understandable unveiling of prophetic truth about the future of the world.

Its Prophetic Character

the things which must soon take place; (1:1e)

The book of Revelation's emphasis on future events sets it apart from all other New Testament books. While they contain references to the future, the Gospels primarily focus on the life and earthly ministry of the Lord Jesus Christ. Acts chronicles the history of the church from its beginnings on the day of Pentecost until the imprisonment at Rome of the apostle Paul. The New Testament epistles, like the Gospels, contain glimpses of the future. Their primary emphasis, however, is explaining the meaning of the life, death, and resurrection of Jesus Christ and applying it to the life of the church in the present. Thus, the first five books of the New Testament are about the past, and the next twenty-one about the present. The last book, though it contains some information about the past (chap. 1) and the present (the seven churches in chaps. 2–3; although actual historical churches of John's day, they depict the types of churches found throughout the church age), focuses on the future (chaps. 4–22).

As in all prophetic literature, there is a dual emphasis in the book of Revelation. It portrays Jesus Christ in His future glory along with the blessedness of the saints. It also depicts the judgment of unbelievers in Jesus Christ leading to their eternal damnation. Commentator Charles Erdman notes:

> This is a book of judgments and of doom. The darker side of the picture is never for a moment concealed. God is just. Sin must be punished. Impenitence and rebellion issue in misery and defeat. Here is no sentimental confusion of right and wrong. Here is no weak tolerance of evil. There is mention of "the Lamb that hath been slain," but also of "the wrath of the Lamb." There is a "river of water of life," but also a "lake of fire." Here is revealed a God of love who is to dwell among men, to wipe away all tears, and to abolish death and sorrow and pain; but first his enemies must be subdued. Indeed, The Revelation is in large measure a picture of the last great conflict between the forces of evil and the power of God. The colors are lurid and are borrowed from the convulsions of nature and from the scenes of human history, with their battles and their carnage. The struggle is titanic. Countless hordes of demonic warriors rise in opposition to him who is "King of Kings, and Lord of Lords." Upon them "woes" are pronounced, "bowls" of wrath are poured out, and overwhelming destruction is visited. A brighter day is to come, but there is thunder before the dawn. (*The Revelation of John* [Philadelphia: Westminster, 1966], 12)

The profound and compelling truths in the book of Revelation are thus bittersweet (cf. 10:9–10).

Soon translates *tachos,* which can mean "in a brief time," or "quickly." It is true that there is a certain brevity to the future events depicted in this book. The unprecedented, unimaginable judgments that sweep the earth do so in a brief period of time. In just seven years, the evil world system is deluged by the horrific wrath of God. Even the thousand-year earthly kingdom is brief by God's standards (cf. 2 Pet. 3:8). It is also true that the Rapture, when Christ returns for His church, takes place "in a moment, in the twinkling of an eye" (1 Cor. 15:52).

But that is not the primary meaning of *tachos* in this context. The idea is not the speed with which Christ moves when He comes, but the nearness of His coming. The use of *tachos* and related words in Revelation supports the understanding of its meaning here as "soon." In 2:16, Jesus warned the church at Pergamum to "repent; or else I am coming to you quickly," while in 3:11 He comforted the faithful church at Philadelphia by telling them, "I am coming quickly." Chapter 11, verse 14, declares, "The second woe is past; behold, the third woe is coming quickly." An angel told John that "the Lord, the God of the spirits of the prophets, sent His angel to show to His bond-servants the things which must soon take place" (22:6). The Lord Jesus Christ three times declared, "I am coming quickly" (22:7, 12, 20). In all those cases *tachos* (or words related to it) clearly refers to the imminence or nearness of an event, not the speed at which it happens. The *tachos* word group is used in a similar sense throughout the New Testament (e.g., Acts 17:15; 25:4; Rom. 16:20; 1 Cor. 4:19; Phil. 2:19, 24; 1 Tim. 3:14; 2 Tim. 4:9; Heb. 13:19, 23; 2 Pet. 1:14). Thus, **the things which must soon take place** about which John wrote do not happen in a brief time span, but are imminent (cf. 1:3; 22:6).

Believers are not to try to set the "times or epochs which the Father has fixed by His own authority" (Acts 1:7). Instead, they are at all times to heed their Lord's warning to "be on the alert, for you do not know which day your Lord is coming" (Matt. 24:42). The knowledge that the events depicted in the book of Revelation are **soon** to **take place** has and should motivate Christians to live holy, obedient lives (2 Pet. 3:14).

ITS SUPERNATURAL DELIVERY

and He sent and communicated it by His angel (1:1*f*)

The book of Revelation is unique in New Testament literature because it is the only book **sent and communicated** to its human author by angels. In 22:16 Jesus reaffirmed the truth taught here, declaring, "I, Jesus, have sent My angel to testify to you these things for the churches." Angels were involved in the giving of the book of Revelation to John just as they were in the giving of the Law to Moses (Acts 7:53; Gal. 3:19; Heb. 2:2). Not only were angels involved in transmitting the book of Revelation to John, but they also play a prominent role in the scenes it depicts. Angels appear in every chapter of Revelation except 4 and 13. The words *angel* or *angels* are used seventy-one times in the book of Revelation—more than in any other book in the Bible. In fact, one out of every four uses in Scripture of those words is in the book of Revelation. This book, then, is an important source of information on the ministry of angels.

ITS HUMAN AUTHOR

to His bond-servant John, who testified to the word of God and to the testimony of Jesus Christ, even to all that he saw. (1:1*g*–2)

The human agent to whom the angelic messengers communicated the book of Revelation is here identified as **His** [Christ's] **bond-**

servant John. As noted in the Introduction, this was John the apostle, the son of Zebedee and brother of James. As also noted in the Introduction, John wrote the book of Revelation while in exile on the island of Patmos (1:9).

The enormity of the visions John received on that barren island staggered him. Throughout his gospel, John never directly referred to himself. Yet here he bookends his vision with the statement, "I, John" (1:9; 22:8)—an exclamation that expressed his amazement that he was receiving such overwhelming visions.

As he had loyally **testified** to the first coming of Christ (John 19:35; 21:24; 1 John 1:2; 4:14), so John faithfully, under the Spirit's inspiration, testified **to all that he saw** concerning His second coming. Specifically, John bore witness **to the word of God and to the testimony of Jesus Christ.** Those phrases appear together again in 1:9 (cf. 12:17), and are used synonymously, since "the testimony of Jesus is the spirit of prophecy" (19:10). The **word of God** expressed in the book of Revelation is **the testimony** about the coming glory of **Jesus Christ** given to His church (cf. 22:16) and recorded by His faithful witness, John.

ITS PROMISED BLESSING

Blessed is he who reads and those who hear the words of the prophecy, and heed the things which are written in it; (1:3*a*)

The book of Revelation is bracketed by promises of blessing (beatitudes, as in Matt. 5:3–12) to those who read and obey it (cf. 22:7; Luke 11:28). But those are only two of the seven promises of blessing the book contains; the rest are equally wonderful: "'Blessed are the dead who die in the Lord from now on!' 'Yes,' says the Spirit, 'so that they may rest from their labors, for their deeds follow with them'" (14:13). "Behold, I am coming like a thief. Blessed is the one who stays awake and keeps his clothes, so that he will not walk about naked and men will not see his shame" (16:15); "blessed are those who are invited to the marriage supper of the Lamb" (19:9); "blessed and holy is the one who has a part in the first resurrection" (20:6); "blessed are those who wash their robes, so that they may have the right to the tree of life, and may enter by the gates into the city" (22:14).

The three participles translated **reads, hear,** and **heed** are in the present tense. Reading, hearing, and obeying the truths taught in the book of Revelation (and in the rest of Scripture) are to be a way of life for believers. The change from the singular **he who reads** to the plural **those who hear the words of the prophecy, and heed the things**

which are written in it depicts a first-century church service. It was common practice when the church gathered for one person to read the Scriptures aloud for all to hear (cf. 1 Tim. 4:13). Dr. Robert L. Thomas explains that "because writing materials were expensive and scarce, so were copies of the books that were parts of the biblical canon. As a rule, one copy per Christian assembly was the best that could be hoped for. Public reading was the only means that rank-and-file Christians had for becoming familiar with the contents of these books" (*Revelation 1–7: An Exegetical Commentary* [Chicago: Moody, 1992], 60). Since only Scripture was to be publicly read, John's "obvious intention that the Apocalypse was to be read publicly argued strongly from the start that it be included among those books that eventually would be recognized as part of the NT canon" (Thomas, *Revelation 1–7*, 62–63).

The book of Revelation is God's final word to man, the culmination of divine revelation. Its writing marked the completion of the canon of Scripture (cf. 22:18–19), and its scope encompasses the entire future sweep of redemptive history (1:19). Therefore it is imperative that believers pay diligent heed to the truths it contains.

ITS COMPELLING URGENCY

for the time is near. (1:3*b*)

This phrase reiterates the truth taught in 1:1, that the events depicted in the book of Revelation are imminent. **Time** does not translate *chronos,* which refers to time on a clock or calendar, but *kairos,* which refers to seasons, epochs, or eras. The next great era of God's redemptive history is **near.**

That the return of Christ is imminent, the next event on God's prophetic calendar, has always been the church's hope. Jesus commanded His followers to watch expectantly for His return:

> Be dressed in readiness, and keep your lamps lit. Be like men who are waiting for their master when he returns from the wedding feast, so that they may immediately open the door to him when he comes and knocks. Blessed are those slaves whom the master will find on the alert when he comes; truly I say to you, that he will gird himself to serve, and have them recline at the table, and will come up and wait on them. Whether he comes in the second watch, or even in the third, and finds them so, blessed are those slaves. But be sure of this, that if the head of the house had known at what hour the thief was coming, he would not have allowed his house to be broken into. You too, be ready; for the Son of Man is coming at an hour that you do not expect. (Luke 12:35–40)

"The night is almost gone," wrote Paul to the Romans, "and the day is near" (Rom. 13:12). The apostle thought that he might be alive when the Lord returns, as his use of the plural pronoun *we* in such passages as 1 Corinthians 15:51–58 and 1 Thessalonians 4:15–18 indicates. The writer of Hebrews exhorted his readers to "[encourage] one another; and all the more as you see the day drawing near" (Heb. 10:25). James encouraged struggling believers with the reality that Christ's return was imminent: "Therefore be patient, brethren, until the coming of the Lord.... You too be patient; strengthen your hearts, for the coming of the Lord is near.... Behold, the Judge is standing right at the door" (James 5:7–9). "The end of all things is near," Peter reminded his readers (1 Pet. 4:7), while in 1 John 2:18 the apostle John added, "Children, it is the last hour."

Despite the skepticism of the scoffers, who demand, "Where is the promise of His coming? For ever since the fathers fell asleep, all continues just as it was from the beginning of creation" (2 Pet. 3:4), the Lord Jesus Christ will return. And His return is **near.**

ITS TRINITARIAN BENEDICTION

John to the seven churches that are in Asia: Grace to you and peace, from Him who is and who was and who is to come, and from the seven Spirits who are before His throne, and from Jesus Christ, the faithful witness, the firstborn of the dead, and the ruler of the kings of the earth. (1:4–5*a*)

Unlike modern letters, in which the senders put their names at the end of the letter, ancient letters sensibly named their writers at the beginning. Thus **John** identifies himself as the writer and names **the seven churches** (listed in 1:11) **that are** in the Roman province of **Asia** (modern Turkey) as the recipients. **Grace to you and peace** was a standard greeting in New Testament letters (cf. Rom. 1:7; 1 Cor. 1:3; 2 Cor. 1:2; Gal. 1:3; Eph. 1:2; Phil. 1:2; Col. 1:2; 1 Thess. 1:1; 2 Thess. 1:2; Philem. 3), but this greeting introduces a benediction from the exalted Trinity (cf. 2 Cor. 13:14).

The phrase **Him who is and who was and who is to come** identifies the first Person of the Trinity, God the Father, described here in anthropomorphic terms. Because it is the only way we can understand, the threefold description (cf. 1:8; 4:8) views God in time dimensions (past, present, and future), although He is timeless. The eternal God is the source of all the blessings of salvation, all grace, and all peace.

The seven Spirits who are before His throne refers to the Holy Spirit. Obviously, there is only one Holy Spirit; the number **seven**

depicts Him in His fullness (cf. 5:6; Isa. 11:2; Zech. 4:1–10). The Holy Spirit in all His glory and fullness sends grace and peace to believers; He is the spirit of grace (Heb. 10:29) and produces peace in believers' lives (Gal. 5:22). Here He is seen in the glory of His place in the Father's presence in heaven.

Grace and peace also flow **from Jesus Christ, the faithful witness, the firstborn of the dead, and the ruler of the kings of the earth.** He, too, is seen in the glory of His exaltation. It is only fitting that John mentions Christ last, and gives a fuller description of Him, since He is the theme of the book of Revelation. A **faithful witness** is one who always speaks and represents the truth, and that certainly characterizes the Lord Jesus Christ. He was a perfect witness to the nature of God. Revelation 3:14 calls Him "The Amen, the faithful and true Witness." "For this I have been born, and for this I have come into the world," He declared to Pilate, "to testify to the truth" (John 18:37). Jesus Christ, the faithful witness who cannot lie and lived and spoke flawlessly the will of God, promises believers salvation's grace and peace.

The second description of Jesus, **the firstborn of the dead,** does not mean He was chronologically the first one to be raised from the dead. There were resurrections before His in the Old Testament (1 Kings 17:17–23; 2 Kings 4:32–36; 13:20–21), and He Himself raised others during His earthly ministry (Matt. 9:23–25; Luke 7:11–15; John 11:30–44). *Prōtotokos* does not mean **firstborn** in time sequence, but rather first in preeminence. Of all who have ever been or ever will be resurrected, He is the premier one. God declares of the Messiah in Psalm 89:27, "I also shall make him My firstborn, the highest of the kings of the earth." The book of Revelation records the unfolding of that promise.

The third title, **the ruler of the kings of the earth,** depicts Christ as absolutely sovereign over the affairs of this world, to which He holds the title deed (cf. 5:1ff.). That Jesus Christ is the sovereign King of the earth is repeatedly taught in Scripture (e.g., 19:16; Ps. 2:6–8; Jer. 23:5; Zech. 9:9; Matt. 2:2; 21:5; Luke 19:38; 23:3; John 1:49). He is Lord, having a name "above every name" (Phil. 2:9–11), who, according to the Father's plan and the Spirit's work, grants believers His royal blessing of grace and peace.

Its Exalted Doxology

To Him who loves us and released us from our sins by His blood—and He has made us to be a kingdom, priests to His God and Father—to Him be the glory and the dominion forever and ever. Amen. (1:5b–6)

The work of Christ on behalf of believers caused John to burst forth in an inspired doxology of praise to Him. In the present, Christ loves believers with an unbreakable love (Rom. 8:35–39). The greatest expression of that love came when He **released us from our sins by His blood**—a reference to the atonement provided by His sacrificial death on the cross on our behalf.

Here is the heart of the gospel. Sinners are forgiven by God, set free from sin, death, and hell by the sacrifice of Jesus Christ on the cross. God made Him our substitute, killing Him for our sins, so that the penalty was fully paid for us. God's justice was satisfied and God was able then to grant righteousness to repentant sinners for whom Christ died.

Christ's love also caused Him to make **us to be a kingdom** (not the millennial kingdom, but the sphere of God's rule which believers enter at salvation; cf. Col. 1:13) in which we enjoy His loving, gracious rule and almighty, sovereign protection. Finally, He made us **priests to His God and Father,** granting us the privilege of direct access to the Father (cf. 1 Pet. 2:9–10).

John concludes his doxology with the only proper response in light of the magnitude of the blessings Christ has given believers: **To Him be the glory and the dominion forever and ever. Amen.** That is to be the response of all who read this marvelous book in which that future glory and dominion is clearly presented.

A Preview of the Second Coming
(Revelation 1:7–8)

2

Behold, He is coming with the clouds, and every eye will see Him, even those who pierced Him; and all the tribes of the earth will mourn over Him. So it is to be. Amen. "I am the Alpha and the Omega," says the Lord God, "who is and who was and who is to come, the Almighty." (1:7–8)

The book of Revelation is the ultimate action thriller. Anyone who loves books filled with adventure and excitement will certainly love this book. The amazing Revelation contains drama, suspense, mystery, passion, and horror. It tells of apostasy by the church. It speaks of unprecedented economic collapse, and of the ultimate war of human history—the war that will truly end all wars. It describes natural disasters rivaled in intensity only by the worldwide Flood of Noah's day, as God will pour out His wrath on the sin-cursed earth. It speaks of the political intrigues that will lead to the ascendancy of the most evil and powerful dictator the world has ever known. Finally, and most terrifying of all, it describes the final judgment and the sentencing of all rebels, angelic and human, to eternal torment in hell. The book of Revelation is thus a book of astounding drama, horror, and pathos. Yet, amazingly, it is also a book of hope and joy with a happy ending, as sin, sorrow, and death are forever banished (21:4; 22:3).

It will take some time for the drama to unfold, so, like any good writer, John gives his readers a preview of what will come later in the book. By so doing, he reveals the theme of the book of Revelation: It is a book about the second coming of the Lord Jesus Christ. In verses 7 and 8 John presents five truths about His second coming: its necessity, glory, scope, response, and certainty.

THE NECESSITY OF THE SECOND COMING

Behold, He is coming (1:7*a*)

After the introduction and greetings (vv. 1–6), verse 7 begins the first great prophetic oracle in the book of Revelation. The exclamation *idou* (**Behold**) is an arresting call to attention. It is intended to arouse the mind and heart to consider what follows. This is the first of its twenty-five uses in Revelation—a book filled with startling truths that demand careful attention. Fittingly, the first thing John calls attention to is the glorious truth that **He** [Jesus] **is coming.** The present tense of *erchomai* (is coming) suggests that Christ is already on the way, and thus that His coming is certain. The present tense also emphasizes the imminency of His coming (cf. the discussion of imminency in chapter one of this volume).

The "coming (or expected) One" was a title for the Messiah. John the Baptist, "while imprisoned, heard of the works of Christ, [and] sent word by his disciples and said to Him, 'Are You the Expected [from *erchomai*] One, or shall we look for someone else?'" (Matt. 11:2–3; cf. Luke 7:19–20; John 3:31; 6:14; 11:27). *Erchomai* is used nine times in Revelation to refer to Jesus Christ; seven times by our Lord in reference to Himself. Thus, the theme of the book of Revelation is the coming One, the Lord Jesus Christ.

Despite the scoffers who deny the Second Coming (2 Pet. 3:3–4), the Bible repeatedly affirms that Jesus will return. That truth appears in more than five hundred verses throughout the Bible. It has been estimated that one out of every twenty-five verses in the New Testament refers to the Second Coming. Jesus repeatedly spoke of His return (e.g., Matt. 16:27; 24–25; 26:64; Mark 8:38; Luke 9:26) and warned believers to be ready for it (e.g., Matt. 24:42, 44; 25:13; Luke 12:40; 21:34–36). The return of the Lord Jesus Christ to this earth is thus a central theme in Scripture.

In addition to the explicit prophecies of the Second Coming, there are several compelling reasons why Christ must return.

First, the promises of God require that Jesus return. Genesis 49:10, the first prophecy of Messiah's rule, reads, "The scepter shall not depart from Judah, nor the ruler's staff from between his feet, until Shiloh comes, and to him shall be the obedience of the peoples." Psalm 2:6–9 declares:

> But as for Me, I have installed My King
> Upon Zion, My holy mountain.
> I will surely tell of the decree of the Lord:
> He said to Me, "You are My Son,
> Today I have begotten You.
> Ask of Me, and I will surely give the nations as Your inheritance,
> And the very ends of the earth as Your possession.
> You shall break them with a rod of iron,
> You shall shatter them like earthenware."

Isaiah also predicted Messiah's earthly rule:

> For a child will be born to us, a son will be given to us;
> And the government will rest on His shoulders;
> And His name will be called Wonderful Counselor, Mighty God,
> Eternal Father, Prince of Peace.
> There will be no end to the increase of His government or of peace,
> On the throne of David and over his kingdom,
> To establish it and to uphold it with justice and righteousness
> From then on and forevermore.
> The zeal of the Lord of hosts will accomplish this. (Isa. 9:6–7)

Jeremiah foresaw Israel's future blessedness under Messiah's reign:

> "Behold, the days are coming," declares the Lord,
> "When I will raise up for David a righteous Branch;
> And He will reign as king and act wisely
> And do justice and righteousness in the land.
> In His days Judah will be saved,
> And Israel will dwell securely;
> And this is His name by which He will be called,
> 'The Lord our righteousness.'"

> "Therefore behold, the days are coming," declares the Lord, "when they will no longer say, 'As the Lord lives, who brought up the sons of Israel from the land of Egypt,' but, 'As the Lord lives, who brought up and led back the descendants of the household of Israel from the north land and from all the countries where I had driven them.' Then they will live on their own soil." (Jer. 23:5–8)

Those predictions and many others that speak of Messiah's earthly reign (e.g., Dan. 7:13–14, 18; Zech. 14:4–9; Mal. 4:1–4) were not fulfilled at Christ's first coming. Therefore, He must come again to fulfill them, since "God is not a man, that He should lie, nor a son of man, that He should repent; Has He said, and will He not do it? Or has He spoken, and will He not make it good?" (Num. 23:19).

Second, the promise of Jesus requires His return. As noted above, Jesus repeatedly predicted that He would return (cf. Rev. 2:16; 3:11; 22:7, 12, 20). John 14:2–3 gives one important reason for His return: "In My Father's house are many dwelling places; if it were not so, I would have told you; for I go to prepare a place for you. If I go and prepare a place for you, I will come again and receive you to Myself, that where I am, there you may be also." In a parable (Luke 19:11–27), Jesus pictured Himself as a nobleman who would one day return to His estate and destroy those who had rejected His rule. Jesus' promises—both to reward those who believe in Him and judge those who reject Him—demand His return.

Third, the guarantee of the Holy Spirit requires that Jesus return. The Holy Spirit is "the Spirit of truth" (John 15:26; 16:13), who would "teach [the inspired authors of the New Testament] all things, and bring to [their] remembrance all that [Jesus] said to [them]" (John 14:26). Thus every New Testament promise of the Second Coming (cf., in addition to those already mentioned 1 Cor. 1:4–8; Phil. 3:20–21; Col. 3:4; 1 Thess. 2:19; James 5:8; 1 Pet. 1:13; 1 John 3:2; etc.) is a promise from the Spirit of truth. Jesus must return because the veracity of the Trinity is at stake.

Fourth, God's program for the church demands that Jesus return. In Revelation 3:10 Jesus promised, "Because you have kept the word of My perseverance, I also will keep you from the hour of testing, that hour which is about to come upon the whole world, to test those who dwell on the earth." To keep that promise, He must return for His church before the onset of "the hour of testing." That event, known as the Rapture of the church, is one aspect of Christ's second coming.

Following the Rapture, Christ will reward His church for its faithful service to Him (Rom. 14:10; 1 Cor. 3:12–15; 4:5; 2 Cor. 5:10; Phil. 1:6, 10; 2 Tim. 1:12, 18; 4:8; Rev. 11:18). That time of reward presupposes that Christ will have already returned for His church.

At the end of the seven-year tribulation period, the glorified church, the bride of Christ (Rev. 19:7–9; cf. 2 Cor. 11:2; Eph. 5:22–30), will return in triumph with Him (Rev. 19:14; cf. v. 8). At that time the church will be vindicated before the unbelieving world, making it evident who truly belongs to the Lord (cf. 2 Tim. 2:19).

God's program for the church—to rescue it from the terrors of the Tribulation, reward it for faithful service, and vindicate it in exaltation in His kingdom before the world—requires that Christ return.

Fifth, Christ's program for the unbelieving nations requires His return. Psalm 2 predicts a time when Christ will rule the nations, something that did not take place at His first coming. Similarly, Joel 3:1–2, 9–17 (cf. Isa. 11:1–5; Mic. 4:1–8; Zeph. 3:8; Matt. 25:31–46) describes His judgment of the unbelieving nations. Since no such judgment took place at Christ's first coming, He must return to carry it out.

Sixth, God's program for Israel demands that Christ return. The Bible teaches that God is not finished with Israel, His covenant people. Although he was the Apostle to the Gentiles (Rom. 11:13; 1 Tim. 2:7), Paul nevertheless wrote, "God has not rejected His people, has He? May it never be! …God has not rejected His people whom He foreknew" (Rom. 11:1–2). Speaking through the prophet Jeremiah, God declared in the strongest terms that He would never permanently set aside Israel:

> Thus says the Lord,
> Who gives the sun for light by day
> And the fixed order of the moon and the stars for light by night,
> Who stirs up the sea so that its waves roar;
> The Lord of hosts is His name:
> "If this fixed order departs
> From before Me," declares the Lord,
> "Then the offspring of Israel also shall cease
> From being a nation before Me forever."
> Thus says the Lord,
> "If the heavens above can be measured
> And the foundations of the earth searched out below,
> Then I will also cast off all the offspring of Israel
> For all that they have done," declares the Lord. (Jer. 31:35–37)

> "Thus says the Lord, 'If My covenant for day and night stand not, and the fixed patterns of heaven and earth I have not established, then I would reject the descendants of Jacob and David My servant, not taking from his descendants rulers over the descendants of Abraham, Isaac and Jacob. But I will restore their fortunes and will have mercy on them.'" (Jer. 33:25–26)

In addition to continued existence as a nation, God promised Israel salvation, peace, prosperity, security, and a kingdom (e.g., Deut. 4:30–31; Isa. 9:6–7; 11:11–12; 60:10–14; Jer. 23:5–8; 30–33; 46:28; Ezek. 36–37; 40–48; Dan. 9:20–27; 12:1–3; Hos. 2:14–23; 3:4–5; 14:4–7; Joel 3:18–21; Amos 9:8–15; Obad. 17, 21; Mic. 4:8; 7:14–20; Zeph. 3:14–20; Zech. 13–14; Matt. 19:28; Acts 1:6–7). Since those promises were not realized at Christ's first coming, He must return to fulfill them.

Seventh, Christ's humiliation demands that He return. At His first coming, He was rejected, reviled, abused, and executed as a common criminal. But that cannot be the way the story ends. One day, "at the name of Jesus every knee will bow, of those who are in heaven and on earth and under the earth, and . . . every tongue will confess that Jesus Christ is Lord, to the glory of God the Father" (Phil. 2:10–11). At His sham trial "the high priest said to Him, 'I adjure You by the living God, that You tell us whether You are the Christ, the Son of God.' Jesus said to him, 'You have said it yourself; nevertheless I tell you, hereafter you will see the Son of Man sitting at the right hand of Power, and coming on the clouds of heaven'" (Matt. 26:63–64). It is inconceivable that the last view the world will have of the Son of God is that of a bleeding, dying, crucified criminal. Jesus Christ must return to reveal His glory.

Eighth, the judgment of Satan demands that Christ return. Satan is the temporary ruler of this world (John 12:31; 14:30; 16:11), the "god of this world" (2 Cor. 4:4), who uses the power of death to enslave men (Heb. 2:14–15). But Jesus, the rightful ruler (cf. Rev. 5:1ff.), will return to destroy him (a process that began with His first coming; Rom. 16:20; 1 John 3:8) and reclaim what is rightfully His.

Ninth, the expectation of believers demands that Christ return. "If we have hoped in Christ in this life only," wrote Paul to the Corinthians, "we are of all men most to be pitied" (1 Cor. 15:19). Believers are those who are constantly "looking for the blessed hope and the appearing of the glory of our great God and Savior, Christ Jesus" (Titus 2:13); those "who have loved His appearing" (2 Tim. 4:8). The hope that Christ will one day return and take believers to heaven to live forever in His presence provides hope and comfort (John 14:1–3; 1 Thess. 4:18).

The Glory of the Second Coming

with the clouds, (1:7*b*)

Clouds in Scripture frequently symbolize God's presence. A cloud was used as the visible manifestation of God's presence with Israel during the wilderness wandering (Ex. 13:21–22; 16:10; Num. 10:34). At the giving of the Law at Mount Sinai, "a thick cloud upon the mountain" symbolized God's presence (Ex. 19:16; cf. 20:21; 24:15–18). When the Lord communicated with Moses at the Tent of Meeting (the tabernacle), "the pillar of cloud would descend and stand at the entrance of the tent; and the Lord would speak with Moses" (Ex. 33:9; cf. 34:5). Both the tabernacle (Ex. 40:34–38) and the temple (1 Kings 8:10–12) were filled with a cloud symbolizing God's glory at their dedications. Jesus ascended to heaven on a cloud (Acts 1:9); believers will ascend with clouds at the Rapture (1 Thess. 4:17), and, as the present verse indicates, Christ will return with **clouds** (cf. Dan. 7:13; Matt. 24:30).

The **clouds** picture Christ's descent from heaven. More significantly, they symbolize the brilliant light that accompanies God's presence—a light so powerful that no one could see it and live (Ex. 33:20). The appearance of the blazing glory of Jesus Christ, "the radiance of [God's] glory and the exact representation of His nature" (Heb. 1:3), and the lesser brilliance of the innumerable angels and the redeemed who accompany Him, will be both an indescribable and terrifying pageant.

THE SCOPE OF THE SECOND COMING

and every eye will see Him, even those who pierced Him; and all the tribes of the earth will mourn over Him. (1:7c)

During the incarnation, Christ's glory was veiled. Only Peter, James, and John caught a glimpse of it at the Transfiguration. But at His second coming **every eye will see Him;** His glory will be obvious to the entire human race.

John divides those who will see the Second Coming into two groups. **Those who pierced Him** does not refer to the Roman soldiers involved in Christ's crucifixion but to the unbelieving Jews who instigated His death. In Zechariah 12:10 God says, "I will pour out on the house of David and on the inhabitants of Jerusalem, the Spirit of grace and of supplication, so that they will look on Me whom they have pierced; and they will mourn for Him, as one mourns for an only son, and they will weep bitterly over Him like the bitter weeping over a firstborn." Peter affirmed that the Jewish people were responsible for Christ's execution, boldly declaring

> Men of Israel, listen to these words: Jesus the Nazarene, a man attested to you by God with miracles and wonders and signs which God performed through Him in your midst, just as you yourselves know—this Man, delivered over by the predetermined plan and foreknowledge of God, you nailed to a cross by the hands of godless men and put Him to death. (Acts 2:22–23; cf. 3:14–15)

Israel's mourning, noted in Zechariah 12:10, will be that of genuine repentance. Many Jews will be saved during the Tribulation, both the 144,000 and their converts. But for many others, the Second Coming will be the time of their salvation. It will be "in that day [that] a fountain will be opened for the house of David and for the inhabitants of Jerusalem, for sin and for impurity" (Zech. 13:1).

John describes the second group as **all the tribes of the earth,** a reference to the unbelieving Gentile nations. Like the Jewish people, they too **will mourn over** Christ. Some of that mourning may relate to the repentance of those who are saved at that time (7:9–10, 14). But unlike the Jewish nation, the Gentiles' mourning will not generally result from genuine repentance. **Mourn** is from *koptō,* which literally means "to cut." The word became associated with mourning due to the pagans' practice of cutting themselves when in extreme grief or despair. First Kings 18:28 records that the frenzied, panicked prophets of Baal "cut themselves according to their custom with swords and lances until the blood gushed out on them" in a desperate attempt to get their god's attention. The Israelites were strictly forbidden to engage in such pagan rituals (Lev. 19:28; Deut. 14:1).

The Gentiles' mourning, for the most part, will be prompted by terror, not repentance. They will mourn not for the Christ they rejected, but over their doom. They will "not repent of their murders nor of their sorceries nor of their immorality nor of their thefts" (9:21).

THE RESPONSE TO THE SECOND COMING

So it is to be. Amen. (1:7*d*)

Having given the response of both believers and unbelievers to Christ's second coming, John interjects his own response. Using the strongest words of affirmation both in Greek (*nai;* **so it is to be**) and Hebrew (**amen**), John pleads for the Lord Jesus Christ to return.

THE CERTAINTY OF THE SECOND COMING

"I am the Alpha and the Omega," says the Lord God, "who is and who was and who is to come, the Almighty." (1:8)

In this verse **the Lord God** puts His signature on the prophecy of the Second Coming recorded in the previous verse. Three of His divine attributes guarantee the certainty of the pledge of Christ's return.

Alpha and the Omega emphasizes God's omniscience. **Alpha** is the first letter of the Greek alphabet, and **Omega** is the last. All knowledge is conveyed through the letters of the alphabet; thus God's designation of Himself as **the Alpha and the Omega** affirms that He has all knowledge. He knows, therefore, the certainty of this promise.

As the one **who is and who was and who is to come,** God's transcendent, eternal presence is not confined by time or space or any feature or event in them. There is no possible contingency of which He is unaware regarding the Second Coming. Thus, His promise that the Lord Jesus Christ will return settles the issue.

The designation of God as **the Almighty** (cf. 4:8; 11:17; 15:3; 16:7, 14; 19:6, 15; 21:22) affirms His omnipotence. Since He is all powerful, nothing can hinder Him from carrying out His sovereign will. No one or no thing can possibly prevent Christ from returning in glory as described in verse 7.

Jesus came the first time in humiliation; He will return in exaltation. He came the first time to be killed; He will return to kill His enemies. He came the first time to serve; He will return to be served. He came the first time as the suffering servant; He will return as the conquering king. The challenge the book of Revelation makes to every person is to be ready for His return.

John Phillips writes,

> One of the most stirring pages in English history tells of the conquests and crusades of Richard I, the Lionhearted. While Richard was away trouncing Saladin, his kingdom fell on bad times. His sly and graceless brother, John, usurped all the prerogatives of the king and misruled the realm. The people of England suffered, longing for the return of the king, and praying that it might be soon. Then one day Richard came. He landed in England and marched straight for his throne. Around that glittering coming, many tales are told, woven into the legends of England. (One of them is the story of Robin Hood.) John's castles tumbled like ninepins. Great Richard laid claim to his throne, and none dared stand in his path. The people shouted their delight. They rang peal after peal on the bells. The Lion was back! Long live the king!
>
> One day a King greater than Richard will lay claim to a realm greater than England. Those who have abused the earth in His absence, seized His domains, and mismanaged His world will all be swept aside. (*Exploring Revelation,* rev. ed. [Chicago: Moody, 1987; reprint, Neptune, N.J.: Loizeaux, 1991], 22–23)

Only those "who have loved His appearing" (2 Tim. 4:8), who love Him and acknowledge Him as the rightful king, will enjoy the blessings of His kingdom.

The Vision of
the Glorified Son
(Revelation 1:9–20)

3

I, John, your brother and fellow partaker in the tribulation and
kingdom and perseverance which are in Jesus, was on the island
called Patmos because of the word of God and the testimony of
Jesus. I was in the Spirit on the Lord's day, and I heard behind me
a loud voice like the sound of a trumpet, saying, "Write in a book
what you see, and send it to the seven churches: to Ephesus and
to Smyrna and to Pergamum and to Thyatira and to Sardis and to
Philadelphia and to Laodicea." Then I turned to see the voice that
was speaking with me. And having turned I saw seven golden
lampstands; and in the middle of the lampstands I saw one like a
son of man, clothed in a robe reaching to the feet, and girded
across His chest with a golden sash. His head and His hair were
white like white wool, like snow; and His eyes were like a flame
of fire. His feet were like burnished bronze, when it has been
made to glow in a furnace, and His voice was like the sound of
many waters. In His right hand He held seven stars, and out of
His mouth came a sharp two-edged sword; and His face was like
the sun shining in its strength. When I saw Him, I fell at His feet
like a dead man. And He placed His right hand on me, saying,
"Do not be afraid; I am the first and the last, and the living One;

and I was dead, and behold, I am alive forevermore, and I have the keys of death and of Hades. Therefore write the things which you have seen, and the things which are, and the things which will take place after these things. As for the mystery of the seven stars which you saw in My right hand, and the seven golden lampstands: the seven stars are the angels of the seven churches, and the seven lampstands are the seven churches." (1:9–20)

By the close of the first century, Christianity had become a hated and despised religious sect in the Roman Empire. Writing to Emperor Trajan early in the second century, Pliny, the Roman governor of Bithynia, scorned Christianity as a "depraved and extravagant superstition." Pliny went on to complain that "the contagion of this superstition [Christianity] has spread not only in the cities, but in the villages and rural districts as well" (cited in Henry Bettenson, ed., *Documents of the Christian Church* [London: Oxford University Press, 1967], 4). The Roman historian Tacitus, a contemporary of Pliny, described Christians as "a class hated for their abominations" (cited in Bettenson, *Documents,* 2), while Suetonius, another contemporary of Pliny, dismissed them as "a set of men adhering to a novel and mischievous superstition" (cited in Bettenson, *Documents,* 2).

Apart from the natural hostility of fallen men to the truth of the gospel, Christians were hated for several more reasons. Politically, the Romans viewed them as disloyal because they refused to acknowledge Caesar as the supreme authority. That disloyalty was confirmed in the eyes of the Roman officials by Christians' refusal to offer the obligatory sacrifices of worship to the emperor. Also, many of their meetings were held privately at night, causing the Roman officials to accuse them of hatching antigovernment plots.

Religiously, Christians were denounced as atheists because they rejected the Roman pantheon of gods and because they worshiped an invisible God, not an idol. Wild rumors, based on misunderstandings of Christian beliefs and practices, falsely accused them of cannibalism, incest, and other sexual perversions.

Socially, Christians, most of whom were from the lower classes of society (cf. 1 Cor. 1:26), were despised by the Roman aristocracy. The Christian teaching that all people are equal (Gal. 3:28; Col. 3:11) threatened to undermine the hierarchical structure of Roman society and topple the elite from their privileged status. It also heightened the Roman aristocracy's fear of a slave rebellion. Christians did not openly oppose slavery, but the perception was that they undermined it by teaching that master and slave were equal in Christ (cf. Philem.). Finally, Christians declined to participate in the worldly amusements that were so much a part of pagan society, avoiding festivals, the theater, and other pagan events.

Economically, Christians were seen as a threat by the numerous priests, craftsmen, and merchants who profited from idol worship. The resulting hostility, first seen in the riot at Ephesus (Acts 19:23ff.), deepened as Christianity became more widespread. In his letter to Emperor Trajan cited earlier, Pliny complained that the pagan temples had been deserted, and that those who sold sacrificial animals found few buyers.

In that superstitious age many Romans feared that natural disasters resulted from the neglect of the pagan gods. The third-century Christian apologist Tertullian remarked sarcastically, "If the Tiber reaches the walls, if the Nile does not rise to the fields, if the sky doesn't move or the earth does, if there is famine, if there is plague, the cry is at once, 'Christians to the lion!' What, all of them to one lion?" (cited in M. A. Smith, *From Christ to Constantine* [Downers Grove, Ill.: InterVarsity, 1973], 86).

During the first few decades after the death of Christ, the Roman government considered Christianity merely a sect of Judaism (cf. Acts 18:12–16). Eventually, it was the hostility the Jews displayed against the Christians that led the Romans to recognize Christianity as a religion distinct from Judaism. That identified Christians as worshipers of an illegal religion (Judaism was a *religio licita,* or legal religion). Yet there was no official persecution by the Roman authorities until the time of Nero. Seeking to divert public suspicion that he had caused the great fire in Rome (July 19, A.D. 64), Nero blamed the Christians for it. As a result, many Christians were executed at Rome (including, according to tradition, both Peter and Paul), but there was yet no empire-wide persecution.

Three decades later, Emperor Domitian instigated an official persecution of Christians. Little is known of the details, but it extended to the province of Asia (modern Turkey). The apostle John had been banished to the island of Patmos, and at least one person, a pastor, had already been martyred (Rev. 2:13). The persecuted, beleaguered, discouraged believers in Asia Minor to whom John addressed the book of Revelation desperately needed encouragement. It had been years since Jesus ascended. Jerusalem had been destroyed and Israel ravaged. The church was losing its first love, compromising, tolerating sin, becoming powerless, and distasteful to the Lord Himself (this is described in Revelation 2 and 3). The other apostles were dead, and John had been exiled. The whole picture looked very bleak. That is why the first vision John received from the inspiring Holy Spirit is of Christ's present ministry in the church.

John's readers took comfort in the knowledge that Christ will one day return in glory and defeat His enemies. The description of those momentous events takes up most of the book of Revelation. But the vision of Jesus Christ that begins the book does not describe Jesus in His future glory, but depicts Him in the present as the glorified Lord of the church. In spite of all the disappointments, the Lord had not abandoned

His church or His promises. This powerful vision of Christ's present ministry to them must have provided great hope and comfort to the wondering and suffering churches to whom John wrote. Verses 9–20 provide the setting for the vision, unfold the vision itself, and relate its effects.

THE SETTING OF THE VISION

I, John, your brother and fellow partaker in the tribulation and kingdom and perseverance which are in Jesus, was on the island called Patmos because of the word of God and the testimony of Jesus. I was in the Spirit on the Lord's day, and I heard behind me a loud voice like the sound of a trumpet, saying, "Write in a book what you see, and send it to the seven churches: to Ephesus and to Smyrna and to Pergamum and to Thyatira and to Sardis and to Philadelphia and to Laodicea." (1:9–11)

This is the third time in the first nine verses of this book that **John** referred to himself by name (cf. vv. 1, 4). This time, his amazement at receiving this vision caused him to add the demonstrative personal pronoun **I.** John was astounded that, despite his utter unworthiness, he had the inestimable privilege of receiving this monumental vision.

John was an apostle, a member of the inner circle of the twelve along with Peter and James, and the human author of a gospel and three epistles. Yet he humbly identified himself simply as **your brother.** He did not write as one impressed with his authority as an apostle, commanding, exhorting, or defining doctrine, but as an eyewitness to the revelation of Jesus Christ that begins to unfold with this vision.

John further humbly identified with his readers by describing himself as their **fellow partaker,** sharing with them first of all in **tribulation.** Like them, John was at that moment suffering severe persecution for the cause of Christ, having been exiled with other criminals. He could thus identify with the suffering believers to whom he wrote. John was part of the same **kingdom** as his readers—the sphere of salvation; the redeemed community over which Jesus reigns as Lord and King (cf. v. 6). He shared a kinship with them as a fellow subject of Jesus Christ. Finally, John identified with his readers in the matter of **perseverance.** *Hupomonē* (**perseverance**) literally means "to remain under." It speaks of patiently enduring difficulties without giving up.

John further described these experiences as **in Jesus.** Suffering persecution for the cause of Christ, belonging to His kingdom, and patiently enduring trials are distinctly Christian experiences.

When he received this vision, John **was** in exile **on the island**

called Patmos. Patmos is a barren, volcanic island in the Aegean Sea, at its extremities about ten miles long and five to six miles wide, located some forty miles offshore from Miletus (a city in Asia Minor about thirty miles south of Ephesus; cf. Acts 20:15–17). According to the Roman historian Tacitus, exile to such islands was a common form of punishment in the first century. At about the same time that John was banished to Patmos, Emperor Domitian exiled his own niece, Flavia Domitilla, to another island (F. F. Bruce, *New Testament History* [Garden City, N.Y.: Doubleday, 1972], 413). Unlike Flavia Domitilla, whose banishment was politically motivated, John was probably sent to Patmos as a criminal (as a Christian, he was a member of an illegal religious sect). If so, the conditions under which he lived would have been harsh. Exhausting labor under the watchful eye (and ready whip) of a Roman overseer, insufficient food and clothing, and having to sleep on the bare ground would have taken their toll on a ninety-year-old man. It was on that bleak, barren island, under those brutal conditions, that John received the most extensive revelation of the future ever given.

John's only crime was faithfulness to **the word of God and the testimony of Jesus.** As noted in the discussion of verse 2 in chapter 1 of this volume, those two phrases appear to be synonymous. John suffered exile for his faithful, unequivocal, uncompromising preaching of the gospel of Jesus Christ.

John received his vision while he **was in the Spirit;** his experience transcended the bounds of normal human apprehension. Under the Holy Spirit's control, John was transported to a plane of experience and perception beyond that of the human senses. In that state, God supernaturally revealed things to him. Ezekiel (Ezek. 2:2; 3:12, 14), Peter (Acts 10:9ff.), and Paul (Acts 22:17–21; 2 Cor. 12:1ff.) had similar experiences.

John received his vision **on the Lord's day.** While some argue that this refers to the time of eschatological judgment called the Day of the Lord, it is best understood as a reference to Sunday. The Greek phrase translated **the Lord's day** (*tē kuriakē hēmera*) is different from the one translated "the Day of the Lord" (*tē hēmerea tou kuriou,* or *hēmerea kuriou;* cf. 1 Cor. 5:5; 1 Thess. 5:2; 2 Thess. 2:2; 2 Pet. 3:10) and appears only here in the New Testament. Further, the vision John received had nothing to do with the eschatological Day of the Lord; it was a vision of Christ's present ministry in the church. Finally, in the second century the phrase *kuriakē hēmera* was widely used to refer to Sunday (cf. R. J. Bauckham, "The Lord's Day," in D. A. Carson, ed., *From Sabbath to Lord's Day* [Grand Rapids: Zondervan, 1982], 221ff.). The phrase **the Lord's day** became the customary way of referring to Sunday because Christ's resurrection took place on a Sunday.

John received his commission to record the vision in dramatic fashion: **I heard behind me a loud voice like the sound of a trumpet, saying, "Write in a book what you see, and send it to the seven churches: to Ephesus and to Smyrna and to Pergamum and to Thyatira and to Sardis and to Philadelphia and to Laodicea."** The **loud voice** (cf. Ezek. 3:12) was that of the Lord Jesus Christ (cf. vv. 12–13, 17–18), sounding to John in its piercing, commanding clarity **like the sound of a trumpet.** Throughout the book of Revelation, **a loud voice** or sound indicates the solemnity of what is about to be revealed (cf. 5:2, 12; 6:10; 7:2, 10; 8:13; 10:3; 11:12, 15; 12:10; 14:2, 15, 18; 16:1, 17; 19:1, 17; 21:3). The scene is reminiscent of the giving of the Law at Sinai: "So it came about on the third day, when it was morning, that there were thunder and lightning flashes and a thick cloud upon the mountain and a very loud trumpet sound, so that all the people who were in the camp trembled" (Ex. 19:16).

The sovereign, powerful voice from heaven commanded John, **"Write in a book** (or scroll) **what you see."** This is the first of twelve commands in the book of Revelation for John to write what he saw (cf. v. 19; 2:1, 8, 12, 18; 3:1, 7, 14; 14:13; 19:9; 21:5); on one other occasion he was forbidden to write (10:4).

After writing the vision, John was to **send it to the seven churches: to Ephesus and to Smyrna and to Pergamum and to Thyatira and to Sardis and to Philadelphia and to Laodicea.** As noted in the discussion of verse 4, these cities were located in the Roman province of Asia (modern Turkey). These seven churches were chosen because they were located in the key cities of the seven postal districts into which Asia was divided. They were thus the central points for disseminating information.

The seven cities appear in the order that a messenger, traveling on the great circular road that linked them, would visit them. After landing at Miletus, the messenger or messengers bearing the book of Revelation would have traveled north to **Ephesus** (the city nearest to Miletus), then in a clockwise circle to **Smyrna, Pergamum, Thyatira, Sardis, Philadelphia,** and **Laodicea.** Copies of Revelation would have been distributed to each church.

The Unfolding of the Vision

Then I turned to see the voice that was speaking with me. And having turned I saw seven golden lampstands; and in the middle of the lampstands I saw one like a son of man, clothed in a robe reaching to the feet, and girded across His chest with a golden sash. His head and His hair were white like white wool, like snow; and His eyes were like a flame of fire. His feet were like burnished bronze, when it has been made to glow in a furnace,

and His voice was like the sound of many waters. In His right hand He held seven stars, and out of His mouth came a sharp two-edged sword; and His face was like the sun shining in its strength. . . . "As for the mystery of the seven stars which you saw in My right hand, and the seven golden lampstands: the seven stars are the angels of the seven churches, and the seven lampstands are the seven churches." (1:12–16, 20)

Having described the circumstances in which he received it, John then related the vision itself. This revealing and richly instructive look at the present work of the glorified Son of God discloses seven aspects of the Lord Jesus Christ's constant ministry to His church: He empowers, intercedes for, purifies, speaks authoritatively to, controls, protects, and reflects His glory through His church.

CHRIST EMPOWERS HIS CHURCH

Then I turned to see the voice that was speaking with me. And having turned I saw seven golden lampstands; and in the middle of the lampstands I saw one like a son of man, . . . the seven lampstands are the seven churches. (1:12–13a, 20b)

At the outset of the vision John had his back to the voice, so he **turned to see the voice that was speaking with** him. As he did so, he first **saw seven golden lampstands,** identified in verse 20 as **the seven churches.** These were like the common portable oil lamps placed on lampstands that were used to light rooms at night. They symbolize churches as the lights of the world (Phil. 2:15). They are **golden** because gold was the most precious metal. The church is to God the most beautiful and valuable entity on earth—so valuable that Jesus was willing to purchase it with His own blood (Acts 20:28). **Seven** is the number of completeness (cf. Ex. 25:31–40; Zech. 4:2); thus, the seven churches symbolize the churches in general. These were actual churches in real places, but are symbolic of the kinds of churches that exist through all of church history.

In the middle of the lampstands John **saw one like a son of man** (cf. Dan. 7:13)—the glorified Lord of the church moving among His churches. Jesus promised His continued presence with His church. In Matthew 28:20 He said, "I am with you always, even to the end of the age." Matthew 18:20 promises Christ's presence during the difficult work of confronting sin in the church. On the night before His death, Jesus promised His disciples, "I will not leave you as orphans; I will come to you.... If anyone loves Me, he will keep My word; and My Father will love him, and We will come to him and make Our abode with him" (John 14:18, 23). Hebrews 13:5 records His promise, "I will never desert you, nor will I ever forsake you."

Christians do not worship a well-meaning martyr, a dead heroic religious leader. The living Christ indwells His church to lead and empower it. Believers personally and collectively have the inestimable privilege of drawing on that power through continual communion with Him. Paul wrote of the Lord's Supper, "Is not the cup of blessing which we bless a sharing in the blood of Christ? Is not the bread which we break a sharing in the body of Christ?" (1 Cor. 10:16). The presence of the Lord Jesus Christ in His church empowers it, enabling believers to say triumphantly with the apostle Paul, "I can do all things through Him who strengthens me" (Phil. 4:13).

CHRIST INTERCEDES FOR HIS CHURCH

clothed in a robe reaching to the feet, and girded across His chest with a golden sash. (1:13b)

The first thing John noted was that Christ was **clothed in a robe reaching to the feet** (cf. Isa. 6:1). Such robes were worn by royalty (e.g., the kings of Midian, Judg. 8:26; Jonathan, 1 Sam. 18:4; Saul, 1 Sam. 24:4; Ahab and Jehoshaphat, 1 Kings 22:10; and Esther, Est. 5:1;) and prophets (cf. 1 Sam. 28:14). But the word translated **robe** was used most frequently (in six of its seven occurrences) in the Septuagint (the Greek translation of the Old Testament) to describe the robe worn by the high priest. While Christ is biblically presented as prophet and king, and His majesty and dignity emphasized, the **robe** here pictures Christ in His role as the Great High Priest of His people. That He was **girded across His chest with a golden sash** reinforces that interpretation, since the high priest in the Old Testament wore such a sash (cf. Ex. 28:4; Lev. 16:4).

The book of Hebrews says much about Christ's role as our Great High Priest. In 2:17–18 the writer of Hebrews notes, "Therefore, He had to be made like His brethren in all things, so that He might become a merciful and faithful high priest in things pertaining to God, to make propitiation for the sins of the people. For since He Himself was tempted in that which He has suffered, He is able to come to the aid of those who are tempted." In Hebrews 3:1 he refers to Christ as the "High Priest of our confession," while in Hebrews 4:14 he reminds believers that "we have a great high priest who has passed through the heavens, Jesus the Son of God." Our Great High Priest is "able also to save forever those who draw near to God through

Him, since He always lives to make intercession for them" (Heb. 7:25). His offering was infinitely superior to that of any human high priest: "But when Christ appeared as a high priest of the good things to come, He entered through the greater and more perfect tabernacle, not made with hands, that is to say, not of this creation; and not through the blood of goats and calves, but through His own blood, He entered the holy place once for all, having obtained eternal redemption" (Heb. 9:11–12).

As our High Priest, Christ once offered the perfect and complete sacrifice for our sins and permanently, faithfully intercedes for us (Rom. 8:33–34). He has an unequaled capacity to sympathize with us in all our dangers, sorrows, trials, and temptations: "For since He Himself was tempted in that which He has suffered, He is able to come to the aid of those who are tempted.... We do not have a high priest who cannot sympathize with our weaknesses, but One who has been tempted in all things as we are, yet without sin" (Heb. 2:18; 4:15). The knowledge that their High Priest was moving sympathetically in their midst to care for and protect His own provided great comfort and hope to the persecuted churches.

CHRIST PURIFIES HIS CHURCH

His head and His hair were white like white wool, like snow; and His eyes were like a flame of fire. His feet were like burnished bronze, when it has been made to glow in a furnace, (1:14–15*a*)

Having described Christ's clothing in verse 13, John described His person in verses 14 and 15. The first few features depict Christ's work of chastening and purifying His church.

The New Testament clearly sets forth the holy standard that Christ has established for His church. "Therefore you are to be perfect," Jesus commanded, "as your heavenly Father is perfect" (Matt. 5:48). In 2 Corinthians 11:2 Paul wrote, "I betrothed you to one husband, so that to Christ I might present you as a pure virgin." He reminded the Ephesians that "Christ . . . loved the church and gave Himself up for her, so that He might sanctify her, having cleansed her by the washing of water with the word, that He might present to Himself the church in all her glory, having no spot or wrinkle or any such thing; but that she would be holy and blameless" (Eph. 5:25–27). In Colossians 1:22 Paul explained that Christ "has now reconciled you in His fleshly body through death, in order to present you before Him holy and blameless and beyond reproach." Peter reminds believers that God expects them to "like the Holy One who called you, be holy yourselves also in all your behavior; because it is written, 'You shall be holy, for I am holy'" (1 Pet. 1:15–16).

To maintain that divine standard, Christ will discipline His church (Matt. 18:15–17; John 15:2; Heb. 12:5ff.)—even to the point of taking the lives of some impenitent, sinning Christians (Acts 5:1–11; 1 Cor. 11:28–30). Even Peter, who well understood the power of temptation, warned, "It is time for judgment to begin with the household of God" (1 Pet. 4:17).

John's description of Christ's **head and . . . hair as white like white wool, like snow** is an obvious reference to Daniel 7:9, where similar language describes the Ancient of Days (God the Father). The parallel descriptions affirm Christ's deity; He possesses the same attribute of holy knowledge and wisdom as the Father. **White** translates *leukos,* which has the connotation of "bright," "blazing," or "brilliant." It symbolizes Christ's eternal, glorious, holy truthfulness.

Continuing his description of the glorified Christ, John noted that **His eyes were like a flame of fire** (cf. 2:18; 19:12). His searching, revealing, infallible gaze penetrates to the very depths of His church, revealing to Him with piercing clarity the reality of everything there is to know. Jesus declared, "There is nothing concealed that will not be revealed, or hidden that will not be known" (Matt. 10:26). In the words of the author of Hebrews, "There is no creature hidden from His sight, but all things are open and laid bare to the eyes of Him with whom we have to do" (Heb. 4:13). The omniscient Lord of the church will not fail to recognize and deal with sin in His church.

That Christ's **feet were like burnished bronze, when it has been made to glow in a furnace,** continues the obvious sequence by making a clear reference to judgment on sinners in the church. Kings in ancient times sat on elevated thrones, so those being judged would always be beneath the king's feet. The feet of a king thus came to symbolize his authority. The red-hot, glowing feet of the Lord Jesus Christ picture Him moving through His church to exercise His chastening authority, ready to deal out remedial pain, if need be, to sinning Christians.

Hebrews 12:5–10 speaks to this matter:

> You have forgotten the exhortation which is addressed to you as sons, "My son, do not regard lightly the discipline of the Lord, nor faint when you are reproved by Him; for those whom the Lord loves He disciplines, and He scourges every son whom He receives." It is for discipline that you endure; God deals with you as with sons; for what son is there whom his father does not discipline? But if you are without discipline, of which all have become partakers, then you are illegitimate children and not sons. Furthermore, we had earthly fathers to discipline us, and we respected them; shall we not much rather be subject to the Father of spirits, and live? For they disciplined us for a short time as seemed best to them, but He disciplines us for our good, so that we may share His holiness.

It is the Lord's love for His redeemed sinners that pursues their holiness.

CHRIST SPEAKS AUTHORITATIVELY TO HIS CHURCH

and His voice was like the sound of many waters. (1:15b)

When Christ spoke again it was no longer with the trumpetlike sound of verse 10. To John, **His voice** now **was like the sound of many waters** (cf. 14:2; 19:6), like the familiar mighty roar of the surf crashing on the rocky shores of Patmos in a storm. The voice of the eternal God was similarly described in Ezekiel 43:2—yet another parallel affirming Christ's deity. This is the voice of sovereign power, the voice of supreme authority, the very voice that will one day command the dead to come forth from the graves (John 5:28–29).

When Christ speaks, the church must listen. At the Transfiguration God said, "This is My beloved Son, . . . listen to Him!" (Matt. 17:5). "God, after He spoke long ago to the fathers in the prophets in many portions and in many ways," wrote the author of Hebrews, "in these last days has spoken to us in His Son" (Heb. 1:1–2). Christ speaks to His church directly through the Holy Spirit-inspired Scriptures.

CHRIST CONTROLS HIS CHURCH

In His right hand He held seven stars . . . the seven stars are the angels of the seven churches, (1:16a, 20a)

As the head of His church (Eph. 4:15; 5:23; Col. 1:18), and the ruler of the "kingdom of [God's] beloved Son" (Col. 1:13), Christ exercises authority in His church. In John's vision, Christ is holding **in His right hand** the **seven stars** (cf. 2:1; 3:1), identified in verse 20 as **the angels of the seven churches**, which symbolized those authorities. That He held them **in His right hand** does not picture safety and protection, but control. *Angeloi* (**angels**) is the common New Testament word for angels, leading some interpreters reasonably to conclude that angels are in view in this passage. But the New Testament nowhere teaches that angels are involved in the leadership of the church. Angels do not sin and thus have no need to repent, as the messengers, along with the congregations they represented, are exhorted to do (cf. 2:4–5, 14, 20; 3:1–3, 15, 17, 19). Dr. Robert L. Thomas notes a further difficulty with this view: "It presumes that Christ is sending a message to heavenly beings through John, an earthly agent, so that it may reach earthly churches through angelic representatives" (*Revelation 1–7: An Exegetical Commentary* [Chicago: Moody, 1992], 117). Therefore, *angeloi* is better rendered "messengers," as in Luke 7:24; 9:52; and James 2:25. Some suggest that these messengers were representatives from each of the seven churches who came to visit John on Patmos and take the book of Revelation back with them. But since Christ is said to hold them in His right hand, they were more likely leading elders and pastors (though not the sole leaders, since the New Testament teaches a plurality of elders), one from each of the seven churches.

These seven men demonstrate the function of spiritual leaders in the church. They are to be instruments through which Christ, the head of the church, mediates His rule. That is why the standards for leadership in the New Testament are so high. To be assigned as an intermediary through which the Lord Jesus Christ controls His church is to be called to a sobering responsibility (cf. 1 Tim. 3:1–7; Titus 1:5–9 for the qualifications for such men).

CHRIST PROTECTS HIS CHURCH

and out of His mouth came a sharp two-edged sword; (1:16*b*)

The Lord Jesus Christ's presence also provides protection for His church. The **sharp two-edged sword that came . . . out of His mouth** is used to defend the church against external threats (cf. 19:15, 21). But here it speaks primarily of judgment against enemies from within the church (cf. 2:12, 16; Acts 20:30). Those who attack Christ's church, those who would sow lies, create discord, or otherwise harm His people, will be personally dealt with by the Lord of the church. His word is potent (cf. Heb. 4:12–13), and will be used against the enemies of His people (cf. 2 Thess. 2:8), so that all the power of the forces of darkness, including death itself (the "gates of Hades"; Matt. 16:18), will be unable to prevent the Lord Jesus Christ from building His church.

CHRIST REFLECTS HIS GLORY THROUGH HIS CHURCH

and His face was like the sun shining in its strength. (1:16*c*)

John's vision of the glorified Lord of the church culminated in this description of the radiant glory evident on **His face,** which John could only describe as **like the sun shining in its strength.** John borrowed that phrase from Judges 5:31, where it describes those who love the Lord (cf. Matt. 13:43). The glory of God through the Lord Jesus Christ shines in and through His church, reflecting His glory to the world (cf. 2 Cor. 4:6). And the result is that He is glorified (Eph. 3:21).

THE EFFECTS OF THE VISION

When I saw Him, I fell at His feet like a dead man. And He placed His right hand on me, saying, "Do not be afraid; I am the first and the last, and the living One; and I was dead, and behold, I am alive forevermore, and I have the keys of death and of Hades. Therefore write the things which you have seen, and the things which are, and the things which will take place after these things." (1:17–19)

The overwhelming vision John witnessed dramatically altered him. Initially, his response was devastating fear, which the Lord removed by assurance and then by giving John a sense of duty.

FEAR

When I saw Him, I fell at His feet like a dead man. (1:17*a*)

In a manner similar to his experience with the glory of Jesus on the Mount of Transfiguration more than six decades earlier (cf. Matt. 17:6), John was again overwhelmed with terror at the manifestation of Christ's glory and **fell at His feet like a dead man.** Such fear was standard for those few who experienced such unusual heavenly visions. When an angel appeared to him, Daniel reported that "no strength was left in me, for my natural color turned to a deathly pallor, and I retained no strength.... and as soon as I heard the sound of his words, I fell into a deep sleep on my face, with my face to the ground" (Dan. 10:8–9; cf. 8:17). Overwhelmed by the vision of God that he saw in the temple, Isaiah cried out, "Woe is me, for I am ruined! Because I am a man of unclean lips, and I live among a people of unclean lips; for my eyes have seen the King, the Lord of hosts" (Isa. 6:5). Ezekiel saw several visions of the Lord's glory and his response was always the same: he fell on his face (Ezek. 1:28; 3:23; 9:8; 43:3; 44:4). After the Angel of the Lord appeared to them and announced the birth of Samson, "Manoah [Samson's father] said to his wife, 'We shall surely die, for we have seen God'" (Judg. 13:22). Job had a similar reaction after God spoke to him: "I have heard of You by the hearing of the ear; but now my eye sees You; therefore I retract, and I repent in dust and ashes" (Job 42:5–6). On his way to Damascus to persecute Christians, Saul of Tarsus (better known as the apostle Paul) "saw on the way a light from heaven, brighter than the sun, shining all around me and those who were journeying with me" (Acts 26:13). In response, Saul and his companions fell prostrate in the road (v. 14). After witnessing the terrifying calamities that follow the opening of the sixth seal, unbelievers during the Tribulation will cry out in terror "to the mountains and to the rocks, 'Fall on us and hide us from the presence of Him who sits on the throne, and from the wrath of the Lamb; for the great day of their wrath has come, and who is able to stand?'" (Rev. 6:16–17).

In stark contrast to the silly, frivolous, false, and boastful claims of many in our own day who claim to have seen God, the reaction of those in Scripture who genuinely saw God was inevitably one of fear. Those brought face-to-face with the blazing, holy glory of the Lord Jesus Christ are terrified, realizing their sinful unworthiness to be in His holy presence. Summarizing the proper response to God's holiness and majesty, the writer of Hebrews exhorts believers to "offer to God an acceptable service with reverence and awe; for our God is a consuming fire" (Heb. 12:28–29).

ASSURANCE

And He placed His right hand on me, saying, "Do not be afraid; I am the first and the last, and the living One; and I was dead, and behold, I am alive forevermore, and I have the keys of death and of Hades. (1:17b–18)

As He had done so long ago at the Transfiguration (Matt. 17:7), Jesus **placed His right hand on** John and comforted him. This is a touch of comfort and reassurance. There is comfort for Christians overwhelmed by the glory and majesty of Christ in the assurance of His gracious love and merciful forgiveness. Jesus' comforting words, **"Do not be afraid,"** (lit. "Stop being afraid") reveal His compassionate assurance of the terrified apostle. Similar words of comfort are God's response throughout Scripture to those overwhelmed by His majestic presence (e.g., Gen. 15:1; 26:24; Judg. 6:23; Matt. 14:27; 17:7; 28:10).

The comfort Jesus offered was based on who He is and the authority He possesses. First, He identified Himself as **I am** (*egō eimi*)—the covenant name of God (cf. Ex. 3:14). It was that name with which He had comforted the terrified disciples who saw Him walking on the Sea of Galilee (Matt. 14:27). Jesus took that name for Himself in John 8:58—a direct claim to deity that was not lost on His opponents (v. 59).

Jesus next identified Himself as **the first and the last** (cf. 2:8; 22:13), a title used of God in the Old Testament (Isa. 44:6; 48:12; cf. 41:4). When all false gods have come and gone, only He remains. He existed before them and will continue to exist eternally, long after they have been forgotten. Jesus' application of that title to Himself is another powerful proof of His deity.

The third title of deity Jesus claimed is that of **the living One** (cf. John 1:4; 14:6). That also is a title used throughout Scripture to describe God (e.g., Josh. 3:10; 1 Sam. 17:26; Ps. 84:2; Hos. 1:10; Matt. 16:16; 26:63; Acts 14:15; Rom. 9:26; 2 Cor. 3:3; 6:16; 1 Thess. 1:9; 1 Tim. 3:15; 4:10; Heb. 3:12; 9:14; 10:31; Rev. 7:2). God is the eternal, uncaused, self–existent One. In John 5:26 Jesus said to His Jewish opponents, "Just as the Father has life in Himself, even so He gave to the Son also to have life in Himself," thus claiming full equality with God the Father.

The One whose presence struck fear into John's heart, the I Am, the first and the last, the living One, the One whose death freed him from his sins (Rev. 1:5) is the very One who comforted and reassured John. In the words of the apostle Paul, "What then shall we say to these things? If God is for us, who is against us?" (Rom. 8:31).

Christ's seemingly paradoxical declaration **I was dead, and behold, I am alive forevermore** provides further grounds for assurance. The Greek text literally reads, "I became dead." The living One, the eternal, self-existent God who could never die, became man and died. As Peter explains in 1 Peter 3:18, Christ was "put to death in the flesh, but made alive in the spirit." In His humanness He died without ceasing to live as God.

Behold introduces a statement of amazement and wonder: **I am alive forevermore.** Christ lives forever in a union of glorified humanity and deity, "according to the power of an indestructible life" (Heb. 7:16). "Christ, having been raised from the dead," wrote Paul, "is never to die again; death no longer is master over Him" (Rom. 6:9). That truth provides comfort and assurance, because Jesus "is able also to save forever those who draw near to God through Him, since He always lives to make intercession for them" (Heb. 7:25). In spite of his sinfulness in the presence of the glorious Lord of heaven, John had nothing to fear because that same Lord had paid by His death the penalty for John's sins (and those of all who believe in Him) and risen to be his eternal advocate.

As the eternal I Am, the first and the last, the living One, Jesus holds **the keys of death and of Hades.** Those terms are essentially synonymous, with **death** being the condition and **Hades** the place. **Hades** is the New Testament equivalent of the Old Testament term *Sheol* and refers to the place of the dead. **Keys** denote access and authority. Jesus Christ has the authority to decide who dies and who lives; He controls life and death. And John, like all the redeemed, had nothing to fear, since Christ had already delivered him from death and Hades by His own death.

Knowing that Christ has authority over death provides assurance, since believers need no longer fear it. Jesus declared, "I am the res-

urrection and the life; he who believes in Me will live even if he dies....
because I live, you will live also." (John 11:25; 14:19). To die, Paul noted, is
"to be absent from the body and to be at home with the Lord" (2 Cor. 5:8;
cf. Phil. 1:23). Jesus conquered Satan and took the keys of death away
from him: "Through death [Christ rendered] powerless him who had the
power of death, that is, the devil, and ... free[d] those who through fear of
death were subject to slavery all their lives" (Heb. 2:14–15). The knowledge that Christ "loves us and released us from our sins by His blood"
(Rev. 1:5) provides the assurance that is the balance to the reverential
fear that His glory and majesty evoke.

DUTY

**Therefore write the things which you have seen, and the things
which are, and the things which will take place after these things.**
(1:19)

The astounding vision John saw inspired in him a healthy ten-
sion between fear and assurance. But to that was added a reminder of his
duty. Christ's earlier command to **write** is now expanded, as John is told
to record three features. First, **the things which you have seen,** the
vision John had just seen and recorded in verses 10–16. Next, **the things
which are,** a reference to the letters to the seven churches in chapters 2
and 3, which describe the present state of the church. Finally, John was to
write **the things which will take place after these things,** the prophetic
revelations of future events unfolded in chapters 4–22. This threefold
command provides an outline for the book of Revelation, encompassing
(from John's perspective) the past, present, and future.
Like John, all Christians have a duty to pass on the truths they
learn from the visions recorded in this book. Those visions may at first be
startling, disturbing, or fascinating. But they, like all Scripture, are "inspired
by God and profitable for teaching, for reproof, for correction, for training
in righteousness; so that the man of God may be adequate, equipped for
every good work" (2 Tim. 3:16–17). As believers study the glory of Christ
reflected in the book of Revelation, "we all, with unveiled face, beholding
as in a mirror the glory of the Lord, [will be] transformed into the same
image from glory to glory, just as from the Lord, the Spirit" (2 Cor. 3:18).

Ephesus: When Loves Grows Cold (Revelation 2:1–7)

4

"To the angel of the church in Ephesus write: The One who holds the seven stars in His right hand, the One who walks among the seven golden lampstands, says this: 'I know your deeds and your toil and perseverance, and that you cannot tolerate evil men, and you put to the test those who call themselves apostles, and they are not, and you found them to be false; and you have perseverance and have endured for My name's sake, and have not grown weary. But I have this against you, that you have left your first love. Therefore remember from where you have fallen, and repent and do the deeds you did at first; or else I am coming to you and will remove your lampstand out of its place—unless you repent. Yet this you do have, that you hate the deeds of the Nicolaitans, which I also hate. He who has an ear, let him hear what the Spirit says to the churches. To him who overcomes, I will grant to eat of the tree of life which is in the Paradise of God.'" (2:1–7)

The late Francis Schaeffer once observed that "the meaning of the word *Christian* has been reduced to practically nothing.... Because the word *Christian* as a symbol has been made to mean so little, it has come to mean everything and nothing" (*The Mark of the Christian* [Downers Grove, Ill: InterVarsity, 1970], 11). The term *Christian* in contemporary usage can mean anyone who is not Jewish, anyone who lives in a "Christian" nation (as opposed, for example, to a Buddhist or an Islamic one), or anyone who claims any kind of allegiance to Jesus Christ. The term *evangelical* is following the same trend toward imprecision.

But though the world may be confused about what a Christian is, the Bible is clear. Christians are those who are savingly united to God through Jesus Christ, those whom "God has chosen ... from the beginning for salvation through sanctification by the Spirit and faith in the truth" (2 Thess. 2:13; cf. Luke 18:7; Rom. 8:33; Eph. 1:4; Col. 3:12; 1 Thess. 1:4; 2 Tim. 2:10; Titus 1:1; 1 Pet. 1:1–2; 2:10). As a result, they have exercised saving faith in the only Savior (Acts 4:12), the Lord Jesus Christ (John 3:15–18, 36; 5:24; 6:47; Rom. 1:16; 4:5; 10:10; 1 John 5:1), and repented of their sins (Rom. 2:4; 2 Pet. 3:9). God has forgiven their sins (Acts 10:43; Eph. 1:7; 1 John 1:7, 9; Rev. 1:5), made them His children (Rom. 8:16–17; Gal. 4:7; Eph. 1:5; 5:1, 8; Phil. 2:15; 1 John 3:2), and transformed them into new creatures (2 Cor. 5:17) indwelt by the Holy Spirit (John 14:17; Rom. 8:4, 9, 11, 14; 1 Cor. 3:16; 6:19; Gal. 4:6; 2 Tim. 1:14; 1 John 3:24).

Many things characterize Christians, including reverential fear of God (2 Cor. 7:1; Phil. 2:12; 1 Pet. 1:17), a desire to imitate Him (Eph. 5:1; 1 John 2:6), holiness (Matt. 5:48; 2 Cor. 7:1; Titus 2:11–12; Heb. 12:14; 1 Pet. 1:15–16; 2:24; 2 Pet. 3:11), and obedience (John 10:27; 14:21; 15:14; Rom. 1:5; 16:26; Heb. 5:9; 1 Pet. 1:2; 1 John 3:24). But the supreme characteristic of a Christian is love for his Lord and God. When challenged to name the single greatest commandment of the law, Jesus replied, " 'You shall love the Lord your God with all your heart, and with all your soul, and with all your mind.' This is the great and foremost commandment" (Matt. 22:37–38). He challenged His disciples to make love for Him the highest priority of their lives: "He who loves father or mother more than Me is not worthy of Me; and he who loves son or daughter more than Me is not worthy of Me. And he who does not take his cross and follow after Me is not worthy of Me" (Matt. 10:37–38). In John 14:21, 23 He added, "He who has my commandments and keeps them is the one who loves Me; and he who loves Me will be loved by My Father, and I will love him and will disclose Myself to him. . . . If anyone loves Me, he will keep My word; and My Father will love him, and We will come to him and make Our abode with him." True children of God, Jesus declared, will love Him (John 8:42; cf. 1 Pet. 1:8) and be known by Him (1 Cor. 8:3). To discern Peter's spiritual condition, Jesus asked him three times, "Do you love Me?" (John 21:15–17). Paul defined Christians as those controlled by "the love of Christ" (2 Cor. 5:14). Those who love Jesus Christ are blessed (Eph. 6:24); those who do not are cursed (1 Cor. 16:22). While love for the Lord Jesus

Christ will always be present in true Christians, it can fluctuate in its intensity. Christians will not always love Jesus Christ with all their heart, soul, mind, and strength, and to fail to do so is sin. There is no better illustration in Scripture of the seriousness of allowing love for Christ to wane than this letter to the church at Ephesus.

The seven churches addressed in chapters 2 and 3 were actual existing churches when John wrote. But while not precisely duplicated, they also represent the types of churches that are generally present throughout the entire church age. Five of the seven churches (Smyrna and Philadelphia being the exceptions) were rebuked for tolerating sin in their midst, not an uncommon occurrence in churches since. The problems in those five churches ranged in severity from waning love at Ephesus to total apostasy at Laodicea. Further, any church in any age could have a mixture of the sins that plagued these five churches.

Though Christ may have addressed the Ephesian church first because it was first on the postal route, it was also the most prominent church of the seven. It was the mother church out of whose ministry the other six were founded (cf. Acts 19:10) and gave its name to the inspired letter of Ephesians penned four decades earlier by the apostle Paul. The contents of this first letter form the pattern for the other six. It contains seven features: the correspondent, the church, the city, the commendation, the concern, the command, and the counsel.

THE CORRESPONDENT

The One who holds the seven stars in His right hand, the One who walks among the seven golden lampstands, (2:1c)

Though the writer is not named, the description makes it obvious who He is. He is the One depicted as the glorious Lord of the church in 1:9–20, the exalted Jesus Christ. The phrases **the One who holds the seven stars in His right hand and the One who walks among the seven golden lampstands** are taken from the description of Christ in John's vision (cf. 1:13, 16). In fact, Christ identifies Himself to each of the first five churches by using phrases from that vision (cf. 2:8 with 1:18; 2:12 with 1:16; 2:18 with 1:14–15; 3:1 with 1:16). That reinforces the truth that He is the author of the letters; they are His direct word, through the apostle John, to those local congregations and to churches like them in years beyond.

As noted in chapter 3 of this volume, **the seven stars** represent leaders from the seven churches. That Christ **holds** them **in His right hand** indicates that they are His ministers, under His power as He mediates His sovereign rule in the church through its human leaders. Christ further describes Himself as **the One who walks among the seven golden lampstands** (the seven churches; 1:20)—scrutinizing, examining, assessing, and evaluating them. As its sovereign ruler, He has the authority to address the church.

THE CHURCH

the church in Ephesus (2:1*a*)

Perhaps no church in history had as rich a heritage as the congregation at Ephesus. The gospel was introduced to that city by Paul's close friends and partners in ministry, Priscilla and Aquila (Acts 18:18–19). They were soon joined by the eloquent preacher and powerful debater Apollos (Acts 18:24–26). Priscilla, Aquila, and Apollos laid the groundwork for Paul's ministry in Ephesus.

The apostle Paul stopped briefly in Ephesus near the end of his second missionary journey (Acts 18:19–21), but his real ministry in that key city took place on his third missionary journey. Arriving in Ephesus, he first encountered a group of Old Testament saints, followers of John the Baptist (Acts 19:1–7). After preaching the gospel to them, he baptized them in the name of the Lord Jesus Christ (Acts 19:5). That began Paul's work of building the church at Ephesus—a work that would last for three years (Acts 20:31). Later, on his way to Jerusalem near the end of his third missionary journey, he taught the elders of the Ephesian church the essential principles of church leadership (Acts 20:17–38), the gist of which he later expanded in his pastoral epistles. Paul's protégé Timothy served as pastor of the church at Ephesus (1 Tim. 1:3). Onesiphorus (2 Tim. 1:16, 18) and Tychicus (2 Tim 4:12), two more of Paul's fellow laborers, also ministered at Ephesus. Finally, according to the testimony of the early church, the apostle John spent the last decades of his life at Ephesus, from which he likely wrote his three epistles in which he calls himself "the elder" (cf. 2 John 1; 3 John 1). He was no doubt leading the Ephesian church when he was arrested and exiled to Patmos.

Dramatic and remarkable events accompanied the birth of the Ephesian church. Paul's ministry profoundly affected not only the city of Ephesus, but also the entire province of Asia (Acts 19:10). As previously noted, it was undoubtedly during this time that the rest of the seven churches were founded. God supernaturally affirmed Paul as His spokesman through a series of spectacular miracles (Acts 19:11–12). Attempting to emulate Paul's success, a group of Jewish would-be exorcists were beaten and humiliated by a demon-possessed individual (Acts 19:13–

16). Their debacle spread consternation and fear throughout the city, causing "the name of the Lord Jesus [to be] magnified" (Acts 19:17). Shocked into realizing the futility of trusting in pagan practices, "many also of those who had believed kept coming, confessing and disclosing their practices. And many of those who practiced magic brought their books together and began burning them in the sight of everyone; and they counted up the price of them and found it fifty thousand pieces of silver" (vv. 18–19). That staggering sum, equivalent to 50,000 days of workers' wages, reveals the magnitude of Ephesus's involvement in the magic arts.

The striking conversions of large numbers of Ephesians posed a severe economic threat to the city's pagan craftsmen. Ephesus was the center of the worship of the goddess Artemis (known to the Romans as Diana), whose ornate temple was one of the Seven Wonders of the Ancient World. At the instigation of a silversmith named Demetrius the craftsmen, who saw their lucrative business endangered, reacted violently. The ensuing riot threw Ephesus into chaos (Acts 19:23–41).

By the time of this letter, four decades had passed since the Ephesian church's tumultuous birth. The apostle Paul was gone, as were many of the first generation of believers converted under his ministry. A new situation called for another inspired letter to the Ephesians, this one from the Lord Himself, penned by the apostle John.

THE CITY

Ephesus (2:1b)

Although not its capital (Pergamum was the province's official capital), Ephesus was the most important city in Asia Minor. (Since the Roman governor resided there, it could be argued that Ephesus was the de facto capital.) Its population in New Testament times has been estimated at between 250,000 and 500,000 people. The city's theater, visible today, into which the frenzied rioters dragged Paul's companions Gaius and Aristarchus (Acts 19:29), held an estimated 25,000 people. Ephesus was a free city (i.e., self-governing, within limits), and no Roman troops were garrisoned there. The city hosted athletic events, rivaling the Olympic games.

Ephesus was the primary harbor in the province of Asia. (By law incoming Roman governors had to enter Asia through Ephesus.) The city was located on the Cayster River, about three miles upriver from where it flowed into the sea. Those disembarking at the harbor traveled along a magnificent, wide, column-lined road (the Arcadian Way) that led to the center of the city. In John's day silt deposited by the Cayster River was slowly filling up the harbor, forcing the city to fight to keep a channel open. That battle would ultimately be lost, and today the ruins of Ephesus are located some six miles inland from the sea.

Ephesus was also strategically located at the junction of four of the most important Roman roads in Asia Minor. That, along with its harbor, prompted the geographer Strabo (a contemporary of Christ) to describe Ephesus as the market of Asia.

But Ephesus was most famous as the center of the worship of the goddess Artemis (Diana)—a point of great civic pride (Acts 19:27, 35). The temple of Artemis was Ephesus's most prominent landmark. Because its inner shrine was supposedly inviolable, the temple served as one of the most important banks in the Mediterranean world. The temple and its environs also provided sanctuary for criminals. Further, the sale of items used in the worship of Artemis provided an important source of income for the city (cf. Acts 19:24). Every spring a month-long festival was held in honor of the goddess, complete with athletic, dramatic, and musical events. Paul may have anticipated this annual event as a unique evangelistic opportunity and have been waiting for it when he wrote the Corinthians that he intended to remain in Ephesus (1 Cor. 16:8).

The worship of Artemis was unspeakably vile. Her idol was a gross, many-breasted monstrosity, popularly believed to have fallen from heaven (Acts 19:35). The temple was attended by numerous priests, eunuchs, and slaves. Thousands of priestesses, who were little more than ritual prostitutes, played a major role in the worship of Artemis. The temple grounds were a chaotic cacophony of priests, prostitutes, bankers, criminals, musicians, dancers, and frenzied, hysterical worshipers. The philosopher Heraclitus was called the weeping philosopher because no one, he declared, could live in Ephesus and not weep over its immorality (see William Barclay, *The Revelation of John* [Philadelphia: Westminster, 1976], 1:60).

Huddled in the midst of such pagan idolatry that characterized Ephesus was a faithful group of Christians. It was to them that Christ addressed this first of the seven letters.

THE COMMENDATION

I know your deeds and your toil and perseverance, and that you cannot tolerate evil men, and you put to the test those who call themselves apostles, and they are not, and you found them to be false; and you have perseverance and have endured for My name's sake, and have not grown weary. . . . Yet this you do have,

that you hate the deeds of the Nicolaitans, which I also hate.
(2:2–3,6)

Oida (**know**) indicates the Lord's knowledge in each of the
seven letters (cf. 2:9; 13, 19; 3:1, 8, 15). In contrast to *ginōskō*, which refers
to a progressive acquisition of knowledge, *oida* refers to complete and
full knowledge. The Lord of the church knows everything there is to
know about the church—both good and bad. Such perfect knowledge is
evident in each letter as the Lord condemns and commends the churches.

Before rebuking them for their failings, the Lord Jesus Christ
commended the Ephesians for what they were doing right. He began by
acknowledging their **deeds**—a general term summarizing all that follows. Specifically, Christ first commended the Ephesian believers for
their **toil.** *Kopos* (**toil**) denotes labor to the point of sweat and exhaus-
tion. It describes an all-out effort, demanding all that a person has to
give—physically, mentally, and emotionally. The Ephesians were diligent
workers for the cause of Christ. Theirs was no spectator mentality; they
did not want merely to be entertained. Nor were they content to eat the
fruit of others' labor, but were willing to plow, plant, and harvest their own
crop. In the midst of the pagan darkness that surrounded them, they were
aggressively evangelizing the lost, edifying the saints, and caring for those
in need.

Perseverance translates *hupomonē*, which denotes patience in
trying circumstances. In contrast, its synonym, *makrothumia*, generally
emphasizes patience with people (cf. Richard C. Trench, *Synonyms of the
New Testament* [reprint; Grand Rapids: Eerdmans, 1983], 195ff.). *Hupomonē*
does not denote a grim, fatalistic resignation, but a courageous accep-
tance of hardship, suffering, and loss. This commendation indicates that,
despite their difficult circumstances, the Ephesian believers remained
faithful to their Lord.

Another praiseworthy aspect of the Ephesian believers was that
they refused to **tolerate evil men.** They held to a high, holy standard of
behavior and were sensitive to sin, undoubtedly following the Lord's
mandate to practice church discipline (Matt. 18:15ff.). Four decades earlier Paul had commanded them not to "give the devil an opportunity"
(Eph. 4:27), and they were still reluctant to do so.

Nor was the Ephesian church lacking in spiritual discernment,
since it **put to the test those who call themselves apostles, and they
are not, and . . . found them to be false.** The Ephesians never forgot
the admonition Paul had addressed to their leaders so many years earlier:

> Be on guard for yourselves and for all the flock, among which the Holy
> Spirit has made you overseers, to shepherd the church of God which

He purchased with His own blood. I know that after my departure sav-age wolves will come in among you, not sparing the flock; and from among your own selves men will arise, speaking perverse things, to draw away the disciples after them. Therefore be on the alert. (Acts 20:28–31)

False teachers pose a constant danger to the church. Jesus warned of "false prophets, who come to you in sheep's clothing, but inwardly are ravenous wolves" (Matt. 7:15). In his second epistle, John warned of the "many deceivers [who] have gone out into the world" (2 John 7) and cautioned believers, "If anyone comes to you and does not bring [true biblical] teaching, do not receive him into your house, and do not give him a greeting" (2 John 10). Paul confronted false "apostles" in Corinth and unmasked them with this description: "Such men are false apostles, deceitful workers, disguising themselves as apostles of Christ. No wonder, for even Satan disguises himself as an angel of light. Therefore it is not surprising if his servants also disguise themselves as servants of righ-teousness, whose end will be according to their deeds" (2 Cor. 11:13–15). The *Didache,* an early Christian manual of church order, also warned of the danger of false teachers:

> Welcome every apostle on arriving, as if he were the Lord. But he must not stay beyond one day. In case of necessity, however, the next day too. If he stays three days, he is a false prophet. On departing, an apostle must not accept anything save sufficient food to carry him till his next lodging. If he asks for money, he is a false prophet. (11.4–6; cited in Cyril C. Richardson, ed., *Early Christian Fathers* [New York: Macmillan, 1970], 176)

The early church father Ignatius, writing not long after John penned the book of Revelation, also commended the Ephesians for their vigilance: "You heed nobody beyond what he has to say truthfully about Jesus Christ. . . . I have heard that some strangers came your way with a wicked teaching. But you did not let them sow it among you. You stopped up your ears to prevent admitting what they disseminated" (*Ephesians* 6.2; 9.1; cited in Richardson, *Early Christian Fathers,* 89, 90).

Through all the difficulties the Ephesians faced over forty years, through all their hard labor and patient enduring of trials, their refusal to tolerate evil, and their spiritual discernment, they maintained their **per-severance.** They **endured,** Jesus declared, for the highest of motives: **for** His **name's sake.** And they had done so without having **grown weary** (cf. Gal. 6:9); they had not yielded to disappointment, ingratitude, or criticism. They remained faithful to the Lord, loyal to His Word and to the work to which He had called them.

Jesus adds a final commendation in verse 6: **Yet this you do have, that you hate the deeds of the Nicolaitans, which I also hate.** The **Nicolaitans,** mentioned also in the letter to Pergamum (2:12–15), cannot be positively identified. The few references to this heresy in the writings of the church fathers link it to Nicolas, one of the seven men appointed to oversee the distribution of food in Acts 6. Some argued that Nicolas was a false believer who became an apostate, but retained influence in the church because of his credentials. Others suggested that the **Nicolaitans** misrepresented his teaching. Whatever its origin, Nicolaitanism led people into immorality and wickedness. The letter to Pergamum links it with Balaam's false teaching that led Israel astray. The **deeds of the Nicolaitans** thus involved sensual temptations leading to sexual immorality and eating things sacrificed to idols (2:14) without regard for the offense of such behavior (cf. Rom. 14:1–15:3)—all in the name of Christian liberty. It has been suggested that "the teaching of the Nicolaitans was an exaggeration of the doctrine of Christian liberty which attempted an ethical compromise with heathenism" (Merrill C. Tenney, *Interpreting Revelation* [Grand Rapids: Eerdmans, 1957], 61). Irenaeus wrote of the Nicolaitans that they "lived lives of unrestrained indulgence" (cited in Tenney, *Interpreting Revelation,* 61). Clement of Alexandria added that the Nicolaitans "abandon themselves to pleasure like goats ... leading a life of self-indulgence" (cited in Barclay, *The Revelation of John,* 1:67).

Unlike the church at Pergamum, the Ephesian church did not tolerate the **Nicolaitans** but hated their heretical teachings. For that the Lord Jesus Christ commended them. Hatred was an appropriate attitude and exactly the opposite reaction to the tolerance of the Pergamum church toward the Nicolaitans (2:14–15). The Bible reveals that God hates impurity (Isa. 61:8; Jer. 44:4; Amos 5:21; Zech. 8:17).

THE CONCERN

But I have this against you, that you have left your first love. (2:4)

Despite all the praiseworthy elements in the Ephesian church, the penetrating, omniscient gaze of the Lord Jesus Christ had spotted a fatal flaw. Though they maintained their doctrinal orthodoxy and continued to serve Christ, that service had degenerated into mechanical orthodoxy. Though at one time they had love (Eph. 1:15; 3:17–19; 6:23), forty years later the affection of the first generation of believers had cooled. The current generation was maintaining the doctrine handed down to them, but they had **left** their **first love.** That love could include love for

God and Christ, love for each other, and love for the lost. It is love defined as obedience (2 John 6). They had sunk to the place where they were carrying out their Christian responsibilities with diminishing love for their Lord and others.

The grave danger of that situation is aptly illustrated by the disaster that ensued when Israel's love for God cooled. Through Jeremiah, God rebuked His people for forsaking Him:

> "Go and proclaim in the ears of Jerusalem, saying, 'Thus says the Lord, "I remember concerning you the devotion of your youth, the love of your betrothals, your following after Me in the wilderness, through a land not sown. Israel was holy to the Lord, the first of His harvest. All who ate of it became guilty; evil came upon them," declares the Lord.'"

> Hear the word of the Lord, O house of Jacob, and all the families of the house of Israel. Thus says the Lord, "What injustice did your fathers find in Me, that they went far from Me and walked after emptiness and became empty? They did not say, 'Where is the Lord who brought us up out of the land of Egypt, who led us through the wilderness, through a land of deserts and of pits, through a land of drought and of deep darkness, through a land that no one crossed and where no man dwelt?' I brought you into the fruitful land to eat its fruit and its good things. But you came and defiled My land, and My inheritance you made an abomination. The priests did not say, 'Where is the Lord?' and those who handle the law did not know Me; the rulers also transgressed against Me, and the prophets prophesied by Baal and walked after things that did not profit. Therefore I will yet contend with you," declares the Lord, "And with your sons' sons I will contend. For cross to the coastlands of Kittim and see, and send to Kedar and observe closely and see if there has been such a thing as this! Has a nation changed gods when they were not gods? But My people have changed their glory for that which does not profit. Be appalled, O heavens, at this, and shudder, be very desolate," declares the Lord. "For My people have committed two evils: they have forsaken Me, the fountain of living waters, to hew for themselves cisterns, broken cisterns that can hold no water." (Jer. 2:2–13)

In a powerful and striking passage Ezekiel also pictured Israel's abandonment of her first love for God:

> "I passed by you and saw you, and behold, you were at the time for love; so I spread My skirt over you and covered your nakedness. I also swore to you and entered into a covenant with you so that you became Mine," declares the Lord God. "Then I bathed you with water, washed off your blood from you and anointed you with oil. I also clothed you with embroidered cloth and put sandals of porpoise skin on your feet; and I wrapped you with fine linen and covered you with silk. I adorned you

with ornaments, put bracelets on your hands and a necklace around your neck. I also put a ring in your nostril, earrings in your ears and a beautiful crown on your head. Thus you were adorned with gold and silver, and your dress was of fine linen, silk and embroidered cloth. You ate fine flour, honey and oil; so you were exceedingly beautiful and advanced to royalty. Then your fame went forth among the nations on account of your beauty, for it was perfect because of My splendor which I bestowed on you," declares the Lord God.

"But you trusted in your beauty and played the harlot because of your fame, and you poured out your harlotries on every passer-by who might be willing." (Ezek. 16:8–15)

As it had in Israel, the honeymoon had ended at Ephesus. The loss of a vital love relationship with the Lord Jesus Christ opened the doors to spiritual apathy, indifference to others, love for the world, compromise with evil, judgment, and, ultimately, the death of the church altogether. Despite its outwardly robust appearance, a deadly spiritual cancer was growing at the heart of the Ephesian church.

THE COMMAND

Therefore remember from where you have fallen, and repent and do the deeds you did at first; or else I am coming to you and will remove your lampstand out of its place—unless you repent. (2:5)

The Great Physician issued a prescription to the Ephesians which, if followed, would cure their spiritual malaise. First, they needed to **remember** (lit. "to keep on remembering") **from where** they had **fallen.** Forgetfulness is frequently the initial cause of spiritual decline, and the Ephesians needed to recognize the seriousness of such a lapse. Second, they needed to **repent** in a deliberate rejection of their sins, because to fail to love God with all one's heart, soul, mind, and strength is sin (Matt. 22:36–38). Finally, they needed to demonstrate the genuineness of their repentance and **do the deeds** they **did at first.** They needed to recapture the richness of Bible study, devotion to prayer, and passion for worship that had once characterized them.

Richard Mayhue writes that Jesus' confrontation of the Ephesian church models how believers are to confront:

First, confronting was done with love and with the goal of restoration (2:4–5).

Second, encouragement preceded correction (2:2–3,6).

Third, Christ openly and concisely stated the problem (2:4–5).

Fourth, He told them how to be restored (2:5): remember your past, repent of your error, return to your best.

Fifth, Christ clearly laid out the consequences if they did not obey (2:5).

Sixth, He wrote with the expectation that they would respond positively (2:7). (*What Would Jesus Say About Your Church?* [Scotland, G.B.: Christian Focus Publishers, 1995], 51)

Underscoring the seriousness of the situation, Christ warns the Ephesians to take the necessary steps to recover their first love for Him. He demanded that they change or be chastened: **I am coming to you and will remove your lampstand out of its place—unless you repent.** The **coming** to which Christ refers is not His second coming, but His coming to them in local judgment on that church. Failure to heed the warning would cause Him to **remove** their **lampstand** (symbolic of the church; Rev. 1:20) **out of its place.** Tragically, Christ threatened divine judgment that would bring an end to the Ephesian church.

THE COUNSEL

He who has an ear, let him hear what the Spirit says to the churches. To him who overcomes, I will grant to eat of the tree of life which is in the Paradise of God. (2:7)

The letter closes with an exhortation and a promise. Christ's exhortation **He who has an ear, let him hear what the Spirit says to the churches** closes each of the seven letters (cf. 2:11, 17, 29; 3:6, 13, 22). It emphasizes the sober responsibility believers have to heed God's voice in Scripture. The use of the plural noun **churches** signifies the universal nature of this invitation each time that it appears. This call cannot be limited just to a group of overcomers in a single church; it must apply to all churches. Every church needs to hear every message.

The promise, as are those associated with the other six letters (cf. 2:11, 17, 26; 3:5, 12, 21), is addressed to **him who overcomes.** The term does not refer to those who have attained to a higher level of the Christian life, but identifies all Christians. The apostle John defines it that way in his first epistle:"For whatever is born of God overcomes the world; and this is the victory that has overcome the world—our faith.Who is the one who overcomes the world, but he who believes that Jesus is the Son of God?" (1 John 5:4–5). All true believers are overcomers, who have by God's grace and power overcome the damning power of the evil world system.

Christ promises the overcomers at Ephesus that they will **eat of the tree of life which is in the Paradise of God.** The **tree of life** is first referred to in Genesis 2:9, where it stands in the Garden of Eden. That earthly tree was lost due to man's sin and he was forbidden to eat of it (Gen. 3:22), but the heavenly tree of life (Rev. 22:2, 14, 19) will last throughout eternity. The **tree of life** thus symbolizes eternal life. The **Paradise of God** is heaven (cf. Luke 23:43; 2 Cor. 12:4).

The example of the Ephesian church warns that doctrinal ortho-doxy and outward service cannot make up for a cold heart. Believers must carefully heed Solomon's counsel:"Watch over your heart with all diligence, for from it flow the springs of life" (Prov. 4:23). Those whose love for God has cooled would do well to heed the exhortation Hosea addressed to backsliding Israel:

> Return, O Israel, to the Lord your God, for you have stumbled because of your iniquity.Take words with you and return to the Lord. Say to Him, "Take away all iniquity and receive us graciously, that we may present the fruit of our lips. Assyria will not save us, we will not ride on horses; nor will we say again, 'Our god,' to the work of our hands; for In You the orphan finds mercy." (Hos. 14:1–3)

And to those who return to Him God promises,"I will heal their apostasy, I will love them freely" (Hos. 14:4).

Smyrna: The Suffering Church (Revelation 2:8–11)

5

"And to the angel of the church in Smyrna write: The first and the last, who was dead, and has come to life, says this: 'I know your tribulation and your poverty (but you are rich), and the blasphemy by those who say they are Jews and are not, but are a synagogue of Satan. Do not fear what you are about to suffer. Behold, the devil is about to cast some of you into prison, so that you will be tested, and you will have tribulation for ten days. Be faithful until death, and I will give you the crown of life. He who has an ear, let him hear what the Spirit says to the churches. He who overcomes will not be hurt by the second death.'" (2:8–11)

Throughout its history, the seemingly paradoxical truth has been that the more the church has been persecuted, the greater has been its purity and strength. For decades, churches in the former Soviet Union and Eastern Europe were oppressed by their atheistic communist governments. Believers continue to be persecuted in Muslim countries and elsewhere to this day. They are forbidden to openly proclaim their faith. Many are imprisoned and some martyred. In the Soviet Union books, even Bibles, were scarce. Yet not only did those churches survive, they prospered. The lifting of the Iron Curtain revealed a powerful, pure church, one characterized by genuine faith, deep spirituality, humility, zeal, love of the truth, and single-minded devotion to the Lord.

Scripture links persecution and spiritual strength. "Consider it all joy, my brethren," wrote James, "when you encounter various trials, knowing that the testing of your faith produces endurance. And let endurance have its perfect result, so that you may be perfect and complete, lacking in nothing" (James 1:2–4). Peter encouraged suffering Christians with the truth that "after you have suffered for a little while, the God of all grace, who called you to His eternal glory in Christ, will Himself perfect, confirm, strengthen and establish you" (1 Pet. 5:10). The purest Christian graces are those forged in the furnace of adversity.

The church at Smyrna displayed the power and purity that comes from successfully enduring persecution. Persecution had purified and purged it from sin and affirmed the reality of its members' faith. Hypocrites do not stay to face persecution, because false believers do not want to endure the pain. Trials and persecution strengthen and refine genuine saving faith, but uncover and destroy false faith.

Though they suffered physical privation and poverty, the Christians at Smyrna clung to their immeasurable spiritual riches. Fittingly, the church at Smyrna is one of the two churches (along with Philadelphia) that received no rebuke in its letter from the Lord Jesus Christ.

As Scripture makes clear, persecution and trials are an inevitable and essential part of the Christian life (Acts 14:22; 2 Tim. 3:12). The example of the church at Smyrna instructs all churches on how to properly respond when they come. Christ's letter of commendation unfolds in six successive stages: the correspondent, the church, the city, the commendation, the command, and the counsel.

THE CORRESPONDENT

The first and the last, who was dead, and has come to life, says this: (2:8c)

As was customary in ancient letters, the writer identifies Himself at the beginning of the letter, instead of signing His name at the end. The depiction of the writer as **the first and the last, who was dead, and has come to life** identifies Him as the glorified, exalted Lord Jesus Christ described by that phrase in the vision of 1:12–20 (cf. 1:18). **The first and the last** is an Old Testament title for God (Isa. 44:6; 48:12; cf. 41:4), and its application here (and in 22:13) to Christ affirms His equality of nature with God. He is the eternal, infinite God, who already existed when all things were created, and who will continue to exist after they are destroyed. Jesus Christ transcends time, space, and the creation.

Yet, amazingly, the eternal God became man and **was dead, and has come to life.** Here is a profound mystery: How can the ever-living One who transcends time, space, and history die? Peter reveals the answer in 1 Peter 3:18: Christ was "put to death in the flesh, but made alive in the spirit." He died in His incarnate humanness as the perfect sacrifice for sin, but now **has come to life** (by His resurrection) and lives forever "according to the power of an indestructible life" (Heb. 7:16; cf. Rom. 6:9).

This designation of Christ was to bring comfort to the persecuted believers at Smyrna. Knowing that they were undergoing difficult times, Christ was reminding them that He transcends temporal matters, and, through their union with Him, so should they. And should they face death at the hands of their persecutors, beside them is the One who conquered death (Heb. 2:14) and who promised, "I am the resurrection and the life; he who believes in Me will live even if he dies, and everyone who lives and believes in Me will never die" (John 11:25–26). Jesus Christ also endured the most unjust and severe persecution anyone ever suffered (cf. Heb. 12:3–4), so He can serve as a compassionate and understanding source of power (Heb. 2:17–18; 4:15). He is the One who addressed this letter of comfort and encouragement to the church at Smyrna.

THE CHURCH

the church in Smyrna (2:8a)

Scripture does not record the founding of the church at Smyrna, nor is the city mentioned in the book of Acts. All that is revealed about this congregation is contained in this letter. Presumably, a church was planted in Smyrna during Paul's Ephesian ministry (Acts 19:10), either by Paul himself, or by his converts.

At the end of the first century, life was difficult and dangerous for the church at Smyrna. The city, long an ally of Rome, was a hotbed of emperor worship. Under Emperor Domitian, it became a capital offense to refuse to offer the yearly sacrifice to the emperor. Not surprisingly, many Christians faced execution. The most famous of Smyrna's martyrs was Polycarp, executed half a century after John's time.

The Greek word translated "Smyrna" was used in the Septuagint to translate the Hebrew word for myrrh, a resinous substance used as a perfume for the living (Matt. 2:11) and the dead (John 19:39). Its association with death perfectly pictures the suffering church at Smyrna. Like myrrh, produced by crushing a fragrant plant, the church at Smyrna, crushed by persecution, gave off a fragrant aroma of faithfulness to God. At Smyrna, unlike Ephesus, there was no waning of love for Jesus Christ. Because the believers at Smyrna loved Him, they remained faithful to Him; because of that faithfulness, they were hated; because they were hated, they were persecuted; that persecution in turn incited them to love Christ more.

THE CITY

Smyrna (2:8b)

Smyrna was an ancient city whose origins are lost in antiquity. It may have been settled as early as 3000 B.C., but the first Greek settlement dates from about 1000 B.C. About 600 B.C. Smyrna was destroyed by the Lydians and lay in ruins for more than three centuries until two of Alexander the Great's successors rebuilt the city in 290 B.C. It was that rebuilt city that was the Smyrna of John's day.

As previously noted, Smyrna was long a staunch ally of Rome. In fact, its citizens were so infatuated with Rome that in 195 B.C. they built a temple in which Rome was worshiped. A century later the Roman general Sulla's ill-clad army faced bitter winter weather. When the Roman soldiers' plight was announced in a general assembly of Smyrna's citizens, they reportedly took off their own clothes to send to them. Rome rewarded Smyrna's loyalty by choosing it above all other applicants as the site of a new temple dedicated to the Emperor Tiberius (A.D. 26). And when an earthquake destroyed the city late in the second century, the Emperor Marcus Aurelius rebuilt it.

Although Ephesus and Pergamum equaled or surpassed it in political and economic importance, Smyrna was said to be the most beautiful city in Asia. It was located on a gulf of the Aegean Sea and, unlike Ephesus, was blessed with an excellent harbor. Smyrna also profited from its location at the western end of the road that ran through the rich Hermus River valley. In addition to the natural beauty of its surroundings, the city itself was well designed. It stretched from the bay up the slopes of the Pagos, a large hill covered with temples and other public buildings. The streets were well laid out, with the outlying ones lined with groves of trees. Smyrna's most famous street, the "Street of Gold," curved around the slopes of the Pagos. At one end was the temple of Cybele, and at the other the temple of Zeus. In between were the temples of Apollo, Asklepios, and Aphrodite.

Smyrna was a noted center of science and medicine. Like Ephesus, it was granted the privilege of being self-governing. It was also one of several cities that claimed to be the birthplace of the poet Homer. As noted in the previous chapter, Ephesus's harbor eventually silted up and the city went out of existence. Smyrna, however, survived numerous earthquakes and fires and exists today as the Turkish city of Izmir.

THE COMMENDATION

I know your tribulation and your poverty (but you are rich), and the blasphemy by those who say they are Jews and are not, but are a synagogue of Satan. (2:9)

Nothing escapes the vision of the glorious Lord of the Smyrna church, who knows every detail about the churches under His care. He began His commendation of those believers by assuring them that He knew their **tribulation.** *Thlipsis* (**tribulation**) literally means "pressure," and is the common New Testament word for persecution or tribulation. The church at Smyrna was facing intense pressure because of their faithfulness to Jesus Christ. There were three reasons for that hostility.

First, as already noted, Smyrna had been fanatically devoted to Rome for several centuries. Not surprisingly, the city was a leading center for the cult of emperor worship. The citizens of Smyrna willingly offered the worship that Emperor Domitian was now demanding of his subjects everywhere. Though the Christians willingly submitted to the emperor's civil authority (cf. Rom. 13:1ff.), they refused to offer sacrifices to him and worship him. For that refusal they were branded rebels and faced the wrath of the Roman government.

Second, the Christians refused to participate in pagan religion in general. As noted above, Smyrna worshiped an eclectic mix of gods, including Zeus, Apollo, Aphrodite, Asklepios, and, especially, Cybele. The Christians' rejection of the pagan pantheon of idols, coupled with their worship of an invisible God, caused them to be denounced as atheists. Much of Smyrna's social life revolved around pagan worship, and Christians were viewed as antisocial elitists for refusing to participate in it.

Finally, the believers at Smyrna faced **blasphemy by those who say they are Jews and are not, but are a synagogue of** the ultimate blasphemer, **Satan.** That shocking statement affirmed that those Jews who hated and rejected Jesus Christ were just as much Satan's followers as pagan idol worshipers (cf. John 8:44). Jesus' use of the strong term **blasphemy,** usually reserved for hostile words against God, indicates the slander's wickedness, intensity, and severity.

Unbelieving Jews commonly accused Christians of cannibalism (based on a misunderstanding of the Lord's Supper), immorality (based on a perversion of the holy kiss with which believers greeted each other; cf. Rom. 16:16; 1 Cor. 16:20; 2 Cor. 13:12; 1 Thess. 5:26), breaking up homes (when one spouse became a Christian and the other did not, it often caused conflict; cf. Luke 12:51–53), atheism (because, as already noted, Christians rejected the pagan pantheon of deities), and political disloyalty and rebellion (because Christians refused to offer the required sacrifices to the emperor). Hoping to destroy the Christian faith, some of Smyrna's wealthy, influential Jews reported these blasphemous, false allegations to the Romans. These haters of the gospel were a **synagogue of Satan,** meaning they assembled to plan their attack on the church, thus doing Satan's will. They may have claimed to be a synagogue of God, but they were just the opposite.

Sadly, the hostility of Smyrna's Jewish population to Christianity was nothing new. The book of Acts frequently records such Satan-inspired opposition (e.g., 2:13; 4:2–3, 18; 5:17–18, 28, 40; 6:9ff.; 7:54–60; 8:1ff.; 9:20–23; 12:1–3; 13:6, 45; 14:2, 19; 17:5ff., 13; 18:6, 12–13; 19:9; 20:3; 21:27ff.; 23:12ff.). In Smyrna, as had happened so often before, the hostile Jewish population poisoned public opinion against the Christians.

Persecution of the church at Smyrna reached its peak half a century after this letter, with the execution of its aged bishop, Polycarp, in which the unbelieving Jews played a major role. A translated second-century document entitled *The Encyclical Epistle of the Church at Smyrna Concerning the Martyrdom of the Holy Polycarp* relates the striking story of Polycarp's martyrdom:

The whole multitude, marveling at the nobility of mind displayed by the devout and godly race of Christians, cried out, "Away with the Atheists; let Polycarp be sought out!"

But the most admirable Polycarp, when he first heard [that he was sought for], was in no measure disturbed, but resolved to continue in the city. However, in deference to the wish of many, he was persuaded to leave it. He departed, therefore, to a country house not far distant from the city. There he stayed with a few [friends], engaged in nothing else night and day than praying for all men, and for the Churches throughout the world, according to his usual custom. And while he was praying, a vision presented itself to him three days before he was taken; and, behold, the pillow under his head seemed to him on fire. Upon this, turning to those that were with him, he said to them prophetically, "I must be burnt alive."

And when those who sought for him were at hand, he departed to another dwelling, whither his pursuers immediately came after him. And when they found him not, they seized upon two youths [that were there], one of whom, being subjected to torture, confessed. It was thus impossible that he should continue hid, since those that betrayed him were of his own household. The Irenarch then (whose office is the same as that of the Cleronomus), by name Herod, hastened to bring him into the stadium. [This all happened] that he might fulfill his special lot, being made a partaker of Christ, and that they who betrayed him might undergo the punishment of Judas himself.

His pursuers then, along with horsemen, and taking the youth with them, went forth at supper-time on the day of the preparation, with their usual weapons, as if going out against a robber. And being come about evening [to the place where he was], they found him lying down in the upper room of a certain little house, from which he might have escaped into another place; but he refused, saying, "The will of God be done." So when he heard that they were come, he went down and spake with them. And as those that were present marveled at his age and constancy, some of them said, "Was so much effort made to capture such a venerable man?" Immediately then, in that very hour, he ordered that something to eat and drink should be set before them, as much indeed as they cared for, while he besought them to allow him an hour to pray without disturbance. And on their giving him leave, he stood and prayed, being full of the grace of God, so that he could not cease for two full hours, to the astonishment of them that heard him, insomuch that many began to repent that they had come forth against so godly and venerable an old man.

Now, as soon as he had ceased praying, having made mention of all that had at any time come in contact with him, both small and great, illustrious and obscure, as well as the whole Catholic Church throughout the world, the time of his departure having arrived, they set him upon an ass, and conducted him into the city, the day being that of the great Sabbath. And the Irenarch Herod, accompanied by his father Nicetes (both riding in a chariot), met him, and taking him up into the chariot, they seated themselves beside him, and endeavored to persuade him, saying, "What harm is there in saying, Lord Caesar, and in sacrificing, with the other ceremonies observed on such occasions, and so make sure of safety?" But he at first gave them no answer; and when they continued to urge him, he said, "I shall not do as you advise me." So they, having no hope of persuading him, began to speak bitter words unto him, and cast him with violence out of the chariot, insomuch that, in getting down from the carriage, he dislocated his leg [by the fall]. But without being disturbed, and as if suffering nothing, he went eagerly forward with all haste, and was conducted to the stadium, where the tumult was so great, that there was no possibility of being heard.

Now, as Polycarp was entering into the stadium, there came to him a voice from heaven, saying, "Be strong, and show thyself a man,

O Polycarp!" No one saw who it was that spoke to him; but those of our brethren who were present heard the voice. And as he was brought forward, the tumult became great when they heard that Polycarp was taken. And when he came near, the proconsul asked him whether he was Polycarp. On his confessing that he was, [the proconsul] sought to persuade him to deny [Christ], saying, "Have respect to thy old age," and other similar things, according to their custom, [such as], "Swear by the fortune of Caesar; repent, and say, Away with the Atheists." But Polycarp, gazing with a stern countenance on all the multitude of the wicked heathen then in the stadium, and waving his hand towards them, while with groans he looked up to heaven, said, "Away with the Atheists." Then, the proconsul urging him, and saying, "Swear, and I will set thee at liberty, reproach Christ"; Polycarp declared, "Eighty and six years have I served Him, and He never did me any injury: how then can I blaspheme my King and my Savior?" And when the proconsul yet again pressed him, and said, "Swear by the fortune of Caesar," he answered, "Since thou art vainly urgent that, as thou sayest, I should swear by the fortune of Caesar, and pretendest not to know who and what I am, hear me declare with boldness, I am a Christian. And if you wish to learn what the doctrines of Christianity are, appoint me a day, and thou shalt hear them." The proconsul replied, "Persuade the people." But Polycarp said, "To thee I have thought it right to offer an account [of my faith]; for we are taught to give all due honor (which entails no injury upon ourselves) to the powers and authorities which are ordained of God. But as for these, I do not deem them worthy of receiving any account from me." The proconsul then said to him, "I have wild beasts at hand; to these will I cast thee, except thou repent." But he answered, "Call them then, for we are not accustomed to repent of what is good in order to adopt that which is evil; and it is well for me to be changed from what is evil to what is righteous." But again the proconsul said to him, "I will cause thee to be consumed by fire, seeing thou despisest the wild beasts, if thou wilt not repent." But Polycarp said, "Thou threatenest me with fire which burneth for an hour, and after a little is extinguished, but art ignorant of the fire of the coming judgment and of eternal punishment, reserved for the ungodly. But why tarriest thou? Bring forth what thou wilt."

While he spoke these and many other like things, he was filled with confidence and joy, and his countenance was full of grace, so that not merely did it not fall as if troubled by the things said to him, but, on the contrary, the proconsul was astonished, and sent his herald to proclaim in the midst of the stadium thrice, "Polycarp has confessed that he is a Christian." This proclamation having been made by the herald, the whole multitude both of the heathen and Jews, who dwelt at Smyrna, cried out with uncontrollable fury, and in a loud voice, "This is the teacher of Asia, the father of the Christians, and the overthrower of our gods, he who has been teaching many not to sacrifice, or to worship the gods." Speaking thus, they cried out, and besought Philip the Asiarch to let loose a lion upon Polycarp. But Philip answered that it was not lawful for him to do so, seeing the shows of wild beasts were already finished. Then it seemed good to them to cry out with one consent, that Polycarp should be burnt alive. For thus it behooved the vision which was revealed to him in regard to his pillow to be fulfilled, when, seeing it on fire as he was praying, he turned about and said prophetically to the faithful that were with him, "I must be burnt alive."

This, then, was carried into effect with greater speed than it was spoken, the multitudes immediately gathering together wood and fagots out of the shops and baths; the Jews especially, according to custom, eagerly assisting them in it. And when the funeral pile was ready, Polycarp, laying aside all his garments, and loosing his girdle, sought also to take off his sandals, — a thing he was not accustomed to do, inasmuch as every one of the faithful was always eager who should first touch his skin. For, on account of his holy life, he was, even before his martyrdom, adorned with every kind of good. Immediately then they surrounded him with those substances which had been prepared for the funeral pile. But when they were about also to fix him with nails, he said, "Leave me as I am; for He that giveth me strength to endure the fire, will also enable me, without your securing me by nails, to remain without moving in the pile."

They did not nail him then, but simply bound him. And he, placing his hands behind him, and being bound like a distinguished ram [taken] out of a great flock for sacrifice, and prepared to be an acceptable burnt-offering unto God, looked up to heaven, and said, "O Lord God Almighty, the Father of thy beloved and blessed Son Jesus Christ, by whom we have received the knowledge of Thee, the God of angels and powers, and of every creature, and of the whole race of the righteous who live before thee, I give Thee thanks that Thou hast counted me, worthy of this day and this hour, that I should have a part in the number of Thy martyrs, in the cup of thy Christ, to the resurrection of eternal life, both of soul and body, through the incorruption [imparted] by the Holy Ghost. Among whom may I be accepted this day before Thee as a fat and acceptable sacrifice, according as Thou, the ever-truthful God, hast fore-ordained, hast revealed beforehand to me, and now hast fulfilled. Wherefore also I praise Thee for all things, I bless Thee, I glorify Thee, along with the everlasting and heavenly Jesus Christ, Thy beloved Son, with whom, to Thee, and the Holy Ghost, be glory both now and to all coming ages. Amen."

When he had pronounced this amen, and so finished his prayer, those who were appointed for the purpose kindled the fire. And as the flame blazed forth in great fury, we, to whom it was given to witness it, beheld a great miracle, and have been preserved that we might report to others what then took place. For the fire, shaping itself into the form of an arch, like the sail of a ship when filled with the wind, encompassed as by a circle the body of the martyr. And he appeared within not like flesh which is burnt, but as bread that is baked, or as gold and silver glowing in a furnace. Moreover, we perceived such a sweet odor [coming from the pile], as if frankincense or some such precious spices had been smoking there.

At length, when those wicked men perceived that his body could not be consumed by the fire, they commanded an executioner to go near and pierce him through with a dagger. And on his doing this, there came forth a dove, and a great quantity of blood, so that the fire was extinguished; and all the people wondered that there should be such a difference between the unbelievers and the elect, of whom this most admirable Polycarp was one, having in our own times been an apostolic and prophetic teacher, and bishop of the Catholic Church which is in Smyrna. For every word that went out of his mouth either has been or shall yet be accomplished.

Jesus' declaration that the Jews who persecuted the Smyrna church **say they are Jews and are not** has caused some to question whether they were racially Jews. Surely they were physical descendants of Abraham, but not true Jews by Paul's definition: "He is not a Jew who is one outwardly, nor is circumcision that which is outward in the flesh. But he is a Jew who is one inwardly; and circumcision is that which is of the heart, by the Spirit, not by the letter; and his praise is not from men, but from God" (Rom. 2:28–29). Though these were by race Jews, they were spiritually pagan. They allied with the Gentile enemies of God in an attempt to stamp out Christianity in Smyrna.

Not only was the Lord aware of the persecution the Smyrna church faced, but also of its **poverty.** In contrast to its synonym *penēs,* which denotes those who struggle to meet their basic needs, *ptocheia* (**poverty**) describes beggars, who live not by their own labor, but by the alms of others (cf. Richard C. Trench, *Synonyms of the New Testament* [reprint; Grand Rapids: Eerdmans, 1983], 128–29). Many of the believers at Smyrna were slaves; most were destitute. Those few who had owned possessions had undoubtedly lost them in the persecution.

The church at Smyrna had every reason, humanly speaking, to collapse. Instead, it remained faithful to its Lord, never (unlike Ephesus) leaving its first love for Him. For that reason, Jesus said to them, **you are rich.** They had what really mattered—salvation, holiness, grace, peace, fellowship, a sympathetic Savior and Comforter. The church at Smyrna was the rich poor church, in contrast to the church at Laodicea, which was the materially rich but spiritually poor church (cf. 3:17). The church at Smyrna typifies the spiritual richness of faithful suffering churches throughout history.

The Command

Do not fear what you are about to suffer. Behold, the devil is about to cast some of you into prison, so that you will be tested, and you will have tribulation for ten days. (2:10*a*)

After commending them for faithfully enduring persecution, Jesus warned the believers that more was coming. Before specifying its nature, He commanded them **not** to **fear what** they were **about to suffer.** He would give them strength to endure it. As He told His disciples in John 16:33, "In the world you have tribulation, but take courage; I have overcome the world." Therefore the suffering believers in that flock could say with David, "In God I have put my trust, I shall not be afraid. What can man do to me?" (Ps. 56:11).

Specifically, the Lord predicted that **the devil** was **about to cast some of** them **into prison.** God's purpose in permitting that imprisonment was **so that** they would **be tested.** By successfully enduring that trial, they would prove the reality of their faith, be strengthened (cf. 2 Cor. 12:9–10)—and prove once again that Satan cannot destroy genuine saving faith.

The supernatural battle in Smyrna was just one skirmish in the age-long war of Satan against God. It has always been Satan's plan to attack God's children and attempt to destroy their faith. That is why one of his titles in Scripture is the "accuser of [the] brethren" (12:10). His attacks on God's true children, however, cannot succeed. Jesus declared, "I give eternal life to them, and they will never perish; and no one will snatch them out of My hand. My Father, who has given them to Me, is greater than all; and no one is able to snatch them out of the Father's hand" (John 10:28–29); and "This is the will of Him who sent Me, that of all that He has given Me I lose nothing, but raise it up on the last day" (John 6:39). As their Great High Priest, Jesus is "able also to save forever those who draw near to God through Him, since He always lives to make intercession for them" (Heb. 7:25). In Romans 8:28–29 Paul traces the unbreakable chain from foreknowledge to predestination to effectual calling to justification to glorification; no one is lost along the way. All who are called will be kept until they are made like Christ in glory.

The knowledge that his efforts to destroy saving faith are doomed to failure does not deter Satan from trying. His most notable attack on saving faith is recorded in the book of Job, where (with God's permission) he took from Job his family, possessions, and physical health. All Job was left with was a cantankerous wife and friends whose inept counsel drove him to distraction. But "through all this Job did not sin nor did he blame God" (Job 1:22; cf. 2:10). Job's triumphant declaration, "Though He slay me, I will hope in Him" (Job 13:15), signaled both the triumph of true saving faith and Satan's utter defeat.

In the New Testament, Satan sought unsuccessfully to destroy Peter's faith. Jesus warned him, "Simon, Simon, behold, Satan has demanded permission to sift you like wheat; but I have prayed for you, that your faith may not fail; and you, when once you have turned again, strengthen your brothers" (Luke 22:31–32). As with the believers at Smyrna, Jesus foretold Satan's attack on Peter, but also that Peter would successfully endure it. Paul also survived the worst Satan could throw at him:

> He has said to me, "My grace is sufficient for you, for power is perfected in weakness." Most gladly, therefore, I will rather boast about my weaknesses, so that the power of Christ may dwell in me. Therefore I am well content with weaknesses, with insults, with distresses, with persecutions, with difficulties, for Christ's sake; for when I am weak, then I am strong. (2 Cor. 12:9–10)

God, who alone sovereignly controls all the circumstances of life, would not permit Satan to torment the Smyrna church for long. Jesus promised that they would **have tribulation for** only **ten days.** Though some see the **ten days** as symbolically representing everything from ten periods of persecution under the Romans, to an undetermined period of time, to a time of ten years, there is no exegetical reason to interpret them as anything other than ten actual days. Satan's major assault on that local church would be intense, but brief.

THE COUNSEL

Be faithful until death, and I will give you the crown of life. He who has an ear, let him hear what the Spirit says to the churches. He who overcomes will not be hurt by the second death. (2:10b–11)

As previously noted, Christ has no reprimand for the faithful church at Smyrna. He closes the letter with some final words of encouraging counsel. Those who prove the genuineness of their faith by remaining **faithful** to the Lord **until death** will receive as their reward **the crown** (*stephanos;* the victor's crown) **of life** (cf. James 1:12). The

crown (reward, culmination, outcome) of genuine saving faith is eternal **life,** and perseverance proves the genuineness of their faith as they endure suffering. The Scriptures teach that true Christians will persevere. That biblical truth was understood by the authors of the Westminster Confession of Faith, who wrote "They, whom God has accepted in His Beloved, effectually called, and sanctified by His Spirit, can neither totally nor finally fall away from the state of grace, but shall certainly persevere therein to the end, and be eternally saved." That is the unmistakable teaching of Scripture (e.g., Matt. 10:22; 24:13; Mark 4:13–20; John 8:31; Col. 1:21–23; 1 John 2:19).

As noted in chapter 4 of this volume, the phrase **He who has an ear, let him hear what the Spirit says to the churches** closes each of the seven letters. It stresses the vital significance of what God says in Scripture, and emphasizes believers' responsibility to heed it. The promise to **he who overcomes** (all Christians; cf. the discussion in chapter 4 of this volume) is that he **will not be hurt by the second death.** Though persecuted believers may suffer the first (physical) death, they will never experience the **second death** (which is not annihilation but conscious, eternal damnation in hell; Rev. 20:14; 21:8). **Not** is the strongest negative the Greek language can express.

The persecuted, suffering, yet faithful church at Smyrna stands for all time as an example of those who "have heard the word in an honest and good heart, and hold it fast, and bear fruit with perseverance" (Luke 8:15). Because they loyally confessed Him before men, Jesus will confess them before the Father (Matt. 10:32).

Pergamum: The Worldly Church (Revelation 2:12–17)

6

"And to the angel of the church in Pergamum write: The One who has the sharp two-edged sword says this: 'I know where you dwell, where Satan's throne is; and you hold fast My name, and did not deny My faith even in the days of Antipas, My witness, My faithful one, who was killed among you, where Satan dwells. But I have a few things against you, because you have there some who hold the teaching of Balaam, who kept teaching Balak to put a stumbling block before the sons of Israel, to eat things sacrificed to idols and to commit acts of immorality. So you also have some who in the same way hold the teaching of the Nicolaitans. Therefore repent; or else I am coming to you quickly, and I will make war against them with the sword of My mouth. He who has an ear, let him hear what the Spirit says to the churches. To him who overcomes, to him I will give some of the hidden manna, and I will give him a white stone, and a new name written on the stone which no one knows but he who receives it.'" (2:12–17)

For many people in today's church, the term *worldliness* has a quaint, old-fashioned ring to it. They associate it with prohibitions against things like dancing, going to the movies, or playing cards. Today's user-friendly, seeker-oriented, market-driven church doesn't preach much against worldliness. To do so might make unbelievers (not to mention many believers) uncomfortable, and is therefore avoided as poor marketing strategy.

But unlike much of the contemporary church, the Bible does not hesitate to condemn worldliness for the serious sin that it is. Worldliness is any preoccupation with or interest in the temporal system of life that places anything perishable before that which is eternal. Since believers are not part of the world system (John 15:19), they must not act as though they were. "Do not be conformed to this world," wrote the apostle Paul, "but be transformed by the renewing of your mind, so that you may prove what the will of God is, that which is good and acceptable and perfect" (Rom. 12:2). Because they have been redeemed by God's grace, believers are called to "deny ungodliness and worldly desires and to live sensibly, righteously and godly in the present age" (Titus 2:12). "Pure and undefiled religion," notes James, consists in keeping "oneself unstained by the world" (James 1:27), because "friendship with the world is hostility toward God[.] Therefore whoever wishes to be a friend of the world makes himself an enemy of God" (James 4:4). First John 2:15–17 makes the believer's duty to avoid worldliness unmistakably clear:

> Do not love the world nor the things in the world. If anyone loves the world, the love of the Father is not in him. For all that is in the world, the lust of the flesh and the lust of the eyes and the boastful pride of life, is not from the Father, but is from the world. The world is passing away, and also its lusts; but the one who does the will of God lives forever.

The church at Pergamum, like much of today's church, had failed to heed the biblical warnings against worldliness. Consequently, it had drifted into compromise and was in danger of becoming intertwined with the world. That would be the next step in the downward spiral from the Ephesian church's loss of its first love for Jesus Christ.

Conforming to the general pattern of the seven letters, the letter to Pergamum unfolds in seven stages: the correspondent, the church, the city, the commendation, the concern, the command, and the counsel.

THE CORRESPONDENT

The One who has the sharp two-edged sword says this: (2:12c)

The holder of **the sharp two-edged sword** is the risen, glorified Lord Jesus Christ, as indicated in 1:16. He, through the inspired apostle

John, is the author of this letter. In this letter, like those to Ephesus and Smyrna, Christ identifies Himself using one of the descriptive phrases from John's vision in 1:12–17.

The **sharp two-edged sword** refers to the Word of God. Hebrews 4:12 notes that "the word of God is living and active and sharper than any two-edged sword, and piercing as far as the division of soul and spirit, of both joints and marrow, and able to judge the thoughts and intentions of the heart." The apostle Paul also uses the metaphor of a sword to describe the Word (Eph. 6:17). That the sword is **two-edged** depicts the Word's potency and power in exposing and judging the innermost thoughts of the human heart. The Word never wields a dull edge.

This description of the Lord Jesus Christ pictures Him as judge and executioner. Describing His appearance at the Second Coming, John writes that "from His mouth comes a sharp sword, so that with it He may strike down the nations, and He will rule them with a rod of iron; and He treads the wine press of the fierce wrath of God, the Almighty" (19:15). This is not a positive, promising introduction; it is a threatening one. It is the first negative introduction of Christ because the Pergamum church faced imminent judgment. Disaster loomed on the horizon for this worldly church; it was and is but a short step from compromising with the world to forsaking God altogether and facing His wrath.

The church at Pergamum is symbolic of the many churches throughout history that have compromised with the world. That spirit of compromise was especially evident during the period from the fourth to the seventh centuries. In A.D. 313 the emperor Constantine issued the Edict of Milan, granting religious freedom to the Christians and ending two and a half centuries of savage persecution. He adopted Christianity and made it the favored religion of the empire. That began the process by which Christianity merged with the Roman state. Heathen priests became Christian priests; heathen temples became Christian churches; heathen feasts became Christian festivals. Christianity was no longer a personal matter, but a national identity. The church married the political system, so that worldliness was synonymous with the church.

Today, in some ways, worldliness is still rampant in the church. Churches, even entire denominations, have departed from the true faith and embraced the world philosophically and morally. And in some places, state churches still exist in spiritually impotent forms. Like the church at Pergamum, they fall under judgment by the Lord of the true church.

THE CHURCH

the church in Pergamum (2:12*a*)

The book of Acts does not record the founding of the church at Pergamum. According to Acts 16:7–8, Paul passed through Mysia (the region in which Pergamum was located) on his second missionary journey, but there is no record that the apostle either preached the gospel or founded a church there at that time. Most likely, the church at Pergamum was founded during Paul's ministry in Ephesus, when the gospel went out from there to be preached throughout the province of Asia (Acts 19:10). Because the church was surrounded by the pagan culture, it was exposed continually to its allurements, strengthened by familiar sins. It also faced severe animosity from the persecuting emperor worshipers.

THE CITY

Pergamum (2:12b)

Pergamum was about one hundred miles north of Ephesus, with Smyrna located about halfway in between. Unlike Ephesus and Smyrna, Pergamum was not a port city but was located about fifteen miles inland from the Aegean Sea. Nor was it on any of the major trade routes. Yet, as its ancient capital, Pergamum was considered Asia's greatest city. The Roman writer Pliny called it "by far the most distinguished city in Asia" (cited in Robert H. Mounce, *The Book of Revelation,* The New International Commentary on the New Testament [Grand Rapids: Eerdmans, 1977], 95). By the time John penned Revelation, Pergamum had been Asia's capital for almost 250 years (since 133 B.C., when its last king bequeathed his kingdom to Rome). Pergamum survives today as the Turkish city of Bergama.

Much of Pergamum was built on a large, conical hill towering some one thousand feet above the plain. So impressive is the site even in modern times that the famed nineteenth-century archaeologist Sir William Ramsay commented, "Beyond all other sites in Asia Minor it gives the traveler the impression of a royal city, the home of authority: the rocky hill on which it stands is so huge, and dominates the broad plain of the Caicus [River valley] so proudly and boldly" (*The Letters to the Seven Churches of Asia* (Albany, Oreg.: AGES Software; reprint of the 1904 edition], 226).

Pergamum's huge library (200,000 handwritten volumes) was second only to that of Alexandria. So impressive was Pergamum's library that Mark Antony later sent it to his lover, Queen Cleopatra of Egypt. According to legend, parchment (or vellum) was invented by the Pergamenes to provide writing material for their library. Seeking to build a library rivaling the one in Alexandria, a third-century B.C. Pergamene king attempted to lure the librarian of the Alexandrian library to his city. Unfortunately, the Egyptian ruler got wind of the plan, refused to allow the librarian to leave, and in retaliation prohibited the further export of papyrus to Pergamum. Out of necessity, the Pergamenes developed parchment, made of treated animal skins, for use as writing material. Though parchment was actually known from a thousand years earlier in Egypt, the Pergamenes were responsible for its widespread use in the ancient world. In fact, the word *parchment* may derive from a form of the word *Pergamum*.

Because of its library, Pergamum was an important center of culture and learning. The physician Galen, second only in prominence to Hippocrates, was born and studied in Pergamum. The city saw itself as the defender of Greek culture in Asia Minor. A large frieze around the base of the altar of Zeus commemorates the victory of the Pergamenes over the invading barbarian Gauls.

Pergamum was an important center of worship for four of the main deities of the Greco-Roman world, and temples dedicated to Athena, Asklepios, Dionysos, and Zeus were located there. But overshadowing the worship of all those deities was Pergamum's devotion to the cult of emperor worship. Pergamum built the first temple devoted to emperor worship in Asia (29 B.C.), in honor of Emperor Augustus. Later, the city would build two more such temples, honoring the emperors Trajan and Septimus Severus. The city thus became the center of emperor worship in the province, and there, more than in any other city in Asia, Christians were in danger of harm from the emperor worship cult. Elsewhere, Christians were primarily in danger on the one day per year they were required to offer sacrifices to the emperor; in Pergamum they were in danger every day. It is likely that the martyr Antipas (2:13) was executed, at least in part, for refusing to worship the emperor.

THE COMMENDATION

I know where you dwell, where Satan's throne is; and you hold fast My name, and did not deny My faith even in the days of Antipas, My witness, My faithful one, who was killed among you, where Satan dwells. (2:13)

Despite the difficult circumstances in which they found themselves, the believers at Pergamum courageously maintained their faith in Jesus Christ. He commended them for continuing to **hold fast** His **name**—even though they lived **where Satan's throne is, where Satan dwells.** Many suggestions have been offered as to the identification of **Satan's throne.** Some identify it with the magnificent altar of Zeus that dominated Pergamum's acropolis. This was not simply an altar, as Edwin Yamauchi notes:

> The word *altar* is somewhat misleading. The structure is a monumental colonnaded court in the form of a horseshoe, 120 by 112 feet. The podium of the altar was nearly 18 feet high. The great frieze, which ran at the base of the structure for 446 feet, depicted a gigantomachy, that is, a battle of the gods and the giants. It was one of the greatest works of Hellenistic art. (*New Testament Cities in Western Asia Minor* [Grand Rapids: Baker, 1980], 35–36)

Such an impressive structure could easily merit the designation **Satan's throne.**

Others connect **Satan's throne** with the worship of the god Asklepios that was prevalent in Pergamum. Asklepios was the god of healing, and people came from all over the ancient world to Pergamum, seeking to be healed at his shrine. Asklepios was depicted as a snake, and nonpoisonous snakes roamed freely in his temple. Suppliants seeking healing either slept or lay down on the temple's floor, hoping to be touched by one of the snakes (symbolically representing the god himself) and thereby be healed. Such symbolism would undoubtedly remind Christians of Satan (cf. Rev. 12:9, 14, 15; 20:2). During the reign of Emperor Diocletian, some Christian stonecutters were executed for refusing to carve an image of Asklepios (Mounce, *Revelation*, 96, n. 36).

Others point out that, as noted above, Pergamum was the leading center of emperor worship in the province of Asia. And the cult of emperor worship certainly posed the gravest threat to the Christians in Pergamum. It was for their refusal to worship the emperor, not the pagan gods, that Christians faced execution. **Satan's throne** could easily be understood as a reference to the might of Rome under the "god of this world" (2 Cor. 4:4), blaspheming the true God by the emperor worship cult.

For any or all of those reasons, Pergamum could justifiably be called the city **where Satan's throne is.** In the midst of those difficult and trying circumstances, the believers continued to **dwell**—a word that speaks of permanent residence as opposed to merely passing through—in Pergamum. In modern terms, they "hung in there." Despite the persecution and suffering they endured, the believers at Pergamum continued to **hold fast** the **name** of Christ, **and did not deny** the **faith.** They did not deviate from fidelity to Christ or to the central truths of the Christian faith. The faithful believers at Pergamum exemplified the truth of Christ's words in Matthew 16:18: "I will build My church; and the gates of Hades will not overpower it." No amount of satanic opposition can destroy genuine saving faith such as those believers possessed.

The church at Pergamum maintained its faithfulness **even in the days of Antipas,** whom Christ described as **My witness, My faithful one, who was killed among you.** Nothing certain is known about Antipas apart from this text. He was probably one of the leaders of the Pergamum church. According to tradition, he was roasted to death inside a brass bull during the persecution instigated by Emperor Domitian. **Witness** translates *martus,* a word that eventually became transliterated into English as the word *martyr,* because so many witnesses for Christ paid with their lives.

Here was a man who paid the ultimate price for his refusal to compromise. Because of his faithfulness, the risen Lord commended Antipas with a title used elsewhere to refer to Himself (Rev. 1:5; 3:14). Antipas's faithfulness and courage were a rebuke to those at Pergamum who were tempted to compromise with the world.

THE CONCERN

But I have a few things against you, because you have there some who hold the teaching of Balaam, who kept teaching Balak to put a stumbling block before the sons of Israel, to eat things sacrificed to idols and to commit acts of immorality. So you also have some who in the same way hold the teaching of the Nicolaitans. (2:14–15)

The church at Pergamum remained loyal to Christ and Christian truth. It faithfully persevered at the very headquarters, as it were, of satanic opposition—even in the face of martyrdom. Yet all was not well at Pergamum. After commending the believers there, Christ informed them, **I have a few things against you.** His concern was that they had **there some who hold** to false **teaching.** While the majority of the believers at Pergamum were faithful and loyal to the truth, there were some associated with the church who came to believe false doctrine. While many in the Christian realm today make light of doctrine, and biblical and theological error are viewed as unimportant, that is not the perspective of the Lord of the church. Our Lord holds it against any in His church who hold to error. Tragically, the rest were tolerating these errorists, instead of confronting them and, if they refused to repent, putting them out of the church (cf. Titus 3:10–11). Like many churches today, the church at Pergamum failed to obey the biblical mandate to practice church discipline (cf. Matt. 18:15–18).

Specifically, Christ was concerned with two heresies being tolerated at Pergamum, one associated with an Old Testament character, the other with a New Testament person. First, some were following the **teaching of Balaam.** The story of Balaam, a notorious Old Testament prophet for hire, is found in Numbers 22–25. Fearful of the Israelites because of what they had done to the Amorites, Balak, king of Moab, hired Balaam to curse them. After trying unsuccessfully three times to curse Israel, Balaam came up with another plan. Since he was unable to curse the Israelites, he decided to corrupt them by **teaching Balak to put a stumbling block before the sons of Israel, to eat things sacrificed to idols and to commit acts of immorality.** He plotted to use Moabite women to lure the Israelites into the behavior of the godless world around them—sexual immorality and idolatry (Num. 25; 31:16). That blasphemous union with Satan and false gods would debase the Israelites and destroy their spiritual power. Balaam's plan succeeded, though not to the extent that he had hoped. God intervened and severely chastened Israel, executing twenty-four thousand (Num. 25:9), including many of the leaders (Num. 25:4–5). That drastic action halted the Israelites' slide into immorality and idolatry.

Like the Israelites who were seduced by Balaam's false teaching, some in the church at Pergamum were lured to mix with the pagan system (cf. Jude 10–11). Peter rebuked the Balaamites in 2 Peter 2:15–16: "Forsaking the right way, they have gone astray, having followed the way of Balaam, the son of Beor, who loved the wages of unrighteousness; but he received a rebuke for his own transgression, for a mute donkey, speaking with a voice of a man, restrained the madness of the prophet." But as God severely chastened Israel for such a union, so the Lord Jesus Christ threatens to do the same in this passage. In 2 Corinthians 6:14–17, the apostle Paul points out the sinful absurdity of believers' seeking to unite with the world:

> Do not be bound together with unbelievers; for what partnership have righteousness and lawlessness, or what fellowship has light with darkness? Or what harmony has Christ with Belial, or what has a believer in common with an unbeliever? Or what agreement has the temple of God with idols? For we are the temple of the living God; just as God said, "I will dwell in them and walk among them; and I will be their God, and they shall be My people. Therefore, come out from their midst and be separate," says the Lord. "And do not touch what is unclean; and I will welcome you."

Despite the graphic example of Israel and the clear teaching of the apostle Paul, with which they were likely familiar, some in Pergamum persisted in following Balaam's teaching. They believed one could attend pagan feasts, with all their debauchery and sexual immorality, and still join the church to worship Jesus Christ. But that is impossible, since "friendship with the world is hostility toward God. Therefore whoever wishes to be a friend of the world makes himself an enemy of God" (James 4:4). "I urge you as aliens and strangers," wrote Peter, "to abstain from fleshly lusts which wage war against the soul" (1 Pet. 2:11). The issue of whether Christians could participate in idolatrous feasts had been settled decades earlier at the Jerusalem Council, which issued a mandate for believers to "abstain from things sacrificed to idols and from blood and from things strangled and from fornication" (Acts 15:29).

Such compromise still goes on today, as people like Balaam appear to speak for God, but motivated by greed and self aggrandizement they lead the church into sin.

A second heresy tolerated at Pergamum involved a New Testament figure. There were **some** there **who in the same way** held **the teaching of the Nicolaitans.** The phrase **in the same way** indicates that the teaching of the **Nicolaitans** led to the same wicked behavior as that of the followers of Balaam. As discussed in chapter 4 of this volume, the **Nicolaitans** derived their name from Nicholas, one of the seven men chosen to oversee the distribution of food in Acts 6. Whether he became an apostate (as some of the early church fathers believed) or the **Nicolaitans,** his followers, perverted his teachings is not known. Abusing the biblical teaching on Christian liberty, the **Nicolaitans** also taught that Christians could participate in pagan orgies. They seduced the church with immorality and idolatry.

The majority of the believers at Pergamum did not participate in the errors of either heretical group. They remained steadfastly loyal to Christ and the Christian faith. But by tolerating the groups and refusing to exercise church discipline, they shared in their guilt, which brought the Lord's judgment.

THE COMMAND

Therefore repent; or else I am coming to you quickly, and I will make war against them with the sword of My mouth. (2:16)

The only remedy for any sinful behavior is to **repent. Repent** is from *metanoeō*, a word used in Scripture to describe a change of mind that results in a change of behavior. While tolerance is lauded in our modern culture, tolerating heretical teaching or sinful behavior in the church is not a virtue but a sin. So serious a matter is it that, should they fail to repent of failure to discipline, Christ warns them **I am coming to you quickly, and I will make war against them with the sword of My mouth** (cf. Num. 22:23). The entire church faced the battle sword of

Christ's judgment, the heretics for practicing their heresy and iniquity, and the rest of the church for tolerating it. The change in pronouns from **you** to **them** reflects an underlying Hebrew idiom commonly found in the Septuagint; both pronouns refer to the entire church.

The church cannot tolerate evil in any form. To the boastful Corinthians, proudly tolerating a man guilty of incest, Paul wrote, "Your boasting is not good. Do you not know that a little leaven leavens the whole lump of dough? Clean out the old leaven so that you may be a new lump, just as you are in fact unleavened" (1 Cor. 5:6–7). Sinning believers should be made to feel miserable in the fellowship and worship of the church by being confronted powerfully with the Word of God. Neither is the goal of the church to provide an environment where unbelievers feel comfortable; it is to be a place where they can hear the truth and be convicted of their sins so as to be saved (Rom. 10:13–17). Gently (cf. 2 Tim. 2:24–26), lovingly, graciously, yet firmly, unbelievers need to be confronted with the reality of their sin and God's gracious provision through the sacrificial death of the Lord Jesus Christ. Error will never be suppressed by compromising with it. Today's nonconfrontive church is largely repeating the error of the Pergamum church on a grand scale, and faces the judgment of the Lord of the church.

THE COUNSEL

He who has an ear, let him hear what the Spirit says to the churches. To him who overcomes, to him I will give some of the hidden manna, and I will give him a white stone, and a new name written on the stone which no one knows but he who receives it. (2:17)

Christ concludes His letter with words of counsel and encouragement. As noted in chapter 4 of this volume, the phrase **he who has an ear, let him hear what the Spirit says to the churches** stresses the vital importance of Christ's words and believers' responsibility to hear and heed them. As is the case with the other six letters, the promises are addressed to **him who overcomes**—a phrase encompassing all believers (1 John 5:4–5). Christ promises three things to the faithful members of the church at Pergamum.

First, He promises to **give** them **some of the hidden manna. Manna** was a honey-flavored bread with which God fed the Israelites during their years of wandering in the wilderness (Ex. 16:14ff.). According to Exodus 16:33, the Israelites were to memorialize that divine provision by keeping a jar of manna inside the Ark of the Covenant during their travels. The **hidden manna** represents Jesus Christ, the Bread of Life who came down from heaven (John 6:48–51). He provides spiritual sustenance for those who put their faith in Him. The **hidden manna** symbolizes all the blessings and benefits of knowing Christ (Eph. 1:3).

There has been much speculation about what the **white stone** symbolizes. Some link it with the Urim and Thummim on the breastplate of the high priest (Ex. 28:15, 30; Lev. 8:8; Num. 27:21; Deut. 33:8). Those stones were used to determine God's will and represented the right of the high priest to request guidance from God for the leader who could not approach God directly, but had to come through the priestly structure. Somehow, God caused those stones to disclose His will in a form beyond just the simple yes and no of casting lots. According to this view, by this **white stone** God promises the overcomers knowledge of His will. Others identify the **white stone** as a diamond, the most precious of stones, symbolizing God's precious gift of eternal life to believers. It seems best, however, to understand the **white stone** in light of the Roman custom of awarding white stones to the victors in athletic contests. A white stone, inscribed with the athlete's name, served as his ticket to a special awards banquet. In this view, Christ promises the overcomers entrance to the eternal victory celebration in heaven.

There will be **a new name written on the stone which no one knows but he who receives it.** As is self-evident from that phrase, we cannot know what that **new name** is until we receive it (cf. Deut. 29:29). *Kainos* (**new**) does not mean new in contrast to old in time, but new in the sense of qualitatively different. The **new name** will serve as each believer's admission pass into eternal glory. It will uniquely reflect God's special love for and adoption of every true child of His.

The Pergamum church faced the same choice that every similar church faces. It could repent and receive all the blessedness of eternal life in the glory of heaven. Or it could refuse to repent and face the terrifying reality of having the Lord Jesus Christ declare war on it. Maintaining the path of compromise ultimately leads to judgment.

Thyatira: The Church that Tolerated Sin (Revelation 2:18–29)

7

"And to the angel of the church in Thyatira write: The Son of God, who has eyes like a flame of fire, and His feet are like burnished bronze, says this: 'I know your deeds, and your love and faith and service and perseverance, and that your deeds of late are greater than at first. But I have this against you, that you tolerate the woman Jezebel, who calls herself a prophetess, and she teaches and leads My bond-servants astray so that they commit acts of immorality and eat things sacrificed to idols. I gave her time to repent, and she does not want to repent of her immorality. Behold, I will throw her on a bed of sickness, and those who commit adultery with her into great tribulation, unless they repent of her deeds. And I will kill her children with pestilence, and all the churches will know that I am He who searches the minds and hearts; and I will give to each one of you according to your deeds. But I say to you, the rest who are in Thyatira, who do not hold this teaching, who have not known the deep things of Satan, as they call them—I place no other burden on you. Nevertheless what you have, hold fast until I come. He who overcomes, and he who keeps My deeds until the end, to him I will give authority over the nations; and he shall rule them with a rod of

iron, as the vessels of the potter are broken to pieces, as I also have received authority from My Father; and I will give him the morning star. He who has an ear, let him hear what the Spirit says to the churches.'" (2:18–29)

The Lord Jesus Christ has called His church to be holy and maintain purity by dealing with sin in its midst. In fact, the very first instruction He gave to the church was about confronting sin. In Matthew 18:15–17 Jesus commanded,

> If your brother sins, go and show him his fault in private; if he listens to you, you have won your brother. But if he does not listen to you, take one or two more with you, so that by the mouth of two or three witnesses every fact may be confirmed. If he refuses to listen to them, tell it to the church; and if he refuses to listen even to the church, let him be to you as a Gentile and a tax collector.

The practice of church discipline that Christ instituted to maintain the holiness of the church has a twofold purpose: to call sinning believers back to righteous behavior, and to purge from the church those who stubbornly cling to their sin. In either case, the purity of the church is maintained.

After the birth of the church on the Day of Pentecost, the Lord demonstrated His commitment to a pure church by executing Ananias and Sapphira (Acts 5:1–11). The Jerusalem Council commanded believers to observe "these essentials: that you abstain from things sacrificed to idols and from blood and from things strangled and from fornication; if you keep yourselves free from such things, you will do well" (Acts 15:28–29).

The apostle Paul also had a passionate concern for the purity of the church. Horrified at the Corinthians' casual attitude toward flagrant sin in their assembly, Paul wrote:

> It is actually reported that there is immorality among you, and immorality of such a kind as does not exist even among the Gentiles, that someone has his father's wife. You have become arrogant and have not mourned instead, so that the one who had done this deed would be removed from your midst. For I, on my part, though absent in body but present in spirit, have already judged him who has so committed this, as though I were present. In the name of our Lord Jesus, when you are assembled, and I with you in spirit, with the power of our Lord Jesus, I have decided to deliver such a one to Satan for the destruction of his flesh, so that his spirit may be saved in the day of the Lord Jesus. (1 Cor. 5:1–5)

Paul himself put two unrepentant sinning leaders out of the Ephesian church: "Hymenaeus and Alexander ... I have handed over to Satan, so that they will be taught not to blaspheme" (1 Tim. 1:20).

In his second epistle to them, Paul explained to the Corinthians what motivated him to desire the church's purity: "For I am jealous for you with a godly jealousy; for I betrothed you to one husband, so that to Christ I might present you as a pure virgin" (2 Cor. 11:2). Ephesians 5:25–27 also teaches that the church is to be a pure bride for the Lord Jesus Christ: "Christ ... loved the church and gave Himself up for her, so that He might sanctify her, having cleansed her by the washing of water with the word, that He might present to Himself the church in all her glory, having no spot or wrinkle or any such thing; but that she would be holy and blameless."

Despite the clear biblical teaching to the contrary, churches throughout history have tolerated sin, following a pattern like the Thyatiran congregation, whose members were engaging in both spiritual and physical adultery. Through the insidious efforts of a false teacher, those sins had become pervasive in the church at Thyatira. The letter Christ addressed to its members was a sobering one, and marks a new phase in the letters to the seven churches. Commentator Charles Erdman offers this perspective on the place of this letter among the seven:

> The letter to the church in Thyatira begins the second group of messages to the churches of Asia. In the first group, the church of Ephesus was characterized by loyalty to Christ which was lacking in love. In the church of Smyrna loyalty was tested by fire. In the church of Pergamum the loyalty was lacking in moral passion. Yet all three churches were true to the faith, and had not yielded to the assaults of evil.
>
> In the case of the church at Thyatira, as of the churches in Sardis and Laodicea, the situation was far more serious. Here not merely a small minority was indifferent, but large numbers had actually yielded to the demoralizing influences of false teaching. (*The Revelation of John* [Philadelphia: Westminster, 1966], 56)

There is a progressive worsening in the character of these seven churches, as they depict becoming more and more influenced by evil. That downward spiral reached its lowest point at Laodicea.

The phrase "the deep things of Satan" (2:24) reveals how far the Thyatira church had slipped in relation to those in Smyrna and Pergamum. The Smyrna church faced hostility from the "synagogue of Satan," that is, from unbelieving Jews (2:9). The Pergamum church existed at the site of Satan's throne (2:13), symbolizing Gentile false religion (particularly the cult of emperor worship). But the church at Thyatira had plunged headlong into the very depths of satanic deception.

The letter to this church is the longest of the seven, though addressed to the church in the smallest of the seven cities. It has an important message for the church today: false doctrine and sin are not to be allowed—even under the banner of love, toleration, and unity. There may be much that is commendable in a church. It may appear on the surface to have an effective ministry, be growing numerically, and even have cordial society. Yet immorality and false doctrine, if not confronted, will bring judgment from the Lord of the church.

The same seven elements constitute the letter to Thyatira: the correspondent, the church, the city, the commendation, the concern, the command, and the counsel.

THE CORRESPONDENT

The Son of God, who has eyes like a flame of fire, and His feet are like burnished bronze, says this: (2:18c)

The title **Son of God** and the two descriptive phrases drawn from the vision of the risen Christ in 1:12–17 identify the writer as the Lord Jesus Christ. As noted, in identifying Himself in the seven letters, Christ chose the phrases from that earlier vision that best fit His approach to each church. The phrases chosen here focus on His role as divine Judge.

Son of God emphasizes Christ's deity, stressing the truth that He is of one essence with the Father (cf. John 5:18). This is a significant change in wording. In the vision recorded in chapter 1, Christ was described as the Son of Man (1:13). That title emphasizes His humiliation, His sympathetic identification with believers as their merciful High Priest. It offers encouragement to persecuted Christians; "He had to be made like His brethren in all things, so that He might become a merciful and faithful high priest in things pertaining to God, to make propitiation for the sins of the people. For since He Himself was tempted in that which He has suffered, He is able to come to the aid of those who are tempted" (Heb. 2:17–18). The title Son of Man views Christ in His ability to sympathize with the needs, trials, and temptations of His church.

In this passage, however, Jesus is identified as **Son of God** (the only time this phrase appears in Revelation); the emphasis is not on His humility, but on His deity, because His approach to the church at Thyatira is not as sympathetic High Priest, but as divine judge. Not comfort, but judgment is in store for the church at Thyatira when Christ's divine power moves against this adulterous assembly.

As the divine Son of God, Jesus Christ **has eyes like a flame of fire.** His piercing, laserlike vision sees all; nothing can be disguised, covered, or hidden from Him. Describing Jesus Christ in His second coming glory, Revelation 19:12 says that "His eyes are a flame of fire" (cf. Dan. 10:6). A church may feel satisfied with itself, have a good reputation in the community, or even with other churches. But the penetrating eyes of the Lord Jesus Christ see it as it really is.

The description of **His feet** as being **like burnished bronze** is reminiscent of Revelation 19:15, where it says of Christ that "He treads the wine press of the fierce wrath of God, the Almighty." That Christ's feet glowed brilliantly **like burnished bronze** depicts His purity and holiness as He tramples out impurity.

This terrifying description of the Lord Jesus Christ must have created shock, consternation, and fear when this letter was read to the congregation at Thyatira. It came as a sobering realization to them, as it should to all sinning Christians, that Christ will judge continual, unrepented sin. In the words of the apostle Peter, "It is time for judgment to begin with the household of God" (1 Pet. 4:17).

THE CHURCH

the church in Thyatira (2:18*a*)

As is the case with the churches at Smyrna and Pergamum, the Bible does not record the founding of the church at Thyatira. According to Acts 16:14, "A woman named Lydia, from the city of Thyatira, a seller of purple fabrics, a worshiper of God," was converted under Paul's ministry at Philippi. Verse 15 records that members of her household also came to saving faith in Christ and were baptized. It is possible that Lydia and her household participated in starting the church at Thyatira. More likely, the church there was founded as an outreach of Paul's ministry at Ephesus (Acts 19:10).

THE CITY

Thyatira (2:18*b*)

From Pergamum, northernmost of the seven cities, the Roman road curved east and then southeast to **Thyatira,** approximately forty miles away. Thyatira was located in a long north-south valley connecting the valleys of the Caicus and Hermus rivers. Unlike Smyrna or Pergamum, Thyatira was built in relatively flat country and lacked an acropolis. Its lack of natural fortifications would play a significant role in its history.

Thyatira was founded by one of Alexander the Great's successors, Seleucus, as a military outpost guarding the north-south road. It later changed hands, and came under the rule of Lysimachus, who ruled Pergamum. Thyatira was the gateway to Pergamum, and the task of the defenders at Thyatira was to delay an attacker and thus buy time for Pergamum. Unfortunately, since Thyatira had no natural defenses, the garrison there could not hope to hold out for long. Thus, the city was repeatedly destroyed and rebuilt; the scanty references to it in ancient literature usually describe its conquest by an invading army.

Finally, about 190 B.C., Thyatira was conquered and annexed by the Romans and enjoyed the Roman peace. The city then became a flourishing commercial center. Its location on the main north-south road, formerly a liability, now became an asset. That road became even more important in Roman times, as it connected Pergamum with Laodicea, Smyrna, and the interior regions of the province of Asia. It also served as the Roman post road. At the time the book of Revelation was written, Thyatira was just entering its period of greatest prosperity.

Thyatira was noted for its numerous guilds (roughly the equivalent of today's labor unions). Thyatira's main industry was the production of wool and dyed goods (especially purple goods, dyed with purple dye extracted from the madder root), but inscriptions also mention guilds for linen workers, makers of outer garments, dyers, leather workers, tanners, potters, bakers, slave dealers, and bronze smiths (William Ramsay, *The Letters to the Seven Churches of Asia* (Albany, Oreg.: AGES Software; reprint of the 1904 edition], 260). Lydia probably represented her guild in Philippi (Acts 16:14), showing that Thyatira's market extended across the Aegean Sea to mainland Greece.

Unlike Pergamum or Smyrna, Thyatira was not an important religious center. The primary god worshiped by the Thyatirans was the Greek sun god, Apollo. Nor does there appear to have been a sizable Jewish population. The pressure faced by the Christians in Thyatira came from the guilds. To hold a job or run a business, it was necessary to be a member of a guild. Each guild had its patron deity, in whose honor feasts were held—complete with meat sacrificed to idols and sexual immorality. Christians faced the dilemma of attending those feasts or possibly losing their livelihood. How some in the Thyatira church were handling the situation caused the Lord Jesus Christ great concern.

The Commendation

I know your deeds, and your love and faith and service and perseverance, and that your deeds of late are greater than at first. (2:19)

As He had with the churches at Ephesus and Pergamum, Christ commended the church at Thyatira before voicing His concerns about it. He assured them that He had not forgotten their righteous **deeds** (cf. Heb. 6:10), which He divided into four categories.

First, the believers at Thyatira were showing **love** for God and for one another—although that love was apparently fragile, since there was not a strong foundation of unified sound doctrine. In some ways, Thyatira was strong where Ephesus was weak; in fact, it is the first of the seven churches to be commended for its love.

Second, Christ commended them for their **faith.** *Pistis* (**faith**) is better translated "fidelity," or "faithfulness." The true Christians in Thyatira were dependable, reliable, and consistent (cf. v. 25). Faith and love are frequently linked in the New Testament (e.g., 1 Cor. 13:2, 13; 2 Cor. 8:7; Gal. 5:6; Eph. 1:15; 3:17; Col. 1:4; 1 Thess. 1:3; 3:6; 5:8; 2 Thess. 1:3; 1 Tim. 1:14; 2:15; 6:11; 2 Tim. 1:13; 2:22; 3:10; Titus 2:2).

Out of faith and love grow **service** and **perseverance.** Those who love will express that love through meeting the needs of others. Those who are faithful will steadfastly persevere in the faith (cf. Matt. 16:24–26; 24:13).

Not only did the Thyatiran Christians possess these virtues, but also their **deeds of late** were **greater** in number **than at first.** Their loving service was becoming more consistent, and their faithful perseverance growing stronger. They were growing in grace, maturing in their Christian lives, and advancing the cause of Christ (cf. 2 Pet. 1:8). For that behavior they were to be commended.

THE CONCERN

But I have this against you, that you tolerate the woman Jezebel, who calls herself a prophetess, and she teaches and leads My bond-servants astray so that they commit acts of immorality and eat things sacrificed to idols. I gave her time to repent, and she does not want to repent of her immorality. Behold, I will throw her on a bed of sickness, and those who commit adultery with her into great tribulation, unless they repent of her deeds. And I will kill her children with pestilence, and all the churches will know that I am He who searches the minds and hearts; and I will give to each one of you according to your deeds. (2:20–23)

Despite the commendation they received, all was not well with the church at Thyatira. The problem was not external persecution, but internal compromise; not vicious wolves from outside the flock, but perverse people from within (cf. Acts 20:29–30). The penetrating gaze of the Lord of the church had discerned serious error, causing Him to warn **I have this against you.** The use of the singular pronoun points this admonition especially to the leader of the congregation. The indictment is **that you tolerate the woman Jezebel, who calls herself a prophetess, and she teaches and leads My bond-servants astray so that they commit acts of immorality and eat things sacrificed to idols.** The sin, apparently involving the majority of the Thyatira church's members, was twofold. First, they violated the biblical teaching that women are not to be teachers or preachers in the church (1 Tim. 2:12). That led them to **tolerate the woman Jezebel, who calls herself a prophetess.** They compounded their error of permitting her to teach by allowing her to teach error. As a result, Jesus declares, **she teaches and leads My bond-servants astray so that they commit acts of immorality and eat things sacrificed to idols.**

Jezebel undoubtedly was not the false prophetess's real name, but like the infamous wife of King Ahab, she was Satan's agent to corrupt God's people. Therefore the Lord branded her with the symbolic name Jezebel. The Old Testament Jezebel was an unspeakably vile woman—so much so that the Bible names marrying her as the most evil thing wicked King Ahab did: "Ahab the son of Omri did evil in the sight of the Lord more than all who were before him. It came about, as though it had been a trivial thing for him to walk in the sins of Jeroboam the son of Nebat, that he married Jezebel the daughter of Ethbaal king of the Sidonians, and went to serve Baal and worshiped him" (1 Kings 16:30–31). Through Jezebel's evil influence, Baal worship became widespread in Israel.

Like her Old Testament counterpart, the woman in Thyatira **who** falsely called **herself a prophetess** succeeded in leading Christ's **bond-servants astray so that they** committed **acts of immorality and ate things sacrificed to idols.** One might speculate that she may have espoused the philosophical dualism so prevalent in contemporary Greek philosophy. When brought into the church, that teaching held that the spirit is good, and the flesh is evil. Since God is only interested in the spirit, its purveyors falsely argued, it doesn't matter what one does with one's body. Thus, according to Jezebel, it did not matter if Christians committed **acts of immorality** or ate **things sacrificed to idols.** She may also have taken a twisted, antinomian view of God's grace, arguing that it did not matter if Christians sinned, since God would graciously forgive them. Perhaps she also encouraged Christians to experience the deep things of Satan so they could better witness to the unsaved. Whatever the specific content of her false teaching, it led the majority of the Thyatiran believers astray from truth and righteousness.

The Bible teaches that true Christians can fall into sexual immorality (cf. 1 Cor. 6:15–20) and idolatry (cf. 1 Cor. 10:21). But to lead other Christians into false doctrine or immoral living is a very serious sin, one meriting the most severe punishment. In Matthew 18:6–10, Jesus graphically described the serious consequences for those who lead other believers into sin:

> Whoever causes one of these little ones who believe in Me to stumble, it would be better for him to have a heavy millstone hung around his neck, and to be drowned in the depth of the sea. Woe to the world because of its stumbling blocks! For it is inevitable that stumbling blocks come; but woe to that man through whom the stumbling block comes! If your hand or your foot causes you to stumble, cut it off and throw it from you; it is better for you to enter life crippled or lame, than to have two hands or two feet and be cast into the eternal fire. If your eye causes you to stumble, pluck it out and throw it from you. It is better for you to enter life with one eye, than to have two eyes and be cast into the fiery hell. See that you do not despise one of these little ones, for I say to you that their angels in heaven continually see the face of My Father who is in heaven.

The "little ones who believe" in Christ are not physical children, but spiritual children—believers. It is so serious to lead another believer into sin that the Lord said death by drowning was a better option. The imagery of maiming oneself is language depicting the need for drastic action in dealing with sin.

In the Old Testament, Jezebel met a gruesome end, befitting her status as one who led Israel astray:

> When Jehu came to Jezreel, Jezebel heard of it, and she painted her eyes and adorned her head and looked out the window. As Jehu entered the gate, she said, "Is it well, Zimri, your master's murderer?" Then he lifted up his face to the window and said, "Who is on my side? Who?" And two or three officials looked down at him. He said, "Throw her down." So they threw her down, and some of her blood was sprinkled on the wall and on the horses, and he trampled her under foot. When he came in, he ate and drank; and he said, "See now to this cursed woman and bury her, for she is a king's daughter." They went to bury her, but they found nothing more of her than the skull and the feet and the palms of her hands. Therefore they returned and told him. And he said, "This is the word of the Lord, which He spoke by His servant Elijah the Tishbite, saying, 'In the property of Jezreel the dogs shall eat the flesh of Jezebel; and the corpse of Jezebel will be as dung on the face of the field in the property of Jezreel, so they cannot say, "This is Jezebel."'" (2 Kings 9:30–37)

Graciously the Lord **gave** the false prophetess at Thyatira **time to repent,** but illustrating the sad truth that people love darkness rather than the light (John 3:19), she did **not want to repent of her immorality.** Her blunt and final refusal to repent would lead to a terrible judgment, introduced by the arresting word **behold.** Because Jezebel refused to repent, Christ declared **I will throw her on a bed of sickness.** The words **of sickness** are not part of the original Greek text, but were supplied as conjecture by the translators. In light of the finality of Jezebel's refusal to repent, it is more likely that the **bed** refers to death and hell—the ultimate resting place for those who refuse to repent.

Divine judgment was about to fall not only on Jezebel, but also on **those who commit adultery with her.** The Lord threatens to cast them **into great tribulation**—not the eschatological tribulation described in Revelation 4–19, but distress or trouble. Since these were the sinning Christians who had believed her lies, the Lord does not threaten to send them to hell as He did the false prophetess. He promises to bring them severe chastening—possibly even physical death (cf. 1 Cor. 11:30; 1 John 5:16)—**unless they repent of her deeds.**

Then Christ names a third group facing divine judgment, declaring, **I will kill her children with pestilence.** Jezebel's **children** were not her biological but her spiritual children. The church was about forty years old when John wrote, so that her false teaching had been around long enough for a second generation of errorists to have arisen. As he did with Ananias and Sapphira, the Lord threatens to **kill** these errorists **with pestilence** (literally "kill them with death"). It was too late for Jezebel; her heart was hardened in unrepentant sin. But the Lord Jesus Christ mercifully warns her disciples to repent while there is still time.

The severe judgment promised to the false prophetess and her followers again reveals Christ's passion for a doctrinally and behaviorally pure church. He will do whatever is necessary to purge His church of sin —even to the point of taking the lives of false teachers. That sobering reality should cause all who purport to be teachers and preachers in the church to be certain they are speaking the truth (cf. James 3:1). It should also warn Christians who are following false teachers to repent of their sins, lest they face divine chastening.

Christ would receive glory when He judged Jezebel and her followers. When that happened, **all the churches** would **know that** He is the One **who searches the minds and hearts.** That phrase offers further confirmation of Christ's deity, since it is used in the Old Testament in reference to God (e.g., 1 Chron. 28:9; Ps. 7:9; Prov. 24:12; Jer. 11:20; 17:10; 20:12). After He judged the Thyatira church, all other churches would be warned against the evil of tolerating sin. They would also realize that nothing can be hidden from the penetrating gaze of the Lord of the churches.

It is not known how many in that congregation responded to Christ's warning, but, tragically, the Thyatira church as a whole apparently did not heed it. History records that it fell prey to the Montanist heresy (a movement led by a false prophet who claimed continuing revelation from God apart from Scripture) and went out of existence by the end of the second century.

Christ then addressed a word of comfort to those true believers in the Thyatira church who had not followed Jezebel's false teaching: **I will give to each one of you according to your deeds.** Christ's unerring judgment would be based on each person's deeds; those who were innocent would not be punished along with the guilty. That everyone will be judged by his or her deeds is a frequent theme in Scripture. In Matthew 7:16 Jesus said of false prophets, "You will know them by their fruits." Speaking of His second coming, Jesus warned, "For the Son of Man is going to come in the glory of His Father with His angels, and will then repay every man according to his deeds" (Matt. 16:27; cf. Rev. 22:12). God is the righteous judge "who will render to each person according to his deeds" (Rom. 2:6). Paul wrote of his bitter opponent Alexander the coppersmith, "The Lord will repay him according to his deeds" (2 Tim. 4:14).

Works have always been the basis for divine judgment. That does not mean, however, that salvation is by works (cf. Eph. 2:8–9; 2 Tim. 1:9; Titus 3:5). People's deeds reveal their spiritual condition. That is what James meant when he said, "I will show you my faith by my works" (James 2:18). Saving faith will inevitably express itself in good works, causing James to declare that "faith, if it has no works, is dead, being by itself" (James 2:17, cf. v. 26). Christians are new creatures (2 Cor. 5:17), "created in Christ Jesus for good works, which God prepared beforehand so that we would walk in them" (Eph. 2:10). Works cannot save, but they do damn.

Judgment must begin with the household of God (1 Pet. 4:17). But Christ's judgment will fairly reflect each person's deeds—a reality that should bring fear to those who teach and practice false doctrine, but comfort and hope to those whose faith is genuine.

The Command

But I say to you, the rest who are in Thyatira, who do not hold this teaching, who have not known the deep things of Satan, as they call them—I place no other burden on you. Nevertheless what you have, hold fast until I come. (2:24–25)

Having warned the practitioners of false doctrine to repent, Christ addressed words of comfort **to the rest who are in Thyatira,**

who did **not hold** to Jezebel's false **teaching.** They are reminiscent of God's words of comfort to those in Malachi's day who feared being swept up in divine judgment:

> Then those who feared the Lord spoke to one another, and the Lord gave attention and heard it, and a book of remembrance was written before Him for those who fear the Lord and who esteem His name. "They will be Mine," says the Lord of hosts, "on the day that I prepare My own possession, and I will spare them as a man spares his own son who serves him." (Mal. 3:16–17)

Christ further defined the true believers as those **who have not known the deep things of Satan, as they call them.** Jezebel and her followers claimed to be plumbing the very depths of Satan's domain and remaining spiritually unscathed. In their perverse, libertine, licentious false theology, they believed they could do so with impunity. This pre-Gnostic teaching said that one was free to engage the sphere of Satan and participate in sins of the body without harming the spirit. Since the spirit belongs to God, their twisted logic went, what does it matter if the body attends idolatrous feasts and engages in sexual immorality? They imagined themselves to be free to explore the satanic sphere and then brazenly come to worship God.

To the true believers who had not experienced the alleged deeper knowledge claimed by these heretics, Christ said, **I place no other burden on you.** Bearing the burden of seeing blatant false teaching and immoral living rampant in their church, and having to resist the incessant solicitation and ridicule from the Jezebel party, was burden enough for them to bear. But lest they become overconfident, Christ exhorts them, **what you have, hold fast until I come** (cf. 1 Cor. 10:12). The use of the strong word *krateō* (**hold fast**) indicates that it would not be easy. The coming of Christ as it related to the Thyatira church was His coming to them in judgment. But in a wider sense, all believers are to "cling to what is good" (Rom. 12:9) until Christ's return.

THE COUNSEL

He who overcomes, and he who keeps My deeds until the end, to him I will give authority over the nations; and he shall rule them with a rod of iron, as the vessels of the potter are broken to pieces, as I also have received authority from My Father; and I will give him the morning star. He who has an ear, let him hear what the Spirit says to the churches. (2:26–29)

To the one **who overcomes** (i.e., a true Christian; cf. 1 John 5:5) **and . . . keeps** Christ's **deeds** (in contrast to those in v. 22 who practiced Jezebel's evil deeds) **until the end** (steadfast obedience marks a genuine Christian), Christ promises two things. First, Christ will **give** such people **authority over the nations; and** they **shall rule them with a rod of iron, as the vessels of the potter are broken to pieces.** That promise, taken from Psalm 2:7–9, is one of participation in the millennial kingdom. Those who remained faithful to Christ despite being beaten and despised in this life will rule with Him in His earthly kingdom. They will exercise **authority over the nations,** ruling **them with a rod of iron** (cf. Rev. 12:5; 19:15). Those nations in the millennial kingdom who rebel against Christ's rule and threaten His people will be destroyed. Those people who rule with Him will help protect His people and promote holiness and righteousness. Christ will delegate authority to them **as** He **also** has **received authority from** His **Father** (cf. John 5:22, 27).

Christ also promised to **give** to His faithful followers **the morning star.** Some connect the morning star with such passages as Daniel 12:3 and Matthew 13:43. The promise would be that believers will reflect Christ's glory. While Christians will reflect Christ's glory, it is better to see the **morning star** as Christ Himself—a title He assumes in Revelation 22:16 (cf. 2 Pet. 1:19). Christ promised believers Himself in all His fullness; the One whom we "now . . . know in part [we will] then . . . know fully just as [we] also have been fully known" (1 Cor. 13:12).

The concluding words, **he who has an ear, let him hear what the Spirit says to the churches,** are a charge to heed the message of the letter to the church at Thyatira. Three important truths stand out. First, this letter reveals the seriousness of practicing and tolerating sin, and that God will judge continued, unrepentant sin in the church. Second, a pattern of obedience marks true Christians. Finally, God's gracious promise to His own is that, in spite of struggles with sin and error in churches, they will experience all the fullness of Christ as they reign with Him in His kingdom. Those churches, like Thyatira, who fail to heed the message will receive divine judgment; those who do heed its message will receive divine blessing.

Sardis: The Dead Church (Revelation 3:1–6)

8

"To the angel of the church in Sardis write: He who has the seven Spirits of God and the seven stars, says this: 'I know your deeds, that you have a name that you are alive, but you are dead. Wake up, and strengthen the things that remain, which were about to die; for I have not found your deeds completed in the sight of My God. So remember what you have received and heard; and keep it, and repent. Therefore if you do not wake up, I will come like a thief, and you will not know at what hour I will come to you. But you have a few people in Sardis who have not soiled their garments; and they will walk with Me in white, for they are worthy. He who overcomes will thus be clothed in white garments; and I will not erase his name from the book of life, and I will confess his name before My Father and before His angels. He who has an ear, let him hear what the Spirit says to the churches.'" (3:1–6)

The vast distances of interstellar space are unimaginably immense. The nearest stars to us are trillions of miles away. Those large distances have forced astronomers to come up with an appropriate measurement unit, the light-year. One light-year equals the distance that light, traveling at more than 186,000 miles per second, travels in one year—more than 6 trillion miles.

The enormous distance to even the nearest stars presents an interesting possibility. If a star thirty light-years away from the earth exploded and died five years ago, we would not be able to tell by looking at it for another twenty-five years. Though no longer in existence, the light from that star would go on shining as if nothing had changed.

That illustration perfectly sums up the situation in many churches. They still shine with the reflected light of a brilliant past. Looking at them from a distance, one might think nothing had changed. Yet the spiritual darkness of false teaching and sinful living has extinguished the light on the inside, though some of their reputation may still remain.

Such a church was the church at Sardis. It was reputed to be alive, but the Lord Jesus Christ pronounced it to be dead. The downward spiral depicted by these churches, beginning with the Ephesian church's loss of its first love for Jesus Christ and continuing with Pergamum's worldliness and Thyatira's toleration of sin, reached a new low at Sardis. The church at Sardis could well be nicknamed "The First Church of the Tares." It was a church dominated by sin, unbelief, and false doctrine. Like the fig tree in Jesus' parable, it bore leaves, but no fruit (Matt. 21:19).

Like the rest of the seven churches, the church at Sardis was an actual, existing church in John's day. Yet it also symbolizes the dead churches that have existed throughout history, and, sadly, continue to exist in our own day. The appearance of light is only an illusion.

The letter from the Lord Jesus Christ to the church at Sardis may be divided into the familiar seven sections: the correspondent, the church, the city, the concern, the commendation, the command, and the counsel.

THE CORRESPONDENT

He who has the seven Spirits of God and the seven stars, says this: (3:1c)

The descriptions of the divine author in each of the seven letters are drawn from the vision of 1:12–17. The letter to Sardis draws an additional component from the salutation in 1:4, where the phrase **seven Spirits** also appears. That phrase may refer to Isaiah 11:2, where the Holy Spirit is described as "the Spirit of the Lord ..., the spirit of wisdom and understanding, the spirit of counsel and strength, the spirit of knowledge and the fear of the Lord." It may also refer to the symbolic depiction of the Holy Spirit as a lampstand with seven lamps (a menorah), presented in Zechariah 4:1–10. In either case, the reference is to the Spirit's fullness. Jesus Christ is represented in His church through the Holy Spirit.

The **seven stars** are the seven messengers or elders (cf. 1:20), one from each of the seven churches, who likely carried a copy of the book of Revelation back to their respective churches. The imagery shows Jesus Christ, the sovereign Lord of the church, mediating His rule through such godly leaders and pastors.

Christ's introduction of Himself does not hint at the severity of the situation in Sardis. Surprisingly, He did not introduce Himself as the divine Judge (as He did in 2:18 to the church at Thyatira), although the church at Sardis faced imminent judgment. Instead, He depicted Himself as the One who sovereignly works in His church through the Holy Spirit and godly leaders. That introduction served as a reminder to the Sardis church of what they lacked. Devoid of the Spirit, the church at Sardis was dead, populated by the unredeemed.

THE CHURCH

the church in Sardis (3:1*a*)

Though the details are not recorded in Scripture, the church at Sardis was probably founded as an outreach of Paul's ministry at Ephesus (Acts 19:10). The most prominent person from the church at Sardis known to history is Melito. He was an apologist (one who wrote in defense of Christianity) who served as bishop of Sardis in the late second century. He also wrote the earliest known commentary on passages from Revelation. The letter does not speak of persecution (why would Satan bother to persecute a dead church?), false doctrine, false teachers, or corrupt living. Yet some combination of those things was obviously present at Sardis, since the church had died.

THE CITY

Sardis (3:1*b*)

To a striking degree, the history of the church at Sardis paralleled that of the city. Founded about 1200 B.C., Sardis had been one of the greatest cities in the ancient world, capital of the fabulously wealthy Lydian kingdom. (The name of that kingdom's most famous king, Croesus, lives on in the saying "As rich as Croesus.") Aesop, the famous writer of fables, may have been from Sardis. Much of Sardis's wealth came from gold taken from the nearby Pactolus River; archaeologists have found hundreds of crucibles, used for refining gold, in the ruins of Sardis (Edwin M.

Yamauchi, *New Testament Cities in Western Asia Minor* [Grand Rapids: Baker, 1980], 65). Gold and silver coins were apparently first minted at Sardis. The city also benefited from its location at the western end of the royal road that led east to the Persian capital city of Susa, and from its proximity to other important trade routes. It was also a center for wool production and the garment industry; in fact, Sardis claimed to have discovered how to dye wool.

Sardis was located about thirty miles south of Thyatira in the fertile valley of the Hermus River. A series of spurs or hills jutted out from the ridge of Mount Tmolus, south of the Hermus River. On one of those hills, some fifteen hundred feet above the valley floor, stood Sardis. Its location made the city all but impregnable. The hill on which Sardis was built had smooth, nearly perpendicular rock walls on three sides. Only from the south could the city be approached, via a steep, difficult path. The one drawback to an otherwise ideal site was that there was limited room for the city to expand. Eventually, as Sardis grew, a new city sprang up at the foot of the hill. The old site remained a refuge to retreat into when danger threatened.

Its seemingly impregnable location caused the inhabitants of Sardis to become overconfident. That complacency eventually led to the city's downfall. Through carelessness, the unimaginable happened: Sardis was conquered. The news of its downfall sent shock waves through the Greek world. Even in John's day, several centuries later, a proverbial saying equated "to capture the acropolis of Sardis" with "to do the impossible" (Colin J. Hemer, *The Letters to the Seven Churches of Asia in Their Local Setting* [Sheffield: JSOT Press, 1986], 133). Dr. Robert L. Thomas relates the account of Sardis's fall:

> Despite an alleged warning against self-satisfaction by the Greek god whom he consulted, Croesus the king of Lydia initiated an attack against Cyrus king of Persia, but was soundly defeated. Returning to Sardis to recoup and rebuild his army for another attack, he was pursued quickly by Cyrus who laid siege against Sardis. Croesus felt utterly secure in his impregnable situation atop the acropolis and foresaw an easy victory over the Persians who were cornered among the perpendicular rocks in the lower city, an easy prey for the assembling Lydian army to crush. After retiring one evening while the drama was unfolding, he awakened to discover that the Persians had gained control of the acropolis by scaling one-by-one the steep walls (549 B.C.). So secure did the Sardians feel that they left this means of access completely unguarded, permitting the climbers to ascend unobserved. It is said that even a child could have defended the city from this kind of attack, but not so much as one observer had been appointed to watch the side that was believed to be inaccessible.

History repeated itself more than three and a half centuries later when Antiochus the Great conquered Sardis by utilizing the services of a sure-footed mountain climber from Crete (195 B.C.). His army entered the city by another route while the defenders in careless confidence were content to guard the one known approach, the isthmus of land connected to Mount Tmolus on the south. (*Revelation 1–7: An Exegetical Commentary* [Chicago: Moody, 1992], 241)

Sardis never regained its independence, eventually coming under Roman control in 133 B.C. A catastrophic earthquake destroyed the city in A.D. 17, but it was rebuilt with the generous financial aid of Emperor Tiberius. In gratitude, the inhabitants of Sardis built a temple in his honor. The city's primary object of worship, however, was the goddess Cybele—the same goddess worshiped at Ephesus as Artemis (Diana). Hot springs not far from Sardis were celebrated as a spot in which the gods manifested their supposed power to give life to the dead—an ironic note for a city whose church was dead. In John's day Sardis was prosperous but decaying, its glory days long past. Both the city and the church it contained had lost their vitality.

THE CONCERN

I know your deeds, that you have a name that you are alive, but you are dead. . . . For I have not found your deeds completed in the sight of My God. (3:1d, 2b)

Because the Sardis church was dead, Christ skipped the usual commendation for the moment and went directly to His concerns for it. Though its outward appearance may have fooled men (it had a **name,** or reputation of being **alive**), the Sardis church could not fool the omniscient Lord Jesus Christ, who knew its **deeds.** With His infallible knowledge, He pronounced the Sardis church to be **dead.** Like so many churches today it was defiled by the world, characterized by inward decay, and populated by unredeemed people playing church.

Spiritual death in the New Testament is always connected with its cause—sin. Ephesians 2:1 describes the unregenerate as "dead in [their] trespasses and sins" (cf. Luke 9:60; 15:24, 32; Col. 2:13; 1 Tim. 5:6; 1 John 3:14). The church at Sardis was like a museum in which stuffed animals are exhibited in their natural habitats. Everything appears to be normal, but nothing is alive. Sin killed the Sardis church.

What are the danger signs that a church is dying? A church is in danger when it is content to rest on its past laurels, when it is more concerned with liturgical forms than spiritual reality, when it focuses on curing social ills rather than changing people's hearts through preaching the life-giving gospel of Jesus Christ, when it is more concerned with material than spiritual things, when it is more concerned with what men think than what God said, when it is more enamored with doctrinal creeds and systems of theology than with the Word of God, or when it loses its conviction that every word of the Bible is the word of God Himself. No matter what its attendance, no matter how impressive its buildings, no matter what its status in the community, such a church, having denied the only source of spiritual life, is dead.

The congregation at Sardis was performing **deeds; they were** going through the motions. But those deeds, Christ declared, were not **completed in the sight of My God.** Though sufficient to give the Sardis church a reputation before men, those deeds were insufficient and unacceptable in God's sight. They were but the pointless, lifeless motion of corpses; the Sardis congregation's good works merely grave clothes of the unregenerate. The spiritual zombies (cf. Eph. 2:1–2) populating the Sardis church were living a lie. They had been weighed on the scales by the Righteous Judge and found wanting (cf. Dan. 5:27).

The Old Testament hero Samson provides an apt illustration of the Sardis church's dilemma. Despite his spectacular feats and his amazing strength, his life came to a sad and tragic end. The temptress Delilah "pressed [Samson] daily with her words and urged him" (Judg. 16:16) to reveal to her the secret of his strength. Eventually, after "his soul was annoyed to death" (v. 16) by her constant prying, Samson told Delilah the truth. She cut his hair, and he lost his great strength, not because of the haircut, but because of his disobedience to God. Then came the saddest moment of the entire tragic story. The Philistines came to seize Samson and, unconcerned, he went to deal with them. They, however, captured him, bound him, and put out his eyes. Tragically, Samson "did not know that the Lord had departed from him" (v. 20). Though he was the same man, with the same name, his power was gone. The result for Samson was imprisonment, blindness, humiliation, and, finally, death.

So also the church at Sardis, once spiritually alive and strong, was now blind and weak, not realizing that God had long since departed.

THE COMMENDATION

But you have a few people in Sardis who have not soiled their garments; and they will walk with Me in white, for they are worthy. (3:4)

In the midst of this dead church, filled with unregenerate people, a **few** true Christians were scattered like flowers in a desert. There were not enough of them, however, to change Christ's overall evaluation of the church as dead. But He had not forgotten those who remained faithful to Him (cf. Mal. 3:16–17; Heb. 6:10).

That God preserves His faithful remnant is a frequent theme of Scripture. Paul writes in Romans 11:1–5:

> I say then, God has not rejected His people, has He? May it never be! For I too am an Israelite, a descendant of Abraham, of the tribe of Benjamin. God has not rejected His people whom He foreknew. Or do you not know what the Scripture says in the passage about Elijah, how he pleads with God against Israel? "Lord, they have killed Your prophets, they have torn down Your altars, and I alone am left, and they are seeking my life." But what is the divine response to him? "I have kept for Myself seven thousand men who have not bowed the knee to Baal." In the same way then, there has also come to be at the present time a remnant according to God's gracious choice.

God had His remnant even in the dead church at Sardis. There were a few sincere among the hypocrites, a few humble among the proud, a few separated among the worldly, and a few stalks of wheat among the tares.

Christ described the faithful remnant as those **who have not soiled their garments. Soiled** is from *molunō*, which means "to stain," "to defile," "to smear," or "to pollute." It was a word that would have been familiar to readers in Sardis because of the city's wool dyeing industry. **Garments** symbolize character in Scripture (e.g., Isa. 64:6; Jude 23). The faithful remnant could come into God's presence because they had not defiled or polluted themselves, but manifested their godly character.

Specifically, Christ says of them that **they will walk with Me in white, for they are worthy.** In ancient times, such garments were worn for celebrations and festivals. Because they refused to defile their garments, Christ would replace those humanly preserved clean garments with divinely pure ones (cf. 7:14). The white robes of purity Christ promises here and in verse 5 (cf. 6:11; 7:9, 13; 19:8, 14) are elsewhere worn by Christ Himself (Matt. 17:2; Mark 9:3) and the holy angels (Matt. 28:3; Mark 16:5; Acts 1:10). Those who have a measure of holiness and purity now will be given perfect holiness and purity in the future.

THE COMMAND

Wake up, and strengthen the things that remain, which were about to die. . . . So remember what you have received and heard;

and keep it, and repent. Therefore if you do not wake up, I will come like a thief, and you will not know at what hour I will come to you. (3:2*a*, 3)

Christ addressed the command to the faithful remnant of true Christians at Sardis; there is no point in talking to those who are dead. If their church was to survive it desperately needed life. Christ laid out for them the path to spiritual restoration by giving them five steps to follow.

First, they needed to **wake up.** There was no time for indifference; they could not just go with the flow, they had to reverse it. The believing remnant needed to look at what was happening in their church, evaluate the situation, get involved in changing things, confront sin and error, and make a difference.

Second, they needed to **strengthen the things that remain, which were about to die. Things** is a neuter noun in the Greek and does not refer to people, but to spiritual realities. Christ exhorted the true Christians at Sardis to fan into flame the dying embers of the remaining spiritual graces in their church.

The third step was for the faithful remnant to **remember what** they had **received and heard.** They needed to go back to the truths of the Word of God, remembering the gospel and the teaching of the apostles. By this time, Paul's letters were in circulation (cf. 2 Pet. 3:15–16) and the rest of the New Testament had been written. The believers at Sardis needed to reaffirm their belief in the truth about Christ, sin, salvation, and sanctification. In the words of Paul to Timothy, they were to guard what had been entrusted to them (1 Tim. 6:20). They needed to establish a solid doctrinal foundation to serve as a base for renewal.

Fourth, having gone back to the truths of Scripture, they needed to **keep** them. Orthodox theology apart from obedient lives would not bring about renewal.

Finally, they needed to **repent.** With remorse and sorrow, the believers at Sardis were to confess and turn away from their sins. These five steps, if diligently practiced, would bring about revival.

The consequences if revival did not come would be severe. Christ warned them **if you do not wake up, I will come like a thief, and you will not know at what hour I will come to you.** The picture of Jesus coming **like a thief** always carries the idea of imminent judgment (Matt. 24:43; Luke 12:39; 1 Thess. 5:2, 4; 2 Pet. 3:10; Rev. 16:15). The threat here is not related to His second coming, but is that the Lord would come and destroy the Sardis church if there is no revival. It can also be extrapolated into a warning of the judgment that faces all dead churches at Christ's return.

The only way to avoid the stricter judgment that awaits those who know the truth and turn away from it (Heb. 10:29–30) is to follow the path to spiritual life.

THE COUNSEL

He who overcomes will thus be clothed in white garments; and I will not erase his name from the book of life, and I will confess his name before My Father and before His angels. He who has an ear, let him hear what the Spirit says to the churches. (3.5–6)

By way of encouragement, Christ described the rewards awaiting those who participated in the revival. True Christians, as already noted, will **be clothed in white garments.** In the ancient world, **white garments** were also worn for festive occasions such as weddings. True Christians will wear theirs at the marriage supper of the Lamb (19:7–9). White robes were also worn by those celebrating victory in battle; all true Christians are victorious through Christ over sin, death, and Satan. But, as noted earlier in the discussion of verse 4, primarily believers' **white garments** represent purity and holiness. Christ promises to clothe Christians in the brilliance of eternal purity and holiness.

Christ further promises every true Christian that He **will not erase his name from the book of life,** but will **confess his name before** the **Father and before His angels.** Incredibly, although the text says just the opposite, some people assume that this verse teaches that a Christian's name can be erased from the **book of life.** They thus foolishly turn a promise into a threat. Exodus 32:33, it is argued by some, supports the idea that God may remove someone's name from the Book of Life. In that passage the Lord tells Moses that "whoever has sinned against Me, I will blot him out of My book." There is no contradiction, however, between that passage and Christ's promise in Revelation 3:5. The book referred to in Exodus 32:33 is not the Book of Life described here, in Philippians 4:3, and later in Revelation (13:8; 17:8; 20:12,15; 21:27). Instead, it refers to the book of the living, the record of those who are alive (cf. Ps. 69:28). The threat, then, is not eternal damnation, but physical death.

In John's day, rulers kept a register of the citizens of a city. If someone died, or committed a serious crime, their name was erased from that register. Christ, the King of heaven, promises never to erase a true Christian's name from the roll of those whose names were "written from the foundation of the world in the book of life of the Lamb who has been slain" (13:8).

On the contrary, Christ will **confess** every believer's **name be-**

fore God the **Father and before His angels.** He will affirm that they belong to Him. Here Christ reaffirmed the promise He made during His earthly ministry: "Everyone who confesses Me before men, I will also confess him before My Father who is in heaven" (Matt. 10:32). The comforting truth that true Christians' salvation is eternally secure is the unmistakable teaching of Scripture. Nowhere is that truth more strongly stated than in Romans 8:28–39:

> And we know that God causes all things to work together for good to those who love God, to those who are called according to His purpose. For those whom He foreknew, He also predestined to become conformed to the image of His Son, so that He would be the firstborn among many brethren; and these whom He predestined, He also called; and these whom He called, He also justified; and these whom He justified, He also glorified. What then shall we say to these things? If God is for us, who is against us? He who did not spare His own Son, but delivered Him over for us all, how will He not also with Him freely give us all things? Who will bring a charge against God's elect? God is the one who justifies; who is the one who condemns? Christ Jesus is He who died, yes, rather who was raised, who is at the right hand of God, who also intercedes for us. Who will separate us from the love of Christ? Will tribulation, or distress, or persecution, or famine, or nakedness, or peril, or sword? Just as it is written, "For Your sake we are being put to death all day long; we were considered as sheep to be slaughtered." But in all these things we overwhelmingly conquer through Him who loved us. For I am convinced that neither death, nor life, nor angels, nor principalities, nor things present, nor things to come, nor powers, nor height, nor depth, nor any other created thing, will be able to separate us from the love of God, which is in Christ Jesus our Lord.

The letter to Sardis ends, like the other six, with an exhortation to heed the counsel, commands, and promises it contains: **He who has an ear, let him hear what the Spirit says to the churches.** The spiritually dead zombies playing church needed to heed Christ's warning of impending judgment. The indifferent believers needed to wake up before it was too late to save their church. And the faithful few could take comfort in the knowledge that their salvation was eternally secure.

What happened to Sardis? Did they heed the warning? Did revival come? That such a prominent man as Melito served as bishop of Sardis several decades after John wrote argues that at least some revival took place in Sardis. Until Christ returns, it is not too late for other dead churches to find the path to spiritual renewal.

Philadelphia: The Faithful Church (Revelation 3:7–13)

9

"And to the angel of the church in Philadelphia write: He who is holy, who is true, who has the key of David, who opens and no one will shut, and who shuts and no one opens, says this: 'I know your deeds. Behold, I have put before you an open door which no one can shut, because you have a little power, and have kept My word, and have not denied My name. Behold, I will cause those of the synagogue of Satan, who say that they are Jews and are not, but lie—I will make them come and bow down at your feet, and make them know that I have loved you. Because you have kept the word of My perseverance, I also will keep you from the hour of testing, that hour which is about to come upon the whole world, to test those who dwell on the earth. I am coming quickly; hold fast what you have, so that no one will take your crown. He who overcomes, I will make him a pillar in the temple of My God, and he will not go out from it anymore; and I will write on him the name of My God, and the name of the city of My God, the new Jerusalem, which comes down out of heaven from My God, and My new name. He who has an ear, let him hear what the Spirit says to the churches.'" (3:7–13)

Occasionally I am asked by young men seeking a church to pastor if I know of a church without any problems. My response to them is "If I did, I wouldn't tell you; you'd go there and spoil it." The point is that there are no perfect churches. Churches struggle because all are made up of imperfect, sinning people. The church is not a place for people with no weaknesses; it is a fellowship of those who are aware of their weaknesses and long for the strength and grace of God to fill their lives. It is a kind of hospital for those who know they are sick and needy.

Like all churches, the one in Philadelphia had its imperfections. Yet the Lord commended its members for their faithfulness and loyalty. They and the congregation at Smyrna were the only two of the seven that received no rebuke from the Lord of the church. In spite of their fleshly struggles, the Christians at Philadelphia were faithful and obedient, serving and worshiping the Lord. They provide a good model of a loyal church.

To aid in understanding the letter to the Philadelphia church, it may be divided into six headings: the correspondent, the church, the city, the commendation, the command, and the counsel.

The Correspondent

He who is holy, who is true, who has the key of David, who opens and no one will shut, and who shuts and no one opens, says this: (3:7c)

The Lord Jesus Christ, the divine author of the seven letters, always introduces Himself with a description reflecting His character. In the previous five letters, those descriptions had come from the vision recorded in 1:12–17. But this description of Him is unique and not drawn from that earlier vision. It has distinctly Old Testament features.

He who is holy refers to God, who alone possesses absolute holiness. The Old Testament repeatedly describes God as the Holy One (e.g., 2 Kings 19:22; Job 6:10; Pss. 71:22; 78:41; Isa. 43:15; 54:5; Hab. 3:3). Isaiah 6:3 solemnly declares, "Holy, Holy, Holy, is the Lord of hosts, the whole earth is full of His glory" (cf. Rev. 4:8). To say that God is holy is to say that He is utterly separate from sin; therefore His character is absolutely unblemished and flawless.

The title "Holy One" is used in the New Testament as a messianic title for the Lord Jesus Christ. In Mark 1:24 a terrified demon screamed, "What business do we have with each other, Jesus of Nazareth? Have You come to destroy us? I know who You are—the Holy One of God!" Announcing His birth to Mary, the angel described Jesus as "the holy Child" (Luke 1:35). In John 6:69 Peter affirmed, "We have believed and have come to know that You are the Holy One of God." Later he rebuked the unbelieving Jews because they "disowned the Holy and Righteous One and asked for a murderer to be granted to [them]" (Acts 3:14).

Jesus' identification of Himself as **He who is holy** can be no less than a direct claim to deity. The Lord Jesus Christ possesses in undiminished, unaltered essence the holy and sinless nature of God. Because Christ is holy, His church must be as well. "Like the Holy One who called you," wrote Peter, "be holy yourselves also in all your behavior" (1 Pet. 1:15). That the omniscient Holy One gave no rebuke, warning, or condemnation to the Philadelphia church speaks very well of them indeed.

Not only is Jesus Christ the Holy One; He also describes Himself as He **who is true.** Truth is used in combination with holiness to describe God in Revelation 6:10; 15:3; 16:7; 19:2, 11. *Alēthinos* (**true**) denotes that which is genuine, authentic, and real. In the midst of the falsehood, perversion, and error that fills the world, the Lord Jesus Christ is the truth (John 14:6).

Third, Christ describes Himself as the One **who has the key of David.** As is clear from Revelation 5:5 and 22:16, **David** symbolizes the messianic office. A **key** in Scripture represents authority; whoever holds a key has control (cf. 1:18; 9:1; 20:1; Matt. 16:19). The term **the key of David** also appears in Isaiah 22:22, where it refers to Eliakim, the steward or prime minister to Israel's king. Because of his office, he controlled access to the monarch. As the holder of **the key of David,** Jesus alone has the sovereign authority to determine who enters His messianic kingdom (cf. John 10:7, 9; 14:6; Acts 4:12). Revelation 1:18 reveals that Jesus has the keys to death and hell; here He is depicted as having the keys to salvation and blessing.

Finally, Jesus identifies Himself as He **who opens and no one will shut, and who shuts and no one opens.** That description stresses Christ's omnipotence; what He does cannot be overturned by someone more powerful. "I act and who can reverse it?" declared the Lord in Isaiah 43:13 (cf. Is. 46:9–11; Jer. 18:6; Dan. 4:35). No one can shut the doors to the kingdom or to blessing if He holds them open, and no one can force them open if He holds them shut. In light of the promise in verse 8, Christ could also be referring to opening and shutting doors for service. In either case, the emphasis is on His sovereign control over His church.

That Jesus Christ, the holy, true, sovereign, omnipotent Lord of the church, found nothing to condemn in the Philadelphia church must have been a joyous encouragement to them.

THE CHURCH

the church in Philadelphia (3:7*a*)

Little is known about the Philadelphia church apart from this passage. Like most of the other seven churches, it was probably founded during Paul's ministry at Ephesus (Acts 19:10). A few years after John wrote Revelation, the early church father Ignatius passed through Philadelphia on his way to martyrdom at Rome. He later wrote the church a letter of encouragement and instruction. Some Christians from Philadelphia were martyred with Polycarp at Smyrna (see chapter 5 of this volume). The church lasted for centuries. The Christians in Philadelphia stood firm even after the region was overrun by the Muslims, finally succumbing in the mid-fourteenth century.

THE CITY

Philadelphia (3:7b)

From the Hermus River valley, where Sardis and Smyrna were located, a smaller valley (that of the Cogamis River) branches off to the southeast. A road through this valley provided the best means of ascending the 2,500 feet from the Hermus valley to the vast central plateau. In this valley, about thirty miles from Sardis, was the city of Philadelphia.

Philadelphia was the youngest of the seven cities, founded sometime after 189 B.C. either by King Eumenes of Pergamum or his brother, Attalus II, who succeeded him as king. In either case, the city derived its name from Attalus II's nickname *Philadelphus* ("brother lover"), which his loyalty to his brother Eumenes had earned him.

Though situated on an easily defensible site on an 800-foot-high hill overlooking an important road, Philadelphia was not founded primarily as a military outpost (as Thyatira had been). Its founders intended it to be a center of Greek culture and language, a missionary outpost for spreading Hellenism to the regions of Lydia and Phrygia. Philadelphia succeeded in its mission so well that by A.D. 19 the Lydian language had been completely replaced by Greek.

Philadelphia benefited from its location at the junction of several important trade routes (as well as from being a stop on the Imperial Post Road), earning it the title "gateway to the East" (Robert H. Mounce, *The Book of Revelation,* The New International Commentary on the New Testament [Grand Rapids: Eerdmans, 1977], 114–15). The city was located on the edge of the *Katakekaumene* (the "burned land"), a volcanic region whose fertile soil was ideally suited for vineyards. Being near such a seismically active region had its drawbacks, however. In A.D. 17 a powerful earthquake rocked Philadelphia, along with Sardis and ten other nearby cities. Though the initial destruction was greater at Sardis,

Philadelphia, being nearer the epicenter, experienced frequent after-shocks during the coming years. That nerve-wracking experience left psychological scars on Philadelphia's inhabitants, as Sir William Ramsay notes:

> Many of the inhabitants remained outside the city living in huts and booths over the vale, and those who were foolhardy enough (as the sober-minded thought) to remain in the city, practiced various devices to support and strengthen the walls and houses against the recurring shocks. The memory of this disaster lived long . . . people lived amid ever threatening danger, in dread always of a new disaster; and the habit of going out to the open country had probably not disappeared when the Seven Letters were written. (*The Letters to the Seven Churches of Asia* [Albany, Oreg.: AGES Software; reprint of the 1904 edition], 316–17)

In gratitude for Caesar Tiberius's financial aid in rebuilding their city, the Philadelphians joined with several other cities in erecting a monument to him. Going beyond the other cities, Philadelphia actually changed its name to Neocaesarea for a number of years. Several decades later, the city again changed its name to Flavia, in honor of the ruling Roman Imperial family. It would be known by both names, Philadelphia and Flavia, throughout the second and third centuries.

THE COMMENDATION

I know your deeds. Behold, I have put before you an open door which no one can shut, because you have a little power, and have kept My word, and have not denied My name. Behold, I will cause those of the synagogue of Satan, who say that they are Jews and are not, but lie—I will make them come and bow down at your feet, and make them know that I have loved you. Because you have kept the word of My perseverance, I also will keep you from the hour of testing, that hour which is about to come upon the whole world, to test those who dwell on the earth. I am coming quickly; (3:8–11*a*)

Finding nothing in their **deeds** that caused Him concern, the Lord Jesus Christ moved on to commend the Christians at Philadelphia for four realities that characterized the congregation.

First, the Philadelphia church had **a little power.** That was not a negative comment on their feebleness, but a commendation of their strength; the Philadelphia church was small in numbers (cf. Luke 12:32), but had a powerful impact on its city. Most of its members may have been poor, from the lower classes of society (cf. 1 Cor. 1:26). But with Paul they could say, "I am well content with weaknesses, with insults, with distresses, with persecutions, with difficulties, for Christ's sake; for when I am weak, then I am strong" (2 Cor. 12:10). Despite its small size, spiritual power flowed in the Philadelphia church. People were being redeemed, lives were being transformed, and the gospel of Jesus Christ was being proclaimed.

The believers at Philadelphia were also marked by obedience; they **kept** Christ's **word.** Like Job, they could say, "I have not departed from the command of His lips; I have treasured the words of His mouth more than my necessary food" (Job 23:12). Like Martin Luther, on trial before the Imperial Diet, they could say, "My conscience is captive to the Word of God." They did not deviate from the pattern of obedience, thus proving the genuineness of their love for Christ (John 14:23–24; 15:13–14).

Christ further commended the Philadelphia congregation for having **not denied** His **name,** despite the pressures they faced to do so. They remained loyal no matter what it cost them. Revelation 14:12 describes the Tribulation saints who refused to take the mark of the beast: "Here is the perseverance of the saints who keep the commandments of God and their faith in Jesus." Like them, the Philadelphia church would not recant its faith.

Finally, Christ commended the Philadelphia church **because** its members had **kept the word of** His **perseverance.** The New International Version's translation clarifies Christ's meaning: "You have kept my command to endure patiently." The Christians at Philadelphia persevered faithfully through all of their trials and difficulties.

The steadfast endurance that marked Jesus' earthly life (Heb. 12:2–4) is to be a model for all Christians. To the Thessalonians Paul wrote, "May the Lord direct your hearts into the love of God and into the steadfastness of Christ" (2 Thess. 3:5). Both Christ's command and example should motivate Christians to patient endurance. Indeed, endurance is an essential aspect of saving faith (Matt. 10:22).

Because of its faithfulness, the Lord Jesus Christ made the Philadelphia church some astounding promises. First, He **put before** them **an open door which no one can shut.** Their salvation was secure; their entrance both into the blessings of salvation by grace and into Christ's future messianic kingdom was guaranteed. The picture of Christ's opening the door also symbolizes His giving the faithful Philadelphia church opportunities for service. Elsewhere in Scripture an open door depicts freedom to proclaim the gospel. Explaining his travel plans to the Corinthians, Paul informed them, "I will remain in Ephesus until Pentecost; for a wide door for effective service has opened to me, and there are many adversaries" (1 Cor. 16:8–9). In his second letter to them he wrote, "Now when I came to Troas for the gospel of Christ and when a door was opened for me in the Lord" (2 Cor. 2:12). To the Colossians Paul wrote, "Devote yourselves to prayer, keeping alert in it with an attitude of thanksgiving; praying at the same time for us as well, that God will open up to us a door for the word" (Col. 4:2–3). Their city's strategic location provided the Christians at Philadelphia with an excellent opportunity to spread the gospel.

Verse 9 records a second promise made by Jesus Christ to the Philadelphia church: **Behold, I will cause those of the synagogue of Satan, who say that they are Jews and are not, but lie—I will make them come and bow down at your feet, and make them know that I have loved you.** As was the case in Smyrna (cf. 2:9), Christians in Philadelphia faced hostility from unbelieving Jews. Ignatius later debated some hostile Jews during his visit to Philadelphia. Because of their rejection of Jesus Christ as the Messiah, they were not at all a synagogue of God, but a **synagogue of Satan.** Though they claimed **that they** were **Jews,** that claim was a **lie.** Racially, culturally, and ceremonially they were Jews, but spiritually they were not. Paul defines a true Jew in Romans 2:28–29: "For he is not a Jew who is one outwardly, nor is circumcision that which is outward in the flesh. But he is a Jew who is one inwardly; and circumcision is that which is of the heart, by the Spirit, not by the letter; and his praise is not from men, but from God" (cf. Rom. 9:6–7).

Amazingly, Christ promised that some of the very Jews who were persecuting the Christians at Philadelphia would **come and bow down at** their **feet, and know that** God had **loved** them. Bowing at someone's feet depicts abject, total defeat and submission. The Philadelphia church's enemies would be utterly vanquished, humbled, and defeated. This imagery derives from the Old Testament, which describes the yet future day when unbelieving Gentiles will bow down to the believing remnant of Israel (cf. Isa. 45:14; 49:23; 60:14). The Philadelphia church's faithfulness would be rewarded by the salvation of some of the very Jews who were persecuting it.

Other faithful churches throughout history have also been enabled by the Lord to reach the Jewish people with the gospel of the Messiah, Jesus Christ. And in the future the day will come when "all Israel will be saved" (Rom. 11:26), when God will "pour out on the house of David and on the inhabitants of Jerusalem, the Spirit of grace and of supplication, so that they will look on Me whom they have pierced; and they will mourn for Him, as one mourns for an only son, and they will weep bitterly over Him like the bitter weeping over a firstborn" (Zech. 12:10).

Verse 10 contains a final promise to the faithful Philadelphia church: **Because you have kept the word of My perseverance, I also will keep you from the hour of testing, that hour which is about to come upon the whole world, to test those who dwell on the earth.** Because the believers in Philadelphia had successfully passed so many tests, Jesus promised to spare them from the ultimate test. The sweeping nature of that promise extends far beyond the Philadelphia congregation to encompass all faithful churches throughout history. This verse promises that the church will be delivered from the Tribulation, thus supporting a pretribulation Rapture. The Rapture is the subject of three passages in the New Testament (John 14:1–4; 1 Cor. 15:51–54; 1 Thess. 4:13–17), none of which speak of judgment, but rather of the church being taken up to heaven. There are three views of the timing of the Rapture in relation to the Tribulation: that it comes at the end of the Tribulation (posttribulationism), in the middle of the Tribulation (midtribulationism), and the view that seems to be supported by this text, that the Rapture takes place before the Tribulation (pretribulationism).

Several aspects of this wonderful promise may be noted. First, the test is yet future. Second, the test is for a definite, limited time; Jesus described it as the **hour of testing.** Third, it is a test or trial that will expose people for what they really are. Fourth, the test is worldwide in scope, since it will **come upon the whole world.** Finally, and most significantly, its purpose is **to test those who dwell on the earth**—a phrase used as a technical term in the book of Revelation for unbelievers (cf. 6:10; 8:13; 11:10; 13:8, 12, 14; 14:6; 17:2, 8). The **hour of testing** is Daniel's Seventieth Week (Dan. 9:25–27), the time of Jacob's trouble (Jer. 30:7), the seven-year tribulation period. The Lord promises to keep His church out of the future time of testing that will come on unbelievers.

Unbelievers will either pass the test by repenting, or fail it by refusing to repent. Revelation 6:9–11; 7:9–10, 14; 14:4; and 17:14 describe those who repent during the Tribulation and are saved, thus passing the test; Revelation 6:15–17; 9:20; 16:11; and 19:17–18 describe those who refuse to repent, thus failing the test, and are damned.

There has been much debate over the meaning of the phrase *tēreō ek* (**keep from**). Those who argue that the church will go through the Tribulation hold that this phrase means preservation in the midst of and emergence from. They believe the church will go through the Tribulation judgments and that God will preserve it in the midst of them, so that the church will thus emerge successfully at the end from the hour of testing. That view is unlikely, however, both on linguistic and biblical grounds. The basic meaning of the preposition *ek* is "from," "out from," or "away from." Had the Lord intended to convey that the church would be preserved in the midst of the Tribulation, the prepositions *en* ("in") or *dia* ("through") would have been more appropriate. *En* is used three times with the verb *tēreō* in the New Testament (Acts 12:5; 1 Pet. 1:4; Jude 21) and *eis* once (Acts 25:4), always implying previous existence within with a view to continuing in. *Tēreō* with *ek* implies just the opposite: continuous existence outside.

The only other time the phrase *tēreō ek* appears in Scripture is in John 17:15. In His High-Priestly prayer, Jesus prayed, "I do not ask You to take them out of the world, but to keep them from the evil one." He certainly did not pray that believers be preserved within Satan's power, for believers have been "rescued … from the domain of darkness" and "transferred … to the kingdom of His beloved Son" (Col. 1:13). Christians are those who have turned "from darkness to light and from the dominion of Satan to God" (Acts 26:18). First John 5:19 says that it is the unregenerate world that lies in Satan's power, not believers.

The meaning of *tēreō ek* in John 17:15, to be kept completely out of, argues strongly for a similar meaning in Revelation 3:10. The apostle John wrote both passages, and both are direct quotes of the Lord Jesus Christ. To interpret *tēreō ek* as a promise of preservation in the midst of the Tribulation poses another difficulty: the Philadelphia church was never in the Tribulation, which is still in the future.

Another obvious objection to interpreting *tēreō ek* as a promise of preservation in the midst of the Tribulation is that believers in that terrible time will not be preserved. In fact, many will be martyred (6:9–11; 7:9–14), leading to the conclusion that promising preservation is meaningless if the believers face the same fate as sinners during the Tribulation.

Some hold that the promise of deliverance is only from God's wrath during the Tribulation. But a promise that God will not kill believers but will allow Satan and Antichrist to do so would provide small comfort to the suffering church at Philadelphia.

The **coming** that Christ refers to differs from those promised to others of the seven churches (e.g., 2:5, 16; 3:3). Those earlier promises were warnings of impending temporal judgment on sinning congregations (cf. Acts 5:1–11; 1 Cor. 11:28–30). The **coming** spoken of here, however, is to bring the hour of testing that culminates in our Lord's second coming. It is Christ's coming to deliver the church (cf. 2 Thess. 2:1), not to bring judgment to it. **Quickly** depicts the imminency of Christ's coming for His church; it could happen at any time. Every believer's response should be, "Amen. Come, Lord Jesus" (22:20).

THE COMMAND

hold fast what you have, so that no one will take your crown. (3:11*b*)

Because of the Lord's imminent return for His church, believers must **hold fast what** they **have.** The members of the Philadelphia church had been faithful and loyal to Christ; He commanded them to remain so. Those who persevere to the end thereby prove the genuineness of their salvation (Matt. 10:22; 24:13).

It is true that believers are eternally secure because of the power of God. Yet the means by which He secures them is by providing believers with a persevering faith. Christians are saved by God's power, but not apart from their constant, undying faith. Paul writes in Colossians 1:22–23 that "He has now reconciled you in His fleshly body through death, in order to present you before Him holy and blameless and beyond reproach—if indeed you continue in the faith firmly established and steadfast, and not moved away from the hope of the gospel that you have heard." According to 1 John 2:19, those who abandon the faith reveal that they were never truly saved to begin with: "They went out from us, but they were not really of us; for if they had been of us, they would have remained with us; but they went out, so that it would be shown that they all are not of us."

Christ's promise to the one who faithfully perseveres is **no one will take your crown** (cf. James 1:12). Revelation 2:10 defines this **crown** as the "crown of life," or as the Greek text literally reads, "the crown which is life." The **crown,** or reward, for those who faithfully endure to the end is eternal life with all its attendant rewards (2 John 8). Second Timothy 4:8 describes it as a crown of righteousness, and 1 Peter 5:4 as one of glory. In our glorified state, we will be perfectly righteous, and thus perfectly able to reflect God's glory. Those whose faithful perseverance marks them as true children of God need never fear losing their salvation.

THE COUNSEL

He who overcomes, I will make him a pillar in the temple of My God, and he will not go out from it anymore; and I will write on him the name of My God, and the name of the city of My God, the new Jerusalem, which comes down out of heaven from My God, and My new name. He who has an ear, let him hear what the Spirit says to the churches. (3:12–13)

As He concluded the letter to the faithful church at Philadelphia, Christ promised four eternal blessings to the one **who overcomes** (another name for a Christian; 1 John 5:5).

The first promise is that Christ **will make him a pillar in the**

temple of God, and he will not go out from it anymore. A **pillar** represents stability, permanence, and immovability. Pillars can also represent honor; in pagan temples they were often carved in such a way as to honor a particular deity. The marvelous promise Christ makes to believers is that they will have an eternal place of honor **in the temple of God** (heaven). To people used to fleeing their city because of earthquakes and enemies, the promise that they **will not go out from** heaven was understood as security in eternal glory.

Christ's second promise to the one who overcomes is that He will **write on him the name of His God.** That depicts ownership, signifying that all true Christians belong to God. It also speaks of the intimate personal relationship we have with Him forever.

Third, Christ promises to write on believers **the name of the city of My God, the new Jerusalem, which comes down out of heaven from My God.** Christians have eternal citizenship in heaven's capital **city, the new Jerusalem,** described at length in Revelation 21. That is yet another promise of security, safety, and glory.

Finally, Christ promises believers His **new name.** Christ's name represents the fullness of His person. In heaven, believers will "see Him just as He is" (1 John 3:2), and whatever we may have known of Him will pale in the reality in which we will then see Him. The **new name** by which we will be privileged to call Him will reflect that glorious revelation of His person.

The exhortation **He who has an ear, let him hear what the Spirit says to the churches** closes all seven letters. Believers must heed the truths found in each letter, since the seven churches represent the types of churches that have existed throughout history. The letter to the faithful Philadelphia church reveals that the holy, true, sovereign, omnipotent God pours out His blessings on churches that remain loyal to Him. He will bless them with open doors for evangelism, eternal salvation, kingdom blessings, and deliverance from the great time of testing that will come on the earth. He will ultimately bring all those who persevere in their faith to the eternal bliss of heaven, where He will reveal Himself fully to them. The promise of those rich blessings should motivate every church and every Christian to follow the Philadelphia church's example of faithfulness.

Laodicea: The Lukewarm Church (Revelation 3:14–22)

10

"To the angel of the church in Laodicea write: The Amen, the faithful and true Witness, the Beginning of the creation of God, says this: 'I know your deeds, that you are neither cold nor hot; I wish that you were cold or hot. So because you are lukewarm, and neither hot nor cold, I will spit you out of My mouth. Because you say, "I am rich, and have become wealthy, and have need of nothing," and you do not know that you are wretched and miserable and poor and blind and naked, I advise you to buy from Me gold refined by fire so that you may become rich, and white garments so that you may clothe yourself, and that the shame of your nakedness will not be revealed; and eye salve to anoint your eyes so that you may see. Those whom I love, I reprove and discipline; therefore be zealous and repent. Behold, I stand at the door and knock; if anyone hears My voice and opens the door, I will come in to him and will dine with him, and he with Me. He who overcomes, I will grant to him to sit down with Me on My throne, as I also overcame and sat down with My Father on His throne. He who has an ear, let him hear what the Spirit says to the churches.'" (3:14–22)

Perhaps the most tragic theme in all of redemptive history is the sad story of wayward Israel. The Jewish people were the recipients of unprecedented spiritual privileges: "the adoption as sons, and the glory and the covenants and the giving of the Law and the temple service and the promises, whose are the fathers, and from whom is the Christ according to the flesh, who is over all, God blessed forever" (Rom. 9:4–5). God chose them from all the world's peoples, rescued them from Egypt, brought them into the Promised Land, loved them, and cared for and protected them (cf. Deut. 4:37; 7:7–8).

Yet despite those privileges, Israel's history was one of continual rebellion against God. After their miraculous deliverance from Egypt, the Israelites' rebellion brought God's severe judgment, as an entire generation perished in the wilderness. The cycle of Israel's sin, God's judgment, and Israel's repentance and restoration runs throughout the book of Judges. The Jewish people's sinful pride led them to reject God as their King and demand a human king. Their first king was the disobedient Saul, and the nation was in turmoil for much of his reign. After a period of relative peace and obedience under David and Solomon, Israel split into two kingdoms. All of the northern kings (of Israel) and most of the southern ones (of Judah) were wicked men, who led their people into the gross abominations of idolatry.

All through its centuries of disobedience, rebellion, and apostasy, God graciously called Israel back to Himself: "Since the day that your fathers came out of the land of Egypt until this day," God declared in Jeremiah 7:25, "I have sent you all My servants the prophets, daily rising early and sending them." But instead of repenting and returning to God, the Israelites "did not listen to [Him] or incline their ear, but stiffened their neck; they did more evil than their fathers" (Jer. 7:26; cf. 25:4; 29:19; 35:15; 44:4–5; Zech. 7:12).

Finally, God brought devastating judgment upon His rebellious and unrepentant people. First Israel fell to the Assyrians, then Judah was carried into captivity by the Babylonians and Jerusalem destroyed. Second Kings 17:7–23 recites the sad litany of sins that brought about God's judgment on His people:

> Now this came about because the sons of Israel had sinned against the Lord their God, who had brought them up from the land of Egypt from under the hand of Pharaoh, king of Egypt, and they had feared other gods and walked in the customs of the nations whom the Lord had driven out before the sons of Israel, and in the customs of the kings of Israel which they had introduced. The sons of Israel did things secretly which were not right against the Lord their God. Moreover, they built for themselves high places in all their towns, from watchtower to fortified city. They set for themselves sacred pillars and Asherim on every high

hill and under every green tree, and there they burned incense on all the high places as the nations did which the Lord had carried away to exile before them; and they did evil things provoking the Lord. They served idols, concerning which the Lord had said to them, "You shall not do this." Yet the Lord warned Israel and Judah through all His prophets and every seer, saying, "Turn from your evil ways and keep My commandments, My statutes according to all the law which I commanded your fathers, and which I sent to you through My servants the prophets." However, they did not listen, but stiffened their neck like their fathers, who did not believe in the Lord their God. They rejected His statutes and His covenant which He made with their fathers and His warnings with which He warned them. And they followed vanity and became vain, and went after the nations which surrounded them, concerning which the Lord had commanded them not to do like them. They forsook all the commandments of the Lord their God and made for themselves molten images, even two calves, and made an Asherah and worshiped all the host of heaven and served Baal. Then they made their sons and their daughters pass through the fire, and practiced divination and enchantments, and sold themselves to do evil in the sight of the Lord, provoking Him. So the Lord was very angry with Israel and removed them from His sight; none was left except the tribe of Judah. Also Judah did not keep the commandments of the Lord their God, but walked in the customs which Israel had introduced. The Lord rejected all the descendants of Israel and afflicted them and gave them into the hand of plunderers, until He had cast them out of His sight. When He had torn Israel from the house of David, they made Jeroboam the son of Nebat king. Then Jeroboam drove Israel away from following the Lord and made them commit a great sin. The sons of Israel walked in all the sins of Jeroboam which he did; they did not depart from them until the Lord removed Israel from His sight, as He spoke through all His servants the prophets. So Israel was carried away into exile from their own land to Assyria until this day.

Israel's apostasy brought grief to God's heart. In the parable of Isaiah 5:1–3, Israel is pictured as a well-cared-for vineyard that nonetheless produced only worthless grapes. In verse 4 the Lord said plaintively, "What more was there to do for My vineyard that I have not done in it? Why, when I expected it to produce good grapes did it produce worthless ones?" In Isaiah 48:18 He exclaimed, "If only you had paid attention to My commandments! Then your well-being would have been like a river, and your righteousness like the waves of the sea." In Psalm 78:40 the psalmist lamented, "How often they rebelled against Him in the wilderness and grieved Him in the desert!" Isaiah echoed that same thought: "They rebelled and grieved His Holy Spirit; therefore He turned Himself to become their enemy, He fought against them" (Isa. 63:10). In Ezekiel 6:9

God said of Israel, "I have been hurt by their adulterous hearts which turned away from Me, and by their eyes which played the harlot after their idols."

The New Testament also records God's sorrow over rebellious Israel. Approaching Jerusalem for the last time, the Lord Jesus Christ cried out, "O Jerusalem, Jerusalem, the city that kills the prophets and stones those sent to her! How often I wanted to gather your children together, just as a hen gathers her brood under her wings, and you would not have it!" (Luke 13:34). The Jews' long history of calloused rejection of God's person, commands, and messengers culminated a few days later when they cried out for their Messiah's execution.

The apostle Paul felt the grief of God over his countrymen's unbelief. To the Romans he wrote, "Brethren, my heart's desire and my prayer to God for them is for their salvation. For I testify about them that they have a zeal for God, but not in accordance with knowledge" (Rom. 10:1–2). In Romans 9:2 he wrote of his "great sorrow and unceasing grief" over Israel's unbelief. So intense was Paul's sorrow over that unbelief that he made the shocking statement that if it were possible, he would be willing to be "accursed, separated from Christ for the sake of my brethren, my kinsmen according to the flesh" (v. 3).

Tragically, the sorrowful unbelief of Israel finds a parallel in the church. There are many people in churches, even entire congregations, who are lost. They may be sincere, zealous, and outwardly religious, but they reject the gospel truth. They have all the rich New Covenant teaching about Christ's life, death, and resurrection contained in Bibles they neither believe nor obey. As a result, they are doomed, just as unbelieving Israel was. Paul described them as those "holding to a form of godliness, although they have denied its power," and then wisely counseled believers to "avoid such men as these" (2 Tim. 3:5).

The church at Laodicea represents such apostate churches as have existed throughout history. It is the last and worst of the seven churches addressed by our Lord. The downward spiral that began at Ephesus, and continued through Pergamum, Thyatira, and Sardis, reached the bottom at Laodicea. Even at Sardis there were some true believers left; as far as can be determined, the church at Laodicea was a totally unregenerate, false church. It has the grim distinction of being the only one of the seven for whom Christ has no positive word of commendation. Due to the drastic nature of the situation at Laodicea, this is also the most threatening of the seven letters.

The contents of this letter may be divided into six headings: the correspondent, the church, the city, the concern, the command, and the counsel.

THE CORRESPONDENT

The Amen, the faithful and true Witness, the Beginning of the creation of God, says this: (3:14c)

As in the letter to the church at Philadelphia, Christ did not identify Himself using any of the phrases from the vision recorded in 1:12–17. Instead, He identified Himself using three divine titles.

First, the Lord Jesus Christ described Himself as **the Amen.** That unique title, used only here in Scripture to describe Christ, is reminiscent of Isaiah 65:16, where God is twice called the "God of truth [Heb. *amen*]." **Amen** is a transliteration of a Hebrew word meaning "truth," "affirmation," or "certainty." It refers to that which is firm, fixed, and unchangeable. **Amen** is often used in Scripture to affirm the truthfulness of a statement (e.g., Num. 5:22; Neh. 8:6; Matt. 6:13; Rom. 16:27; 1 Cor. 16:24; and also Matt. 5:18; 6:2; Mark 9:1; Luke 4:24; John 1:51; 3:3, 5, 11; 5:19; where the underlying Greek *amen* is rendered "verily" in the KJV and "truly" in the NASB). Whatever God says is true and certain; therefore, He is the God of truth.

Christ is certainly the **Amen** in the sense that He is the God of truth incarnate. But there is more in this rich title than just an affirmation of His deity. In 2 Corinthians 1:20 Paul writes concerning Jesus Christ, "For as many as are the promises of God, in Him they are yes; therefore also through Him is our Amen to the glory of God through us." It is through the person and work of Christ that all God's promises and covenants are fulfilled and guaranteed. All the Old Testament promises of forgiveness, mercy, lovingkindness, grace, hope, and eternal life are bound up in Jesus Christ's life, death, and resurrection. He is the **Amen** because He is the One who confirmed all of God's promises.

Christ also identified Himself as **the faithful and true Witness.** That title further elucidates the thought expressed in the first title. Not only is Jesus the Amen because of His work, but also because everything He speaks is the truth. He is completely trustworthy, perfectly accurate, and His testimony is always reliable. Jesus Christ is "the way, *and the truth*, and the life" (John 14:6; emphasis added).

This was an appropriate way to begin the letter to the Laodiceans because it affirmed to them that Christ had accurately assessed their unredeemed condition. It also affirmed that His offer of fellowship and salvation in verse 20 was true, because God's promises were confirmed through His work.

Finally, Christ referred to Himself as **the Beginning of the creation of God.** The English translation is somewhat ambiguous and misleading. As a result, false teachers seeking to deny Christ's deity have attempted to use this verse to prove He is a created being. There is no ambiguity in the Greek text, however. *Archē* (**Beginning**) does not mean that Christ was the first person God created, but rather that Christ Himself is the source or origin of creation (cf. Rev. 22:13). Through His power everything was created (John 1:3; Heb. 1:2).

This letter to the Laodiceans has much in common with Paul's letter to the Colossian church. Colossae was not far from Laodicea, so it is likely that the same heresy plaguing the Colossians had made its way to Laodicea (cf. Col. 4:16). That heresy, a form of incipient gnosticism (from the Greek word *gnōsis*, "knowledge"), taught that Christ was a created being, one of a series of emanations from God. Its proponents also claimed that they possessed a secret, higher spiritual knowledge above and beyond the simple words of Scripture. Combating that heresy Paul wrote of Christ,

> He is the image of the invisible God, the firstborn of all creation. For by Him all things were created, both in the heavens and on earth, visible and invisible, whether thrones or dominions or rulers or authorities— all things have been created through Him and for Him. He is before all things, and in Him all things hold together. (Col. 1:15–17)

"Firstborn" (*prōtotokos*) is not limited to the first one born chronologically, but refers to the supreme or preeminent one, the one receiving the highest honor (cf. Ps. 89:27). Christ is thus the source (*archē*) of the creation, and the supreme person (*prōtotokos*) in it.

This damning heresy about the person of Christ was the reason the Laodicean church was spiritually dead. Their heretical Christology had produced an unregenerate church. False teaching about Christ, specifically the denial of His deity, is a hallmark of modern cults as well.

THE CHURCH

the church in Laodicea (3:14*a*)

The New Testament does not record anything about the founding of the church at Laodicea. Like most of the other six churches, it was likely established during Paul's ministry at Ephesus (Acts 19:10). Paul did not found it, since when he wrote Colossians some years later he still had not visited Laodicea (Col. 2:1). Since Paul's coworker Epaphras founded the church in nearby Colossae (Col. 1:6–7), he may well have founded the Laodicean church as well. Some have suggested that Archippus, Philemon's son (Philem. 2), was its pastor (cf. Col. 4:17), since the fourth-century *Apostolic Constitutions* names Archippus as the bishop of Laodicea (vii, 46).

THE CITY

Laodicea (3:14*b*)

One of a triad of cities (with Colossae and Hierapolis) in the Lycus valley, about one hundred miles east of Ephesus, Laodicea was the southeasternmost of the seven cities, about forty miles from Philadelphia. Its sister cities were Colossae, about ten miles to the east, and Hierapolis, about six miles to the north. Located on a plateau several hundred feet high, Laodicea was geographically nearly impregnable. Its vulnerability to attack was due to the fact that it had to pipe in its water from several miles away through aqueducts that could easily be blocked or diverted by besieging forces.

Laodicea was founded by the Seleucid ruler Antiochus II and named after his first wife. Since he divorced her in 253 B.C., the city was most likely founded before that date. Though its original settlers were largely from Syria, a significant number of Jews also settled there. A local governor once forbade the Jews from sending the temple tax to Jerusalem. When they attempted to do so in spite of the prohibition, he confiscated the gold they intended for that tax. From the amount of the seized shipment, it has been calculated that 7,500 Jewish men lived in Laodicea; there would have been several thousand more women and children. Even the Talmud spoke scornfully of the life of ease and laxity lived by the Laodicean Jews.

With the coming of the Pax Romana (peace under Rome's rule), Laodicea prospered. It was strategically located at the junction of two important roads: the east-west road leading from Ephesus into the interior, and the north-south road from Pergamum to the Mediterranean Sea. That location made it an important commercial city. That the first-century B.C. Roman statesman and philosopher Cicero cashed his letters of credit there reveals Laodicea to have been a strategic banking center. So wealthy did Laodicea become that it paid for its own reconstruction after a devastating earthquake in A. D. 60, rejecting offers of financial aid from Rome.

The city was also famous for the soft, black wool it produced. The wool was made into clothes and woven into carpets, both much sought after. Laodicea was also an important center of ancient medicine. The nearby temple of the Phrygian god Men Karou had an important medical school associated with it. That school was most famous for an eye salve that it had developed, which was exported all over the Greco-Roman world. All three industries, finance, wool, and the production of eye salve, come into play in this letter to the Laodicean church.

The Concern

I know your deeds, that you are neither cold nor hot; I wish that you were cold or hot. So because you are lukewarm, and neither hot nor cold, I will spit you out of My mouth. Because you say, "I am rich, and have become wealthy, and have need of nothing," and you do not know that you are wretched and miserable and poor and blind and naked, (3:15–17)

Since there was nothing for which to commend this unregenerate church, Christ launched directly into His concerns. **Deeds** always reveal people's true spiritual state, as indicated by the Lord's words "you will know them by their fruits" (Matt. 7:16; cf. Rom. 2:6–8). Though salvation is wholly by God's grace through faith alone, **deeds** confirm or deny the presence of genuine salvation (James 2:14ff.). The omniscient Lord Jesus Christ knew the Laodiceans' deeds and that they indicated an unregenerate church.

Christ rebuked them for being **neither cold nor hot** but **lukewarm.** His metaphorical language is drawn from Laodicea's water supply. Because it traveled several miles through an underground aqueduct before reaching the city, the water arrived foul, dirty, and tepid. It was not hot enough to relax and restore, like the hot springs at Hierapolis. Nor was it cold and refreshing, like the stream water at Colossae. Laodicea's lukewarm water was in a useless condition.

Comparing its spiritual state to the city's foul, tepid water, Christ gave the Laodicean church a powerful, shocking rebuke: **because you are lukewarm, and neither hot nor cold, I will spit you out of My mouth.** Some churches make the Lord weep, others make Him angry; the Laodicean church made Him sick.

Hot people are those who are spiritually alive and possess the fervency of a transformed life. The spiritually **cold,** on the other hand, are best understood as those who reject Jesus Christ. The gospel leaves them unmoved; it evokes in them no spiritual response. They have no interest in Christ, His Word, or His church. And they make no pretense about it; they are not hypocrites.

The **lukewarm** fit into neither category. They are not genuinely saved, yet they do not openly reject the gospel. They attend church and claim to know the Lord. Like the Pharisees, they are content to practice a self-righteous religion; they are hypocrites playing games. The Lord Jesus Christ described such people in Matthew 7:22–23: "Many will say to Me on that day, 'Lord, Lord, did we not prophesy in Your name, and in Your name cast out demons, and in Your name perform many miracles?' And then I will declare to them, 'I never knew you; depart from Me, you who practice lawlessness.'" The lukewarm are like the unbelieving Jews of whom Paul lamented, "For I testify about them that they have a zeal for God, but not in accordance with knowledge" (Rom. 10:2). They are those who "[hold] to a form of godliness, although they have denied its power" (2 Tim. 3:5). Such obnoxious hypocrisy nauseates Christ.

These smug, self-righteous hypocrites are far more difficult to reach with the gospel than cold-hearted rejecters. The latter may at least be shown that they are lost. But those who self-righteously think that they are saved are often protective of their religious feelings and unwilling to recognize their real condition. They are not cold enough to feel the bitter sting of their sin. Consequently, there is no one further from the truth than the one who makes an idle profession but never experiences genuine saving faith. No one is harder to reach for Christ than a false Christian. Jesus' paralleling critique of the self-righteous, self-deceived Pharisees and Sadducees was that "the tax collectors and prostitutes [would] get into the kingdom of God before [them]" (Matt. 21:31).

Unfortunately, such lukewarm churches are common today, making the letter to the Laodiceans especially relevant. As John R. W. Stott notes,

> Perhaps none of the seven letters is more appropriate to the twentieth-century church than this. It describes vividly the respectable, sentimental, nominal, skin-deep religiosity which is so widespread among us today. Our Christianity is flabby and anaemic. We appear to have taken a lukewarm bath of religion. (*What Christ Thinks of the Church* [Grand Rapids: Eerdmans, 1980], 116)

The Laodiceans' lukewarmness was compounded by their self-deception. Christ rebuked them for their disastrously inaccurate self-assessment: **Because you say, "I am rich, and have become wealthy, and have need of nothing," and you do not know that you are wretched and miserable and poor and blind and naked.** Their deeds gave the lie to their empty words. "Not everyone who says to Me 'Lord, Lord,' will enter the kingdom of heaven," declared Jesus, "but he who does the will of My Father who is in heaven will enter" (Matt. 7:21). Like the rich young ruler (Matt. 19:16–22), they were deceived about their actual spiritual condition.

As previously noted, Laodicea was a very wealthy city. That wealth gave the members of its church a false sense of security as they imagined that their spiritual wealth mirrored their city's material wealth. They were rich in spiritual pride but bankrupt in saving grace. Believing they were to be envied, they were in fact to be pitied. Their incipient gnosticism, discussed earlier, led them to believe they had attained an exalted level of knowledge. They no doubt looked down on the unsophisticated people who fully accepted and were satisfied with the biblical teaching on the person and work of Jesus Christ. But the reality was, as Jesus pointed out, that they were spiritually **wretched and miserable and poor and blind and naked.**

THE COMMAND

I advise you to buy from Me gold refined by fire so that you may become rich, and white garments so that you may clothe yourself, and that the shame of your nakedness will not be revealed; and eye salve to anoint your eyes so that you may see. Those whom I love, I reprove and discipline; therefore be zealous and repent. Behold, I stand at the door and knock; if anyone hears My voice and opens the door, I will come in to him and will dine with him, and he with Me. (3:18–20)

The Lord Jesus Christ could have instantly judged and destroyed this church filled with unredeemed hypocrites. Instead, He graciously offered them genuine salvation. Christ's threefold appeal played on the three features the city of Laodicea was most noted for and proud of: its wealth, wool industry, and production of eye salve. Christ offered them spiritual gold, spiritual clothes, and spiritual sight.

The Lord, of course, did not teach that salvation may be earned by good works; lost sinners have nothing with which to **buy** salvation (Isa. 64:5–6). The buying here is the same as that of the invitation to salvation in Isaiah 55:1: "Ho! Every one who thirsts, come to the waters; and you who have no money come, buy and eat. Come, buy wine and milk without money and without cost." All sinners have to offer is their wretched, lost condition. In exchange for that, Christ offers His righteousness to those who truly repent.

Christ advised the Laodiceans to **buy from** Him three things, all of which symbolize true redemption. First, they needed to purchase **gold refined by fire so that** they might **become rich.** They needed gold that was free of impurities, representing the priceless riches of true salvation. Peter wrote of a "faith ... more precious than gold" (1 Pet. 1:7), while Paul defined saving faith as "rich in good works," having the "treasure of a good foundation for the future" (1 Tim. 6:18–19). Christ offered the Laodiceans a pure, true salvation that would bring them into a real relationship with Him.

Second, Christ advised them to buy **white garments so that** they might **clothe** themselves, **and that the shame of** their **nakedness** would **not be revealed.** Laodicea's famed black wool symbolized the filthy, sinful garments with which the unregenerate are clothed (Isa. 64:6; Zech. 3:3–4). In contrast, God clothes the redeemed with **white garments** (3:4–5; 4:4; 6:11; 7:9, 13–14; cf. Isa. 61:10), symbolizing the righteous deeds that always accompany genuine saving faith (19:8).

Finally, Christ offered them **eye salve to anoint** their **eyes so that** they might **see.** Though they prided themselves on their allegedly superior spiritual knowledge, the Laodiceans were in fact spiritually stone blind. Blindness represents lack of understanding and knowledge of spiritual truth (cf. Matt. 15:14; 23:16–17, 19, 24, 26; Luke 6:39; John 9:40–41; 12:40; Rom. 2:19; 2 Cor. 4:4; 1 John 2:11). Like all unregenerate people, the Laodiceans desperately needed Christ to "open their eyes so that they [might] turn from darkness to light and from the dominion of Satan to God, that they may receive forgiveness of sins and an inheritance among those who have been sanctified by faith in [Him]" (Acts 26:18; cf. 1 Pet. 2:9).

Some argue that the language of Christ's direct appeal to the Laodiceans in verse 19, **those whom I love, I reprove and discipline,** indicates that they were believers. Verses 18 and 20, however, seem better suited to indicate that they were unregenerate, desperately in need of the gold of true spiritual riches, the garments of true righteousness, and the eye salve that brings true spiritual understanding (v. 18).

Christ has a unique and special **love** for His elect. Yet, such passages as Mark 10:21 and John 3:16 reveal that He also loves the unredeemed. Because the Laodiceans outwardly identified with Christ's church and His kingdom, they were in the sphere of His concern. To **reprove** means to expose and convict. It is a general term for God's dealings with sinners (cf. John 3:18–20; 16:8; 1 Cor. 14:24; Titus 1:9; Jude 15). **Discipline** refers to punishment (cf. Luke 23:16, 22) and is used of God's convicting of unbelievers (2 Tim. 2:25). Thus, the terminology of verse 19 does not demand that Christ be referring to believers. The Lord compassionately, tenderly called those in this unregenerate church to come to saving faith, lest He convict and judge them (cf. Ezek. 18:30–32; 33:11).

But in order for the Laodiceans to be saved, they would have to **be zealous and repent.** That is tantamount to the attitude of mourning over sin and hungering and thirsting for righteousness of which Jesus spoke (Matt. 5:4, 6). While repentance is not a meritorious work, the New Testament call to salvation always includes it (e.g., Matt. 3:2, 8; 4:17; Mark 6:12; Luke 13:3, 5; 15:7, 10; Acts 2:38; 3:19; 8:22; 11:18; 17:30; 20:21; 26:20; Rom. 2:4; 2 Cor. 7:10; 2 Tim. 2:25; 2 Pet. 3:9). In repentance, the sinner turns from his sin to serve God (1 Thess. 1:9).

> Repentance means that you realize that you are a guilty, vile sinner in the presence of God, that you deserve the wrath and punishment of God, that you are hell-bound. It means that you begin to realize that this

thing called sin is in you, that you long to get rid of it, and that you turn your back on it in every shape and form. You renounce the world whatever the cost, the world in its mind and outlook as well as its practice, and you deny yourself, and take up the cross and go after Christ. (D. Martyn Lloyd-Jones, *Studies in the Sermon on the Mount* [Grand Rapids: Eerdmans, 1974], 2:248)

The message to this lost church, as it is to all the unsaved, is to zealously pursue the "repentance that leads to life" (Acts 11:18).

The Lord Jesus Christ followed the call to repentance in verse 19 with a tender, gracious invitation in verse 20. The apostate Laodicean church could only have expected Christ to come in judgment. But the startling reality, introduced by the arresting word **behold,** was that Christ stood **at the door** of the Laodicean church **and knock**ed; **if anyone** in the church would hear His **voice and open the door,** He would **come in to him and dine with him, and he with** Christ.

Though this verse has been used in countless tracts and evangelistic messages to depict Christ's knocking on the door of the sinner's heart, it is broader than that. The door on which Christ is knocking is not the door to a single human heart, but to the Laodicean church. Christ was outside this apostate church and wanted to come in—something that could only happen if the people repented.

The invitation is, first of all, a personal one, since salvation is individual. But He is knocking on the door of the church, calling the many to saving faith, so that He may enter the church. If one person (**anyone**) opened the door by repentance and faith, Christ would enter that church through that individual. The picture of Christ outside the Laodicean church seeking entrance strongly implies that, unlike Sardis, there were no believers there at all.

Christ's offer to **dine** with the repentant church speaks of fellowship, communion, and intimacy. Sharing a meal in ancient times symbolized the union of people in loving fellowship. Believers will dine with Christ at the marriage supper of the Lamb (19:9), and in the millennial kingdom (Luke 22:16, 29–30). **Dine** is from *deipneō*, which refers to the evening meal, the last meal of the day (cf. Luke 17:8; 22:20; 1 Cor. 11:25, where the underlying Greek is rendered "sup," "supper," and "supped," respectively). The Lord Jesus Christ urged them to repent and have fellowship with Him before the night of judgment fell and it was too late forever.

The Counsel

He who overcomes, I will grant to him to sit down with Me on My throne, as I also overcame and sat down with My Father on His throne. He who has an ear, let him hear what the Spirit says to the churches. (3:21–22)

The wonderful promise to **he who overcomes** (all believers; 2:7, 11, 26; 3:5, 12; 1 John 5:5) is that Christ **will grant to him to sit down with Him on His throne, as** He **also overcame and sat down with** the **Father on His throne.** To enjoy fellowship with Christ in the kingdom and throughout eternity is sufficient blessing beyond all comprehension. But Christ offers more, promising to seat believers on the throne He shares with the Father (cf. Matt. 19:28; Luke 22:29–30). That symbolizes the truth that we will reign with Him (2 Tim. 2:12; Rev. 5:10; 20:6; cf. 1 Cor. 6:3).

The right to sit with Christ on His heavenly throne is but one of the many promises made to overcomers in the letters to the seven churches. Overcomers are also promised the privilege of eating from the tree of life (2:7), the crown of life (2:10), protection from the second death (2:11), the hidden manna (2:17), a white stone with a new name written on it (2:17), authority to rule the nations (2:26–27), the morning star (2:28), white garments, symbolizing purity and holiness (3:5), the honor of having Christ confess their names before God the Father and the holy angels in heaven (3:5), to be made a pillar in God's temple (3:12), and to have written on them the name of God, of the new Jerusalem, and of Christ (3:12).

As did the other six letters, the letter to the Laodiceans closed with Christ's exhortation, **He who has an ear, let him hear what the Spirit says to the churches.** The message to the apostate church is obvious: repent, and open up to Christ before the night of judgment falls. The implication for true believers is that, like Christ, we must compassionately call those in the apostate church to repent and receive salvation in Jesus Christ (cf. Jude 23).

A Trip
to Heaven
(Revelation 4:1–11)

11

After these things I looked, and behold, a door standing open in heaven, and the first voice which I had heard, like the sound of a trumpet speaking with me, said, "Come up here, and I will show you what must take place after these things." Immediately I was in the Spirit; and behold, a throne was standing in heaven, and One sitting on the throne. And He who was sitting was like a jasper stone and a sardius in appearance; and there was a rainbow around the throne, like an emerald in appearance. Around the throne were twenty-four thrones; and upon the thrones I saw twenty-four elders sitting, clothed in white garments, and golden crowns on their heads. Out from the throne come flashes of lightning and sounds and peals of thunder. And there were seven lamps of fire burning before the throne, which are the seven Spirits of God; and before the throne there was, something like, a sea of glass like crystal; and in the center and around the throne, four living creatures full of eyes in front and behind. The first creature was like a lion, and the second creature like a calf, and the third creature had a face like that of a man, and the fourth creature was like a flying eagle. And the four living creatures, each one of them having six wings, are full of eyes around and

within; and day and night they do not cease to say, "Holy, holy, holy is the Lord God, the Almighty, who was and who is and who is to come." And when the living creatures give glory and honor and thanks to Him who sits on the throne, to Him who lives forever and ever, the twenty-four elders will fall down before Him who sits on the throne, and will worship Him who lives forever and ever, and will cast their crowns before the throne, saying, "Worthy are You, our Lord and our God, to receive glory and honor and power; for You created all things, and because of Your will they existed, and were created." (4:1–11)

There is an unprecedented fascination these days among both Christians and non-Christians with the afterlife. Books on supposed after- or near-death experiences and angels top the bestseller lists. TV programs explore the mysterious realm of the supernatural, often focusing on angels and their alleged interaction with humans. Many people, both those who profess to be Christians and those who do not, claim to have visited heaven and returned to tell of their experiences.

In contrast to the fanciful, bizarre, often silly fabrications of those who falsely claim to have visited heaven (which I critique in my books *Charismatic Chaos* [Grand Rapids: Zondervan, 1992] and *The Glory of Heaven* [Wheaton, Ill.: Crossway, 1996]), the Bible records the accounts of two people who actually were taken there in visions. In 2 Corinthians 12, the apostle Paul wrote of being transported to the third heaven (the abode of God). But he was forbidden to speak of what he saw there (2 Cor. 12:4).

The apostle John also had the inestimable privilege of visiting heaven. Unlike Paul, John was permitted to give a detailed description of his vision, which he did in chapters 4 and 5 of Revelation. In those two chapters, John recorded the second vision he saw, the first being his vision of the glorified Lord Jesus Christ in 1:12–17. The Bible refers to heaven more than five hundred times, and others, such as Paul (2 Cor. 12) and Ezekiel (Ezek. 1), wrote descriptions of it. Yet John's description in chapters 4 and 5 is the most complete and informative in all of Scripture. Escorted by the beloved apostle, readers are carried far beyond the mundane features of this temporal realm to behold the realities of eternal heaven. Through John's vision, believers have the privilege of previewing the place where they will live forever.

The first occurrence of the phrase **after these things** (v. 1) relates to John's personal chronology. It notes that this second vision followed immediately after John's vision of the risen, glorified Christ (1:9–20) and the letters to the seven churches (2:1–3:22). The phrase **after these things** is used throughout Revelation to mark the beginning of a new vision (cf. 7:9; 15:5; 18:1; 19:1).

The second occurrence of **after these things** relates to God's chronology. Its use marks an important transition in the book of Revelation from the church age (the "things which are"; 1:19), described in chapters 2–3, to the third great division of the book (the "things which will take place"; 1:19), found in chapters 4–22. The scene shifts from matters concerning the church (which is nowhere mentioned in chaps. 4–19) on earth to a dramatic scene in heaven. That scene centers on the throne of God and forms the prologue to the future historical events (the Tribulation, millennial kingdom, and eternal state) that unfold in chapters 6–22. In keeping with the Lord's promise to spare His church from the hour of testing (the outpouring of wrath before the Lord returns) given in 3:10, the church will be raptured before that time of tribulation (described in detail in chapters 6–19) begins.

As John **looked,** to his astonishment (indicated by the exclamation **behold**) he saw **a door standing open in heaven** (cf. Ezek. 1:1; Acts 7:56). That already open door admitted John into the third **heaven** (cf. 2 Cor. 12:2; the first being the earth's atmosphere and the second interplanetary and interstellar space)—to the very throne room of God. It was **heaven** to which Christ ascended after His resurrection and where He has since been seated at the right hand of God (John 14:2–3; Acts 1:9–11; 3:20–21; 7:55–56; Rom. 10:6; Col. 3:1; 1 Thess. 4:16). Heaven became John's vantage point for most of the remainder of the book of Revelation.

After noticing the open door, the **first voice** John **heard** was the familiar voice **like the sound of a trumpet** that had spoken to him in his first vision (1:10). As noted in the discussion of that passage in chapter 3 of this volume, this was the voice of the risen, exalted Lord Jesus Christ. His voice is likened to **the sound of a trumpet** because of its commanding, authoritative quality. The Lord specifically ordered John to **come up here,** that is, to heaven. John was not swept away into some mystical fantasyland, but transported spiritually into the reality of heaven. Some see in this command a reference to the Rapture of the church. However, the verse does not describe the church ascending to heaven in resurrected glorification, but John going to heaven to receive revelation.

The central theme of John's vision is the throne of God, mentioned eleven times in this chapter. All the features of the chapter can be outlined based on how they relate to that throne of divine glory. After describing the throne, John tells us who is on the throne, what is going on around the throne, what comes from the throne, what stands before the throne, who is in the center and around the throne, and what is directed toward the throne.

THE THRONE

Immediately I was in the Spirit; and behold, a throne was standing in heaven, (4:2*a*)

Most modern-day people who claim to have had visions of heaven tend to emphasize the trivial and the bizarre. But John's vision focused on the glorious throne of God and the ineffable majesty of the One who sits on it. As he was taken out of the familiar dimension of space and time and into the heaven of God's presence **in the Spirit**'s power (cf. 1:10), John was amazed and astounded by what he saw, causing him to exclaim **behold.**

The cause of John's amazement was the **throne** of God that he saw **standing in heaven.** This was not a piece of furniture, but a symbol of God's sovereign rule and authority (cf. Pss. 11:4; 103:19; Isa. 66:1) located in the temple in heaven (cf. 7:15; 11:19; 14:15, 17; 15:6–8; 16:17). According to Revelation 21:22 the heavenly temple is not an actual building: "the Lord God the Almighty and the Lamb" are the temple. The use of the term *temple* symbolizes God's presence. The throne was said to be **standing** because God's sovereign rule is fixed, permanent, and unshakable. A vision of God's immovable throne reveals He is in permanent, unchanging, and complete control of the universe. That is a comforting realization in light of the horror and trauma of the end-time events about to be revealed (chaps. 6–19). In much the same way, Isaiah was comforted during a traumatic time in Israel's history by his vision of God's glory (Isa. 6).

ON THE THRONE

and One sitting on the throne. And He who was sitting was like a jasper stone and a sardius in appearance; (4:2*b*–3*a*)

The whimsical, mindless, purposeless forces of random chance do not, as many foolishly believe, govern the universe. Instead, the sovereign, omnipotent Creator of the universe is **sitting on** His **throne** as its ruler. Unlike its use in Hebrews (cf. Heb. 1:3; 10:12; 12:2), where it depicts Christ's posture of rest, the term **sitting** here indicates the posture of reigning. The thought is not resting because the work of redemption has been accomplished, but reigning because judgment is about to take place.

Though John does not name the One sitting on the throne, it is obvious who He is. He is the One Isaiah saw in his vision: "I saw the Lord sitting on a throne, lofty and exalted, with the train of His robe filling the temple" (Isa. 6:1). The prophet Micaiah also saw Him on His glorious throne: "I saw the Lord sitting on His throne, and all the host of heaven standing by Him on His right and on His left" (1 Kings 22:19). "God reigns over the nations," declared the psalmist, "God sits on His holy throne" (Ps. 47:8). Daniel also saw a vision of the heavenly throne room:

> I kept looking until thrones were set up, and the Ancient of Days took His seat; His vesture was like white snow and the hair of His head like pure wool. His throne was ablaze with flames, its wheels were a burning fire. A river of fire was flowing and coming out from before Him; thousands upon thousands were attending Him, and myriads upon myriads were standing before Him. (Dan. 7:9–10)

But perhaps the most detailed look at God on His heavenly throne outside of Revelation is that given by Ezekiel:

> Now above the expanse that was over their heads there was something resembling a throne, like lapis lazuli in appearance; and on that which resembled a throne, high up, was a figure with the appearance of a man. Then I noticed from the appearance of His loins and upward something like glowing metal that looked like fire all around within it, and from the appearance of His loins and downward I saw something like fire; and there was a radiance around Him. As the appearance of the rainbow in the clouds on a rainy day, so was the appearance of the surrounding radiance. Such was the appearance of the likeness of the glory of the Lord. (Ezek. 1:26–28)

In sharp contrast to the casual, flippant, proud, almost blasphemous accounts of those today who claim visions of God, Isaiah (Isa. 6:5), Ezekiel (Ezek. 1:28), and Daniel (Dan. 7:15) were terrified and humbled by their visions.

John described **He who was sitting** on the throne as being **like a jasper stone and a sardius in appearance.** That description is reminiscent of the flashing light, blazing fire, and vivid colors in Ezekiel's vision. Revelation 21:11 describes **jasper** as "crystal-clear"; therefore, it is best to identify this stone as a diamond. All the shining, flashing facets of the glory of God are compared to a diamond, brilliantly refracting all the colors of the spectrum. A sardius, from which the city of Sardis got its name, is a fiery, bloodred ruby. It too expresses the shining beauty of God's glory, and may also symbolize God's blazing wrath, about to be poured out on the sinful, rebellious world (chaps. 6–19).

There is a possible further symbolism in the choice of these two stones. The **sardius** and the **jasper** were the first and last stones on the high priest's breastplate (Ex. 28:17–20; "ruby," "jasper"), representing the firstborn (Reuben) and lastborn (Benjamin) of the twelve sons of Jacob.

It may be that those stones depict God's covenant relationship with Israel; His wrath and judgment will not abrogate that relationship. In fact, it is during the Tribulation that, largely through the zealous evangelistic efforts of the 144,000 (Rev. 7:3ff.), "all Israel will be saved" (Rom. 11:26). It is also possible that the names of Reuben ("behold, a son") and Benjamin ("son of my right hand") picture God the Son, the Lord Jesus Christ, sitting at His Father's right hand in glory.

John's vision of God's throne is not one of peace and comfort. Its flashing, glorious, splendorous magnificence reveals the terrors of God's judgment. Truly, "our God is a consuming fire" (Heb. 12:29; cf. Deut. 4:24).

AROUND THE THRONE

and there was a rainbow around the throne, like an emerald in appearance. Around the throne were twenty-four thrones; and upon the thrones I saw twenty-four elders sitting, clothed in white garments, and golden crowns on their heads. (4:3b–4)

Moving away from his description of the throne to describe what was around it, John noted first that **there was a rainbow around** it. That John described it as being **like an emerald in appearance** reveals that green was the dominant color. This again is introduced to show the many-splendored glory of God (cf. Ezek. 1:28). The **rainbow** provides a comforting balance to the fiery flashings of judgment earlier seen emanating from God's throne. According to Genesis 9:13–17, a rainbow symbolizes God's covenant faithfulness, mercy, and grace. God's attributes always operate in perfect harmony. His wrath never operates at the expense of His faithfulness; His judgments never abrogate His promises. God's power and holiness would cause us to live in abject terror were it not for His faithfulness and mercy. God said of the faithful remnant of Israel who feared being swept away in His judgment of the nation, "They will be Mine . . . on the day that I prepare My own possession, and I will spare them as a man spares his own son who serves him" (Mal. 3:17).

John also saw around the throne **twenty-four thrones; and upon the thrones** he **saw twenty-four elders sitting, clothed in white garments, and golden crowns on their heads.** The identity of the **twenty-four elders** has been much debated. While some see them as an order of angelic beings, it seems best to view them as human representatives of the church. Several lines of evidence point to that conclusion.

First, the reference to the **twenty-four thrones** on which the **twenty-four elders** sat indicates that they reign with Christ. Nowhere in Scripture do angels sit on thrones, nor are they pictured ruling or reigning.

Their role is to serve as "ministering spirits, sent out to render service for the sake of those who will inherit salvation" (Heb. 1:14; cf. Matt. 18:10). The church, on the other hand, is repeatedly promised a co-regency with Christ (2:26–27; 3:21; 5:10; 20:4; Matt. 19:28; Luke 22:30; 1 Cor. 6:2–3; 2 Tim. 2:12).

Presbuteroi (**elders**) is never used in Scripture to refer to angels, but always to men. It is used to speak of older men in general, and the rulers of both Israel and the church. There is no indisputable use of *presbuteroi* outside of Revelation to refer to angels. (Some believe that "elders" in Isaiah 24:23 refers to angels, but it could as well refer to humans.) Further, "elder" would be an inappropriate term to describe angels, who do not age.

While angels do appear in white (e.g., John 20:12; Acts 1:10), **white garments** more commonly are the dress of believers. That is particularly true in the immediate context of Revelation. Christ promised the believers at Sardis that they would "be clothed in white garments" (3:5). He advised the apostate Laodiceans to "buy from Me . . . white garments so that you may clothe yourself" (3:18). At the marriage supper of the Lamb, His bride will "clothe herself in fine linen, bright and clean" (19:8). **White garments** symbolize Christ's righteousness imputed to believers at salvation.

That the elders wore **golden crowns on their heads** provides further evidence that they were humans. Crowns are never promised in Scripture to angels, nor are angels ever seen wearing them. *Stephanos* (**crown**) is the victor's crown, worn by those who successfully endured the trial, those who competed and won the victory. Christ promised such a crown to the loyal believers at Smyrna: "Be faithful until death, and I will give you the crown of life" (2:10). "Everyone who competes in the games exercises self-control in all things," wrote Paul. "They then do it to receive a perishable wreath [*stephanos*], but we an imperishable" (1 Cor. 9:25). He wrote of that imperishable crown again in 2 Timothy 4:8: "In the future there is laid up for me the crown of righteousness, which the Lord, the righteous Judge, will award to me on that day; and not only to me, but also to all who have loved His appearing." James wrote of "the crown of life which the Lord has promised to those who love Him" (James 1:12), and Peter of "the unfading crown of glory" (1 Pet. 5:4). Holy angels do not personally struggle with and triumph over sin; thus, the overcomer's crown, the crown of those who successfully ran the race and finished victorious, would not be appropriate for them.

Assuming, then, that the twenty-four elders are humans, the question remains as to which humans they represent. First, it should be noted that the number twenty-four is used in Scripture to speak of completion and representation. There were twenty-four officers of the sanctuary representing the twenty-four courses of the Levitical priests (1 Chron. 24:4–

5, 7–18), as well as twenty-four divisions of singers in the temple (1 Chron. 25). Whoever the twenty-four elders are, then, they likely represent a larger group.

Some believe the elders represent Israel. But while individual Jews have been and will continue to be redeemed throughout history, at the time of this vision the nation as a whole had not yet been redeemed. Their national judgment and salvation (Rom. 11:26) comes during the Tribulation (chaps. 6–19), largely as a result of the evangelistic efforts of the 144,000 (introduced in chap. 7). When the twenty-four elders are first introduced, those events are yet to take place.

Similarly, the elders cannot be Tribulation saints, since they too had not yet been converted. The elders are already in heaven when the Tribulation saints arrive. Revelation 7:11–14 describes the scene:

> And all the angels were standing around the throne and around the elders and the four living creatures; and they fell on their faces before the throne and worshiped God, saying, "Amen, blessing and glory and wisdom and thanksgiving and honor and power and might, be to our God forever and ever. Amen." Then one of the elders answered, saying to me, "These who are clothed in the white robes, who are they, and where have they come from?" I said to him, "My lord, you know." And he said to me, "These are the ones who come out of the great tribulation, and they have washed their robes and made them white in the blood of the Lamb."

The elders are also seen in heaven when other momentous events of the Tribulation take place, such as when the kingdoms of the world become the kingdom of Christ (11:15–18), when the 144,000 gather on Mount Zion (14:1–3), and when God destroys the Babylonian economic and religious system (19:1–4).

Some would split the twenty-four elders into two groups of twelve, one representing the church and the other Israel. There is no compelling exegetical reason, however, for so dividing them. In all their appearances in Revelation they appear as a unified group of twenty-four, never as two groups of twelve.

It is unlikely, then, that the twenty-four elders are angels, or that they represent Israel, the Tribulation saints, or a combination of Israel and the church. That leaves one most acceptable possibility, that they represent the raptured, glorified, coronated church, which sings the song of redemption (5:8–10). They have their crowns and live in the place prepared for them, where they have gone to be with Jesus (cf. John 14:1–4).

FROM THE THRONE

Out from the throne come flashes of lightning and sounds and peals of thunder. (4:5*a*)

Flowing out from God's presence, symbolized by the **throne,** John saw a precursor to the firestorm of divine fury about to burst on the sinful world. **Flashes of lightning and sounds and peals of thunder** are associated with God's presence in Exodus 19:16 and Ezekiel 1:13. They are also associated with God's judgment during the Tribulation. In Revelation 8:5 "the angel took the censer and filled it with the fire of the altar, and threw it to the earth; and there followed peals of thunder and sounds and flashes of lightning." In Revelation 11:19 "the temple of God which is in heaven was opened; and the ark of His covenant appeared in His temple, and there were flashes of lightning and sounds and peals of thunder." When the seventh angel pours out his bowl there will be "flashes of lightning and sounds and peals of thunder" (16:18). John saw a preview of the divine wrath that will be poured out on the earth, described in chapters 6–19.

BEFORE THE THRONE

And there were seven lamps of fire burning before the throne, which are the seven Spirits of God; and before the throne there was, something like, a sea of glass like crystal; (4:5*b*–6*a*)

As he looked at the scene in heaven John saw two things **before the throne.** First **were seven lamps of fire.** Unlike the lampstands mentioned in 1:12–13, these were outdoor torches, giving off not the soft, gentle light of an indoor lamp, but the fierce, blazing light of a fiery torch. John identifies them as **the seven Spirits of God.** As noted in the discussion of 1:4 in chapter 1 of this volume, that phrase describes the Holy Spirit in all His fullness (cf. Isa. 11:2; Zech. 4:1–10). The sevenfold representation of the Holy Spirit in Isaiah speaks of wisdom, understanding, counsel, strength, knowledge, reverence, and deity; in Zechariah of power; in Revelation 1:4 of grace and peace; and here of fiery judgment. Torches are associated with war in Judges 7:16, 20 and Nahum 2:3–4. John's vision depicts God as ready to make war on sinful, rebellious mankind and the Holy Spirit as His war torch. The Comforter of those who love Christ will be the Consumer of those who reject Him.

Also in front of God's throne **was something like a sea of glass like crystal.** That **sea** is metaphorical, since there is no sea in heaven

(21:1). What John saw at the base of the throne was a vast pavement of **glass,** shining brilliantly like sparkling **crystal.** Exodus 24:10 records a similar scene when Moses, Aaron, and the elders of Israel "saw the God of Israel; and under His feet there appeared to be a pavement of sapphire, as clear as the sky itself" (cf. Ezek. 1:22, 26). Heaven is not a shadowy world of mists and indistinct apparitions. It is a world of dazzlingly brilliant light, refracting and shining as through jewels and crystal in a manner beyond our ability to describe or imagine (cf. Rev. 21:10–11, 18).

IN AND AROUND THE THRONE

and in the center and around the throne, four living creatures full of eyes in front and behind. The first creature was like a lion, and the second creature like a calf, and the third creature had a face like that of a man, and the fourth creature was like a flying eagle. And the four living creatures, each one of them having six wings, are full of eyes around and within; (4:6b–8a)

This passage introduces **the four living creatures** who will play a significant role in the events that unfold in Revelation. That they are said to be both **in the center and around the throne** means that their station is in the inner circle nearest the throne. The similar passage in Ezekiel 1:12, 17 suggests they are in constant motion about it. The translation **living creatures** is somewhat misleading, since these are not animals. The phrase derives from a single word in the Greek text, the noun form of the verb *zaō*, which means "to live."

Ezekiel gives a detailed description of these incredible beings and of the glorious magnificence of heaven and God's throne:

> As I looked, behold, a storm wind was coming from the north, a great cloud with fire flashing forth continually and a bright light around it, and in its midst something like glowing metal in the midst of the fire. Within it there were figures resembling four living beings. And this was their appearance: they had human form, each of them had four faces and four wings. Their legs were straight and their feet were like a calf's hoof, and they gleamed like burnished bronze. Under their wings on their four sides were human hands. As for the faces and wings of the four of them, their wings touched one another; their faces did not turn when they moved, each went straight forward. As for the form of their faces, each had the face of a man; all four had the face of a lion on the right and the face of a bull on the left, and all four had the face of an eagle. Such were their faces. Their wings were spread out above; each had two touching another being, and two covering their bodies. And

each went straight forward; wherever the spirit was about to go, they would go, without turning as they went. In the midst of the living beings there was something that looked like burning coals of fire, like torches darting back and forth among the living beings. The fire was bright, and lightning was flashing from the fire. And the living beings ran to and fro like bolts of lightning.

Now as I looked at the living beings, behold, there was one wheel on the earth beside the living beings, for each of the four of them. The appearance of the wheels and their workmanship was like sparkling beryl, and all four of them had the same form, their appearance and workmanship being as if one wheel were within another. Whenever they moved, they moved in any of their four directions without turning as they moved. As for their rims they were lofty and awesome, and the rims of all four of them were full of eyes round about. Whenever the living beings moved, the wheels moved with them. And whenever the living beings rose from the earth, the wheels rose also. Wherever the spirit was about to go, they would go in that direction. And the wheels rose close beside them; for the spirit of the living beings was in the wheels. Whenever those went, these went; and whenever those stood still, these stood still. And whenever those rose from the earth, the wheels rose close beside them; for the spirit of the living beings was in the wheels.

Now over the heads of the living beings there was something like an expanse, like the awesome gleam of crystal, spread out over their heads. Under the expanse their wings were stretched out straight, one toward the other; each one also had two wings covering its body on the one side and on the other. I also heard the sound of their wings like the sound of abundant waters as they went, like the voice of the Almighty, a sound of tumult like the sound of an army camp; whenever they stood still, they dropped their wings. And there came a voice from above the expanse that was over their heads; whenever they stood still, they dropped their wings. (Ezek. 1:4–25)

Ezekiel's description appears incomprehensible, almost incoherent, as he struggled to make sense out of the spectacular, supernatural scene that he witnessed. Both Ezekiel's description and that in Revelation 4 describe what could be called the divine war machine ready to unleash judgment.

Ezekiel 10:15 specifically identifies these four living beings: "Then the cherubim rose up. They are the living beings that I saw by the river Chebar." The **four living creatures** are thus cherubim, an exalted order of angels frequently associated in Scripture with God's holy power (e.g., 1 Sam. 4:4; 2 Sam. 6:2; 22:11; Pss. 80:1; 99:1; Isa. 37:16). After Adam and Eve sinned, God drove them out of Eden and stationed cherubim at the entrance to keep them from returning (Gen. 3:24). Two carved cherubim were placed in the Holy of Holies (also called the Most Holy Place), symbolically guarding God's holiness (1 Kings 6:23–28). Satan, before his fall, was the "the anointed cherub who covers"; his duty was to attend God's throne (Ezek. 28:14; cf. v. 16).

John, like Ezekiel, struggled to capture the reality in comprehensible terms to describe the indescribable scene before him. First, he said the living creatures were **full of eyes in front and behind** (cf. v. 8; Ezek. 1:18; 10:12), symbolizing their awareness, alertness, and comprehensive knowledge. Though they are not omniscient, nothing pertaining to their duties escapes their scrutiny.

Ezekiel's description of these angels notes that each one possessed all four facial features (Ezek. 1:6). But from John's vantage point, **the first creature was like a lion, and the second creature like a calf, and the third creature had a face like that of a man, and the fourth creature was like a flying eagle.** Those descriptions view the four cherubim in relation to the created world; the **lion** represents wild creatures, the **calf** domestic animals, the **eagle** flying creatures, and **man** the pinnacle of creation. Symbolically, the **lion** represents strength, the **calf** service, the **man** reason, and the **eagle** speed. The Talmud saw in these four creatures the four primary forms of life in God's creation. It also noted that the twelve tribes of Israel camped under these four banners; some with Reuben (symbolized by a man), others with Dan (symbolized by an eagle), others with Ephraim (symbolized by the calf, or ox), and the rest with Judah (symbolized by a lion).

The **four living creatures,** like angels in general (Matt. 13:40–43, 49; 25:31ff.; Rev. 15:1, 7), are deeply involved with the coming judgments of the Tribulation, in which they will play an integral role. They will be there at the outset of divine judgments as one of their number calls forth the rider on the white horse (6:1–2). Another will decree economic disaster upon the earth (6:6), while another will give the seven angels involved in the bowl judgments their bowls (15:7).

Their **six wings** denote that their supreme responsibility and privilege is to constantly worship God. From Isaiah's vision, we learn that the seraphim (possibly the same beings as the cherubim) used their six wings in the following manner: "with two [they] covered [their faces], and with two [they] covered [their] feet, and with two [they] flew" (Isa. 6:2). Four of their six wings related to worship; with two they covered their faces, since even the most exalted created beings cannot look on the unveiled glory of God without being consumed. They also used two wings to cover their feet, since they stood on holy ground. Worship is thus their privilege, calling, and permanent occupation.

TOWARD THE THRONE

and day and night they do not cease to say, "Holy, holy, holy is the Lord God, the Almighty, who was and who is and who is to come." And when the living creatures give glory and honor and thanks to Him who sits on the throne, to Him who lives forever and ever, the twenty-four elders will fall down before Him who sits on the throne, and will worship Him who lives forever and ever, and will cast their crowns before the throne, saying, "Worthy are You, our Lord and our God, to receive glory and honor and power; for You created all things, and because of Your will they existed, and were created." (4:8b–11)

Fittingly, the scene in heaven culminates in worship directed toward God on His throne. In this passage and in chapter 5 are five great hymns of praise, during the singing of which the size of the choir gradually increases. The hymns of praise begin in verse 8 with a quartet—the four living creatures. In verse 10, the twenty-four elders join in, and in 5:8, harps are added to the vocal praise. The rest of the angels add their voices in 5:11. Finally, in 5:13, all created beings in the universe join in the mighty chorus of praise to God. Worship is reserved for God alone, since there is no one in the universe like Him. In 1 Chronicles 17:20 David prayed, "O Lord, there is none like You, nor is there any God besides You" (cf. Pss. 86:8–10; 89:6–8).

This mighty oratorio of praise and worship may be divided into two movements: the hymn of creation (chap. 4), and the hymn of redemption (chap. 5). The hymn of creation, the first movement, may be divided into several elements.

The four living creatures begin the oratorio of worship by focusing on God's holiness; **day and night they do not cease to say, "Holy, holy, holy is the Lord God."** The threefold repetition of holy is also found in Isaiah 6:3; holiness is the only one of God's attributes so repeated, since it is the summation of all that He is. God's holiness is His utter and complete separation from evil in any and every form. He is absolutely untainted by any evil, error, or wrongdoing—unlike angels (some of whom sinned) or humans (all of whom sinned). In 1 Samuel 2:2 Hannah declared, "There is no one holy like the Lord," because He alone is "majestic in holiness" (Ex. 15:11). The prophet Habakkuk praised God because "[His] eyes are too pure to approve evil, and [He] can not look on wickedness with favor" (Hab. 1:13). "God sits on His holy throne," declared the psalmist (Ps. 47:8), while Psalm 111:9 adds, "Holy and awesome is His name." In 1 Peter 1:16, God Himself declared, "You shall be holy, for I am holy."

But on this occasion, the praise is for God's holiness specifically exhibited through judgment. Being holy, God hates sin, and pours out His wrath on it. "Will not His majesty terrify you?" Job asked his would-be counselors (Job 13:11). After God executed some of the men of Beth-shemesh for irreverently peering into the Ark, the survivors exclaimed, "Who is able to stand before the Lord, this holy God?" (1 Sam. 6:20). After Uzzah was executed for touching the Ark, "David was afraid of the Lord that day; and he said, 'How can the ark of the Lord come to me?'" (2 Sam. 6:9). Overwhelmed by his vision of God's majestic holiness Isaiah cried out, "Woe is me, for I am ruined! Because I am a man of unclean lips, and I live among a people of unclean lips" (Isa. 6:5).

Because of His grace and mercy, God refrains from worldwide judgment on all sinners, as they deserve. But in the future time of Tribulation, the opportunity for mercy and grace will be past, and the sinful, rebellious world will feel the full fury of God's wrath. So terrifying will that time be that unrepentant sinners will cry "to the mountains and to the rocks, 'Fall on us and hide us from the presence of Him who sits on the throne, and from the wrath of the Lamb; for the great day of their wrath has come, and who is able to stand?'" (6:16–17).

Not only is God's holiness cause for worship, but also His power. In their song of praise, the four living creatures refer to God as **the Almighty**—a title by which God identified Himself to Abraham (Gen. 17:1). That term identifies God as the strongest, most powerful being, utterly devoid of any weakness, whose conquering power and overpowering strength none can oppose. Because God is Almighty, He can effortlessly do whatever His holy will purposes to do (cf. Isa. 40:28). In the midst of his trials Job affirmed, "If it is a matter of power, behold, He is the strong one!" (Job 9:19). The psalmist declared, "Our God is in the heavens; He does whatever He pleases" (Ps. 115:3). In Isaiah 46:10 God said, "My purpose will be established, and I will accomplish all My good pleasure." After experiencing God's devastating and humiliating judgment, King Nebuchadnezzar acknowledged, "He does according to His will in the host of heaven and among the inhabitants of earth; and no one can ward off His hand or say to Him, 'What have You done?'" (Dan. 4:35). Jesus taught that "with God all things are possible" (Matt. 19:26).

God's power is seen in creation. Psalm 33:9 says, "He spoke, and it was done; He commanded, and it stood fast." Having created the universe, God also controls it. In 1 Chronicles 29:11–12 David declared,

> Yours, O Lord, is the greatness and the power and the glory and the victory and the majesty, indeed everything that is in the heavens and the earth; Yours is the dominion, O Lord, and You exalt Yourself as head over all. Both riches and honor come from You, and You rule over all, and in Your hand is power and might; and it lies in Your hand to make great and to strengthen everyone.

The phrase "He is able" expresses God's power toward His elect, redeemed children. In Ephesians 3:20 Paul praises God for being "able to do [far more] abundantly beyond all that we ask or think, according to the power that works within us," adding in 2 Corinthians 9:8, "God is able to make all grace abound to you, so that always having all sufficiency in everything, you may have an abundance for every good deed." Paul wrote to Timothy expressing his confidence in God's power working on his behalf: "I know whom I have believed and I am convinced that He is able to guard what I have entrusted to Him until that day" (2 Tim. 1:12). Hebrews 2:18 reveals that the Lord Jesus Christ "is able to come to the aid of those who are tempted," while Hebrews 7:25 reassures believers that "He is able also to save forever those who draw near to God through Him, since He always lives to make intercession for them." Jude closes his brief epistle with a doxology of praise: "Now to Him who is able to keep you from stumbling, and to make you stand in the presence of His glory blameless with great joy, to the only God our Savior, through Jesus Christ our Lord, be glory, majesty, dominion and authority, before all time and now and forever. Amen" (Jude 24–25).

But as was the case with His holiness, the aspect of God's power most clearly in view here is His power exhibited in judgment. For example, He judged Satan and the sinning angels, expelling them from heaven; drowned the world in the Flood; destroyed Sodom, Gomorrah, and the cities of the plain; drowned Pharaoh's army; and shattered the most powerful king in the world, Nebuchadnezzar, reducing him to eating grass like an animal for seven years. Many times God's power has destroyed the wicked. And it will be God's power that unleashes the terrible, irresistible judgments on sinful mankind during the Tribulation before the Lord's return.

Speaking of God's judgment power, the prophet Nahum declared, "Who can stand before His indignation? Who can endure the burning of His anger? His wrath is poured out like fire and the rocks are broken up by Him" (Nah. 1:6; cf. Mal. 3:2). God will judge those human rulers who foolishly think they can stand against Him (Ps. 2:2–6). "Who understands the power of Your anger," asked Moses, "and Your fury, according to the fear that is due You?" (Ps. 90:11). "Wail, for the day of the Lord is near!" cried Isaiah. "It will come as destruction from the Almighty" (Isa. 13:6). In Joel 1:15 Joel also warned of God's coming judgment: "Alas for the day! For the day of the Lord is near, and it will come as destruction from the Almighty."

The four living creatures also praise God for His eternity, extolling Him as He **who was and who is and who is to come** (cf. the discussion of this phrase in chaps. 1 and 2 of this volume), **who lives forever and ever** (cf. 10:6; 15:7; Dan. 4:34). Scripture repeatedly affirms God's eternity, that He transcends time, having neither beginning nor ending (e.g., Pss. 90:2; 93:2; 102:24–27; Isa. 57:15; Mic. 5:2; Hab. 1:12; 1 Tim. 1:17; 6:15–16). That sets Him apart from animals, who have both a beginning and an ending, and angels and humans, who had a beginning, but will have no ending.

To know that God is eternal provides comfort for His children, since, unlike a human father, He will always be there to take care of them. God's eternity guarantees that our eternal life in heaven will never cease, that we will receive "an eternal weight of glory far beyond all comparison" (2 Cor. 4:17). But it also means that the punishment of the wicked in hell will last forever, that their weeping, wailing, and gnashing of teeth will never cease, that "the smoke of their torment goes up forever and ever" (Rev. 14:11). Such destruction of sinners is a vindication of the righteousness of God.

The praise of the four living creatures, as they **give glory and honor and thanks to Him who sits on the throne,** triggers a response from the **twenty-four elders.** They **will fall down before Him who sits on the throne, and will worship Him who lives forever and ever.** This is the first of six times that the elders prostrate themselves before God (5:8, 14; 7:11; 11:16; 19:4). Such a posture is one of reverential worship, a natural response to the majestic, holy, awe-inspiring glory of God (cf. Gen. 17:3; Josh. 5:14; Ezek. 1:28; 3:23; 43:3; 44:4; Matt. 17:6; Acts 9:4).

Amazingly, after prostrating themselves the twenty-four elders **cast their crowns before the throne.** They are not preoccupied with their own excellence. They are not concerned about their own holiness, honor, or reward. All those things pale into insignificance and become meaningless in light of the glory of God.

The elders add their own note to the chorus of praise initiated by the four living beings, crying out, **"Worthy are You, our Lord and our God, to receive glory and honor and power; for You created all things, and because of Your will they existed, and were created."** *Axios* (**worthy**) was used of the Roman emperor when he marched in a triumphal procession. The focus of the elders' song is on God's glory manifested in creation; He is presented as Creator throughout Scripture (cf. 10:6; Gen. 1:1; Ex. 20:11; Isa. 40:26, 28; Jer. 10:10–12; 32:17; Col. 1:16). The elders are acknowledging that God has the right both to redeem and to judge His creation. Their song anticipates paradise lost becoming paradise regained.

This first movement of the oratorio of praise pictures God about to judge Satan, demons, and sinners and take back His creation. Both the living creatures and the twenty-four elders can only worship in awe and wonder as God prepares to bring about the glorious day of which Paul wrote:

For the anxious longing of the creation waits eagerly for the revealing of the sons of God. For the creation was subjected to futility, not willingly, but because of Him who subjected it, in hope that the creation itself also will be set free from its slavery to corruption into the freedom of the glory of the children of God. For we know that the whole creation groans and suffers the pains of childbirth together until now. (Rom. 8:19–22)

A Vision of the Lamb (Revelation 5:1–14)

12

I saw in the right hand of Him who sat on the throne a book written inside and on the back, scaled up with seven seals. And I saw a strong angel proclaiming with a loud voice, "Who is worthy to open the book and to break its seals?" And no one in heaven or on the earth or under the earth was able to open the book or to look into it. Then I began to weep greatly because no one was found worthy to open the book or to look into it; and one of the elders said to me, "Stop weeping; behold, the Lion that is from the tribe of Judah, the Root of David, has overcome so as to open the book and its seven seals." And I saw between the throne (with the four living creatures) and the elders a Lamb standing, as if slain, having seven horns and seven eyes, which are the seven Spirits of God, sent out into all the earth. And He came and took the book out of the right hand of Him who sat on the throne. When He had taken the book, the four living creatures and the twenty-four elders fell down before the Lamb, each one holding a harp and golden bowls full of incense, which are the prayers of the saints. And they sang a new song, saying, "Worthy are You to take the book and to break its seals; for You were slain, and purchased for God with Your blood men from every tribe and tongue

and people and nation. You have made them to be a kingdom and priests to our God; and they will reign upon the earth." Then I looked, and I heard the voice of many angels around the throne and the living creatures and the elders; and the number of them was myriads of myriads, and thousands of thousands, saying with a loud voice, "Worthy is the Lamb that was slain to receive power and riches and wisdom and might and honor and glory and blessing." And every created thing which is in heaven and on the earth and under the earth and on the sea, and all things in them, I heard saying, "To Him who sits on the throne, and to the Lamb, be blessing and honor and glory and dominion forever and ever." And the four living creatures kept saying, "Amen." And the elders fell down and worshiped. (5:1–14)

Throughout history there have been many pretenders to earth's throne who have sought to conquer and rule the world. The first and most powerful and notorious usurper was Satan. After his rebellion against God was crushed, he and his angelic followers were thrown out of heaven (Luke 10:18; Rev. 12:3–4), and he became the "god of this world" (2 Cor. 4:4). He inspired a host of humans to try their hand at conquest, men such as Nebuchadnezzar, Darius, Alexander the Great, the emperors of Rome, Attila the Hun, Genghis Khan, Napoleon, Lenin, Stalin, and Hitler. In the future will come the most powerful Satan-possessed human conqueror of all, the final Antichrist.

All of those men, and a host of lesser lights, have one thing in common: they failed. Only one individual has the right, the power, and the authority to rule the earth: the Lord Jesus Christ. He will one day take back what is rightfully His from Satan the usurper, and all the rebels, demonic and human. No one else is worthy or capable of ruling the world—no evil man, no good man, no demon, and no holy angel. Revelation 5 introduces Jesus Christ, earth's rightful ruler, who is pictured about to return to redeem the world from sin, Satan, death, and the curse. He is the central theme of John's second vision of heaven.

The events of chapter 5 occur right after those of chapter 4. The scene, as in chapter 4, is the throne of God in heaven. Present are the cherubim, the twenty-four elders (representing the raptured, glorified church), and the Holy Spirit in His sevenfold glory (4:5). The events described in these two chapters anticipate the holocaust of divine judgment about to be poured out on the sinful, rebellious, cursed earth (chaps. 6–19). Awestruck by the indescribable majesty of God's throne, and the flashes of lightning and peals of thunder that proceed from it, the cherubim and elders begin a series of hymns of praise to God. Those hymns celebrate God as creator and redeemer, and rejoice that He is about to take back what is rightfully His. This is the moment that all Christians (Eph. 1:14) and the entire creation (Rom. 8:19–22) long for.

As that moment approaches, God begins to stir. The phrase **I saw,** or "I looked," introduces the various scenes described in this chapter (cf. vv. 2, 6, 11) and stresses John's status as an eyewitness. In his vision, John **saw in the right hand of Him who sat on the throne a book written inside and on the back, sealed up with seven seals.** God stretched out His hand, as it were, and in it He held a **book.** *Biblion* (**book**) does not refer to a book in the modern sense, but to a scroll (cf. 6:14). A scroll was a long piece of papyrus or animal skin, rolled from both ends into the middle. Such scrolls were commonly used before the invention of the codex, or modern-style book, consisting of square pages bound together.

While Roman wills were **sealed up with seven seals,** this scroll is not a will but a deed or contract. Dr. Robert L. Thomas explains:

> This kind of contract was known all over the Middle East in ancient times and was used by the Romans from the time of Nero on. The full contract would be written on the inner pages and sealed with seven seals. Then the content of the contract would be described briefly on the outside. All kinds of transactions were consummated this way, including marriage-contracts, rental and lease agreements, release of slaves, contract-bills, and bonds. Support also comes from Hebrew practices. The Hebrew document most closely resembling this scroll was a title-deed that was folded and signed, requiring at least three witnesses. A portion of text would be written, folded over and sealed, with a different witness signing at each fold. A larger number of witnesses meant that more importance was assigned to the document. (*Revelation 1–7: An Exegetical Commentary* [Chicago: Moody, 1992], 378)

Jeremiah 32 provides a good illustration of the use of such a document. In the waning days of the southern kingdom, shortly before the fall of Jerusalem, Jeremiah's cousin Hanamel approached him. Hanamel was desperate to sell a field he owned in Jeremiah's hometown of Anathoth, not far from Jerusalem. Hanamel knew that once the Babylonian army conquered (actually, the Babylonians may have already occupied the land in question; cf. Jer. 32:2, 24–25), he would lose his plot of ground. Jeremiah, in obedience to God's command (Jer. 32:6–7), purchased the field in spite of its potential loss as a sign that the Babylonian captivity would not be permanent (Jer. 32:15). Jeremiah 32:9–15 records the details of his purchase:

> I bought the field which was at Anathoth from Hanamel my uncle's son, and I weighed out the silver for him, seventeen shekels of silver. I

signed and sealed the deed, and called in witnesses, and weighed out the silver on the scales. Then I took the deeds of purchase, both the sealed copy containing the terms and conditions and the open copy; and I gave the deed of purchase to Baruch the son of Neriah, the son of Mahseiah, in the sight of Hanamel my uncle's son and in the sight of the witnesses who signed the deed of purchase, before all the Jews who were sitting in the court of the guard. And I commanded Baruch in their presence, saying, "Thus says the Lord of hosts, the God of Israel, 'Take these deeds, this sealed deed of purchase and this open deed, and put them in an earthenware jar, that they may last a long time.'" For thus says the Lord of hosts, the God of Israel, 'Houses and fields and vineyards will again be bought in this land.'"

The scroll John saw in God's hand is the title deed to the earth, which He will give to Christ. Unlike other such deeds, however, it does not record the descriptive detail of what Christ will inherit, but rather how He will regain His rightful inheritance. He will do so by means of the divine judgments about to be poured out on the earth (6:1ff.). While the scroll is a scroll of doom and judgment, it is also a scroll of redemption. It tells how Christ will redeem the world from the usurper, Satan, and those men and demons who have collaborated with him. Ezekiel describes this same scroll in his vision of heaven: "Then I looked, and behold, a hand was extended to me; and lo, a scroll was in it. When He spread it out before me, it was written on the front and back, and written on it were lamentations, mourning and woe" (Ezek. 2:9–10).

The chapter divides naturally into three sections: the search for the worthy one, the selection of the worthy one, and the song of the worthy one.

THE SEARCH FOR THE WORTHY ONE

And I saw a strong angel proclaiming with a loud voice, "Who is worthy to open the book and to break its seals?" And no one in heaven or on the earth or under the earth was able to open the book or to look into it. Then I began to weep greatly because no one was found worthy to open the book or to look into it; (5:2–4)

The **strong angel** (cf. 10:1; 18:21) is not named. Some identify him as Gabriel, others as Michael, but since the text does not name him, he must remain anonymous. He spoke **with a loud voice** so that his proclamation would penetrate to every corner of the universe. The angel sought someone both **worthy** and able **to open the book** and **to break its seals.** Who, he asked, has the innate, virtuous worthiness of character and the divine right that would qualify him to break the seals? And who has the power to defeat Satan and his demon hosts, to wipe out sin and its effects, and to reverse the curse on all of creation?

But as the echoes of his cry recede there is only silence. The powerful archangels Michael and Gabriel do not answer. Uncounted thousands of other angels remain silent. All the righteous dead of all the ages, including Abraham, Isaac, Jacob, Joseph, Job, Moses, David, Solomon, Elijah, Elisha, Isaiah, Jeremiah, Ezekiel, Daniel, Peter and the rest of the apostles, Paul, and all the others from the church age, say nothing. **No one in heaven or on the earth or under the earth was able to open the book or to look into it.** A search of the entire universe, from hell to heaven and all points in between, turns up no one worthy to open the scroll.

Overwhelmed with grief and dismay at this turn of events, John **began to weep greatly because no one was found worthy to open the book or to look into it. Weep** is from *klaiō*, the same word used to describe Jesus' weeping over Jerusalem (Luke 19:41), and Peter's bitter weeping after betraying the Lord (Luke 22:62). It is thus a word that expresses strong, unrestrained emotion. This is the only time in Scripture that tears are seen in heaven (cf. 7:17; 21:4). W. A. Criswell explains why John wept:

> [John's tears] represent the tears of all God's people through all the centuries. Those tears of the Apostle John are the tears of Adam and Eve, driven out of the Garden of Eden, as they bowed over the first grave, as they watered the dust of the ground with their tears over the silent, still form of their son, Abel. Those are the tears of the children of Israel in bondage as they cried unto God in their affliction and slavery. They are the tears of God's elect through the centuries as they cried unto heaven. They are the sobs and tears that have been wrung from the heart and soul of God's people as they looked on their silent dead, as they stand beside their open graves, as they experience in the trials and sufferings of life, heartaches and disappointments indescribable. Such is the curse that sin has laid upon God's beautiful creation; and this is the damnation of the hand of him who holds it, that usurper, that interloper, that intruder, that alien, that stranger, that dragon, that serpent, that Satan-devil. "And I wept audibly," for the failure to find a Redeemer meant that this earth in its curse is consigned forever to death. It meant that death, sin, damnation and hell should reign forever and ever and the sovereignty of God's earth should remain forever in the hands of Satan. (*Expository Sermons on Revelation* [Grand Rapids: Zondervan, 1969], 3:69–70)

John's weeping, though sincere, was premature. He need not have wept, for God was about to take action. Similarly, Jesus told the widow at Nain (Luke 7:13) and those weeping over the death of the synagogue ruler's daughter (Luke 8:52) that their tears were inappropriate because of what He was about to do. John wept because he wanted to see the world rid of evil, sin, and death. He wanted to see Satan vanquished and God's kingdom established on earth. He wanted to see Israel saved and Christ exalted. John knew that the Messiah had been executed, Jerusalem destroyed, and the Jewish people massacred and scattered. He was well aware that the church faced intense persecution and was infected with sin (chaps. 2–3). Everything seemed, from his perspective, to be going badly. Would no one step forward to change this? Was no one going to unroll the scroll and redeem God's creation? But John need not have wept, because the search for the one worthy to open the scroll was about to end.

THE SELECTION OF THE WORTHY ONE

and one of the elders said to me, "Stop weeping; behold, the Lion that is from the tribe of Judah, the Root of David, has overcome so as to open the book and its seven seals." And I saw between the throne (with the four living creatures) and the elders a Lamb standing, as if slain, having seven horns and seven eyes, which are the seven Spirits of God, sent out into all the earth. And He came and took the book out of the right hand of Him who sat on the throne. (5:5–7)

Because his tears were inappropriate, **one of the elders** told John to **stop weeping.** Then he drew John's attention to a new Person emerging on the scene, **the Lion that is from the tribe of Judah, the Root of David.** No human and no angel can redeem the universe, but there is One who can. This Person, of course, is the glorified, exalted Lord Jesus Christ, described here by two of His messianic titles. The title **the Lion that is from the tribe of Judah** derives from Jacob's blessing on the tribe of Judah given in Genesis 49:8–10:

> Judah, your brothers shall praise you; your hand shall be on the neck of your enemies; your father's sons shall bow down to you. Judah is a lion's whelp; from the prey, my son, you have gone up. He couches, he lies down as a lion, and as a lion, who dares rouse him up? The scepter shall not depart from Judah, nor the ruler's staff from between his feet, until Shiloh comes, and to him shall be the obedience of the peoples.

Out of the lionlike tribe of Judah would come a strong, fierce, and deadly ruler—the Messiah, Jesus Christ (Heb. 7:14). The Jews of Jesus' day expected the Messiah to be powerful and to liberate them from the heavy hand of their oppressors, at that time the Roman rulers. It was partly because Jesus failed to live up to those expectations that they rejected and killed Him. He had no political aspirations (cf. John 6:15; 18:36), nor did He use His miraculous powers against the Roman oppressors. Instead, He offered a spiritual kingdom.

Tragically, the Jews completely misjudged their Messiah. He *is* a lion, and will tear up and destroy their enemies. But He will do so according to His timetable, not theirs. His lionlike judgment of His enemies awaits the yet-future day that He has chosen—the day that begins to unfold in Revelation chapter 5.

Jesus is also seen here as **the Root** or descendant **of David** (cf. 22:16; Jer. 23:5–6; 33:15–17). That messianic title derives from Isaiah 11:1, 10: "Then a shoot will spring from the stem of Jesse, and a branch from his roots will bear fruit. . . . Then it will come about in that day that the nations will resort to the root of Jesse, who will stand as a signal for the peoples; and His resting place will be glorious." As the genealogies of Matthew 1 and Luke 3 reveal, Jesus was a descendant of David both on His father's and on His mother's side. In Romans 1:3 the apostle Paul said that Jesus was "born of a descendant of David according to the flesh." The term "Son of David" is a messianic title used frequently in the Gospels (e.g., Matt. 9:27; 12:23; 15:22; 20:30–31; 21:9, 15; 22:42; Mark 12:35).

Jesus is the One worthy to take the scroll because of who He is, the rightful King from David's loins; what He is, the Lion from Judah's tribe with the power to destroy His enemies; and also because of what He has done—He **has overcome**. At the cross He defeated sin (Rom. 8:3), death (Heb. 2:14–15), and all the forces of hell (Col. 2:15; 1 Pet. 3:19). Believers are overcomers through His overcoming (Col. 2:13–14; 1 John 5:5).

As he looked at the incredible scene before him, the glowing, blazing reflection of God's glory emanating from the throne, the bright green rainbow surrounding it, the brilliant pavement on which it sat, the flashes of lightning and peals of thunder foreshadowing fearsome divine judgment, the worshiping four living creatures and twenty-four elders, John's attention was irresistibly drawn to what he **saw between the throne (with the four living creatures) and the elders.** Instead of the anticipated mighty Lion of the Tribe of Judah, the all-conquering Davidic King, John saw **a Lamb.** The Lord Jesus could not be the Lion of judgment, or the King of glory, unless He was first "the Lamb of God who takes away the sin of the world" (John 1:29).

Arnion (**Lamb**), the diminutive form of *arnos*, refers to a little lamb, or a pet lamb. The imagery derives from the Passover, when Jewish families were required to keep the sacrificial lamb as a household pet for four days before sacrificing it (Ex. 12:3–6). While every lamb sacrificed under the Old Covenant pointed toward Christ, He is only referred to as a lamb once in the Old Testament (Isa. 53:7). In the New Testament outside of Revelation, He is only called a lamb four times (John 1:29, 36; Acts 8:32; 1 Pet. 1:19). But in Revelation He appears as the Lamb thirty-one times.

Several features indicate that this was no ordinary lamb. First, He was **standing,** alive, on His feet, yet looking **as if** He had been **slain.** The scars from the deadly wound this Lamb received were clearly visible; yet He was alive. Though demons and wicked men conspired against Him and killed Him, He rose from the dead, thus defeating and triumphing over His enemies.

At first glance it seems a disastrous mismatch to pit a lamb against a dragon (12:9) and the hordes of hellish locusts (9:3), frogs (16:13), and human soldiers (19:19) who follow the dragon. But this Lamb is more than just a willing sacrificial offering for sin; He is also a Lion and the "King of kings, and Lord of lords" (19:16). He has already defeated Satan (1 John 3:8; cf. John 12:31; 16:11; Rom. 16:20; Heb. 2:14) and his forces (Col. 2:15; 1 Pet. 3:22) at the cross and is about to consummate that victory.

Another feature about this Lamb that John noted was that it had **seven horns.** In imagery drawn from the animal world, **horns** in Scripture symbolize strength and power (e.g., 1 Sam. 2:1, 10; 2 Sam. 22:3; Pss. 18:2; 75:10; 89:17, 24; Jer. 48:25; Mic. 4:13). **Seven,** the number of perfection, symbolizes the Lamb's complete, absolute power. The Lamb in John's vision also had **seven eyes,** again denoting perfect omniscience and complete understanding and knowledge. Those eyes, John noted, represented the **seven Spirits of God, sent out into all the earth.** As noted in the discussions of 1:4 and 4:5 earlier in this volume, the phrase **seven Spirits of God** describes the Holy Spirit in all His fullness. Here, as in 4:5, the Holy Spirit's fullness is seen in relation to judgment, as He goes **out into all the earth** searching for guilty, unrepentant sinners to be judged (cf. John 16:8).

Verse 7 records the final, monumental act in the heavenly scene. Everything John has been describing since this vision began in 4:1 had been building toward this moment. This views the great, culminating act of history, the act that will signal the end of man's day. The ultimate goal of redemption is about to be seen; paradise will be regained, Eden restored. Before John's wondering eyes the Lamb **came and took the book out of the right hand of Him who sat on the throne.**

This is the same scene described by Daniel in Daniel 7:13–14, although Daniel does not mention the scroll:

> I kept looking in the night visions, and behold, with the clouds of heaven One like a Son of Man was coming, and He came up to the Ancient

of Days and was presented before Him. And to Him was given dominion, glory and a kingdom, that all the peoples, nations and men of every language might serve Him. His dominion is an everlasting dominion which will not pass away; and His kingdom is one which will not be destroyed.

The worthy One has arrived to take back what is rightfully His.

THE SONG OF THE WORTHY ONE

When He had taken the book, the four living creatures and the twenty four elders fell down before the Lamb, each one holding a harp and golden bowls full of incense, which are the prayers of the saints. And they sang a new song, saying, "Worthy are You to take the book and to break its seals; for You were slain, and purchased for God with Your blood men from every tribe and tongue and people and nation. You have made them to be a kingdom and priests to our God; and they will reign upon the earth." Then I looked, and I heard the voice of many angels around the throne and the living creatures and the elders; and the number of them was myriads of myriads, and thousands of thousands, saying with a loud voice, "Worthy is the Lamb that was slain to receive power and riches and wisdom and might and honor and glory and blessing." And every created thing which is in heaven and on the earth and under the earth and on the sea, and all things in them, I heard saying, "To Him who sits on the throne, and to the Lamb, be blessing and honor and glory and dominion forever and ever." And the four living creatures kept saying, "Amen." And the elders fell down and worshiped. (5:8–14)

The appearance of the Lamb as He moves to take the scroll causes praise to break out from everywhere in the universe. The praise accelerates in an ascending crescendo of worship as the oratorio of redemption reaches its climax. To the two majestic doxologies of chapter 4 are added three more in chapter 5. The spontaneous outburst of worship results from the realization that the long-anticipated defeat of sin, death, and Satan is about to be accomplished and the Lord Jesus Christ will return to earth in triumph and establish His glorious millennial kingdom. The curse will be reversed, the believing remnant of Israel will be saved, and the church will be honored, exalted, and granted the privilege of reigning with Christ. All of the pent-up anticipation of millennia finally bursts out at the prospect of what is about to take place.

As they began their song of praise and worship, **the four living creatures and the twenty-four elders fell down before the Lamb.** That they offer the same worship to Christ that they did to the Father in 4:10 offers convincing proof of Christ's deity, since only God is to be worshiped (cf. 19:10; Matt. 4:10).

After Jesus accomplished redemption by bearing sin on the cross, God raised Him from the dead and exalted Him to His right hand. Jesus received back the glory He had had in the Father's presence before the world began (John 17:5). To the Ephesians Paul wrote of Christ, "[God] raised Him from the dead and seated Him at His right hand in the heavenly places, far above all rule and authority and power and dominion, and every name that is named, not only in this age but also in the one to come. And He put all things in subjection under His feet, and gave Him as head over all things to the church" (Eph. 1:20–22).

But though exalted to the Father's right hand, Jesus Christ is not yet fully reigning. Psalm 2:6–12 speaks of the future day when Christ rules on the earth:

> But as for Me, I have installed My King upon Zion, My holy mountain. I will surely tell of the decree of the Lord: He said to Me, "You are My Son, today I have begotten You. Ask of Me, and I will surely give the nations as Your inheritance, and the very ends of the earth as Your possession. You shall break them with a rod of iron, You shall shatter them like earthenware." Now therefore, O kings, show discernment; take warning, O judges of the earth. Worship the Lord with reverence and rejoice with trembling. Do homage to the Son, that He not become angry, and you perish in the way, for His wrath may soon be kindled.

Dr. Donald Gray Barnhouse once observed that there are four things out of place in the universe: the church, which should be in heaven; Israel, which should be living in peace occupying all the land promised to her; Satan, who belongs in the lake of fire; and Christ, who should be seated on His throne reigning. All four of those anomalies will be set right when Christ takes the scroll from His Father's hand.

But before He begins to unroll it in chapter 6 comes the song of praise in chapter 5. As they prostrated themselves before the Lamb in worship, John noticed that **each one** of the twenty-four elders was **holding a harp and golden bowls full of incense, which are the prayers of the saints.** (The grammatical structure of the Greek text seems to indicate that it was only the elders, not the living creatures, who held those two items.) **Harps** were frequently associated in the Old Testament with worship (e.g., 2 Sam. 6:5; 1 Chron. 15:16, 20, 28; 16:5; 2 Chron. 5:12; 29:25; Pss. 33:2; 71:22; 92:1–4; 144:9; 150:3; cf. Rev. 14:2; 15:2), but they were also closely linked to prophecy. In 1 Samuel 10:5 Samuel said to

Saul, "Afterward you will come to the hill of God where the Philistine garrison is; and it shall be as soon as you have come there to the city, that you will meet a group of prophets coming down from the high place with harp, tambourine, flute, and a lyre before them, and they will be prophesying." Similarly, when about to prophesy, Elisha said, "'Now bring me a harpist.' While the harpist was playing, the hand of the Lord came upon Elisha." (2 Kings 3:15 NIV). First Chronicles 25:1 records that "David and the commanders of the army set apart for the service some of the sons of Asaph and of Heman and of Jeduthun, who were to prophesy with lyres, harps and cymbals" (cf. vv. 3, 6). The harps held by the elders probably symbolize all of prophecy, which culminates in the momentous events about to take place.

In addition to the harps, the elders were also holding **golden bowls full of incense.** These wide-mouthed bowls were used in the tabernacle and the temple (1 Kings 7:40, 45, 50; 2 Kings 12:13–14; 1 Chron. 28:17; 2 Chron. 4:22; Jer. 52:19; Zech. 14:20), where they were connected with the altar. They symbolized the priestly work of intercession for the people. Scripture elsewhere associates the burning of incense with the prayers of the saints in Psalm 141:2; Luke 1:9–10; and Revelation 8:3–4 (cf. 6:9–10). The incense in these bowls represents the prayers of believers through the ages that God's prophesied and promised redemption of the earth might come. Taken together, the harps and the bowls indicate that all that the prophets ever prophesied and all that God's children ever prayed for is finally to be fulfilled.

As the elders brought before God the desires and prayers of the saints, **they sang a new song.** Since (with the possible exception of Job 38:7) the Bible nowhere records angels singing, it is best to see only the elders as singing here. (Adopting the variant reading found in many manuscripts "You . . . have redeemed us to God," as the *New King James Version* does, further reinforces that point, since the four living creatures are holy angels who have no need to be redeemed.) That is consistent with the rest of Scripture, which pictures the redeemed singing praise to God (cf. Judg. 5:3; 2 Chron. 5:13; Neh. 12:46; Pss. 7:17; 9:2; 61:8; 104:33; 146:2; Acts 16:25; Eph. 5:19) and angels speaking it (cf. Luke 2:13–14). Throughout Scripture the **new song** is a song of redemption (Pss. 33:3; 40:3; 96:1; 98:1; 144:9; 149:1; Isa. 42:10; Rev. 14:3).

The song opens with a reaffirmation that Christ is **worthy . . . to take the book and to break its seals.** He is worthy because He is the Lamb, the Lion of the tribe of Judah, and the King of kings and Lord of lords. To **break** the book's **seals** means to enact the judgments written in it. Then, further reinforcing Christ's worthiness, the song continues, **for You were slain, and purchased for God with Your blood men from every tribe and tongue and people and nation.** That phrase elaborates on the statement of verse 6 that the Lamb had been slain, explaining the significance of His death. It was Christ's substitutionary, sacrificial death that **purchased for God . . . men from every tribe and tongue and people and nation. Purchased** is from *agorazō*, a rich New Testament word for redemption that pictures slaves purchased in the marketplace and then set free. At the cross, the Lord Jesus Christ paid the purchase price (His own **blood;** 1 Pet. 1:18–19) to redeem **men from every tribe** (descent) **and tongue** (language) **and people** (race) **and nation** (culture) from the slave market of sin (cf. 1 Cor. 6:20; 7:23; Gal. 3:13). Those four terms appear together also in Revelation 7:9; 11:9; 13:7; and 14:6 and encompass all of humanity.

It must have been a thrilling, exhilarating realization for John that the redeemed would one day include people from all over the world. In a day when the church was small, isolated, struggling, and sinful, John must have been concerned about its future—especially because five of the seven churches addressed in chapters 2–3 had such serious and potentially fatal problems. The knowledge that persecution and sin would not extinguish the spreading flame of Christianity must have brought joy and hope to the apostle's heart.

The song moves on to express the results of redemption: **You have made them to be a kingdom and priests to our God; and they will reign upon the earth.** The use of **them** instead of "us" indicates the vastness and comprehensiveness of redemption. The twenty-four elders move beyond themselves to sweep up all the saints of all the ages into their paean of praise and adoration. The redeemed are a part of God's **kingdom** (cf. 1:6), a community of believers under God's sovereign rule. They are also **priests to our God** (cf. 20:6), signifying their complete access to God's presence for worship and service. The present priesthood of believers (1 Pet. 2:5, 9) foreshadows that future day when we will have total access to and perfect communion with God. During the millennial kingdom, believers **will reign upon the earth** with Christ (20:6; 2 Tim. 2:12).

In verse 11 John says for the fourth time in the chapter that he saw something. As he **looked, he heard the voice of many angels around the throne and the living creatures and the elders; and the number of them was myriads of myriads, and thousands of thousands** (cf. Dan. 7:10). To the voices of the four living creatures and the twenty-four elders are now added those of innumerable angels. **Myriad** means "ten thousand," apparently the highest number for which the Greeks had a word. The phrase **myriads and myriads** describes an uncountable host. Hebrews 12:1 also says that the number of holy angels cannot be counted. They number at least twice as many as the fallen angels (demons) according to Revelation 12:3–4.

The vast host began **saying with a loud voice** (cf. Neh. 9:4; Pss. 33:3, "shout"; 98:4, "shout") the familiar doxology, **Worthy is the Lamb that was slain to receive power and riches and wisdom and might and honor and glory and blessing.** Once again, the emphasis is on Christ's death providing a perfect redemption, because of which He must be given worship, praise, and adoration. He is worthy to receive recognition because of His **power** and omnipotence. He is worthy to receive recognition because of the spiritual and material **riches** that He possesses —He owns everything (Ps. 50:10–12). He is worthy to receive recognition because of His **wisdom** and omniscience. For all those things and all His other absolute perfections, Jesus Christ is worthy of all **honor and glory and blessing.**

As the great hymn of praise reaches a crescendo, **every created thing which is in heaven and on the earth and under the earth and on the sea, and all things in them** joins in. This all-inclusive statement is reminiscent of Psalm 69:34: "Let heaven and earth praise Him, the seas and everything that moves in them," and the concluding verse of the Psalms, "Let everything that has breath praise the Lord. Praise the Lord!" (Ps. 150:6). This mighty chorus cries out, **"To Him who sits on the throne, and to the Lamb, be blessing and honor and glory and dominion forever and ever."** Endless blessing, endless honor, endless praise, endless glory, and endless worship belong to God the Father and the Lord Jesus Christ. The creation is unable to contain its joy over its imminent redemption (cf. Rom. 8:19–22).

Lost in wonder, love, and praise, the four living creatures could only keep **saying, "Amen."** That solemn affirmation means "let it be," "make it happen" (cf. 1:6–7). And **the elders fell down** once again **and worshiped.**

Soon, this mighty host would march out of heaven to execute judgment, gather the elect, and return with Christ when He sets up His earthly kingdom. The stage is set.

The Beginning of the End: The First Four Seals
(Revelation 6:1–8)

13

Then I saw when the Lamb broke one of the seven seals, and I heard one of the four living creatures saying as with a voice of thunder, "Come." I looked, and behold, a white horse, and he who sat on it had a bow; and a crown was given to him, and he went out conquering and to conquer. When He broke the second seal, I heard the second living creature saying, "Come." And another, a red horse, went out; and to him who sat on it, it was granted to take peace from the earth, and that men would slay one another; and a great sword was given to him. When He broke the third seal, I heard the third living creature saying, "Come." I looked, and behold, a black horse; and he who sat on it had a pair of scales in his hand. And I heard something like a voice in the center of the four living creatures saying, "A quart of wheat for a denarius, and three quarts of barley for a denarius; and do not damage the oil and the wine." When the Lamb broke the fourth seal, I heard the voice of the fourth living creature saying, "Come." I looked, and behold, an ashen horse; and he who sat on it had the name Death; and Hades was following with him. Authority was given to them over a fourth of the earth, to kill with sword and with famine and with pestilence and by the wild beasts of the earth. (6:1–8)

The Bible teaches that the world is headed inexorably not toward peace and unity, but toward a final, cataclysmic war, the battle of Armageddon (16:14–16). Until that climactic holocaust, things will continue to deteriorate as the world falls deeper and deeper into chaos, confusion, and sin. As the end approaches, wars will increase, crime will escalate, there will be economic upheavals, and unprecedented natural disasters, such as earthquakes, floods, famines, and diseases (cf. Matt. 24:6–8). All those calamities will mark the outpouring of God's wrath on the fallen, rebellious world.

The Old Testament prophets spoke of this terrifying time of future judgment. Describing Israel's sufferings during that time, Jeremiah wrote, "Alas! for that day is great, there is none like it; and it is the time of Jacob's distress" (Jer. 30:7). Describing the coming judgment of the Gentile nations, Isaiah wrote,

> Draw near, O nations, to hear; and listen, O peoples! Let the earth and all it contains hear, and the world and all that springs from it. For the Lord's indignation is against all the nations, and His wrath against all their armies; He has utterly destroyed them, He has given them over to slaughter. So their slain will be thrown out, and their corpses will give off their stench, and the mountains will be drenched with their blood. And all the host of heaven will wear away, and the sky will be rolled up like a scroll; all their hosts will also wither away as a leaf withers from the vine, or as one withers from the fig tree. (Isa. 34:1–4)

In Revelation 5:1–7, Christ received from God the Father a scroll sealed with seven seals until opened by the One with authority to do so. The scroll contained the title deed to the earth. Unlike normal title deeds, it did not contain a description of Christ's inheritance, but rather details how He will execute His reclaiming of what is rightfully His. Beginning in chapter 6, that scroll is unrolled and its seals broken. The unrolling of the scroll marks the beginning of God's wrath and judgment on sinful mankind as the Lord takes back creation from the usurper, Satan.

Each of the scroll's seven seals (cf. 5:1) represents a specific divine judgment that will be poured out sequentially on the earth. The seals encompass the entire period of the Tribulation (3:10), culminating with the return of Christ. It seems best to understand the first four seals as taking place during the first half of the Tribulation, the fifth stretching from the first into the second half, (called the "great tribulation" in 7:14 and lasting three and one-half years; 11:2; 12:6; 13:5) and the sixth and seventh taking place during that "great tribulation." Apparently the seventh seal contains the seven trumpet judgments (8:1–11:19) and the seventh trumpet (11:15) contains the seven bowl judgments (16:1–21). The seven seals thus contain all the judgments to the end when Jesus Christ returns.

The unfolding of the seven seals parallels our Lord's chronology of Tribulation events found in Jesus' own message describing the end times and His return, recorded in Matthew 24. The first seal describes a brief, false peace that will precede the final holocaust. In Matthew 24:4–5, Jesus also spoke of that peace, warning of the deceiving, false christs who will promote it. The second seal depicts worldwide war, which Jesus also predicted (Matt. 24:6–7). The third seal, famine, finds a parallel in Matthew 24:7. In that same verse Jesus predicted earthquakes, representative of natural disasters; the fourth seal represents death by such natural disasters, including earthquakes and plagues. The fifth seal, revealing the martyrs under the altar, finds a parallel in Jesus' warning that believers will be martyred during the Tribulation (Matt. 24:9). During the unfolding of the sixth seal, the sky goes black—just as Jesus predicted it would (Matt. 24:29). The seventh seal reveals the final cataclysmic judgments, including all the devastation from the trumpet and bowl judgments, leading up to His second coming (Matt. 24:37ff.).

Just as a mother's birth pains increase in frequency and intensity as the time to give birth approaches, so the judgments depicted by the seals will intensify throughout the Tribulation until they culminate in the arrival of the Lord Jesus Christ in blazing judgment glory. The first four seals cover the period Jesus described as "the beginning of birth pangs" (Matt. 24:8). As terrible as those four judgments are, they are but the preliminary outpouring of God's final wrath in the last three seals.

THE FIRST SEAL: FALSE PEACE

Then I saw when the Lamb broke one of the seven seals, and I heard one of the four living creatures saying as with a voice of thunder, "Come." I looked, and behold, a white horse, and he who sat on it had a bow; and a crown was given to him, and he went out conquering and to conquer. (6:1–2)

Chapters 4 and 5 described the praise offered in heaven to God the Father and the Lord Jesus Christ. Chapter 4 extols God as creator (cf. 4:11) while chapter 5 extols Jesus Christ as redeemer (cf. 5:9–10). Suddenly, as the seals begin to be opened in chapter 6, the praise ceases in anticipation of the coming judgment. The scene now shifts from heaven to earth, which will be the focus of events through the return of Christ in chapter 19 and the establishment of His earthly kingdom in chapter 20.

Having received from His Father the title deed to the earth (5:7), the **Lamb** (the Lord Jesus Christ) **broke** the first **of the seven seals.** As each seal is broken in the vision, what is written on the scroll is not read, but acted out. Immediately, John **heard one of the four living creatures** (cherubim; an exalted order of angels—cf. Ezek. 10:15 and see the discussion of 4:6–8 in chapter 11 of this volume) **saying with** a powerful, shattering **voice of thunder, "Come."** In response to the angelic summons, **a white horse** came forth bearing its rider. The first four seals involve horses and riders (the so-called four horsemen of the Apocalypse). Horses in Scripture are associated with triumph, majesty, power, and conquest (e.g., 19:11, 14; Job 39:19–25; Prov. 21:31; Isa. 43:17; Jer. 6:23; Zech. 9:10; 10:3).

Some, seeing a parallel with 19:11, identify the one **who sat on** the white horse as Christ. But since Christ opens the sealed scroll, He cannot be the rider. Further, this rider wears a *stephanos,* a crown won as a prize; in 19:12 Christ wears many *diadēmas,* royal crowns. Unlike this rider, who carries a bow, Christ carries a sword (19:15). Finally, Christ returns at the end of the Tribulation, not at its beginning.

Others identify the rider as Antichrist. But since the other three riders represent not individual persons but impersonal forces (war, famine, and death), it is best to view the first one as a force as well. That force is best defined as a worldwide peace, shattered during the second seal by the second rider; 6:4). However Antichrist, as will be seen, will play a leading role in promoting this worldwide obsession with seeking peace.

So before the terrors of the Tribulation break loose and lead to the battle of Armageddon there will come a period of world peace. But it will be a deceptive peace, as the world is lulled into a false sense of security followed by war, famine, and death. The world's desperate desire for international peace will serve as the bait for the satanic trap. That longing for security and safety will play into the hands of Antichrist, Satan's ruler, who will convince the world that he can provide them. He will particularly deceive Israel, whose people have for so long desired peace, and he "will make a firm covenant with the many [Israel] for one week" (Dan. 9:27). Antichrist's peace pact and protection of Israel will not last, however: "in the middle of the week [the Seventieth Week of Daniel's prophecy; the Tribulation] he will put a stop to sacrifice and grain offering; and on the wing of abominations will come one who makes desolate, even until a complete destruction, one that is decreed, is poured out on the one who makes desolate" (Dan. 9:27). The false peace that Antichrist brings will come to an abrupt halt at the midpoint of the Tribulation when he desecrates the temple in Jerusalem, betrays the Jewish people, and launches deadly attacks on them (cf. Matt. 24:4–10). There can and will be no peace until the Prince of Peace sets up His earthly kingdom (20:1–6).

The Bible repeatedly warns of the deadly lure of false peace. Jeremiah described those in his day who pronounced "'Peace, peace,' but there is no peace" (Jer. 6:14; 8:11). He cried out to the Lord, "'Ah, Lord God!' I said, 'Look, the prophets are telling them, "You will not see the sword nor will you have famine, but I will give you lasting peace in this place"'" (Jer. 14:13). The Lord replied, "The prophets are prophesying falsehood in My name. I have neither sent them nor commanded them nor spoken to them; they are prophesying to you a false vision, divination, futility and the deception of their own minds" (v. 14). Writing of the deceitfulness of this future false peace Paul said, "While they are saying, 'Peace and safety!' then destruction will come upon them suddenly like labor pains upon a woman with child, and they will not escape" (1 Thess. 5:3).

It may seem incredible that the world, hovering on the brink of final disaster, could be so totally deceived. Yet that is precisely what happened on a smaller scale before the outbreak of the most devastating war to date, World War II. Adolf Hitler spelled out in detail his plans for conquest in his book *Mein Kampf,* published more than a decade before World War II began. Yet, incredibly, the Western allies (particularly Britain and France) persisted in believing Hitler's false claim to be a man of peace. They stood idly by as he reoccupied the Rhineland (demilitarized after World War I), thus abrogating the Versailles Treaty, then annexed Austria, the Sudetenland, and Czechoslovakia. Desperate to appease Hitler and avoid war, British Prime Minister Neville Chamberlain met with the Nazi dictator at Munich in 1938. Upon his return to England, Chamberlain triumphantly waved a piece of paper (containing a worthless pledge of peace from Hitler) which he claimed guaranteed "peace with honor . . . peace for our time." When Winston Churchill (one of the few never taken in by Hitler) rose in the House of Commons to declare that England had suffered a total, unmitigated defeat he was shouted down by angry members of Parliament. The deception was nearly universal; almost everyone misread Hitler's intentions. Only after he invaded Poland in September 1939 did the allies finally acknowledge the truth. By then it was too late to avoid the catastrophe of the Second World War.

That the rider **had a bow** but no arrows, and that he was honored with **a crown** that **was** freely **given to him,** reveals that his **conquering** will involve bloodless victories. His crown (*stephanos*) is a winner's crown. He is no real king and has no real monarch's crown (*diadēma*), but has won a crown from the world for his triumphant achievements leading to world peace. He will not **conquer** by military force, but by cunning and deceit (cf. 2 Thess. 2:9–11). His conquest will be a "cold war" victory, a peace won by agreement, not conflict (Dan. 9:24–27). Even as the final doom of the world approaches, Antichrist will promise a golden age of peace and prosperity. In gratitude, the world will honor him and elevate him to the position of supreme leadership. But both the accolades and the peace will be short-lived.

THE SECOND SEAL: WAR

When He broke the second seal, I heard the second living creature saying, "Come." And another, a red horse, went out; and to him who sat on it, it was granted to take peace from the earth, and that men would slay one another; and a great sword was given to him. (6:3–4)

The world's euphoric mood of peace and harmony will be rudely shattered as the second horse and rider appear on the scene. Just as World War II followed the deceptive peace promoted by Hitler, so devastating wars will spread throughout the world following the collapse of Antichrist's false peace. Here the story turns ugly and remains that way until the true King returns to establish His kingdom.

As the Lamb **broke the second seal** John **heard the second living creature** summoning the second horseman, **saying, "Come."** Immediately **a red horse went out. Red,** the color of fire and blood, depicts war. God's judgment descends and the short-lived, false peace led by Antichrist dissolves in a bloody holocaust.

John first notes, concerning the rider, that **to him . . . it was granted to take peace from the earth.** All that happens will be under God's sovereign control. He allows the false peace, and He ends it and brings war on the earth. Contrary to the teaching of some, the judgments of the Tribulation do not reflect the wrath of men or the wrath of Satan; they can only express God's wrath poured out on the world. It is He who holds the seven-sealed scroll and the Lamb who unrolls it. Sometime early in the first half of the Tribulation, during the beginning of the birth pains (cf. Matt. 24:8; Mark 13:7–8; Luke 21:9), world peace turns to worldwide conflict as **peace** vanishes from **the earth.** Describing this time Jesus said, "You will be hearing of wars and rumors of wars.... Nation will rise against nation, and kingdom against kingdom" (Matt. 24:6–7). **Men** will **slay one another** on an unprecedented scale. Violent slaughter will become commonplace. While Scripture does not give the details, the advances in modern weaponry suggest a terrible, unimaginable holocaust.

John also noted that **a great sword was given to** the rider. *Machaira* (**sword**) refers to the short, stabbing sword a Roman soldier carried into battle. It was also a weapon used by assassins. The vision depicts a **great** sword to describe the extent of the war. Antichrist's false peace, then, will dissolve in a maelstrom of battle, assassination, rebellion, revolt, and massacre.

As he was prominent in promoting the false peace, the final Antichrist will play a major role in the wars that follow it. Though the chief architect of the false peace, when wars break out all over the world he will have no choice but to resort to war himself in order to preserve his authority and power. Antichrist will be as skillful at war as he was at promoting the false peace. Daniel 8:24 describes his career as a warrior: "He will destroy to an extraordinary degree and prosper and perform his will; he will destroy mighty men and the holy people." Among his victims will be many of God's people (cf. 6:9; Matt. 24:9).

Antichrist's setting up of the abomination of desolation (Dan. 11:31; 12:11; Matt. 24:15) will touch off a massive conflict, described in detail in Daniel 11:36–45:

> Then the king will do as he pleases, and he will exalt and magnify himself above every god and will speak monstrous things against the God of gods; and he will prosper until the indignation is finished, for that which is decreed will be done. He will show no regard for the gods of his fathers or for the desire of women, nor will he show regard for any other god; for he will magnify himself above them all. But instead he will honor a god of fortresses, a god whom his fathers did not know; he will honor him with gold, silver, costly stones and treasures. He will take action against the strongest of fortresses with the help of a foreign god; he will give great honor to those who acknowledge him and will cause them to rule over the many, and will parcel out land for a price. At the end time the king of the South will collide with him, and the king of the North will storm against him with chariots, with horsemen and with many ships; and he will enter countries, overflow them and pass through. He will also enter the Beautiful Land, and many countries will fall; but these will be rescued out of his hand: Edom, Moab and the foremost of the sons of Ammon. Then he will stretch out his hand against other countries, and the land of Egypt will not escape. But he will gain control over the hidden treasures of gold and silver and over all the precious things of Egypt; and Libyans and Ethiopians will follow at his heels. But rumors from the East and from the North will disturb him, and he will go forth with great wrath to destroy and annihilate many. He will pitch the tents of his royal pavilion between the seas and the beautiful Holy Mountain; yet he will come to his end, and no one will help him.

As the head of a Western confederacy, Antichrist, as noted above, will initially portray himself as a champion of peace. He will even appear to do what no one has been able to do, bring peace to the troubled Middle

East. He will make a treaty with Israel, posing as their protector and defender. But all too soon his true colors will show, and his desire for dominance will provoke rebellion. Antichrist's attempts to crush his enemies and rule them with an iron hand will touch off wars that will last throughout the remainder of the Tribulation. Finally, when earth's true King, the Lord Jesus Christ, returns, Antichrist will be cast into the lake of fire forever (20:10).

The wars that begin with the opening of the second seal will last for the brief remaining time before the coming of the millennial kingdom.

THE THIRD SEAL: FAMINE

When He broke the third seal, I heard the third living creature saying, "Come." I looked, and behold, a black horse; and he who sat on it had a pair of scales in his hand. And I heard something like a voice in the center of the four living creatures saying, "A quart of wheat for a denarius, and three quarts of barley for a denarius; and do not damage the oil and the wine." (6:5–6)

As the Lamb **broke the third seal,** the mighty voice of the **third living creature** heralded the coming of the third horse and rider. John's use of the word **behold** reveals how startled and shocked he was by the rider's ominous appearance. The color **black** is associated with famine in Lamentations 5:10 (KJV). Famine is a logical consequence of worldwide war as food supplies are destroyed and those involved in food production are killed. Jesus also predicted this future famine in Matthew 24:7: "For nation will rise against nation, and kingdom against kingdom, and in various places there will be famines and earthquakes." God has used famine as a means of judgment in the past (e.g., Lev. 26:26; Deut. 32:24; 2 Kings 8:1; Ps. 105:16; Isa. 3:1; Jer. 16:4; Ezek. 4:16–17; 5:16; 14:13; Hag. 1:11), but this will be the most devastating famine in all of human history.

The **pair of scales** the rider carried **in his hand** pictures the rationing that will result from the famine. As in the United States during the Depression, in Europe in the aftermath of World War II, and today in many war-torn third-world nations, there will be starving people standing in food lines. But they will not find enough food to live on, as the fourth seal in John's vision reveals. Following the appearance of the black horse and its rider, John **heard something like a voice in the center of the four living creatures.** Since the **four living creatures** were stationed around the throne (4:6), this is likely the voice of God, the One sitting on the throne (4:2–3). God also speaks in connection with the fifth seal (6:11). He speaks here as a reminder that the famine is a direct judgment from Him.

God's pronouncements reveal how devastating the famine conditions will be. **A quart of wheat** is barely enough to sustain one person for one day, while a denarius represents one day's wages for an average worker. People's labor will barely provide enough food for themselves and not enough to feed their families. Those with families will be able to purchase **three quarts of barley for a denarius.** That will provide food for their families, but barley was low in nutritional value and commonly fed to livestock. Thus, a person's wages will barely feed three people with low quality food. Both of those scenarios represent starvation wages, and signify severe famine conditions.

In light of those extreme conditions, God cautions people **not** to **damage** (waste) **the oil and the wine.** Basic food staples will become priceless luxuries. Olive **oil** and **wine,** used in the preparation and cooking of food, as well as the purification of water, will need to be carefully protected.

A deceptive peace followed by worldwide wars and a resultant devastating global famine will combine to escalate the universal chaos. All this will take place during the first half of the Tribulation, while the worst will be yet to come.

THE FOURTH SEAL: DEATH

When the Lamb broke the fourth seal, I heard the voice of the fourth living creature saying, "Come." I looked, and behold, an ashen horse; and he who sat on it had the name Death; and Hades was following with him. Authority was given to them over a fourth of the earth, to kill with sword and with famine and with pestilence and by the wild beasts of the earth. (6:7–8)

The fourth seal in the vision follows the pattern of the first three. The **Lamb** broke the **seal** and the **fourth living creature** summoned the fourth horse and its rider. John described the final horse as **an ashen horse.** *Chlōros* (**ashen**), from which the English words "chlorophyll" and "chlorine" derive, refers to a sickly, pale, yellow-green color. It describes green vegetation in its only other New Testament uses (8:7; 9:4; Mark 6:39). The horse's color vividly portrays the pale-green pallor of death characteristic of the decomposition of a corpse. Fittingly, the rider **who sat on it had the** ominous **name Death.** Death on a massive scale is the inevitable consequence of widespread war and famine. In this macabre and terrifying scene, John saw **Hades . . . following with** Death. **Hades** (here representing the grave) becomes, as it were, the grave digger, burying the remains of Death's victims. Death and Hades are also paired in 1:18 and 20:13, 14.

The extent of the death and destruction wrought by war and famine is then quantified; **authority was given to** Death and Hades to destroy **a fourth of the** population of the **earth.** At the world's current population of nearly 6 billion, that would amount to the staggering total of almost 1.5 billion deaths. In an age of nuclear, chemical, and biological weapons, such a total is terrifyingly plausible. Death will use four tools in his grim task. The first three elements, the **sword, famine,** and **pestilence,** are often linked together in Scripture (e.g., 1 Chron. 21:12; 2 Chron. 20:9; Jer. 14:12; 24:10; 44:13; Ezek. 6:11), and all four elements appear in Ezekiel 14:12–21.

The **sword** (war) and **famine** have already been discussed in connection with the second and third seals; the fourth seal exacerbates these conditions. **Pestilence** translates *thanatos,* the same word translated "Death" earlier in verse 8. Here it may primarily refer to disease as the cause of death (cf. 2:23; 18:8) but is broad enough to encompass natural disasters such as the earthquakes predicted by Jesus (Matt. 24:7), floods, and volcanic eruptions. It could also refer to the effects of biological and chemical weapons.

Throughout human history, disease has killed people on a far more massive scale than war. More Union and Confederate soldiers died from disease during the Civil War than were killed in battle. An estimated 30 million people died during the great influenza epidemic of 1918–19 —more than three times as many as the estimated 8.5 million soldiers who died in battle during World War I. In addition, several million more died at about that same time in an outbreak of typhus in Russia, Poland, and Romania. In a world ravaged by war and famine, it is inevitable that such disease will be widespread.

At first glance, the inclusion of **wild beasts** with war, famine, and disease seems puzzling, since most creatures dangerous to man are either extinct or isolated in unpopulated regions. But one explanation may be that the most deadly creature of all, the rat, thrives in all populated areas. Rats have been responsible for uncounted millions of deaths throughout history, both by eating food supplies, and especially by spreading disease. The most infamous and devastating occurrence of rat-borne disease was the Black Death, a fourteenth-century outbreak of bubonic plague that wiped out one-fourth to one-third of Europe's population. In a world ravaged by war, famine, and disease, the rat population may run wild.

The first four seals clearly describe awe-inspiring, frightening judgments without parallel in human history. There is nothing that has happened since John had this vision that could be the fulfillment of these judgments. These doomsday prophecies cannot be applied to the destruction of Jerusalem in A.D. 70 (which was before John had these visions, since he wrote Revelation about A.D. 96) or any other event since that one. Nothing this devastating has happened, yet these first four seal judgments are just the beginning of the horrific, worldwide woes that the sinful, rebellious world will experience. Far worse is still to come in the remainder of the seals, the trumpets, and the bowls. At that time the world of sinners will realize that "it is a terrifying thing to fall into the hands of the living God" (Heb. 10:31). There will be no escape for impenitent unbelievers from the terrors of the Tribulation, or from the infinitely worse terrors of hell. In the words of the writer of Hebrews, "How will we escape if we neglect so great a salvation?" (Heb. 2:3).

Prayers for Vengeance: The Fifth Seal (Revelation 6:9–11)

14

When the Lamb broke the fifth seal, I saw underneath the altar the souls of those who had been slain because of the word of God, and because of the testimony which they had maintained; and they cried out with a loud voice, saying, "How long, O Lord, holy and true, will You refrain from judging and avenging our blood on those who dwell on the earth?" And there was given to each of them a white robe; and they were told that they should rest for a little while longer, until the number of their fellow servants and their brethren who were to be killed even as they had been, would be completed also. (6:9–11)

It has been observed that God created man in His image and man has returned the favor. People have created gods in whatever form pleases them and accommodates their sinful lifestyles. In the cynical words of British author D. H. Lawrence, "God is only a great imaginative experience" (cited in *The Columbia Dictionary of Quotations*, Copyright © 1993, 1995 by Columbia University Press). God rebuked such foolish people in Psalm 50:21: "You thought that I was just like you; I will reprove you and state the case in order before your eyes." God is who He has revealed Himself to be in Scripture and not what people imagine Him to be.

While Scripture reveals that God is loving, merciful, and gracious —a savior of sinners, one truth about Him that is decidedly unpopular today is that He is a God of vengeance against those who reject Him and salvation in His Son. The Bible repeatedly affirms that to be the case. In Deuteronomy 32:35 God declared, "Vengeance is Mine, and retribution" (cf. vv. 41, 43). In several psalms, known as the imprecatory (from the verb *imprecate,* meaning "to call down calamity on someone") psalms, the psalmists cry out for God to take vengeance on the wicked. One such passage is found in Psalm 64:7–9, where David says of the wicked that "God will shoot at them with an arrow; suddenly they will be wounded. So they will make him stumble; their own tongue is against them; all who see them will shake the head. Then all men will fear, and they will declare the work of God, and will consider what He has done." Psalm 79:10 reads, "Let there be known among the nations in our sight, vengeance for the blood of Your servants which has been shed." In Psalm 94, the psalmist prayed, "O Lord, God of vengeance, God of vengeance, shine forth! Rise up, O Judge of the earth, render recompense to the proud. . . . He has brought back their wickedness upon them and will destroy them in their evil; the Lord our God will destroy them" (vv. 1–2, 23). Other imprecatory psalms include 7, 35, 40, 55, 58, 59, 69, 109, 137, 139, and 144.

The prophets, too, spoke of God's vengeance. Isaiah wrote,

> Draw near, O nations, to hear; and listen, O peoples! Let the earth and all it contains hear, and the world and all that springs from it. For the Lord's indignation is against all the nations, and His wrath against all their armies; He has utterly destroyed them, He has given them over to slaughter. So their slain will be thrown out, and their corpses will give off their stench, and the mountains will be drenched with their blood. . . . For the Lord has a day of vengeance, a year of recompense for the cause of Zion. (Isa. 34:1–3, 8)

Speaking of God, Isaiah declared, "He put on righteousness like a breastplate, and a helmet of salvation on His head; and He put on garments of vengeance for clothing and wrapped Himself with zeal as a mantle. According to their deeds, so He will repay, wrath to His adversaries, recompense to His enemies; to the coastlands He will make recompense" (Isa. 59:17–18). One of the things the Servant (the Lord Jesus Christ) will proclaim is "the day of vengeance of our God" (Isa. 61:2), while in 63:4 God speaks of having a day of vengeance in His heart.

Speaking of a time when God would take vengeance on Israel's enemies Jeremiah declared, "For that day belongs to the Lord God of hosts, a day of vengeance, so as to avenge Himself on His foes; and the sword will devour and be satiated and drink its fill of their blood; for there will be a slaughter for the Lord God of hosts, in the land of the north by the river Euphrates" (Jer. 46:10). The prophet Micah records God's promise to "execute vengeance in anger and wrath on the nations which have not obeyed" (Mic. 5:15), while Nahum 1:2 describes God as "a jealous and avenging God . . . the Lord is avenging and wrathful. The Lord takes vengeance on His adversaries, and He reserves wrath for His enemies."

In the midst of judgment, God spares those who are His. Malachi 4:1–2 says,

> "For behold, the day is coming, burning like a furnace; and all the arrogant and every evildoer will be chaff; and the day that is coming will set them ablaze," says the Lord of hosts, "so that it will leave them neither root nor branch. But for you who fear My name, the sun of righteousness will rise with healing in its wings; and you will go forth and skip about like calves from the stall."

Isaiah comforted the fearful among his people by urging them, "Take courage, fear not. Behold, your God will come with vengeance; the recompense of God will come, but He will save you" (Isa. 35:4).

Nor is God's vengeance limited to the Old Testament. Jesus described the future time of God's judgment during the time of Tribulation as the "days of vengeance" (Luke 21:22). To the Thessalonians Paul wrote,

> For after all it is only just for God to repay with affliction those who afflict you, and to give relief to you who are afflicted and to us as well when the Lord Jesus will be revealed from heaven with His mighty angels in flaming fire, dealing out retribution to those who do not know God and to those who do not obey the gospel of our Lord Jesus. These will pay the penalty of eternal destruction, away from the presence of the Lord and from the glory of His power. (2 Thess. 1:6–9)

Both Paul (Rom. 12:19) and the writer of Hebrews (Heb. 10:30) quote Deuteronomy 32:35, which affirms that vengeance belongs to the Lord.

God's vengeance is not to be equated with petty human vindictiveness and bitter desire for revenge. God's holiness, righteousness, and justice demand that He take vengeance on unrepentant sinners. Vengeance belongs to God alone because all sin is ultimately against Him and an offense to Him (cf. Ps. 51:4).

The knowledge that God will one day execute vengeance on those who reject Him does not justify any personal vengeance on the part of believers. Proverbs 25:21 commands, "If your enemy is hungry, give him food to eat; and if he is thirsty, give him water to drink." Paul echoed that thought in Romans 12:19–20: "Never take your own revenge, beloved, but leave room for the wrath of God, for it is written, 'Vengeance is Mine, I will repay," says the Lord. 'But if your enemy is hungry, feed him, and if he is thirsty, give him a drink; for in so doing you will heap burning coals on his head.'" Neither Jesus (Luke 23:34), Stephen (Acts 7:60), nor Paul (1 Cor. 4:12) sought personal vengeance on their oppressors. Even God Himself declares, "I take no pleasure in the death of the wicked, but rather that the wicked turn from his way and live" (Ezek. 33:11), because "The Lord . . . is patient toward you, not wishing for any to perish but for all to come to repentance" (2 Pet. 3:9).

The realization that the Day of the Lord is coming in which God will take vengeance on the wicked is a bittersweet one for believers. On the one hand we rejoice, because God's glory will be put on display, sin will be done away with, the world will be taken back from the usurper, Satan, and God will be vindicated. But on the other hand, that day will bring about the destruction of the ungodly and their sentencing to eternal punishment.

That bittersweet, almost ambivalent attitude toward God's judgment is pictured in Revelation 10:8–10:

> And the voice which I heard from heaven, I heard again speaking with me, and saying, "Go, take the book which is open in the hand of the angel who stands on the sea and on the land." So I went to the angel, telling him to give me the little book. And he said to me, "Take it and eat it; it will make your stomach bitter, but in your mouth it will be sweet as honey." I took the little book out of the angel's hand and ate it, and in my mouth it was sweet as honey; and when I had eaten it, my stomach was made bitter.

John's initial reaction to the judgments described in the little book was the sweet realization that God will be vindicated and His glory put on display. But the sobering realization of the horrors that would be inflicted on unbelievers nauseated him.

God is patient to penitent sinners who embrace the gospel, but there will come a time when He will no longer withhold His judgment on those who reject it. He gave the sinful pre-Flood world 120 years to repent (Gen. 6:3), proclaiming the message of salvation to them through Noah. But at the end of that time, the judgment of the Flood came and destroyed them all. Similarly, in the future there will come a day when grace will end and judgment will fall on everyone. "Therefore having overlooked the times of ignorance," the apostle Paul declared to the philosophers on Mars Hill in Athens, "God is now declaring to men that all people everywhere should repent, because He has fixed a day in which He will judge the world in righteousness through a Man whom He has appointed, having furnished proof to all men by raising Him from the dead" (Acts 17:30–31).

It is the anticipation of that coming great day of God's wrath known as the Day of the Lord (see the discussion of the Day of the Lord in chapter 15 of this volume) that is in view in the fifth seal. That day will come during the seven-year period of Tribulation (the Seventieth Week of Dan. 9:27), particularly during the last three-and-one-half-year period that Jesus described as the "great tribulation, such as has not occurred since the beginning of the world until now, nor ever will" (Matt. 24:21; cf. Rev. 7:14). As indicated in chapter 13 of this volume, the first four seals, false peace, war, famine, and death, will take place during the first three and one-half years of the Tribulation, the period Jesus called "the beginning of birth pangs" (Matt. 24:8). Just as a woman's labor pains increase in intensity as the time to give birth draws near, so also will the terrifying events of God's judgment increase in painful intensity as the return of Jesus Christ approaches. The full force of God's wrath will be unleashed during the second half of the Tribulation.

The fifth seal marks the midpoint of the Tribulation period in bridging the gap between the beginning of God's wrath in the first half of the Tribulation and its full fury revealed in the second half. Like the horsemen of the first four seals, it also portrays a force. That force is the prayers of God's saints for Him to exact vengeance on rebellious mankind. Three features become evident as the fifth seal is unveiled: the persons involved, the petition they have, and the promise they receive.

THE PERSONS

When the Lamb broke the fifth seal, I saw underneath the altar the souls of those who had been slain because of the word of God, and because of the testimony which they had maintained; (6:9)

As with the first four seals, **when the Lamb** (the Lord Jesus Christ, who alone has authority to take back the universe; cf. 5:4–5) **broke the fifth seal** another sequence in the unfolding of divine judgment was revealed, in which John **saw underneath the altar the souls of those who had been slain.** These are martyrs, killed during the time of all the judgments. In addition to divine judgment through the false peace, war, famine, and disease dominating the unbelieving world, there will be widespread persecution of believers led by Satan, his demons, and the final Antichrist.

Jesus taught that identical sequence of events in His Olivet Discourse in Matthew 24. As noted in chapter 13 of this volume, the first seven verses of Matthew 24 describe the events of the first four seals. Just as the fifth seal describes martyrs, so also does Jesus in Matthew 24:9: "Then they will deliver you to tribulation, and will kill you, and you will be hated by all nations because of My name." The event that marks the midpoint of the Tribulation, the setting up of the "abomination of desolation," does not occur until verse 15 of Matthew 24. Therefore the persecution Jesus spoke of (that associated with the fifth seal) will begin in the first half of the Tribulation and escalate in the second half, after the abomination of desolation. The "abomination of desolation" is referred to three times in Daniel's prophecy (Dan. 9:27; 11:31; 12:11) to describe the desecration of the temple in the second century B. C. by the Syrian king Antiochus Epiphanes. The yet future "abomination of desolation" Jesus described in Matthew 24:15 will be similar to Antiochus's act. At that time, the final Antichrist will set himself up in the temple to be worshiped as God (2 Thess. 2:3–4). (For further discussion of the "abomination of desolation," see *Matthew 24–28,* MacArthur New Testament Commentary [Chicago: Moody, 1989], 34–37.) The removal of what now restrains him (2 Thess. 2:6–7) will permit Antichrist and his evil followers to run rampant. The power that will keep Antichrist from fully manifesting his evil can be none other than the power of God. He will keep Antichrist from manifesting himself before God's appointed time. He will then remove the restraining force and allow that Satan-possessed false christ to fully manifest his apostasy.

The persecution will, even in its initial phase, be worldwide in scope. Jesus warned, "You will be hated by all nations because of My name" (Matt. 24:9). That verse also implies that the persecution will be tolerated, if not actively led, by the world's governments. It will also be religious in nature, led by the false, worldwide, ecumenical religious system involved in worshiping the Antichrist (cf. Rev. 17:1–6). The world's hatred for God the Father and the Lord Jesus Christ will motivate them to persecute believers (cf. 16:9, 11, 21).

Inevitably, the persecution will sift those who outwardly identify with Jesus Christ. As has been true throughout the history of the church, there will be tares mingled with the wheat (Matt. 13:24–43). But the persecution, as it always does, will reveal who is truly redeemed and who is not. Jesus described this sifting process in Matthew 24:10–12: "At that time many will fall away and will betray one another and hate one another. Many false prophets will arise and will mislead many. Because lawlessness is increased, most people's love will grow cold." False believers will reveal their lack of genuine saving faith by defecting. First John 2:19 describes such people: "They went out from us, but they were not really of us; for if they had been of us, they would have remained with us; but they went out, so that it would be shown that they all are not of us." Genuine believers, on the other hand, will, as always, remain loyal to Jesus

Christ, since "the one who endures to the end, he will be saved" (Matt. 24:13). The redeemed persevere through any trial, including persecution and martyrdom.

The world's hostility toward Jesus Christ and His followers will not be able to prevent the "gospel of the kingdom" from being "preached in the whole world for a witness to all the nations" (Matt. 24:14). The preachers will include 144,000 Jewish evangelists (7:1–8; 14:1–5), two powerful preachers known as the two witnesses (11:3ff.), and an angel flying through the sky (14:6–7). So effective will their preaching be that those who will respond to it and are saved are described in Revelation 7:9 as "a great multitude which no one could count."

As noted earlier in this chapter, the "abomination of desolation" will be the event that causes the persecution to greatly increase in intensity. It will occur halfway through the seven-year tribulation period when Antichrist defiles the temple by setting up in it an idol of himself and demanding that the world worship him as God. With that blasphemous act, Antichrist will be unmasked for the Satan-possessed false christ that he is.

At that point the world will no longer view Antichrist as merely a political leader and deliverer. Because his "coming is in accord with the activity of Satan, with all power and signs and false wonders" (2 Thess. 2:9), the world will be deceived into worshiping him as a deity. Revelation 13:3–4 teaches that this worldwide worship of Antichrist will be motivated by the power of Satan: "The whole earth was amazed and followed after the beast [Antichrist]; they worshiped the dragon [Satan] because he gave his authority to the beast; and they worshiped the beast, saying, 'Who is like the beast, and who is able to wage war with him?'" Antichrist will exalt himself, speaking "arrogant words and blasphemies," and be granted by God authority to carry out his blasphemous enterprise for forty-two months (13:5)—the second half of the Tribulation.

The persecution of believers, which began early in the first half of the Tribulation, will intensify dramatically after Antichrist sets himself up as God. At that time he will "make war with the saints and ... overcome them" (13:7). With the whole world worshiping Antichrist as God, believers will be considered blasphemers for opposing him. That will bring upon them persecution from Antichrist's false religious system. Revelation 9:21 speaks of the proliferation of murders at this time; many of the victims will no doubt be believers, the victims of mob violence.

In His Olivet Discourse Jesus also spoke of the intensifying persecution that will mark this time:

> Then those who are in Judea must flee to the mountains; whoever is on the housetop must not go down to get the things out that are in his

house. Whoever is in the field must not turn back to get his cloak. But woe to those who are pregnant and to those who are nursing babies in those days! But pray that your flight will not be in the winter, or on a Sabbath. For then there will be a great tribulation, such as has not occurred since the beginning of the world until now, nor ever will. Unless those days had been cut short, no life would have been saved; but for the sake of the elect those days will be cut short. (Matt. 24:16–22)

The only defense against the sudden onslaught of persecution, Jesus said, will be immediate flight. Those unable to flee quickly enough, such as pregnant and nursing women, will be slaughtered. Inclement winter weather and Sabbath-day restrictions on travel could also hinder those attempting to flee. So severe will the persecution become that none would survive unless God shortened the time of persecution. Revelation 7:9–14 indicates that the slaughter will be on a massive scale, resulting in victims from every nation too numerous to count.

John described the martyrs he **saw underneath the altar** as **souls** because their bodily resurrection had not yet taken place (cf. 20:4). They are the firstfruits of those who will be saved throughout the Tribulation. Some of them will be Jewish, foreshadowing the salvation of Israel as a whole at the end of the Tribulation (Zech. 12:10; 14:1; Rom. 11:26–29).

The text does not define which **altar** is in view, nor does the scene in heaven parallel the earthly temple (or tabernacle), which had no throne (cf. 4:2). The altar John saw is most likely emblematic of the altar of incense in the Old Testament (Ex. 40:5), because of the association of incense with prayer (cf. 5:8; 8:3–4; Ps. 141:2; Luke 1:10).

John gives two reasons why the martyrs will be slain: **because of the word of God, and because of the testimony which they had maintained.** They will correctly interpret what they see going on around them in the world in the light of Scripture. They will proclaim from the Bible God's judgment and call on people to repent and believe the gospel. Antichrist and his followers, however, will not tolerate their bold preaching and will persecute and kill them. **Because of the testimony which they had maintained** refers to their loyalty to Jesus Christ (cf. 1:2, 9; 12:17; 19:10; 20:4), which was demonstrated by their proclamation of the Word of God in the face of life-threatening hatred and hostility. In a world bereft of the restraining influence of the Holy Spirit, merciless men will murder those who faithfully and courageously proclaim the message of judgment and salvation.

The Petition

and they cried out with a loud voice, saying, "How long, O Lord, holy and true, will You refrain from judging and avenging our blood on those who dwell on the earth?" (6:10)

The fifth seal is not martyrdom, as some suggest, because martyrdom could not be judgment from God. The seals depict God's wrath and judgment on the evil and ungodly—not His children. The force, then, that is involved in the fifth seal is the prayers of the Tribulation martyrs for God to enact vengeance on their Christ-rejecting murderers.

Prayer will play a vital role in the outpouring of God's judgments on the earth. This prayer is very different from the one by the martyr Stephen (Acts 7:60) in which he prayed for his killers to not be held guilty by God. This prayer of the martyrs is more like the imprecatory Psalms. A prayer for pardon is appropriate in a time of grace. But when grace is finished and judgment comes, prayers for divine, holy retribution are fitting. Such prayers are not from a desire for revenge, but are a protest against all that is sinful, unholy, dishonoring to God, and destructive to His creation.

Many Christians act as if prayer were a mere formality that has little effect. Yet, amazingly, the prayers of the Tribulation martyrs will move God's hand of judgment. Jesus illustrated that same principle in the parable of the persistent widow and the unrighteous judge: "Will not God bring about justice for His elect who cry to Him day and night, and will He delay long over them? I tell you that He will bring about justice for them quickly" (Luke 18:7–8). The prayers of the Tribulation martyrs will participate in activating the torments of the sixth and seventh seals along with the trumpet and bowl judgments which follow.

God's hand of judgment will move in response to the martyrs because their prayers will be urgent, fervent, impassioned, and consistent with His purpose and will. *Krazō* (**cried out**) is a strong word that emphasizes the urgent need and denotes strong emotions (cf. Matt. 9:27; 14:26, 30; 15:22; 20:30–31; Mark 9:24). The twenty-four elders and the angels loudly praised God (5:12), and the Tribulation martyrs will petition Him **with a loud voice.** In keeping with their call for vengeance and justice, they address Him as the **Lord, holy and true. Lord** does not translate *kurios,* the common New Testament word for Lord, but the stronger term *despotēs* ("master," "ruler"). It speaks of God the Father's might, power, majesty, and authority.

The martyrs base their appeal for vengeance on two of God's attributes. Because God is **holy,** He must judge sin (cf. Ps. 5:4–5; Hab. 1:13; Acts 10:42; 17:31; Rom. 2:16; 3:6; 2 Tim. 4:1); because He is **true,** He must be faithful to His word and keep His promises (Num. 23:19; 1 Sam. 15:29; Luke 21:33). Revelation 3:7 applies this phrase **holy and true** to Jesus Christ, thus affirming His deity and full equality with His Father.

The martyrs' question **"How long . . . will You refrain from judging and avenging our blood on those who dwell on the earth?"** does not reflect a personal vendetta on their part. They are not trying to tell God what to do or when to do it; they are asking Him the question because they have a holy desire to see Satan and Antichrist destroyed, iniquity defeated, the wicked judged, and Jesus Christ reigning in glory on the earth. **How long** is a well-known cry of suffering Israel, reflecting the perplexing question of the righteous as to when their pain will end (cf. Pss. 13:1; 35:17). The phrase **those who dwell on the earth** is a technical one which refers throughout Revelation to the ungodly (cf. 3:10; 8:13; 11:10; 13:8, 12; 17:2, 8). As was the case with murdered Abel, the very ground cries out for their **blood** to be required at the hands of their killers.

The time of grace is nearing its end. No longer do God's people ask God to forgive their enemies. The time is fast approaching when God will judge His enemies, and the Lord Jesus Christ will take His rightful place as earth's ruler. But since these martyrs are from the first half of the Tribulation, the "beginning of birth pangs," that time is still a little way off.

THE PROMISE

And there was given to each of them a white robe; and they were told that they should rest for a little while longer, until the number of their fellow servants and their brethren who were to be killed even as they had been, would be completed also. (6:11)

Two elements make up God's response to His martyred saints: a symbolic gift, and a spoken word. The gift that **was given to each of them** by God as they arrived in heaven was **a white robe** (*stolē;* a long robe flowing to the feet). These long, brilliant white robes were a reward of grace (cf. 7:9, 14), symbolizing God's gift of eternal righteousness, blessedness, dignity, and honor (cf. 3:5). They symbolize all the glory that redeemed saints will enjoy in heaven. These were not actual robes, since what is depicted in this vision is before the resurrection of the bodies of the redeemed, which occurs for Tribulation saints at Christ's return (20:4–5).

Along with this gift came God's spoken word, namely **that they should rest for a little while longer.** That is not a rebuke for impatience, since impatience is a sin and perfected people in heaven do not sin. Rather, it is an invitation to stop the cry for vengeance and to continue to enjoy the bliss of heavenly **rest** until God's time for wrath arrives. The phrase **for a little while longer** (cf. John 7:33; 12:35) indicates that that time will not be long delayed. As indicated earlier, this seal is best seen as describing a period in the middle of the seven years of tribulation. There is a verbal similarity to the phrase in Revelation 10:6, "there will be delay no longer," which obviously ends the delay of which God spoke to the martyrs in 6:11. Some time will clearly elapse between 6:11 and 10:6. God's day of judgment and vengeance is about three and a half years ahead, and will not come **until the number of their fellow servants and their brethren who were to be killed even as they had been, would be completed also.** God sovereignly predetermined the exact number of those who would be killed. The petitioners were told to enjoy heaven's rest until that number had been reached. Robert L. Thomas notes,

> The word to the souls under the altar gives them reassurance that God will eventually avenge their blood, but the time for the culmination of that vengeance has not yet arrived. One feature that must yet transpire beforehand is the increase of their number through additional martyrdoms. The earth dwellers under the dawning leadership of the beast from the sea will take an even greater toll of human lives before Christ finally intervenes through His personal arrival back on earth. Until then, the already martyred are told to rest and enjoy their state of blessedness already attained. (*Revelation 1–7: An Exegetical Commentary* [Chicago: Moody, 1992], 499)

Fellow servants and **brethren** are two classes of people. The first group was alive and willing to die like the martyrs, though they may not. The second group were those who will be killed.

The world is not too enlightened, humane, civilized, educated, or sophisticated to avoid repeating the atrocities of the past. In fact, the atrocities of the Tribulation will far exceed any that have gone before. With God's supernatural restraint on sin removed and the forces of hell running rampant, the slaughter of that time will be without precedent in human history. But out of those dark and evil days will come thousands who sealed their testimony for the Word of God and the lordship of Jesus Christ with their own blood.

Fear of the Wrath to Come: The Sixth Seal (Revelation 6:12–17)

15

I looked when He broke the sixth seal, and there was a great earthquake; and the sun became black as sackcloth made of hair, and the whole moon became like blood; and the stars of the sky fell to the earth, as a fig tree casts its unripe figs when shaken by a great wind. The sky was split apart like a scroll when it is rolled up, and every mountain and island were moved out of their places. Then the kings of the earth and the great men and the commanders and the rich and the strong and every slave and free man hid themselves in the caves and among the rocks of the mountains; and they said to the mountains and to the rocks, "Fall on us and hide us from the presence of Him who sits on the throne, and from the wrath of the Lamb; for the great day of their wrath has come, and who is able to stand?" (6:12–17)

One of the central prophetic themes in Scripture is the coming of the final day of God's wrath known as the Day of the Lord. While it is true that "God is angry with the wicked every day" (Ps. 7:11 NKJV), the Day of the Lord is an expression used to describe periods when God specially intervenes in human history for judgment. The phrase "Day of the Lord" appears nineteen times in the Old Testament and four times in the

New. It is a unique time when God's power and holiness are unveiled, bringing terror and death to His enemies. The prophets describe the Day of the Lord as "destruction from the Almighty" (Isa. 13:6; Joel 1:15), a time of "fury and burning anger" (Isa. 13:9), a "time of doom" (Ezek. 30:3), "great and very awesome" (Joel 2:11), and "darkness and not light" (Amos 5:18; cf. v. 20).

The phrase "the Day of the Lord" is not limited to future, final wrath, but sometimes refers to imminent historical judgments, which occurred during Old Testament history (e.g., Isa. 13:6–22; Ezek. 30:2–19; Joel 1:15; Amos 5:18–20; Obad. 11–14; Zeph. 1:14–18). These historical Day of the Lord judgments were usually preceded by some preliminary judgments of lesser severity. They acted as warnings by providing sample previews of the far more devastating judgments to come when the Day actually arrived.

An example of one of these preliminary judgments comes from the prophet Joel. In Joel 2:28–32 the final, eschatological Day of the Lord is described. But the sequence leading up to that Day is very informative. Joel 1:4–12 describes an actual locust plague that came on Judah. This was a preview of the near historical Day of the Lord to come on Judah in the future Babylonian invasion seen in Joel 2:1–17. This historical Day of the Lord invasion was also a preview of the ultimate eschatological Day discussed in 2:28–32.

There is another illustration in Ezekiel of preliminary judgments leading to the Day of the Lord judgments. In Ezekiel 13:5, the prophet declares that the Day of the Lord is coming on Judah. Clearly, he was warning about the Babylonian captivity and the total destruction of Jerusalem—the disruption of the nation's life in the land of promise and the beginning of seventy years of captivity in pagan Babylon. Though that Day had not yet come, Ezekiel was already in exile, one of the ten thousand Jews deported to Babylon in 597 B.C. There had been an earlier deportation of Jews in 605 B.C. in which Daniel and his friends had been taken captive. Those first two deportations (judgments) were previews of the coming Day of the Lord in 586 B.C., when the Babylonians completely destroyed Jerusalem and put an end to the nation of Israel as it had existed in the land. That again illustrates that God sends preliminary judgments before the actual Day of the Lord judgments.

Other times the phrase "Day of the Lord" refers directly to God's final, eschatological judgments at the end of human history (e.g., Joel 2:28–32; Zech. 14:1; Mal. 4:1, 5; Acts 2:20; 1 Thess. 5:2; 2 Thess. 2:2; 2 Pet. 3:10). This final Day of the Lord will also have its preliminary judgments in the first five seals, before it begins with the opening of the sixth seal (6:17). That Day will unfold in two stages, first during the Tribulation (1 Thess. 5:2), and then at the end of the Millennium (2 Pet. 3:10). Those two stages are separated by a thousand years. It is noteworthy that Peter, as if to erase any questions about that separation, reminds the reader that "with the Lord one day is like a thousand years, and a thousand years like one day (2 Pet. 3:8)."

The most detailed New Testament exposition of the coming Day of the Lord is found in 1 Thessalonians 5:1–4:

> Now as to the times and the epochs, brethren, you have no need of any-
> thing to be written to you. For you yourselves know full well that the
> day of the Lord will come just like a thief in the night. While they are
> saying, "Peace and safety!" then destruction will come upon them sud-
> denly like labor pains upon a woman with child, and they will not
> escape. But you, brethren, are not in darkness, that the day would over-
> take you like a thief.

The Thessalonians had apparently asked Paul about the timing and sequence of events relating to the Day of the Lord. Many of the Thessalonian Christians were confused about the state of those who died before Christ's return, which they believed would happen in their life-time. Having taught them all that God intended them to know about the Rapture (1 Thess. 4:13–18), the apostle cautioned the Thessalonians to live godly lives in light of God's coming judgment (cf. 1 Thess. 5:4–8). To focus on esoteric speculation into the details of prophetic timing at the expense of growing in grace was (and is) unprofitable.

God has not chosen to disclose the precise time of the final Day of the Lord or the return of Jesus Christ (cf. Matt. 24:36; Acts 1:7). Unfortu-nately, the practice of date setting continues unabated in our own time.

Since the Day of the Lord will come unexpectedly and without warning ("like a thief in the night"; 1 Thess. 5:2; cf. 2 Pet. 3:10), believers alive during the Tribulation are to live in anticipation and expectation of its imminent arrival. Speaking of His return, which will climax the first phase of the Day of the Lord, Jesus said, "Be on the alert, for you do not know which day your Lord is coming" (Matt. 24:42; cf. v. 50). Later in the Olivet Discourse, He cautioned, "Be on the alert then, for you do not know the day nor the hour" (Matt. 25:13; cf. Luke 12:35–40). Every genera-tion must be ready for the Day of the Lord. Peter adds, "Since you look for these things, be diligent to be found by Him in peace, spotless and blameless" (2 Pet. 3:14).

Even those alive during the Tribulation will not know the precise time that the Day of the Lord will begin. They will be duped by false prophets, who will reassure them that judgment is not near; rather "peace and safety" are at hand—just as their predecessors falsely reassured rebellious Israel (Mic. 3:5; cf. Jer. 6:14; 8:11). These lying deceivers will scoff at the idea that Christ will return, demanding mockingly, "Where is the promise of His coming? For ever since the fathers fell asleep, all continues just as it was from the beginning of creation" (2 Pet. 3:4). Deceived by the false prophets, the world will plunge blindly into the Day of the Lord and face disastrous, hopeless ruin.

Like the first five seals, the sixth seal (which introduces the arrival of the Day of the Lord, calling it "the great day of … wrath"; 6:17) is associated with a force. That force is fear, a feeling which is among the most powerful of human emotions, capable of seizing control of the mind and will. Fear can produce everything from cowardice to heroism, strength to weakness, aggression to passivity, reason to confusion, clear thinking to total panic. Fear can strengthen the heart and make it beat faster—or stop it dead.

There are fears that affect many people, such as fear of disease, injury, death, loss of a loved one, loss of a job, and public speaking. In addition, there are other fears (usually called phobias) that some people are susceptible to, including fear of spiders, insects, snakes, mice, dogs, being alone, enclosed spaces, flying, and heights.

People fear all kinds of things, but rarely what they ought to fear most. In Luke 12:5 Jesus said, "I will warn you whom to fear: fear the One who, after He has killed, has authority to cast into hell; yes, I tell you, fear Him!" The writer of Hebrews adds "For we know Him who said, 'Vengeance is Mine, I will repay.' And again, 'The Lord will judge His people.' It is a terrifying thing to fall into the hands of the living God" (Heb. 10:30–31). But instead of fearing Him, most people either view God as some sort of benign grandfather, or deny His existence altogether. One day, however, people will have a consuming, debilitating, uncontrollable fear of the judgments of the living God. Describing that coming day, Jesus spoke in Luke 21:26 of "men fainting from fear and the expectation of the things which are coming upon the world." "Fainting" is from *apopsuchō*, which literally means "to stop breathing," or "to expire." When the Day of the Lord comes, sinners will be so terrified that some will faint and others will drop dead. The sixth seal reveals that the ones who are left will be so terrified that they will cry for the mountains and rocks to hide them from the fury of God's devastating wrath.

Three features describe the overwhelming fear associated with the sixth seal: the reason for fear, the range of fear, and the reaction of fear.

The Reason for Fear

I looked when He broke the sixth seal, and there was a great earthquake; and the sun became black as sackcloth made of hair, and the whole moon became like blood; and the stars of the sky fell to the earth, as a fig tree casts its unripe figs when shaken by

a great wind. The sky was split apart like a scroll when it is rolled up, and every mountain and island were moved out of their places. (6:12–14)

Unlike the first five seals, each of which involved humans in one way or another (the four horsemen and the saints under the altar), in **the sixth seal** God acts alone. By the time this seal is opened, the midpoint of the Tribulation has passed and the world is in the final three-and-one-half-year period known as the "great tribulation" (Matt. 24:21). By then the final Antichrist has desecrated the temple in Jerusalem (the "abomination of desolation"), the world worships him, and a massive persecution of Jews and Christians has broken out. Incredibly, in the midst of all the turmoil and chaos from the divine judgments on the world, it will be business as usual for most people. Speaking of this time, Jesus said, "For the coming of the Son of Man will be just like the days of Noah. For as in those days before the flood they were eating and drinking, marrying and giving in marriage, until the day that Noah entered the ark, and they did not understand until the flood came and took them all away; so will the coming of the Son of Man be" (Matt. 24:37–39). The warnings that the traumatic events of the first five seals are the beginning of God's judgment will go unheeded. But the events of the sixth seal will be so devastating and terrifying that they will be attributable only to God. The world will be forced to acknowledge that the Christian preachers' warnings of divine judgment were precisely accurate.

As has been previously noted in this volume, the seals parallel the sequence of events given by Jesus in the Olivet Discourse. The Lord described the events associated with the sixth seal in Matthew 24:29: "Immediately after the tribulation of those days the sun will be darkened, and the moon will not give its light, and the stars will fall from the sky, and the powers of the heavens will be shaken." Luke's account of the Olivet Discourse adds, "There will be great earthquakes, and in various places plagues and famines; and there will be terrors and great signs from heaven" (Luke 21:11). And Luke further writes: "There will be signs in sun and moon and stars, and on the earth dismay among nations, in perplexity at the roaring of the sea and the waves, men fainting from fear and the expectation of the things which are coming upon the world; for the powers of the heavens will be shaken" (Luke 21:25–26).

The Old Testament prophets also spoke of frightening natural disasters in connection with the Day of the Lord. Joel wrote, "Let all the inhabitants of the land tremble, for the day of the Lord is coming; surely it is near, a day of darkness and gloom, a day of clouds and thick darkness. . . . The earth quakes, the heavens tremble, the sun and the moon grow dark and the stars lose their brightness" (Joel 2:1–2, 10; cf. 2:31; 3:16).

Ezekiel wrote of violent weather accompanying the Day of the Lord (Ezek. 13:5–16), and Zephaniah described it as "a day of trouble and distress, a day of destruction and desolation, a day of darkness and gloom, a day of clouds and thick darkness" (Zeph. 1:15). John recorded six frightening natural disasters associated with the opening of the sixth seal.

First, **there was a great earthquake.** There have been many earthquakes in recorded history and there will be more during the first half of the Tribulation (Matt. 24:7). But the cataclysmic event John saw in this seal is to be far more powerful and devastating than any previous earthquake. In fact, this one will shake more than just the earth (6:13–14). *Seismos* (**earthquake**) literally means "a shaking." In Matthew 8:24 it describes a great storm on the Sea of Galilee, and the Septuagint uses it in Joel 2:10 to describe the heavens trembling.

God has often made His presence felt in human history by shaking the earth. He did so when He gave the Law to Israel at Mt. Sinai (Ex. 19:18; Ps. 68:8), when Elijah called on Him (1 Kings 19:11–12), at the death of His Son (Matt. 27:51, 54), and when He released Paul and Silas from jail in Philippi (Acts 16:26). Both Isaiah (Isa. 29:6) and Ezekiel (Ezek. 38:19) associate earthquakes with God's judgment. This event, however, causes far more than the earth to be shaken. It will shake the heavens as well as the earth.

Earthquakes have always frightened people. Many who reside in earthquake country live in constant fear of the "big one." After experiencing an earthquake some people are so unnerved that they camp outdoors for days, or even weeks, afraid to stay in their houses. Some permanently move out of an earthquake-prone area altogether. The number of appointments in psychiatrist's and psychologist's offices also rises, as those who remain struggle to overcome their fears.

But the fears caused by this earthquake will be incalculably greater than those caused by any previous earthquake. Not only will this be the most powerful earthquake the world has ever seen, but it will also come at a time of unprecedented troubles. The people who experience this earthquake will have survived worldwide war, devastating famine, and widespread epidemics of deadly diseases. The removal of the restrainer, the Holy Spirit, the divine One who has held back Satan and Antichrist until God's appointed season (2 Thess. 2:6–8), will allow the world to plunge headlong into immorality, vice, wickedness, and godlessness. Antichrist will be worshiped as God and his false prophet will be proclaiming that utopia is at hand—as soon as the believers in the true God are done away with. In an instant, however, the lie of Satan is exposed and the world's false hopes are shattered by the violent shaking of the very earth under their feet.

On the heels of the earthquake came a second disaster, as **the**

sun became black as sackcloth made of hair. Sackcloth was rough cloth worn by mourners, usually made from the hair of **black** goats. Following the violent earthquake that devastates the earth, the sun will turn as black as a mourner's robe. Scientist Dr. Henry M. Morris explains what could cause that phenomenon:

> The great earthquake described here . . . for the first time in history is worldwide in scope. Seismologists and geophysicists in recent years have learned a great deal about the structure of the earth and about the cause and nature of earthquakes. The earth's solid crust is traversed with a complex network of faults, with all resting upon a plastic mantle whose structure is still largely unknown. Whether the crust consists of great moving plates is a current matter of controversy among geophysicists, so the ultimate cause of earthquakes is still not known. In all likelihood, the entire complex of crustal instabilities is a remnant of the phenomena of the great Flood, especially the breakup of the fountains of the great deep.
>
> In any case, the vast worldwide network of unstable earthquake belts around the world suddenly will begin to slip and fracture on a global basis and a gigantic earthquake will ensue. This is evidently, and naturally, accompanied by tremendous volcanic eruptions, spewing vast quantities of dust and steam and gases into the upper atmosphere. It is probably these that will cause the sun to be darkened and the moon to appear blood-red. (*The Revelation Record* [Wheaton, Ill.: Tyndale, 1983], 121)

The prophet Joel spoke of these same phenomena in connection with the Day of the Lord: "The sun will be turned into darkness and the moon into blood before the great and awesome day of the Lord comes" (Joel 2:31; cf. Isa. 13:9–10; Matt. 24:29; Mark 13:24–25; Luke 21:25). Darkness is associated with judgment elsewhere in Scripture (e.g., Ex. 10:21–22; Matt. 27:45).

The third disaster is closely connected with the darkening of the sun, as **the whole moon became like blood.** There will be vast clouds of ash and smoke spewed out by the volcanic activity associated with the great worldwide earthquake. That ash and smoke will eclipse the moon, coloring it bloodred as it attempts to pierce the smoke-darkened sky.

Isaiah also described this strange and terrifying phenomenon, writing in Isaiah 13:10, "The sun will be dark when it rises and the moon will not shed its light." Joel adds, "the sun and the moon grow dark" (Joel 2:10). And, in the passage quoted above, Joel spoke of the sun being darkened and the moon being turned into blood (Joel 2:31; cf. Acts 2:20). These phenomena will affect every aspect of life as the normal cycle of daylight and darkness is disrupted. The total eclipse of the sun and moon will add more reason for the world to be in panic.

Then, out of the darkened sky came the fourth disaster; John records that the **stars of the sky fell to the earth.** *Asteres* (**stars**) can refer to actual stars, but can also describe any heavenly body other than the sun and the moon. Obviously, in this context it does not refer to actual stars, since they are far too large to fall to the earth and would incinerate it long before striking it. Also, the stars are still in place later when the fourth trumpet sounds (8:12). This is most likely a reference to asteroid or meteor showers bombarding the earth. There has been much speculation among scientists recently about the effects of a large asteroid striking the earth. Modern experts believe that the impacts of asteroids, comets, and meteors striking the earth would be devastating and cause unprecedented destruction. There will be so many such bodies hitting the earth that John, in a vivid analogy, likens the scene to **a fig tree** that **casts its unripe figs when shaken by a great wind.** With the whole earth being pummeled by fiery balls plunging out of the blackness there will be nowhere for people to flee, nowhere for them to hide.

The fifth disaster in this seal affects in some way the earth's atmosphere, because from man's perspective **the sky** appears to **split apart like a scroll when it is rolled up.** This is the human perception of the magnitude of this judgment, but is not the final dissolving of heaven which comes later (21:1; 2 Pet. 3:10). Here is a culminating feature of the "terrors and great signs from heaven" (Luke 21:11) that will terrify people. John likens the sky to an unrolled scroll that splits in the middle and rolls up on either side. This vivid picture finds a parallel in Isaiah 34:4: "All the host of heaven will wear away, and the sky will be rolled up like a scroll; all their hosts will also wither away as a leaf withers from the vine, or as one withers from the fig tree." God will strike a blow at the domain of Satan, the "prince of the power of the air" (Eph. 2:2).

Returning in his vision to events on the earth, John describes a sixth devastating natural phenomenon, noting that **every mountain and island were moved out of their places.** The whole unstable crust of the earth begins to move and shift. Dr. Morris also explains how this could happen:

> The earth's crust, highly unstable ever since the great Flood, will be so disturbed by the impacting asteroids, the volcanic explosions, and the worldwide earthquakes, that great segments of it will actually begin to slip and slide over the earth's deep plastic mantle. Geophysicists for many years have been fascinated with the idea of "continental drift" (although strong evidence has been accumulating against any such phenomenon occurring in the present age). Several have published theories of a past naturalistic catastrophism involving what they call "the earth's shifting crust." Some such phenomenon may actually be triggered under this judgment of the sixth seal, dwarfing the damage

occasioned by all the mighty earthquakes of the past. (*The Revelation Record,* 123)

The devastating natural disasters accompanying the sixth seal will be the most terrifying events ever to affect the earth. Their cumulative impact will be far more destructive than any of the current doomsday scenarios about asteroids hitting the earth. And the even more intense trumpet and bowl judgments are still to come! The total flattening of all mountains will come later at the seventh bowl judgment (16:20).

THE RANGE OF FEAR

Then the kings of the earth and the great men and the commanders and the rich and the strong and every slave and free man (6:15a)

This verse indicates that the debilitating fear caused by the disasters associated with the sixth seal will affect all unbelievers. These seven categories embrace all classes of society. **The kings of the earth** refers to the heads of state throughout the world. **The great men** (*megistanes*) are the high-ranking officials in government. **The commanders** are the military leaders, while **the rich** are those who control commerce and business **and the strong** may well be the influential. Together, they comprise the elite elements of human society. Ironically, these are the very people who ignored the warnings of God's impending judgment and persecuted those who proclaimed it. Neither political power, military authority, riches, nor influence will exempt anyone from God's judgment (cf. Prov. 11:4; Zeph. 1:18). Nor will the common people, the lower classes, escape; **every slave and free man** will be as terrified as the influential and wealthy.

THE REACTION OF FEAR

hid themselves in the caves and among the rocks of the mountains; and they said to the mountains and to the rocks, "Fall on us and hide us from the presence of Him who sits on the throne, and from the wrath of the Lamb; for the great day of their wrath has come, and who is able to stand?" (6:15b–17)

The reaction of the unbelieving world to the terrors unleashed by the sixth seal will not be one of repentance (cf. 9:21; 16:11), but of mindless panic. They will finally acknowledge what believers have been saying all along, that the disasters they have experienced are God's judgment. Yet, like the demons of whom James wrote (James 2:19), they will believe and fear but will not repent. They will follow Satan, believe his lies, and embrace his messenger, Antichrist. As a result, God will judicially abandon them: "For this reason God will send upon them a deluding influence so that they will believe what is false, in order that they all may be judged who did not believe the truth, but took pleasure in wickedness" (2 Thess. 2:11–12). Those who repeatedly harden their hearts will have their hearts hardened by God; they will be unable to repent and believe.

The panic-stricken sinners will react irrationally, foolishly attempting to hide **themselves in the caves and among the rocks of the mountains** (cf. Isa. 2:17–21)—the very places that are being shaken. They are no doubt seeking refuge from the swarms of meteors and asteroids bombarding the earth. But in light of the massive earthquake and its continuing aftershocks, the widespread volcanic eruptions, and the other disturbances to the earth's crust, such hiding places will offer no safety. Further, it is impossible to hide from God or evade His judgment. Speaking of rebellious Israel, God said, "Though they dig into Sheol, from there shall My hand take them; and though they ascend to heaven, from there will I bring them down. Though they hide on the summit of Carmel, I will search them out and take them from there; and though they conceal themselves from My sight on the floor of the sea, from there I will command the serpent and it will bite them" (Amos 9:2–3; cf. Ps. 139:7–12).

The terrifying events prompt a worldwide prayer meeting, but the prayers are to Mother Nature, not to God. As the unbelievers frantically burrow into the earth in their futile attempt to hide themselves, **they** will say **to the mountains and to the rocks, "Fall on us and hide us from the presence of Him who sits on the throne, and from the wrath of the Lamb; for the great day of their wrath has come, and who is able to stand?"** Too late, the people alive at that time will finally realize that all the disasters that have come upon them and their world are the result of God's wrath. Unwilling and unable to repent, they will scream for the mountains and rocks to fall on them and crush them. Two similar cries can be seen in Scripture (Hos. 10:8; Luke 23:30), both in a time of national calamity for Israel. They are, to some degree, prophetic of the time referred to in the sixth seal. People will be so terrified that they would rather die than face wrath of a holy God—foolishly ignoring the fact that death will provide absolutely no escape from divine judgment, rather a casting into the eternal lake of fire (cf. 20:11–15).

Him who sits on the throne refers to God (4:2, 3, 9, 10). They will have, by then, come to a clear understanding that God has been behind all the judgments.

More specifically, they fear **the wrath of the Lamb.** The Lamb, the Lord Jesus Christ (5:6–8), is the agent of direct judgment. The wrath of the incarnate Jesus was seen only twice before in Scripture, when He cleansed the temple (John 2:13–17; cf. Matt. 21:12–13). In the future, He will judge like a lion (5:5). The panic-stricken people of the world will recognize the Lamb as the executioner.

The great day of their (God's and Christ's) **wrath** is another term for the Day of the Lord. Apparently the world will understand that final wrath has come.

The primary Old Testament passages from which the images in the sixth seal are drawn prove that **the great day** must be the Day of the Lord (Isa. 2:10–11, 19–21; 13:9–13; 34:4, 8; Ezek. 32:7–8; Hos. 10:8; Joel 2:11, 30; Zeph. 1:14; Mal. 4:5).

These Day of the Lord horrors precede the coming of the Lord and even anticipate the worst that is yet to come in the seventh seal, which includes the trumpet (8:1–9:21) and bowl (16:1–21) judgments.

The scene closes with the asking of the rhetorical question **who is able to stand?** The answer is "no one." The prophet Nahum wrote, "Who can stand before His indignation? Who can endure the burning of His anger?" (Nah. 1:6). First Thessalonians 5:3 declares that "destruction will come upon them suddenly like labor pains upon a woman with child, and they will not escape." The ungodly will not be able to evade divine judgment.

This picture, horrifying and frightening as it is, is not altogether hopeless. The church will be delivered from that time (3:10). Great multitudes of people will be saved in the midst of the terrors of divine judgment, both Gentiles (7:9) and Jews (Rom. 11:26). But for the rest the sobering words of the writer of Hebrews will apply: "For if we go on sinning willfully after receiving the knowledge of the truth, there no longer remains a sacrifice for sins, but a terrifying expectation of judgment and the fury of a fire which will consume the adversaries. . . . It is a terrifying thing to fall into the hands of the living God" (Heb. 10:26–27, 31).

Survivors of the Wrath of God (Revelation 7:1–8)

16

After this I saw four angels standing at the four corners of the earth, holding back the four winds of the earth, so that no wind would blow on the earth or on the sea or on any tree. And I saw another angel ascending from the rising of the sun, having the seal of the living God; and he cried out with a loud voice to the four angels to whom it was granted to harm the earth and the sea, saying, "Do not harm the earth or the sea or the trees until we have sealed the bond-servants of our God on their foreheads." And I heard the number of those who were sealed, one hundred and forty-four thousand sealed from every tribe of the sons of Israel: from the tribe of Judah, twelve thousand were sealed, from the tribe of Reuben twelve thousand, from the tribe of Gad twelve thousand, from the tribe of Asher twelve thousand, from the tribe of Naphtali twelve thousand, from the tribe of Manasseh twelve thousand, from the tribe of Simeon twelve thousand, from the tribe of Levi twelve thousand, from the tribe of Issachar twelve thousand, from the tribe of Zebulun twelve thousand, from the tribe of Joseph twelve thousand, from the tribe of Benjamin, twelve thousand were sealed. (7:1–8)

The previous chapter of Revelation (6) looked at a time of unprecedented disaster, unrelieved terror, and unimaginable slaughter that lies ahead for the world. Commonly known as the Tribulation, it will be the time when Jesus Christ takes back the earth from the usurper, Satan. That action is symbolized in the book of Revelation by His unrolling of a seven-sealed scroll. As He breaks each seal, a new divine judgment is poured out on the earth. The judgments of the first five seals were severe. But the disasters associated with the sixth seal (the beginning of the Day of the Lord) will far surpass those of the first five seals. And the judgments of the seventh seal, which contains the even more intense trumpet and bowl judgments, will be the worst of all.

The world will refuse to acknowledge that the disasters of the first five seals are God's judgment—despite the warnings from believers that they are. But the events of the sixth seal will be so horrific that all will be forced to acknowledge them as the judgment of God. In their terror, amid their futile attempts to hide from the terrible presence of God the Father and the Lamb, people will cry out, "The great day of their wrath has come, and who is able to stand?" (6:17).

Chapter 7 forms a parenthetical section between the sixth (6:12–17) and seventh (8:1) seals to answer that question, introducing two groups who will survive the fury of divine judgment. The first, those described in verses 1–8, are the Jewish evangelists who will be preserved on earth. They will survive the holocaust of divine wrath unleashed by the seal, trumpet, and bowl judgments. God will also protect them from the murderous efforts of Antichrist and his henchmen to wipe out believers in the true God. Having survived the wars, famine, unprecedented natural disasters, disease, rampant, unchecked sinfulness, and savage persecution of the Tribulation, they will enter the millennial kingdom alive. The second group to escape divine fury (vv. 9–17) are those who will be martyred and thereby ushered into the blissful rest of heaven, where they will be preserved. After the horrific events of the sixth seal, and before the opening of the seventh seal in chapter 8, the Holy Spirit provided this chapter as an interlude for the reader to catch his breath. It is also a reminder that in the midst of His wrath, God will remember mercy (cf. Hab. 3:2).

This pair of visions contrasts the preparedness of believers, who will be delivered from wrath, with the panic and devastation of the unbelievers, who will not survive that wrath. First Thessalonians 5:3 declares that "destruction will come upon them suddenly like labor pains upon a woman with child, and they will not escape." In his second letter to the Thessalonians Paul adds, "The Lord Jesus will be revealed from heaven with His mighty angels in flaming fire, dealing out retribution to those who do not know God and to those who do not obey the gospel of our

Lord Jesus. These will pay the penalty of eternal destruction, away from the presence of the Lord and from the glory of His power" (2 Thess. 1:7–9). Later in that epistle the apostle wrote, "For this reason God will send upon them a deluding influence so that they will believe what is false, in order that they all may be judged who did not believe the truth, but took pleasure in wickedness" (2 Thess. 2:11–12). The Bible offers no hope that any ungodly person in that Day will escape God's judgment. The Day of the Lord will eventually destroy all the ungodly who do not know God and do not obey the gospel of Christ.

That God will preserve His people in the time of judgment is a familiar theme in Scripture. David triumphantly exulted, "The righteous cry, and the Lord hears and delivers them out of all their troubles. The Lord is near to the brokenhearted and saves those who are crushed in spirit. Many are the afflictions of the righteous, but the Lord delivers him out of them all" (Ps. 34:17–19). In Psalm 91:3–10 the psalmist relates God's promise to preserve the godly:

> For it is [God] who delivers you from the snare of the trapper and from the deadly pestilence. He will cover you with His pinions, and under His wings you may seek refuge; His faithfulness is a shield and bulwark. You will not be afraid of the terror by night, or of the arrow that flies by day; of the pestilence that stalks in darkness, or of the destruction that lays waste at noon. A thousand may fall at your side and ten thousand at your right hand, but it shall not approach you. You will only look on with your eyes and see the recompense of the wicked. For you have made the Lord, my refuge, even the Most High, your dwelling place. No evil will befall you, nor will any plague come near your tent.

Malachi describes God's comforting of those who feared being swept away by the judgments of the Day of the Lord:

> Then those who feared the Lord spoke to one another, and the Lord gave attention and heard it, and a book of remembrance was written before Him for those who fear the Lord and who esteem His name. "They will be Mine," says the Lord of hosts, "on the day that I prepare My own possession, and I will spare them as a man spares his own son who serves him. So you will again distinguish between the righteous and the wicked, between one who serves God and one who does not serve Him. For behold, the day is coming, burning like a furnace; and all the arrogant and every evildoer will be chaff; and the day that is coming will set them ablaze," says the Lord of hosts, "so that it will leave them neither root nor branch. But for you who fear My name, the sun of righteousness will rise with healing in its wings; and you will go forth and skip about like calves from the stall...."

Behold, I am going to send you Elijah the prophet before the coming
of the great and terrible day of the Lord. He will restore the hearts of
the fathers to their children and the hearts of the children to their
fathers, so that I will not come and smite the land with a curse." (Mal.
3:16–4:2, 5–6)

When God destroyed the world in the Flood, He preserved Noah
and his family. When He destroyed Sodom and Gomorrah, He preserved
Lot and his daughters. When He destroyed Jericho, He preserved Rahab
and her household. And when He destroyed Egypt, He preserved the
nation of Israel.

The Tribulation is revealed to be a time of unparalleled judgment, disaster, and death. But it will also be for many the time of salvation. Some of those redeemed out of the Tribulation have already been
mentioned in connection with the fifth seal (6:9–11). They were martyrs,
killed because of their faithfulness to the Word of God and to the Lord
Jesus Christ (cf. 7:9–17). Many believers will surely die from the wars,
famine, and natural disasters (6:3–8, 12–14) that God brings in judgment
on the earth. Countless others will die as a result of Antichrist's persecution (13:7–10; 14:12–13; 17:6; 20:4). Their physical deaths are not, however, a result of God's wrath (1 Thess. 1:10; 5:9) any more than when a
believer dies today. God's judgments on the world and Antichrist's persecution are just the means by which God ushers them into His presence.

Many believers, however, will not die, but will survive to populate
the millennial kingdom. Jesus taught that truth in His description of the
sheep and goat judgment (Matt. 25:31ff.). The goats (the unsaved) will be
cast into hell (vv. 41–46), but to the sheep (the saved) Jesus will say,
"Come, you who are blessed of My Father, inherit the kingdom prepared
for you from the foundation of the world" (v. 34). Believers who are alive
at the Lord's second coming will live on in His earthly kingdom.

Many of those who enter the millennial kingdom alive will be
Gentiles (cf. Isa. 2:2–4; Mic. 4:1–5; Zech. 8:20–23). But the Tribulation is also
the time of Israel's national salvation, of which the prophets spoke. The
most detailed description of that event is found in Zechariah's prophecy:

"I [the Lord] will pour out on the house of David and on the inhabitants of Jerusalem, the Spirit of grace and of supplication, so that they
will look on Me whom they have pierced; and they will mourn for Him,
as one mourns for an only son, and they will weep bitterly over Him
like the bitter weeping over a firstborn. In that day there will be great
mourning in Jerusalem, like the mourning of Hadadrimmon in the
plain of Megiddo. The land will mourn, every family by itself; the family of the house of David by itself and their wives by themselves; the family of the house of Nathan by itself and their wives by themselves; the

family of the house of Levi by itself and their wives by themselves; the family of the Shimeites by itself and their wives by themselves; all the families that remain, every family by itself and their wives by themselves. In that day a fountain will be opened for the house of David and for the inhabitants of Jerusalem, for sin and for impurity. . . .

"It will come about in all the land," declares the Lord, "that two parts in it will be cut off and perish; but the third will be left in it. And I will bring the third part through the fire, refine them as silver is refined, and test them as gold is tested. They will call on My name, and I will answer them; I will say, 'They are My people,' and they will say, 'The Lord is my God.'" (Zech. 12:10–13:1, 8–9)

This is the time of which the apostle Paul spoke when he wrote "And so all Israel will be saved; just as it is written, 'The Deliverer will come from Zion, He will remove ungodliness from Jacob'" (Rom. 11:26).

Revelation 7:1–8 introduces the group of survivors (for others see 12:16–17), preserved in the midst of the maelstrom of the Tribulation, who have been redeemed for some time but, as the final fury hits, are set apart for special service and given special protection.

John's vision of this special group of people contains three features: wrath restrained, saints sealed, and Israelites identified.

WRATH RESTRAINED

After this I saw four angels standing at the four corners of the earth, holding back the four winds of the earth, so that no wind would blow on the earth or on the sea or on any tree. (7:1)

The phrases **after this** and "after these things," usually followed by some form of the verb *eidon* ("to see"), are used several times in Revelation to introduce a new vision (cf. 4:1; 7:1; 7:9; 15:5; 18:1; 19:1, "heard"). The use of **after this** in this passage signifies that the vision of the sixth seal has ended and John is about to see a new vision. It may also indicate that this new vision depicts events that come after the sixth seal chronologically. The scene now shifts from judgment on the ungodly to special protection for the godly.

As the vision unfolded, John first **saw four angels. Angels** are frequently associated in Scripture with God's judgment (cf. 8:2ff.; 9:1ff.; 11:15–19; 14:15ff.; 15:1ff.; 16:1ff.; 18:1ff.; 19:17–18; 2 Sam. 24:16–17; 2 Kings 19:35; Ps. 78:49; Matt. 13:39–42, 49–50; 16:27; 25:31; 2 Thess. 1:7–8). These **four** are given power over the elements of nature (cf. 14:18; 16:5); they are seen **standing at the four corners of the earth holding back the**

four winds of the earth (cf. Jer. 49:36; Matt. 24:31). Unsophisticated skeptics imagine that John's poetic reference to the **four corners of the earth** reflects a primitive notion that the earth is flat and square. But the phrase actually refers to the whole earth by designating the four primary points on the compass (north, south, east, and west), from which directions **the four winds** (i.e., all the winds) **of the earth** originate. Dr. Henry M. Morris comments,

> This verse has long been derided as reflecting a naive "prescientific" concept of earth structure, one that supposedly viewed the earth as flat with four corners. . . . In terms of modern technology, it is essentially equivalent to what a mariner or geologist would call the four quadrants of the compass, or the four directions. This is evident also from the mention of the "four winds" which, in common usage, would of course be the north, west, south, and east winds.
>
> Parenthetically, accurate modern geodetic measurements in recent years have proved that the earth actually does have four "corners." These are protuberances standing out from the basic "geoid," that is, the basic spherical shape of the earth. The earth is not really a perfect sphere, but is slightly flattened at the poles. Its equatorial bulge is presumably caused by the earth's axial rotation, and its four "corners" protrude from that. (*The Revelation Record* [Wheaton, Ill.: Tyndale, 1983], 126)

From their key positions on the earth, these powerful angels ensured **that no wind would blow on the earth or on the sea or on any tree.** The four winds are often associated in Scripture with God's judgment (cf. Jer. 49:36; Dan. 7:2; Hos. 13:15). For the duration of the interlude described in chapter 7 judgment will be held back as the angels turn off the essential engine of earth's atmosphere. There will be no wind, no breeze, no waves breaking on the shore, no movement of clouds in the sky; everything will be deathly still. That is an incredible display of power, since

> [the] circulation of the atmosphere is a mighty engine, driven by energy from the sun and from the earth's rotation. The tremendous powers involved in this operation become especially obvious when they are displayed in the form of great hurricanes and blizzards and tornadoes. These winds of the earth make life possible on earth through the hydrologic cycle, transporting waters inland from the ocean with which to water the earth. Yet the angels—only four of them—had turned off this gigantic engine. (Morris, *The Revelation Record*, 126)

Holding back is from *krateō*, a strong word that suggests that the winds are struggling to break free from their restraint. The angelic restraining of the wind also symbolizes the withholding of the plagues associated with the imminent trumpet judgments (8:5ff.). So the next phase of God's wrath is restrained for the moment. The winds of judgment are gathering force, soon to be released.

SAINTS SEALED

And I saw another angel ascending from the rising of the sun, having the seal of the living God; and he cried out with a loud voice to the four angels to whom it was granted to harm the earth and the sea, saying, "Do not harm the earth or the sea or the trees until we have sealed the bond-servants of our God on their foreheads." (7:2–3)

The reason for the temporary restraining of God's judgment becomes clear as John sees **another angel** in addition to the four holding back the winds. Some have identified this angel as Jesus Christ, but that is unlikely because *allos* (**another**) means another in numerical sequence, another of the same kind as the first four angels. Though Christ appeared in the Old Testament as the Angel of the Lord, He is not in essence of nature an angel. In addition, by using the plural pronoun "we" in verse 3 the fifth angel identifies with the first four in the work of sealing God's servants.

John saw the angel **ascending from the rising of the sun.** That is a poetic way of saying from the east, the point of the compass in which the sun rises. From John's perspective on the isle of Patmos, the east would be toward the land of Israel, the land where God's promised salvation came through Jesus the Messiah, and from where the twelve tribes of Israel came—members of which are about to be sealed.

The angel had with him **the seal of the living God.** *Sphragis* (**seal**) often referred to a signet ring. Kings or other officials would use such rings to stamp into wax on documents or other items, thereby affirming their authenticity and guaranteeing their security (cf. Gen. 41:42; Est. 3:10; 8:2, 8; Dan. 6:17; Matt. 27:66). A **seal** thus denoted ownership and protection (cf. John 6:27; 2 Cor. 1:22; Eph. 1:13; 4:30).

In contrast to the seals of petty earthly rulers, the seal borne by the angel was that of **the living God.** The Bible frequently identifies God as the living God (cf. 4:9–10; 10:6; 15:7; Deut. 5:26; Josh. 3:10; 1 Sam. 17:26; 2 Kings 19:4; Pss. 42:2; 84:2; Jer. 10:10; 23:36; Dan. 6:20; Hos. 1:10; Matt. 16:16; Rom. 9:26; 2 Cor. 3:3; 6:16; 1 Tim. 3:15; 4:10; Heb. 3:12; 9:14; 10:31; 12:22) to distinguish Him from the dead idols worshiped by unbelievers. His eternality guarantees that He will accomplish all His will. The most prominent false deity of the Tribulation period, Antichrist, will seal his followers (13:16–17; 14:9–11; 16:2; 19:20; 20:4), and the true and living God will seal His. Revelation 14:1 identifies the mark left by God's seal as the names of Christ and the Father.

In the Old Testament, God marked Israel with blood on their doorposts and lintels to spare them when He killed Egypt's firstborn. He marked Rahab with a scarlet cord to keep her and those with her from being killed. But the illustration that most nearly parallels the present passage comes from Ezekiel 9:3–6:

> Then the glory of the God of Israel went up from the cherub on which it had been, to the threshold of the temple. And He called to the man clothed in linen at whose loins was the writing case. The Lord said to him, "Go through the midst of the city, even through the midst of Jerusalem, and put a mark on the foreheads of the men who sigh and groan over all the abominations which are being committed in its midst." But to the others He said in my hearing, "Go through the city after him and strike; do not let your eye have pity and do not spare. Utterly slay old men, young men, maidens, little children, and women, but do not touch any man on whom is the mark."

Those with God's mark on them would be spared in the coming destruction of Jerusalem. Similarly, these servants of God whom the angel will mark with God's seal will be protected from and preserved through the judgments yet to come (cf. 9:4).

Urgently, authoritatively, the fifth angel **cried out with a loud voice to the four angels to whom it was granted to harm the earth and the sea, saying, "Do not harm the earth or the sea or the trees until we have sealed the bond-servants of our God on their foreheads."** The **harm** or damaging devastation that will come to the **earth, the sea,** and the **trees** will occur when the four angels suddenly release the judgment (symbolized by the winds) they have been restraining. But that judgment (and the trumpet and bowl judgments to follow) had to wait until the angels had **sealed the bond-servants of God on their foreheads.** That they are referred to as **bond-servants** indicates they are already redeemed. They will have remained faithful to God and the Lord Jesus, and will have probably been powerfully and effectively preaching His Word in the midst of the chaos of the first six seals. At this point they are to be protected so they can continue to proclaim the Word of God and the truth about His Son Jesus Christ during the most severe times. After the sealing is complete the judgments can begin, from which those sealed will be exempt.

Revelation 14:1–5 describes their morally pure, undefiled character and their devotion to Jesus Christ. They are the most faithful, loyal, diligent, holy servants of God during these dark days; they are the cream of the crop. They are also described as having been "purchased from among men as first fruits to God and to the Lamb" (14:4). They will also be the most effective missionaries the world has ever seen, and will be instrumental in the conversion of both their own countrymen and the nations.

ISRAELITES IDENTIFIED

And I heard the number of those who were sealed, one hundred and forty-four thousand sealed from every tribe of the sons of Israel: from the tribe of Judah, twelve thousand were sealed, from the tribe of Reuben twelve thousand, from the tribe of Gad twelve thousand, from the tribe of Asher twelve thousand, from the tribe of Naphtali twelve thousand, from the tribe of Manasseh twelve thousand, from the tribe of Simeon twelve thousand, from the tribe of Levi twelve thousand, from the tribe of Issachar twelve thousand, from the tribe of Zebulun twelve thousand, from the tribe of Joseph twelve thousand, from the tribe of Benjamin, twelve thousand were sealed. (7:4–8)

These Jewish believers and evangelists are the firstfruits of Israel, which as a nation will be redeemed before Christ returns (Zech. 12:10–13:1, 8–9; Rom. 11:26). The 144,000 are not all Jewish believers at that time, but a unique group selected to proclaim the gospel in that day (cf. 12:17; 14:1–5). Despite the plain and unambiguous declaration of the text that the **one hundred and forty-four thousand** who are to be **sealed** will come **from every tribe of the sons of Israel,** many persist in identifying them as the church. They cite several New Testament passages that allegedly identify the church as Israel to support that interpretation. But the identification of Israel with the church in those passages is tenuous and disputed. Thus, they can offer no support for such an identification in the present passage. The fact is that "no clear-cut example of the church being called 'Israel' exists in the NT or in ancient church writings until A.D. 160.... This fact is crippling to any attempt to identify Israel as the church in Rev. 7:4" (Robert L. Thomas, *Revelation 1–7: An Exegetical Commentary* [Chicago: Moody, 1992], 476). Further, "such an attempt becomes even more ridiculous because it necessitates typological interpretation that divides the church into twelve tribes to coincide with the listing of Rev. 7:5–8, even with all the irregularities in that list" (Thomas, *Revelation 1–7,* 476). The term **Israel** must be interpreted in accordance with its normal Old and New Testament usage as a reference to the physical descendants of Abraham, Isaac, and Jacob. Nor is there any exegetical reason not to interpret the numbers 144,000 and 12,000 literally.

That there were 12,000 **sealed from every tribe of the sons of Israel** speaks of God's elective purpose. Mere random human choice would not come up with such an even division. While the tribal records were lost when the Romans sacked Jerusalem in A.D. 70, God knows who belongs to each tribe. This passage also teaches that the so-called "ten lost tribes" were, in fact, never lost (cf. 21:12; Matt. 19:28; Luke 22:30; James 1:1). Instead, representatives from the ten northern tribes filtered south and intermingled with the two southern tribes (cf. 2 Chron. 30:1–11; 34:1–9) and thus were preserved.

The specific tribal names in this list raise some interesting questions. First, however, it should be noted that there is no standard way of listing the twelve tribes. There are at least nineteen different ways of listing them in the Old Testament, none of which agree with the list given here:

> In the Old Testament lists, sometimes the order of birth is followed (Gen. 29:32–35:18). At other times, it is the order of Jacob's blessing them (Gen. 49:3–27), the order of encampment (Num. 2:3–31), the order of the census before the invasion of Canaan (Num. 26:4–51), the order of blessing and cursing (Deut. 27:12–13), the order of Moses' blessing (Deut. 33:6–25), the order of "the princes" (Num. 1:5–15), the order of inheritance (Josh. 13:7–22:34), the order by the wives and concubines (1 Chron. 2:1–8:40), and the order of the gates of the city (Ezek. 48:31–34). (Thomas, *Revelation 1–7,* 479)

Although Reuben was the firstborn (Gen. 46:8), Judah is listed first. Reuben forfeited his birthright as punishment for his sexual misconduct with his father's concubine (1 Chron. 5:1). The omission of the tribe of Dan in favor of the priestly tribe of Levi is also unusual. Dan was evidently omitted due to the tribe's penchant for idolatry (cf. Deut. 29:18–21)—which was even worse than that of the rest of the nation (cf. Judg. 18; Amos 8:14). While Dan will share in the millennial blessings (Ezek. 48:1–2, 32) the tribe will not be selected for this duty nor protected during the Tribulation. Similarly, the name of Ephraim is omitted in favor of his father Joseph because Ephraim defected from the ruling house of Judah (Isa. 7:17). Also Ephraim, like Dan, was consumed with idolatry (Hos. 4:17). His brother Manasseh is included because he was the faithful son of Joseph.

This critical passage reinforces the biblical truth that God is not through with the nation of Israel (cf. Rom. 9–11). Though Israel failed in its mission to be a witness nation in the Old Testament, that will not be the case in the future. From the Jewish people will come the greatest missionary force the world has ever known. The result of their effort will be a redeemed Israel, as promised by God, and innumerable redeemed Gentiles.

Tribulation
Saints
(Revelation 7:9–17)

17

After these things I looked, and behold, a great multitude which
no one could count, from every nation and all tribes and peoples
and tongues, standing before the throne and before the Lamb,
clothed in white robes, and palm branches were in their hands;
and they cry out with a loud voice, saying, "Salvation to our God
who sits on the throne, and to the Lamb." And all the angels were
standing around the throne and around the elders and the four
living creatures; and they fell on their faces before the throne
and worshiped God, saying, "Amen, blessing and glory and wisdom and thanksgiving and honor and power and might, be to our
God forever and ever. Amen." Then one of the elders answered,
saying to me, "These who are clothed in the white robes, who are
they, and where have they come from?" I said to him, "My lord,
you know." And he said to me, "These are the ones who come out
of the great tribulation, and they have washed their robes and
made them white in the blood of the Lamb. For this reason, they
are before the throne of God; and they serve Him day and night
in His temple; and He who sits on the throne will spread His
tabernacle over them. They will hunger no more, nor thirst anymore; nor will the sun beat down on them, nor any heat; for the

Lamb in the center of the throne will be their shepherd, and will guide them to springs of the water of life; and God will wipe every tear from their eyes." (7:9–17)

There have been many times of great response to the gospel throughout history, including the church's birth on the Day of Pentecost, the Reformation in Europe in the sixteenth century, and the Great Awakening in America in the eighteenth century. During those powerful movements of God's saving grace, thousands came to faith in Jesus Christ. It has ever been the prayer of God's people that God would bring in such great harvests of souls, and often He has answered.

But there is coming in the future a worldwide response to the gospel that will far exceed any other in history and maybe all others combined. It will sweep the globe in just a few short years and produce a vast multitude of redeemed people from all the nations, making it the greatest movement of God's saving power the world will ever see.

Anticipation of that great "revival" is consistent with the fact that God is a merciful, gracious God who is by nature a Savior and desires people to be saved. First Timothy 2:4 declares that He "desires all men to be saved and to come to the knowledge of the truth." Second Peter 3:9 adds, "The Lord is not slow about His promise, as some count slowness, but is patient toward you, not wishing for any to perish but for all to come to repentance." The common biblical designation of God as Savior reflects His desire that people be saved (e.g., Ps. 106:21; Isa. 43:3, 11; 45:15, 21; 49:26; 60:16; 63:8; Hos. 13:4; Luke 1:47; 2:11; 1 Tim. 2:3; 2 Tim. 1:10; Titus 1:3; 2:10, 13; 3:4, 6; 2 Pet. 1:1).

In 1 Timothy 4:10 God is designated as the "Savior of all men, especially of believers." He is the "Savior of all men" in a temporal, physical (common grace) sense; that is, He allows sinners deserving of instant death and hell to continue to live on earth. The fact that He does not destroy them in hell immediately when they sin indicates His saving disposition. He is the Savior of believers, however, in an eternal and spiritual sense. To those who receive the gospel He gives eternal heaven and existence in its glories forever.

In the future, God will put His spiritual and eternal salvation on display at a most unexpected time. In fact, He will do so during the worst time in all of human history. It will be the time of Satan's fury, as he and his demon hosts ravage the world. It will be the time of unparalleled wickedness, as the Holy Spirit removes His restraining influence (2 Thess. 2:7). It will be the time when Antichrist's worldwide reign of terror is occurring alongside the pouring out of God's wrath and the Day of the Lord in a historically unequaled series of powerful, devastating judgments. It will be in the midst of that time of horrors and fear that God will save people to an extent previously unknown.

God's saving work during that future time will be twofold. First, it will be the time of Israel's national salvation, which Zechariah (Zech. 12:10ff.) in the Old Testament and Paul (Rom. 11:25–27) in the New Testament predicted. The firstfruits of Israel's salvation will be the 144,000 Jewish evangelists (7:1–8), who will preach the gospel both to their countrymen and to the Gentiles.

It is the salvation of those Gentiles that is in view in 7:9–17—a salvation promised in Scripture. The Abrahamic Covenant, in which God promised to bless Israel, also promised salvation to the Gentiles:

> Now the Lord said to Abram, "Go forth from your country, and from your relatives and from your father's house, to the land which I will show you; and I will make you a great nation, and I will bless you, and make your name great; and so you shall be a blessing; and I will bless those who bless you, and the one who curses you I will curse. And in you all the families of the earth shall be blessed." (Gen. 12:1–3)

God from the beginning chose Israel to be a channel through which His blessings of salvation would flow to the whole world. That truth is affirmed in many Old Testament passages. In Psalm 67 the psalmist prayed: "God be gracious to us and bless us, and cause His face to shine upon us" (v. 1). But that blessing was not to stop with them; the psalmist implored God to bless Israel so "that Your way may be known on the earth, Your salvation among all nations. . . . God blesses us, that all the ends of the earth may fear Him (vv. 2, 7)." Psalm 98:3 declares, "He has remembered His lovingkindness and His faithfulness to the house of Israel; all the ends of the earth have seen the salvation of our God." Chosen to be the instrument of God in the salvation of the nations, Israel tragically failed in that mission. The church has intervened and is that channel in this age.

In the future, God will graciously grant Israel a second opportunity to be His witness nation, and at that time they will not fail. Led by the 144,000 evangelists (cf. 7:1–8), Israel will be a light to the nations during the darkest hour of earth's history. God's promise to bless the nations of the world through Abraham's descendants will be fulfilled on a massive scale.

Speaking of that future time of Gentile salvation Isaiah wrote, "In that day . . . the nations will resort to the root of Jesse, who will stand as a signal for the peoples; and His resting place will be glorious" (Isa. 11:10). In Isaiah 49:6 God promised the Servant (the Lord Jesus Christ) that people from the nations will be added to His flock: "It is too small a thing that You should be My Servant to raise up the tribes of Jacob and to restore the preserved ones of Israel; I will also make You a light of the nations so that My salvation may reach to the end of the earth." In Isaiah 45:22 God commands, "Turn to Me and be saved, all the ends of the earth." Isaiah 52:10 adds, "The Lord has bared His holy arm in the sight of all the nations, that all the ends of the earth may see the salvation of our God." In a familiar passage, quoted by Peter in his sermon on the Day of Pentecost (Acts 2:17–21), Joel also speaks of the future salvation of the nations:

> It will come about after this that I will pour out My Spirit on all mankind; and your sons and daughters will prophesy, your old men will dream dreams, your young men will see visions. Even on the male and female servants I will pour out My Spirit in those days. I will display wonders in the sky and on the earth, blood, fire and columns of smoke. The sun will be turned into darkness and the moon into blood before the great and awesome day of the Lord comes. And it will come about that whoever calls on the name of the Lord will be delivered. (Joel 2:28–32)

Jesus taught that before His return at the end of the Tribulation "this gospel of the kingdom shall be preached in the whole world for a witness to all the nations, and then the end will come" (Matt. 24:14). John 11:50–52 records one of the most unusual prophecies in Scripture (because it was revealed through a bitter enemy of Christ, the high priest Caiaphas):

> "It is expedient for you that one man die for the people, and that the whole nation not perish." Now he did not say this on his own initiative, but being high priest that year, he prophesied that Jesus was going to die for the nation, and not for the nation only, but in order that He might also gather together into one the children of God who are scattered abroad.

"Is God the God of Jews only? Is He not the God of Gentiles also?" asked Paul. Then, answering his own rhetorical question, the apostle added, "Yes, of Gentiles also" (Rom. 3:29).

Revelation 7:9–17 describes that vast multitude of people from all the nations of the world who will be saved during the coming time of tribulation. This could include those of Israel who are saved during the preaching of the 144,000. There is nothing in the terminology of the passage that excludes Jews. Rather, the phrase "every nation" could include them.

Eight key words introduce this group: their description, location, action, association, origination, function, protection, and provision.

DESCRIPTION

After these things I looked, and behold, a great multitude which no one could count, from every nation and all tribes and peoples and tongues . . . clothed in white robes, and palm branches were in their hands; (7:9a, c)

As it does throughout Revelation (cf. 4:1; 7:1; 15:5; 18:1; 19:1), the phrase **after these things** introduces a new vision, distinct from the one in 7:1–8. The exclamation **behold** reveals this vision to be a shocking, startling one to John. The aged apostle, the last survivor of the twelve, must have felt isolated and alone in his exile on the isle of Patmos. He had seen Gentiles come to Christ, through his own ministry in Asia Minor and the ministries of Paul, Timothy, Titus, and others. Gentile churches had been founded, yet they were for the most part small, beleaguered, and persecuted. Further, five of the seven churches in Asia Minor to which the Lord wrote earlier in this great book (2:1–3:22) had fallen into serious and threatening patterns of sin. To see in his vision a vast, triumphant multitude of the redeemed singing praises to God was a profoundly thrilling experience for John, who had seen the severe failures of the churches in Asia Minor and the threats of judgment from the Lord (chaps. 2–3). This vision must surely have renewed his joy and hope, as he realized that the church would survive and, in the end, people from the nations would be saved in great numbers.

That the group introduced in this passage is distinct from the 144,000 (7:1–8) is evident from several considerations. First, as noted above, the phrase **after these things** introduces a new vision. Second, this group is described as **a great multitude which no one could count;** no specific number is mentioned. Third, the 144,000 came from the twelve tribes of Israel (7:4–8); this group came **from every nation and all tribes and peoples and tongues.** That phrase describes people from every culture, descent, race, and language (cf. 5:9). It depicts the mass of humanity, crossing all barriers and dividing lines. Finally, the 144,000 are beyond the reach of persecutors because they are sealed for protection from persecution on earth (7:3); this group is beyond the reach of any persecutors because it is already in heaven. Verse 14 describes and identifies them: "These are the ones who come out of the great tribulation, and they have washed their robes and made them white in the blood of the Lamb."

The redeemed were **clothed in white robes.** *Leukos* (**white**) describes a dazzling, brilliant, shining white. In ancient times, such clothing was worn for festivals and celebrations. **Robes** is from *stolē*, which depicts a long, full-length robe. These long, radiant white robes are the same ones worn by the martyrs in 6:9–11. That fact suggests that the group in view in this passage is part of that earlier group of martyred believers. As the Tribulation wears on, the number of martyrs will increase, as will the number of believers who die naturally or violently, eventually accumulating into the vast, uncountable multitude depicted in heaven in this passage. The **white robes** are symbolic rather than literal, since the saints do not as yet have their resurrected bodies (6:9; 20:4). The robes picture especially their exaltation, victory, and rejoicing. Such white robes, also symbolic of holiness, are reserved for Christ (Matt. 17:2; Mark 9:3), angels (Matt. 28:3; Mark 16:5), and the glorified church (19:8, 14).

The saints also held **palm branches . . . in their hands. Palm branches** are associated in Scripture with celebration, deliverance, and joy. They were especially prominent during the Feast of Tabernacles, the Old Testament commemorative celebration of God's provision for Israel during their wilderness wandering (Lev. 23:40), being employed in the construction of the booths the people lived in during that feast (Neh. 8:15–17). During Jesus' triumphal entry the joyous crowd waved palm branches as they welcomed Him into Jerusalem, shouting, "Hosanna! Blessed is He who comes in the name of the Lord, even the King of Israel" (John 12:13). The palm branches in the hands of these redeemed saints are a fitting celebrative symbol of the unequaled provision of salvation from the world, Satan, Antichrist, sin, death, and hell provided for them by the Lord Jesus Christ.

LOCATION

standing before the throne and before the Lamb (7:9*b*)

John saw this vast, uncountable crowd of victorious, joyous saints **standing before the throne** of God in heaven (cf. 4:2). They were also in the presence of the **Lamb,** whom John saw in his earlier vision standing near the throne (5:6). Many had suffered death at the hands of Antichrist (cf. 20:4, where "beheaded" speaks of violent death) for refusing to take his mark or worship him. They are no longer seen under the altar praying for divine vengeance (cf. 6:9–11), which has already begun, but standing triumphantly before the throne of God, "the spirits of the righteous made perfect" (Heb. 12:23).

ACTION

and they cry out with a loud voice, saying, "Salvation to our God who sits on the throne, and to the Lamb." (7:10)

As do all in heaven, the redeemed martyrs constantly **cry out with a loud voice** (cf. 5:12; 6:10; 11:12, 15; 12:10; 14:7; 16:1; 19:1; 21:3) in joyous, exuberant worship. The Lord desires loud praise (Pss. 66:1; 100:1). Their prayers of intercession have ceased and they are glorifying and praising God, the One responsible for their triumph. Salvation is the theme of their worship, as it is throughout Revelation. In his vision of God's throne recorded in 5:8–10 John noted:

> When He had taken the book, the four living creatures and the twenty-four elders fell down before the Lamb, each one holding a harp and golden bowls full of incense, which are the prayers of the saints. And they sang a new song, saying, "Worthy are You to take the book and to break its seals; for You were slain, and purchased for God with Your blood men from every tribe and tongue and people and nation. You have made them to be a kingdom and priests to our God; and they will reign upon the earth."

In 12:10 John "heard a loud voice in heaven, saying, 'Now the salvation, and the power, and the kingdom of our God and the authority of His Christ have come, for the accuser of our brethren has been thrown down, he who accuses them before our God day and night.'" In 19:1 John wrote, "After these things I heard something like a loud voice of a great multitude in heaven, saying, 'Hallelujah! Salvation and glory and power belong to our God.'" As in the worship recorded in 5:13ff., the occupation of those in heaven is continual, eternal praise of the Almighty God (whose sovereignty is indicated by the comment that He **sits on the throne**) and the **Lamb.** They identify God as **our God,** claiming, as do all the redeemed, God as their own.

ASSOCIATION

And all the angels were standing around the throne and around the elders and the four living creatures; and they fell on their faces before the throne and worshiped God, saying, "Amen, blessing and glory and wisdom and thanksgiving and honor and power and might, be to our God forever and ever. Amen." (7:11–12)

The innumerable believers before God's throne were not alone in their loud worship. The first group identified along with them in praise was **all the angels** who **were standing around the throne.** Their number, too, was uncountable to John. In his earlier vision of God's throne, John could only describe the number of angels as "myriads of myriads, and thousands of thousands" (5:11). Deuteronomy 33:2 reads,

"The Lord came from Sinai, and dawned on them from Seir; He shone forth from Mount Paran, and He came from the midst of ten thousand holy ones." In a vision of God on His heavenly throne Daniel saw "thousands upon thousands ... attending Him, and myriads upon myriads ... standing before Him" (Dan. 7:10). The writer of Hebrews also saw "myriads of angels" in heaven (Heb. 12:22). Jude 14 speaks of "many thousands of His holy ones." That the angels joined the spirits of heavenly saints in praising God is not surprising, since they were created for the purpose of worshiping and serving Him (Ps. 103:20; Col. 1:16).

That wretched, unworthy sinners can freely mingle with the pristine, holy angels is a triumph of God's grace that makes the angels glorify God all the more. These people had turned their backs on God, rejected the gospel (or in some cases never heard it), and not being part of the church, they had missed the Rapture. So in the midst of God's wrath and judgment during the Tribulation, He will remember mercy and gather them to Himself. The wonder of God's gracious salvation (a subject about which angels are curious, having never experienced it themselves; cf. 1 Pet. 1:12) displayed before the angels stimulates them to praise and worship Him (cf. Eph. 3:8–10). Though angels do not experience salvation, they rejoice at the salvation of humans (Luke 15:7, 10).

The angels ringing God's glorious, magnificent throne (cf. 4:1–6, 5:1, 6) also surrounded the other two groups involved in worshiping God, **the elders and the four living creatures.** The twenty-four **elders** are best viewed as representatives of the raptured church (see the discussion in chapter 11 of this volume). In 5:8–10 they sang the song of redemption, while here they are seen praising the God of redemption. As noted in chapter 11's discussion, the **four living creatures** are cherubim, an exalted order of angels. These two groups frequently appear together (cf. 5:6, 8, 11, 14; 14:3; 19:4).

Overwhelmed by God's majesty, glory, and the splendor surrounding His throne, all present **fell on their faces before the throne and worshiped God.** It is the appropriate reaction of all creatures, including those who are holy and perfect, to prostrate themselves in humble adoration before the unequaled glorious and majestic presence of the only true and holy God (cf. 4:10; 5:8, 14; 11:16; 19:4; Gen. 17:3; Lev. 9:24; Josh. 5:14; Judg. 13:20; 1 Kings 18:39; 2 Chron. 20:18; Ezek. 1:28; 3:23; Matt. 17:6; Phil. 2:9–10). Then, recognizing God's sovereignty, supremacy, holiness, and majesty, the worshipers in John's vision utter a benediction bracketed front and back with the solemn affirmation **amen,** which means, "so let it be." Their prayer is that **blessing and glory and wisdom and thanksgiving and honor and power and might be** attributed **to our God forever and ever** (cf. 4:11; 5:12).

Worship is the constant occupation of those in heaven. There was praise in chapters 4 and 5, before the seals were opened and judgment began. Now, as the final climactic judgments approach, there is praise again, praise not for judgment anticipated but for judgment realized. The mounting crescendo of praise began with the four living creatures, then grew as the twenty-four elders, the angels, and the ever-increasing number of tribulation martyrs joined in. Finally, all heaven rings with praise to God.

The phrase **forever and ever** indicates, as did the doxology of 5:13ff., that this praise is not temporary or momentary, but will continue eternally. What is described here is worship that will never cease through all of endless eternity.

ORIGINATION

Then one of the elders answered, saying to me, "These who are clothed in the white robes, who are they, and where have they come from?" I said to him, "My lord, you know." And he said to me, "These are the ones who come out of the great tribulation, and they have washed their robes and made them white in the blood of the Lamb." (7:13–14)

John became an active participant in the vision when one of the twenty-four **elders** asked him, **"These who are clothed in the white robes, who are they, and where have they come from?"** The elder was not asking for information because he did not know, but to underscore his point both for John and all readers of John's record. Dr. Robert Thomas comments on the significance of the elder's question: "This exemplifies the dialogue format used from time to time to convey an explanation of a vision (cf. Jer. 1:11, 13; Amos 7:8; 8:2; Zech. 4:2, 5). This tool shows that visions were not given for the purpose of spectacular displays, but to convey revelation, the details of which were not to be missed (*Revelation 1–7: An Exegetical Commentary* [Chicago: Moody, 1992], 493).

The elder's question specifies and emphasizes the truth that people will be saved during the time of tribulation. Some may doubt that, given the intensity of God's judgments during that terrible time. And there will come a point in the Tribulation when those who continue to reject the gospel will be confirmed in that rejection. Revelation 9:20–21 reads, "And the rest of mankind, who were not killed by these plagues, did not repent of the works of their hands, so as not to worship demons, and the idols of gold and of silver and of brass and of stone and of wood, which can neither see nor hear nor walk; and they did not repent of their murders nor of their sorceries nor of their immorality nor of their thefts."

Revelation 16:9 reiterates that truth: "Men were scorched with fierce heat; and they blasphemed the name of God who has the power over these plagues, and they did not repent so as to give Him glory." Paul wrote of those who will "perish, because they did not receive the love of the truth so as to be saved. For this reason God will send upon them a deluding influence so that they will believe what is false, in order that they all may be judged who did not believe the truth, but took pleasure in wickedness" (2 Thess. 2:10–12).

Some argue that the redeemed Tribulation martyrs and others seen in heaven will be people who never lived during the church age. That cannot be true, however, for the obvious reason that since the Tribulation lasts seven years (Dan. 9:27) and the Great Tribulation half of that (Rev. 11:2–3; 12:6; 13:5), they would all have to be younger than seven years of age. Others hold that these are people who never heard the gospel during their lifetimes and received the opportunity to repent after death. That interpretation is also impossible, "inasmuch as it is appointed for men to die once and after this comes judgment" (Heb. 9:27; cf. John 8:21–24). People have the opportunity to repent and believe the gospel only during their lifetimes; these are people whose lifetimes will extend past the Rapture into the Tribulation.

John's bewildered reply to the elder is emphatic: **"My lord, you know,"** and is both a confession of ignorance and a request for further revelation. John's calling the elder **lord** did not ascribe deity to him; he was using the word *kurios* (**lord**) in the common manner as a title of great respect. This is the sort of respect John shows heavenly beings in 19:10 and 22:8–9. John had been taught by the Lord that few would be saved (Matt. 7:13–14; 22:14) and had seen the churches in decline, so that this great crowd of the redeemed may have been incomprehensible to him. The heavenly elder's reply confirmed the identity of these believers as **the ones who come out of the great tribulation** (cf. Matt. 24:21). They lived into it, were redeemed during it, and have now come out of it through death by violence, natural causes, and martyrdom. The phrase **the ones who come out** translates the present durative participle of the verb *erchomai*. It depicts a prolonged process; this group will keep growing as people keep dying during the Tribulation (especially the last half, the **great tribulation**). Therefore the Rapture of the church is not in view in this verse, since it is a single, instantaneous, and sudden event (cf. 1 Cor. 15:51–52). The elder's description of these believers as having **come out of the great tribulation** clearly distinguishes them from any other group of redeemed people in history. The term **great tribulation** refers to a specific time in the future that is unique in all of human history. It refers to the future eschatological day of divine judgment immediately before Jesus Christ returns to establish His earthly kingdom. All the judgments described during this time, from the sixth seal through the trumpet and bowl judgments, have no parallel in human history. Never has such worldwide devastation happened. The term **great tribulation** cannot describe the destruction of Jerusalem in A.D. 70 or any other historical event. This term must describe a future time of divine punishment on the whole fallen world; the "great day of [the] wrath" of God and the Lamb (6:17). Jesus Himself coined the phrase "great tribulation" (Matt. 24:21) and limited it to the second half of Daniel's Seventieth Week (Matt. 24:13–22; Mark 13:14–20; cf. Dan. 9:27). Its limit will be forty-two months or 1,260 days (11:2–3). Of this period Thomas writes,

> It is the superlatively great crisis of trial through which all rebels against God must pass just before Christ's second coming. The servants of God will not suffer the direct effects of God's wrath. They will be untouched by it (Caird). The saints on earth will not be exempt from the ire of God's enemies during this period, however. During both the Great Tribulation and the three-and-one-half years of tribulation before it, they will bear the brunt of suffering caused by anti-God animosities. The intensity of persecution will be a marked increase over that experienced before this end-time arrives and will increase again when the seven-year period reaches its midpoint. Some will have already been martyred by the end of the sixth seal (cf. 6:9–11) and many more persecuted in other ways. (*Revelation 1–7*, 497)

If these believers were part of the church, why would the elder not have so identified them? There would appear to be little reason to distinguish this group from others in the church if the church is on earth both before and during the Tribulation. If that were the case, the elder could simply have referred to them as the church.

The elder further described the redeemed and heavenly Tribulation believers as to how they gained the privilege of being in the presence of God and the holy angels. It is because they are **clothed in the white robes,** which **they have washed** and made **white in the blood of the Lamb.** Their dazzling, brilliant **white robes** were first mentioned in verse 9, where they primarily symbolized celebration, victory, and exaltation; here they primarily emphasize righteousness, holiness, and purity. Soiled garments in Scripture symbolize the defilement of sin (cf. Isa. 64:6; Zech. 3:3), and salvation is often pictured as a washing (cf. 22:14; Ps. 51:7; Isa. 1:18; Titus 3:5). That anything could be cleansed by washing it in blood seems strange to consider, but not to those who are familiar with the Old Testament. To them such a washing was required for spiritual cleansing; there had to be a blood sacrifice to cleanse people from their sins. The blood of the Old Testament animal sacrifices did not provide that cleansing from sin (Heb. 10:4), but pictured the need for a sacrifice that could—the sacrifice that would once for all cleanse from sin; **the blood of the Lamb.** That is a frequent metaphor in Scripture for Christ's sacrificial death on the cross which provided cleansing from sin for every believing sinner in every age (cf. 1:5; 5:9; 12:11; Matt. 26:28; Acts 20:28; Rom. 3:25; 5:9; Eph. 1:7; 2:13; Col. 1:20; Heb. 9:12–14; 10:19; 13:12; 1 Pet. 1:2, 19; 1 John 1:7). Christ's substitutionary death atoned for the Tribulation believers' sins, and by repentant faith they were justified and reconciled to God (Rom. 5:10; 2 Cor. 5:18–21).

FUNCTION

For this reason, they are before the throne of God; and they serve Him day and night in His temple; (7:15a)

The **reason** these Tribulation believers were allowed to stand **before the throne of God** is that they were purified and cleansed from their sins by the sacrifice of the Lamb of God on their behalf. They were thus fitted for the presence of God that they might **serve Him day and night.** Serve is from *latreuō*, a word often used to describe priestly service (cf. Luke 2:37; Heb. 8:5; 13:10); they were rendering a "spiritual service of worship" (Rom. 12:1) to God. **Day and night** is an idiomatic way to indicate their continuous occupation; there is no actual night and day in God's eternal heaven (22:3–5). The location of that service is **in His temple** (cf. 11:19; 14:15, 17; 15:5–8; 16:1, 17). There is currently a temple in heaven, and there will be one on earth during the millennial kingdom of Christ on earth (cf. Ezek. 40–48). In the eternal state, however, there will no longer be a need for a temple, "for the Lord God the Almighty and the Lamb are its temple" (Rev. 21:22). The heavenly temple currently is the holy domain where God's presence dwells outside the fallen universe, but that will be unnecessary in the new heavens and new earth where sin has been forever done away with. There will no longer be a temple building, because God will occupy all places, and all believers everywhere throughout the eternal state will continue to worship and serve Him forever.

PROTECTION

and He who sits on the throne will spread His tabernacle over them. (7:15b)

In a wonderful, comforting picture, God, described as **He who sits on the throne** (cf. 4:1–3; 5:1, 13; 7:10), promises to **spread** the

232

tabernacle, or tent (cf. 21:3), of His Shechinah presence over these persecuted believers. **Tabernacle** is a word John likes to use (cf. 13:6; 15:5; 21:3; the related verb translated *dwelt* appears in John 1:14) which reflects the sheltering presence of the Lord. It corresponds to the Old Testament promises of God's protective presence (cf. Lev. 26:11–12; Ezek. 37:27; Zech. 2:10–11; 8:3, 8). These believers will have witnessed unspeakable suffering and indescribable horrors as God's judgments were poured out on the world. They will have suffered terrible persecution at the hands of Antichrist and his followers. But when they enter God's presence, they will come to a heavenly sanctuary, the most secure place. There they will receive shelter from the terrors of the fallen world that are to come as God continues to unleash His devastating and destructive judgments.

PROVISION

They will hunger no more, nor thirst anymore; nor will the sun beat down on them, nor any heat; for the Lamb in the center of the throne will be their shepherd, and will guide them to springs of the water of life; and God will wipe every tear from their eyes. (7:16–17)

This comforting promise of further provision is drawn from and almost identical to the words of Isaiah 49:10. As they experienced the horrors of the Tribulation, these sufferers of the Great Tribulation had endured **hunger, thirst,** and scorching heat as **the sun beat down on them,** a phenomenon which will occur in the Tribulation (16:9). But all the tormenting physical and spiritual elements of earthly life they will experience no longer, but rather will enjoy eternal satisfaction, **for the Lamb in the center of the throne** (cf. 5:6) **will be their shepherd, and will guide them to springs of the water of life; and God will wipe every tear from their eyes.** The picture of God as the Shepherd of His people is one of the most beloved and common in the Old Testament (cf. Pss. 23; 80:1; Isa. 40:11; Ezek. 34:23), and Jesus is depicted as the Shepherd of His people in the New Testament (John 10:11ff.; Heb. 13:20; 1 Pet. 2:25; 5:4). Interestingly, the other three uses of *poimainō* **(shepherd)** in Revelation (2:27; 12:5; 19:15; "rule" or "shepherd" in all three cases) reveal Christ in a destroying mode, crushing sinners with a rod of iron, as in Psalm 2:9. The Great Shepherd **will guide** His flock **to springs of the water of life** (cf. 21:6; 22:1, 17). He will also **wipe every tear from their eyes** (cf. 21:4; Isa. 25:8), for in heaven there will be no pain, sorrow, or suffering to cause them.

In this age when Christianity is under siege on all sides, seemingly losing its grip on divine truth and apparently headed for defeat, it is comforting to be reassured of the ultimate triumph of God's saving grace. In the midst of an even worse situation in the future before Christ's return, God will redeem His people. That thought should bring present-day believers great comfort, and motivate all to praise God for the greatness of His redemptive plan. And ultimately, in the eternal state, all these promises will come true for all believers.

The Seventh Seal
(Revelation 8:1–5)

18

When the Lamb broke the seventh seal, there was silence in heaven for about half an hour. And I saw the seven angels who stand before God, and seven trumpets were given to them. Another angel came and stood at the altar, holding a golden censer; and much incense was given to him, so that he might add it to the prayers of all the saints on the golden altar which was before the throne. And the smoke of the incense, with the prayers of the saints, went up before God out of the angel's hand. Then the angel took the censer and filled it with the fire of the altar, and threw it to the earth; and there followed peals of thunder and sounds and flashes of lightning and an earthquake. (8:1–5)

The future Day of the Lord will be the climactic time of judgment that ends man's day and Satan's rule on earth. During that time, God will take back the earth in a final holocaust of wholesale destruction. The first five seals (false peace, war, famine, death, and vengeance) describe the preliminary judgments leading to the full outpouring of divine wrath during the Day of the Lord. As horrifying as those preliminary judgments are, they pale before the terrors of the sixth seal, which marks the beginning of the Day of the Lord. So terrifying are the judgments of the sixth seal that people are finally forced to acknowledge God as the source of the calamities. At that point they will cry "to the mountains and to the rocks, 'Fall on us and hide us from the presence of Him who sits on the throne, and from the wrath of the Lamb; for the great day of their wrath has come, and who is able to stand?'" (6:16–17).

When the Lamb opens the seventh and last seal on the little scroll that was the title deed to the earth (5:1), the judgments of the Day of the Lord will intensify and expand dramatically. This final seal contains within it the full sweep of the remaining divine judgments of the time of the Great Tribulation, including the trumpet and bowl judgments. Though some believe the events of the trumpet and bowl judgments happen simultaneously with those of the sixth seal, it seems better to understand them as telescoping out of each other sequentially. That the seventh seal contains the seven trumpet judgments seems clear, since there is no description of judgment in the seventh seal, but an anticipation of severe judgment followed immediately in the text by the seven trumpet judgments. In a similar manner, the seventh trumpet does not describe a judgment (10:7; 11:15–17), but rather contains the anticipation of heavenly rejoicing over the judgment to come, which will lead to the final destruction and establishment of the rule of the Lord Jesus Christ. As 10:7 indicates, the seventh trumpet is the "finish." Chapter 15 verse 1 makes clear that the seventh trumpet, which finishes the work of judgment, contains the final fury of God's wrath, which the pouring out of seven plague judgments pictures: "Then I saw another sign in heaven, great and marvelous, seven angels who had seven plagues, which are the last, because in them the wrath of God is finished." Chapter 16, verse 1, identifies these seven plagues as "seven bowls of the wrath of God." They are then described in detail in the remainder of chapter 16 (vv. 2–21).

The progressive judgments within the seventh seal will take place over an indefinite period of time; the effects of the fifth trumpet, for example, will last for five months (9:10). While the exact timetable for the trumpet and bowl judgments is not revealed, their escalating devastation indicates that they all occur during the last half of the Tribulation. Therefore, the seventh seal encompasses all of God's final wrath up to the triumphant return of the Lord Jesus Christ in glory.

Four key words may be used to describe the events associated with the opening of the seventh seal: silence, sounding, supplication, and storm.

SILENCE

When the Lamb broke the seventh seal, there was silence in heaven for about half an hour. (8:1)

As the rightful heir to the universe, **the Lamb** took the scroll (the title deed to the earth) from the Father's hand (5:7). As He unrolled it and broke the first six seals, divine judgments were poured out on the earth. But when He **broke the seventh seal** a unique response occurred: **there was silence in heaven for about half an hour.** A review of the visions up to this point makes it clear that John had heard a good deal of noise in heaven. Emanating from God's throne were "sounds and peals of thunder" (4:5). "The four living creatures ... [did] not cease to say, 'Holy, holy, holy is the Lord God, the Almighty, who was and who is and who is to come'" (4:8), while the twenty-four elders added their song of praise (4:11). In 5:2 John heard a "strong angel proclaiming with a loud voice, 'Who is worthy to open the book and to break its seals?'" In response to the Lamb's taking of the title deed to the earth (5:5–7), first the four living creatures and the twenty-four elders (5:9–10), then an innumerable host of angels (5:11–12), and finally all of creation (5:13) joined in praising God. When the Lamb opened the first seal, John "heard one of the four living creatures saying as with a voice of thunder, 'Come'" (6:1)—as he would when the second (6:3), third (6:5), and fourth (6:7) seals were opened. With the opening of the fifth seal came the cries of the martyrs for vengeance (6:9–10), while the breaking of the sixth seal brought the loud roar of a powerful earthquake (6:12). In the interlude between the sixth and seventh seals, an angel "cried out with a loud voice to the four angels to whom it was granted to harm the earth and the sea, saying, 'Do not harm the earth or the sea or the trees until we have sealed the bond-servants of our God on their forchcads'" (7:2–3). Later in that interlude John saw

> a great multitude which no one could count, from every nation and all tribes and peoples and tongues, standing before the throne and before the Lamb, clothed in white robes, and palm branches were in their hands; and they [cried] out with a loud voice, saying, "Salvation to our God who sits on the throne, and to the Lamb." And all the angels were standing around the throne and around the elders and the four living creatures; and they fell on their faces before the throne and worshiped God, saying, "Amen, blessing and glory and wisdom and thanksgiving and honor and power and might, be to our God forever and ever. Amen." (7:9–13)

But after all that loudness, as the full fury of the final judgments is about to be released, **silence** falls on the heavenly scene. The implication is that when the judgment about to happen becomes visible as the seventh seal is broken and the scroll unrolled, both the redeemed and the angels are reduced to silence in anticipation of the grim reality of the destruction they see written on the scroll. The **half an hour** of silence is the calm before the storm. It is the silence of foreboding, of intense expectation, of awe at what God is about to do.

And silence is the only proper response to such divine judgment. In Psalm 76:8–9 the psalmist wrote, "The earth feared and was still when God arose to judgment." Habakkuk declared, "The Lord is in His holy temple. Let all the earth be silent before Him" (Hab. 2:20). "Be silent before the Lord God!" exhorted Zephaniah, "for the day of the Lord is near" (Zeph. 1:7). Zechariah 2:13 commands, "Be silent, all flesh, before the Lord; for He is aroused from His holy habitation."

While eternal heaven has no time, the apostle John who is seeing the vision does. Each minute of that half hour of silence must have increased the sense of agonizing suspense for John. Heaven, which had resounded with loud praises from the vast crowd of redeemed people and angels, became deathly still. The hour of God's final judgment had come—the hour when the saints will be vindicated, sin punished, Satan vanquished, and Christ exalted. The greatest event since the Fall is about to take place and all heaven is seen waiting in suspenseful expectancy.

SOUNDING

And I saw the seven angels who stand before God, and seven trumpets were given to them. (8:2)

Following the half hour of heaven's silence, John experienced a new feature of the seventh seal, namely **the seven angels who stand before God.** The use of the definite article appears to set them apart as a unique group, which some have called the "presence angels." The verb translated **stand** is in the perfect tense, which indicates that they were in the presence of God and had been there for a time. Scripture describes various ranks and orders of angels, such as cherubim (Gen. 3:24), seraphim (Isa. 6:2), archangels (1 Thess. 4:16; Jude 9), thrones, dominions, rulers, authorities (Col. 1:16), and powers (Eph. 6:12). These seven appear to be one such order of high-ranking angels. Gabriel, who appeared to Zacharias and Mary, may have been one of them, since he identified himself to Zacharias as "Gabriel, who stands in the presence of God" (Luke 1:19).

As John watched, **seven trumpets were given to** these angels, in preparation for the trumpet judgments that will shortly follow. As they did in the seal judgments (6:1,3,5,6,7) and will in the bowl judgments (16:2,3,4,8, 10,12,17), angels participate in the trumpet judgments. That involvement is consistent with the teaching of Jesus that angels will play an important role in God's eschatological judgments (e.g., Matt. 13:39–41,49–50; 16:27; 25:31).

Trumpets are the most significant musical instruments in Scripture, being associated with many different events. In the Old Testament, trumpets were used to summon the congregation of Israel (Num. 10:2), to sound the alarm in time of war (Num. 10:9; 2 Chron. 13:12; Ezek. 33:3), at religious feasts (Num. 10:10; Ps. 81:3), to announce news (1 Sam. 13:3), to acclaim new kings (1 Kings 1:34, 39), and in worship (1 Chron. 16:6, 42; 2 Chron. 5:12–13). Zephaniah 1:14–16 associates trumpets with the Day of the Lord. The New Testament teaches that a trumpet will announce the Rapture (1 Cor. 15:52; 1 Thess. 4;16) and this chapter associates them with the judgments of that Day (8:6ff.).

Each of the seven trumpets unleashes a specific judgment of greater intensity than the first six seals, but not as destructive as the seven bowls (16:1–21). The first four trumpets destroy the earth's ecology (8:6–12), the next two produce demonic destruction of humanity (8:13; 9:1–11, 13–19), and the seventh trumpet introduces the final outpouring of God's wrath contained in the seven bowl judgments.

When the first angel blew his trumpet, "a third of the earth was burned up, and a third of the trees were burned up, and all the green grass was burned up" (8:7). At the sounding of the second trumpet, "a third of the sea became blood" (8:8). The blowing of the third trumpet destroyed "a third of the rivers and...the springs of waters" (8:10). When the fourth angel blew his trumpet, "a third of the sun ... moon and ...stars were struck" (8:12). At the sounding of the fifth trumpet, John saw demons being belched out of hell to torment humanity (9:1–6). When the sixth trumpet sounded, John saw four powerful demons "who had been prepared for the hour and day and month and year, [and] were released, so that they would kill a third of mankind" (9:13–15). And with the sounding of the seventh trumpet (11:15) came the unleashing of the seven bowl judgments more severe than anything before them (16:2–21).

Having been introduced and given their trumpets, the seven angels did not immediately blow them. They had to wait for other important events to transpire.

SUPPLICATION

Another angel came and stood at the altar, holding a golden censer; and much incense was given to him, so that he might add it to the prayers of all the saints on the golden altar which was before the throne. And the smoke of the incense, with the prayers of the saints, went up before God out of the angel's hand. (8:3–4)

John's attention was drawn from the seven angels with their trumpets to another figure. As he watched, **another angel came and stood at the altar** of incense (cf. 6:9). Because of his priestly work, some identify him as the Lord Jesus Christ. That identification is unlikely, however, for several reasons. First, Christ is already identified in the heavenly scene as the Lamb (5:6; 6:1; 7:17), distinguishing Him from this angel. Second, while the pre-incarnate Christ appeared as the Angel of the Lord in the Old Testament, Jesus is nowhere identified as an angel in the New Testament. Third, the reference in verse 2 to the seven actual angels defines the meaning of the term in this context. The angel in verse 3 is described as **another** (*allos;* another of the same kind; cf. 7:2) angel like those in verse 2. Finally, everywhere He appears in Revelation, Jesus is clearly identified. He is called "the faithful witness, the firstborn of the dead, and the ruler of the kings of the earth" (1:5), the son of man (1:13), the first and the last (1:17), the living One (1:18), the Son of God (2:18), "He who is holy, who is true" (3:7), "the Amen, the faithful and true Witness, the Beginning of the creation of God" (3:14), "the Lion that is from the tribe of Judah, the Root of David" (5:5), the Lamb (6:1, 16; 7:17; 8:1), Faithful and True (19:11), the Word of God (19:13), and "King of Kings, and Lord of Lords" (19:16). If He were the One at the altar, it is reasonable to assume that He would be specifically identified.

John notes that the angel **came and stood at the altar** (cf. v. 5). That altar is the heavenly counterpart to the altar of incense in the temple, which also was made with gold (Ex. 30:3). It was the same golden incense altar seen by Isaiah in his vision (Isa. 6:6) and by Ezekiel (cf. Ezek. 10:2). The further description of this altar as **before the throne** assures John's readers that the altar of incense was the earthly counterpart to this heavenly incense altar. That is evident because the altar of incense in the tabernacle and the temple was the nearest thing to the Holy of Holies where God's glory dwelt (Ex. 30:6). Consistent with that identification is that fact that the angel held in his hand **a golden censer,** or firepan. In the Old Testament era, the priests would twice daily (morning and evening) take hot, fiery coals from the brazen altar (where sacrifices were offered) and transport them into the Holy Place to the incense altar (Ex. 30:7, 8; 2 Chron. 29:11; cf. 1 Kings 7:50; 2 Kings 25:15; Jer. 52:18–19). They then ignited the incense, which rose toward heaven, emblematic of the prayers of the saints (cf. 5:8). A New Testament illustration of this comes from the story of Zacharias, the father of John the Baptist: "Now it happened that while he was performing his priestly service before God in the appointed order of his division, according to the custom of the priestly office, he was chosen by lot to enter the temple of the Lord [the Holy Place] and burn incense. And the whole multitude of the people were in prayer outside at the hour of the incense offering"

(Luke 1:8–10). While the people stood outside praying, Zacharias burned incense inside, symbolizing the ascending of those prayers to God.

The angel took the **much incense** (symbolizing the multiplied prayers of God's people; 5:8; 6:9–11) that **was given to him,** perhaps by God. Though it does not say who gave the angel the incense, the verb *didōmi* (**was given**) frequently in Revelation refers to something given by God (e.g., 6:2, 4, 8, 11; 7:2, 9:1, 3, 5; 11:1, 2; 13:5, 7, 14, 15; 16:8; 19:8; 20:4). The purpose of the angel's being given the **incense** was **so that he might add it to the prayers of all the saints** already rising from the altar. Those prayers were for Satan to be destroyed, sin to be defeated, their deaths to be avenged (cf. 6:9–11), and Christ to come. As the angel added his incense to that already burning on the altar, the **smoke of the incense, with the prayers of the saints, went up before God out of the angel's hand.** These are undoubtedly the cries of believers in the Great Tribulation against their persecutors and all who blaspheme God and Christ in that time. Their prayers, affirmed by the heavenly incense which God has provided, show that He is in agreement with the cries of the saints as they come into His presence, from which the seven trumpet judgments will be released. There is a sense of anticipation as these prayers rise before God. They will shortly be answered; God's wrath and His people's prayers are connected. The question of 6:10, "How long?" is about to be answered.

Storm

Then the angel took the censer and filled it with the fire of the altar, and threw it to the earth; and there followed peals of thunder and sounds and flashes of lightning and an earthquake. (8:5)

Heaven's half hour of silence is abruptly shattered and judgment resumes as a divine firestorm bursts upon this planet. The **angel** standing before the golden incense altar **took** his **censer and,** removing the coals from the altar, **filled it with the fire of the altar.** Then, in an act that must have stunned John and the assembled multitude in heaven, the angel **threw it to the earth.** The results are catastrophic, as God's judgment falls upon the earth like a massive fireball out of the sky.

The **censer . . . filled with the fire of the altar,** usually linked with the prayers of God's people, becomes here a symbol of divine wrath. The angel's act of throwing it to earth reveals that God's judgment will come in direct response to those prayers. James 5:16 notes that "the effective prayer of a righteous man can accomplish much." The cumulative effect of the prayers of innumerable righteous men will be very powerful.

The immediate effects of the firestorm of wrath that bursts upon the earth are **peals of thunder and sounds and flashes of lightning and an earthquake,** in direct contrast to the silence (8:1). **Peals of thunder and sounds and flashes of lightning** are associated with the awesome majesty of God's glorious throne in 4:5; 11:19; 16:18 (cf. Ex. 19:16–19). No details are given about the **earthquake,** but it will probably be at least as powerful as the one associated with the sixth seal (6:12). And following the earthquake will come the horrors of the trumpet and bowl judgments. By the end of those judgments, God's purging judgment of His creation will be complete.

Despite all the terrifying judgments, which by this time all will acknowledge to be from God (6:15–17), and the worldwide preaching of the gospel (Matt. 24:14) by the 144,000 and others, people will still refuse to believe (cf. 9:20–21; 16:9, 11). It seems incredible that, having experienced the fury of God's judgment and heard the message of salvation, people will stubbornly cling to their sin. But the sad truth is that "the Light has come into the world, and men loved the darkness rather than the Light, for their deeds were evil. For everyone who does evil hates the Light, and does not come to the Light for fear that his deeds will be exposed" (John 3:19–20).

The unbelieving world rejected Jesus when He came, it rejects the life-giving message of the gospel now, and will continue to reject the truth even during the future outpouring of God's wrath and judgment. Having gone on "sinning willfully after receiving the knowledge of the truth," wicked people have nothing to look forward to except "a terrifying expectation of judgment and the fury of a fire which will consume the adversaries" (Heb. 10:26–27).

But for those who repent of their sins and come to saving faith in the Lord Jesus Christ, the blessed reality is that "God so loved the world, that He gave His only begotten Son, that whoever believes in Him shall not perish, but have eternal life," because "He who believes in Him is not judged" (John 3:16, 18; cf. John 5:24; Rom. 5:1; 8:1, 34).

Divine Destruction of Earth's Ecology: The First Four Trumpets (Revelation 8:6–13)

19

And the seven angels who had the seven trumpets prepared themselves to sound them. The first sounded, and there came hail and fire, mixed with blood, and they were thrown to the earth; and a third of the earth was burned up, and a third of the trees were burned up, and all the green grass was burned up. The second angel sounded, and something like a great mountain burning with fire was thrown into the sea; and a third of the sea became blood, and a third of the creatures which were in the sea and had life, died; and a third of the ships were destroyed. The third angel sounded, and a great star fell from heaven, burning like a torch, and it fell on a third of the rivers and on the springs of waters. The name of the star is called Wormwood; and a third of the waters became wormwood, and many men died from the waters, because they were made bitter. The fourth angel sounded, and a third of the sun and a third of the moon and a third of the stars were smitten, so that a third of them would be darkened and the day would not shine for a third of it, and the night in the same way. Then I looked, and I heard an eagle flying in midheaven, saying with a loud voice, "Woe, woe, woe to those who dwell

on the earth, because of the remaining blasts of the trumpet of the three angels who are about to sound!" (8:6–13)

People today are very concerned about saving the environment. Fears about the depletion of the ozone layer, pollution, the destruction of the rain forests, and global warming are constantly in the news. There is a passionate concern to save endangered species, everything from whales to spotted owls to California condors, and a host of lesser-known species. For many, protecting the environment has become far more than a concern for health and safety; it has become an issue of idolatry, as they worship "Mother Nature" by trying to protect and perpetuate the earth.

There is no question that fallen man has failed in his responsibility to properly care for God's creation (cf. Gen. 2:15). But the damage man has done to the earth pales in comparison to what God will one day do to it. The powerful judgments of the future time of tribulation will utterly devastate the earth, causing wholesale, unimaginable destruction of the environment. Eventually, after the Millennium, God will completely destroy (or uncreate) the present heaven and earth (2 Pet. 3:10), and, after the whole universe has gone completely out of existence, He will replace it with a new heaven and a new earth (Rev. 21:1ff.).

There is a sense in which the present age is man's day; he is free to do what he wants within certain limitations. It is also Satan's day, during which the "god of this world" (2 Cor. 4:4) has been granted certain liberties within the parameters of God's purposeful, sovereign tolerance. But God will not permit the present state of affairs to continue forever. He will end man's day, overthrow the usurper, Satan, destroy the present evil world system, and establish the earthly kingdom of the Lord Jesus Christ. That future time of judgment is known, appropriately, as the Day of the Lord (see the discussion in chapter 15 of this volume). That Day involves a complete renovation of the universe and the earth by judgment and restoration.

As the time for the trumpet judgments to begin approaches, the world will have already experienced for years the frightening and relentless reality of God's wrath. As that seven-year tribulation period unfolds there will be wars, famines, plagues, devastating earthquakes, fiery celestial objects smashing into the earth, and a worldwide reign of terror by Antichrist. But the trumpet judgments will be even worse.

As noted in the previous chapter of this volume, 8:1 depicts a brief, half-hour interlude in heaven in response to the opening of the seventh and final seal. So horrifying are the trumpet and bowl judgments contained within the seventh seal that its opening stuns the heavenly host of angels and redeemed people into silence.

That half hour of silence came to an abrupt end when the angel who stood before the altar flung his censer to the earth. The resulting powerful earthquake (8:5) was the signal for **the seven angels who had the seven trumpets,** and they **prepared themselves to sound them.** The serial judgments the trumpets unleash will hit the earth and its wicked people just as they are crawling out of the caves and rocks where they futilely attempted to hide from the fury of God's wrath during the sixth seal (6:15–17). Thinking that things are returning to normal, they will be hit with the terrifying, rapid-paced trumpet terrors, followed by the bowl judgments. These final judgments are likely the ones held back until the sealing of the 144,000 (7:3).

The first four trumpets are described in a brief and straightforward manner; far more detail is given about the last three. The first four trumpets all deal directly with the earth. They do not symbolize political, social, or economic judgment; those types of judgment come later in Revelation. Nor do they describe any judgment that has ever happened in history in some locale or region. The trumpet judgments are actual, literal, physical events that will affect the whole earth. God will use nature to punish sinners in that day. The partial destruction described by the repeated use of the word "third" in each of the first four trumpet judgments indicates that these are not the final judgments.

The First Trumpet

The first sounded, and there came hail and fire, mixed with blood, and they were thrown to the earth; and a third of the earth was burned up, and a third of the trees were burned up, and all the green grass was burned up. (8:7)

Hail is frequently associated in Scripture with divine judgment (cf. Ex. 9:13–25; Job 38:22–23; Ps. 105:32; Isa. 28:2; Hag. 2:17), as is **fire** (cf. Gen. 19:24; Ps. 11:6; Ezek. 38:22). The combination of **fire mixed with blood** is reminiscent of Joel 2:30, which also describes the Day of the Lord. The specific cause of the **hail and fire . . . thrown to the earth** is not revealed, but from a scientific standpoint an earthquake of the magnitude and extent of the one in 8:5 would likely trigger worldwide volcanic eruptions. Besides spewing vast quantities of flaming lava (which could be bloodred in appearance) into the atmosphere, the atmospheric disturbances caused by those eruptions could trigger violent thunderstorms that would produce large hail. Such thunderstorms would be in keeping with the imagery of 8:5; after the angel hurled his censer to earth "there followed peals of thunder and sounds and flashes of lightning." Dr.

Henry Morris suggests that the **blood** may be actual blood, or John may be using descriptive language: "The masses of water vapor blown skyward might well condense in the intense updrafts as hailstones. . . . The blood of entrapped men and animals might be mingled with them, or possibly showers of liquid water drops might be so contaminated with dust and gases as to appear blood-red" (*The Revelation Record* [Wheaton, Ill.:Tyndale, 1983], 146).

Morris also offers an alternative explanation for the fiery phenomena:

> It may be possible that angelic hosts will divert the path of one of the many comets with which the solar system abounds so that the earth will pass through its tail. The most spectacular comet with which we are familiar—Halley's Comet—would not need to stray too far from its normal orbit to envelop Earth in its fiery train. Whether such an experience would produce the phenomena described in this passage we do not know, since our scientists have no experimental data to go on yet. (Morris, *Revelation Record,* 146)

Whatever the scientific explanation, this deluge of death was **thrown to the earth** by God with devastating effects. The shocking result was that **a third of the earth was burned up,** rendering the soil in which crops are cultivated unusable. Then **a third of the trees were burned up,** destroying fruit all over the earth. Finally **all** the **green grass was burned up.** Commenting on the difficulty posed by the destruction of all, rather than a third, of the green grass, Robert Thomas writes

> This poses a dilemma, because grass still exists when the fifth trumpet arrives (9:4). It is hermeneutically wrong to see this as an inconsistency retained to preserve artistic effect. . . . Two considerations help to resolve the quandary. First, a time lapse between the first and fifth trumpets allows time for grass to be regrown after the burning, but before the assault of the fifth [trumpet]. Second, in most parts of the earth grass is not green the year round, but is seasonal. Burning of all the grass that is green during a particular season would leave the remainder untouched until its season of dormancy is over. . . . Whether the affected portion was one-third or some other percentage, the text does not say. The description simply says "all" that is green at the time of the plague. Either of these two explanations allows for taking "all" in its literal sense without contradicting 9:4. (*Revelation 8–22: An Exegetical Commentary* [Chicago: Moody, 1995], 17–18)

The fire falling from the sky kindled raging infernos that consumed one-third of the earth's vegetation and forests (cf. Ex. 9:25, which records the destruction of vegetation in Egypt).

The effects of such catastrophic fires would be widespread and devastating, including destruction of crops, death of animals on a massive scale, loss of wood for construction, and the destruction of watersheds. That is a fitting judgment for those who "exchanged the truth of God for a lie, and worshiped and served the creature rather than the Creator" (Rom. 1:25). Fallen mankind has failed to recognize and honor God as Creator, choosing instead to make a god out of the earth. But the environmental, evolutionary pantheism that devalues man, elevates animals and plants, and ignores the Creator will be severely judged. "Earth Day" that year will be a gloomy and dismal affair; in a scorched and ravaged world there will be little of the environment left to celebrate. And worse judgments are still to fall.

THE SECOND TRUMPET

The second angel sounded, and something like a great mountain burning with fire was thrown into the sea; and a third of the sea became blood, and a third of the creatures which were in the sea and had life, died; and a third of the ships were destroyed. (8:8–9)

While the earth's population was still trying to recover from the devastating fire falls, John saw an even more terrifying sign of doom appearing in the sky. As **the second angel sounded** his trumpet, **something like a great mountain burning with fire was thrown into the sea.** The judgment of the first trumpet fell on the land, that of the second trumpet on the sea. God created the sea to be a blessing to mankind, to provide food, oxygen (much of Earth's oxygen comes from the phytoplankton and algae in the world's oceans), and water from the rainstorms on the land that is originally gathered up by evaporation from the oceans. But people have repaid God's gracious provision with ingratitude and idolatry, revering the sea as the supposed source of their remotest evolutionary ancestors. As He had devastated the land environment, the true God judges the sea.

The massive object plunging through the sky looked to the terrified observers on earth **like a great mountain burning with fire.** This is evidently a giant meteorite or asteroid, surrounded by flaming gases set ablaze by the friction of the earth's atmosphere, on a collision course with the earth. The current doomsday scenarios about an asteroid hitting the earth will come true with a vengeance. Everyone will see it, either live or on television, and as the world's telescopes see it coming, many predictions will no doubt be made about whether it will hit the earth or not. It will hit, striking somewhere in the world's oceans with an explosive power far greater than that of an atomic bomb. Because all the world's oceans are connected, the devastation from that hit will spread across one-third of the ocean waters, causing **a third of the sea** to become **blood.**

Three catastrophic, supernaturally designed effects result from the collision: **a third of the sea became blood,** as a result of that effect **a third of the creatures which were in the sea and had life, died.** As with the first trumpet, it is impossible to say whether the **blood** was the miraculous deposit of actual blood. Perhaps more likely, the death of countless billions of sea creatures as **a third of the creatures which were in the sea and had life, died,** could certainly account for the reddish tinge of the water. (This is reminiscent of the plague in which the waters of the Nile turned to blood; Ex. 7:20–21; cf. Zeph. 1:3.) The reddish hue of the sun shining through the pall of smoke from the impact might also give the oceans' surface a bloodred appearance.

The impact will also generate unimaginably huge tsunamis (tidal waves). Those giant waves will destroy **a third of the ships** on the world's oceans, capsizing huge ocean-going vessels and completely swamping ports. The resulting disruption of commerce and transportation will cause economic chaos.

So the first two trumpets will bring devastating judgment on both the land and the sea, which are the beginning of the final catastrophes God will unleash on the sinful, rebellious world.

THE THIRD TRUMPET

The third angel sounded, and a great star fell from heaven, burning like a torch, and it fell on a third of the rivers and on the springs of waters. The name of the star is called Wormwood; and a third of the waters became wormwood, and many men died from the waters, because they were made bitter. (8:10–11)

As **the third angel sounded** his trumpet another flaming object hurtled toward the earth. John described this latest of the "terrors and great signs from heaven" (Luke 21:11) as **a great star** that **fell from heaven.** *Astēr* (**star**) can refer to any celestial body other than the sun and moon. The massive object that smashed into the ocean remained intact, but this object (possibly a comet or a meteor because of its fiery tail) disintegrated as it reached Earth's atmosphere. The fact that it is described as **burning like a torch** supports that interpretation, since *lampas* (**torch**) was used in ancient times to describe meteors and comets. The celestial object's fiery debris **fell on a third of the rivers and on the springs of waters,** polluting the fresh water around the globe. This also is reminiscent of the polluting of Egyptians' drinking water (Ex. 7:21, 24).

Because of its deadly effects, **the star** will be **called Worm-wood,** although the text does not reveal who will name it. **Wormwood** translates *apsinthos,* a word used only here in the New Testament. Wormwood is a shrub whose leaves are used in the manufacture of absinthe, a liqueur so toxic that its manufacture is banned in many countries. Wormwood is mentioned eight times in the Old Testament, where it is associated with bitterness, poison, and death (Deut. 29:18; Prov. 5:4; Jer. 9:15; 23:15; Lam. 3:15, 19; Amos 5:7; 6:12). In three of those uses, wormwood is connected with poisoned water. In Jeremiah 9:15, for example, God says of rebellious Israel, "Behold, I will feed them, this people, with wormwood and give them poisoned water to drink" (cf. Jer. 23:15; Lam. 3:15).

Whatever the poison represented by the name **Wormwood** is, it is lethal, since **a third of the** fresh **waters became** poisonous like **wormwood.** This is the reverse of the miracle at Marah, where the Lord made bitter waters sweet (Ex. 15:25). It is also reminiscent of the first plague on Egypt, when "all the water that was in the Nile was turned to blood" (Ex. 7:20) and became unfit to drink. The repeated pattern of one-third destruction (one-third of the earth and the trees burned up, v. 7; one-third of the sea turned to blood, v. 8; one-third of the sea creatures killed and one-third of the ships destroyed, v. 9) demonstrates clearly that these are not random natural events, but divine judgments.

No human deaths were mentioned with the first two trumpet judgments, although they undoubtedly will take a severe toll of human lives. But with the third trumpet judgment, John records that **many men died from the waters, because they were made bitter.** The rivers will run with deadly poison; the wells will become springs of death; the lakes and reservoirs will be filled with toxic waters. People will be able to survive, for a time, the destruction of food supplies caused by the first two trumpet judgments, living off stored provisions. But people cannot long survive without fresh water, and the loss of a significant portion of the world's fresh water supply will cause widespread death.

The devastation caused by the first three trumpet judgments will leave the earth's inhabitants in a state of shock and fear. Still, God has not finished pouring out His wrath on sinful mankind. The death of **many** is only an indirect result of these first three blasts. The direct killing of sinners comes with the sixth trumpet (9:15).

THE FOURTH TRUMPET

The fourth angel sounded, and a third of the sun and a third of the moon and a third of the stars were smitten, so that a third of them would be darkened and the day would not shine for a third

of it, and the night in the same way. Then I looked, and I heard an eagle flying in midheaven, saying with a loud voice, "Woe, woe, woe to those who dwell on the earth, because of the remaining blasts of the trumpet of the three angels who are about to sound!" (8:12–13)

As **the fourth angel sounded,** the focus of divine judgment shifted from the earth to the heavens. Still reeling from the effects of the first three ecological judgments, people will be desperately seeking answers to the crisis. There will no doubt be seminars, conferences, emergency sessions of the United Nations, discussions among scientists—all desperately and futilely seeking to cope with the damage to the earth's ecosystems.

In the midst of all that frenzied activity comes a new disaster in the sky, as **a third of the sun and a third of the moon and a third of the stars were smitten.** *Plēssō* (**were smitten**) is the verb from which the noun "plague" (cf. 11:6; 16:21) derives. The heavenly bodies are hit with a plague from God **so that a third of them would be darkened and the day would not shine for a third of it, and the night in the same way.** This partial eclipse, reminiscent of the ninth Egyptian plague (Ex. 10:21–22), is temporary, as God will later increase the amount of heat coming from the sun (cf. 16:8–9). At this point, however, the loss of heat from the sun will cause temperatures to plunge drastically all over the world. That will severely disrupt the earth's weather patterns and the seas' tides, leading to violent, unpredictable storms and tides, the destruction of crops, and further loss of animal and human lives.

The Old Testament prophets associated such signs in the heavens with the Day of the Lord. Isaiah wrote, "Behold, the day of the Lord is coming, cruel, with fury and burning anger, to make the land a desolation; and He will exterminate its sinners from it. For the stars of heaven and their constellations will not flash forth their light; the sun will be dark when it rises and the moon will not shed its light" (Isa. 13:9–10). Speaking through the prophet Ezekiel, God declared, "I will cover the heavens and darken their stars; I will cover the sun with a cloud and the moon will not give its light. All the shining lights in the heavens I will darken over you and will set darkness on your land" (Ezek. 32:7–8). "The heavens tremble," wrote Joel, "the sun and the moon grow dark and the stars lose their brightness.... The sun will be turned into darkness and the moon into blood before the great and awesome day of the Lord comes.... The sun and moon grow dark and the stars lose their brightness" (Joel 2:10, 31; 3:15). "'It will come about in that day,' declares the Lord God, 'That I shall make the sun go down at noon and make the earth dark in broad daylight'" (Amos 8:9). The Lord Jesus Christ added His own prediction to that of the prophets, warning, "There will be signs in sun and moon and stars" (Luke 21:25; cf. Mark 13:24).

The dimming of the celestial lights sets the stage for a startling and ominous announcement. As John **looked, he heard an eagle flying in midheaven, saying with a loud voice, "Woe, woe, woe to those who dwell on the earth, because of the remaining blasts of the trumpet of the three angels who are about to sound!"** The imagery is that of a strong bird of prey rushing to consume its victim, in this case referring to the rapid approach of God's final vengeance (cf. Deut. 28:49; Hos. 8:1; Hab. 1:8). Depicted in the vision as **flying in midheaven,** the bird would be at the height of the midday sun, thus visible to all. His loud voice assures that all will be able to hear his pronouncements. The eagle's dire warning is that the last three trumpet judgments will be even more devastating than the first four.

While double woes are used for emphasis (cf. 18:10, 16, 19; Ezek. 16:23), the eagle's triple pronouncement of **woe, woe, woe** introduces one threat for each of the remaining three trumpets **about to sound** (9:1–21; 11:15ff.). **Woe** is used throughout Scripture, an expression of judgment, destruction, and condemnation (cf. Num. 21:29; 1 Sam. 4:7–8; Job 10:15; Ps. 120:5; Eccl. 10:16; Isa. 3:9; Jer. 4:13; Lam. 5:16; Ezek. 13:3; Hos. 7:13; Amos 6:1; Mic. 2:1; Nah. 3:1; Hab. 2:6; Zeph. 2:5; Matt. 11:21; Jude 11). God's wrath and judgment will come upon **those who dwell on the earth.** That descriptive phrase is used in Revelation as a technical term for those who reject the gospel (cf. 6:10; 11:10; 13:8, 12, 14; 17:2, 8). Although they will acknowledge that the disasters they have experienced have come from God (6:15–17), they will not repent. Later in Revelation John records that "the rest of mankind, who were not killed by these plagues, did not repent of the works of their hands, so as not to worship demons, and the idols of gold and of silver and of brass and of stone and of wood, which can neither see nor hear nor walk; and they did not repent of their murders nor of their sorceries nor of their immorality nor of their thefts" (9:20–21; cf. 16:9, 11). They will be destroyed because they fail to heed the warning God addresses to all sinners: "Therefore, just as the Holy Spirit says, 'Today if you hear His voice, do not harden your hearts'" (Heb. 3:7–8).

Hell on Earth: The Fifth Trumpet (Revelation 9:1–12)

20

Then the fifth angel sounded, and I saw a star from heaven which had fallen to the earth; and the key of the bottomless pit was given to him. He opened the bottomless pit, and smoke went up out of the pit, like the smoke of a great furnace; and the sun and the air were darkened by the smoke of the pit. Then out of the smoke came locusts upon the earth, and power was given them, as the scorpions of the earth have power. They were told not to hurt the grass of the earth, nor any green thing, nor any tree, but only the men who do not have the seal of God on their foreheads. And they were not permitted to kill anyone, but to torment for five months; and their torment was like the torment of a scorpion when it stings a man. And in those days men will seek death and will not find it; they will long to die, and death flees from them. The appearance of the locusts was like horses prepared for battle; and on their heads appeared to be crowns like gold, and their faces were like the faces of men. They had hair like the hair of women, and their teeth were like the teeth of lions. They had breastplates like breastplates of iron; and the sound of their wings was like the sound of chariots, of many horses rushing to battle. They have tails like scorpions, and stings; and in their tails

is their power to hurt men for five months. They have as king over them, the angel of the abyss; his name in Hebrew is Abaddon, and in the Greek he has the name Apollyon. The first woe is past; behold, two woes are still coming after these things. (9:1–12)

Because our world is the theater where the glorious, God-honoring story of redemption is played out, Satan and his demon hosts have attacked the human race, turning the earth into the main battleground in their cosmic war against God, the holy angels, and the elect. Satan launched his first assault in the Garden of Eden, where he successfully tempted Adam and Eve to disobey God. The disastrous consequences were that "sin entered into the world, and death through sin, and so death spread to all men, because all sinned" (Rom. 5:12).

After the Fall, God graciously promised a Savior who would come to destroy Satan and deliver people from his power (Gen. 3:15). Satan countered by sending demons to cohabitate with human women, attempting to produce a hybrid demon/human race of people for whom the God-Man could not atone (Gen. 6:1–4). In response, God destroyed that race and the whole sinful world in the powerful judgment of the universal Flood—the single greatest catastrophe the earth has yet seen.

Satan's tormenting of righteous Job reveals his hatred for the godly. Satan sought to destroy Job's faith—to take him from God's kingdom back to his own kingdom of darkness. With God's permission, Satan destroyed Job's possessions, killed his children, and ruined his health. Job was left with an embittered wife (Job 2:9), friends whose inept counsel drove him to distraction, and many unanswered questions about why God allowed him to suffer. But Job remained loyal to God, proving that saving faith is permanent and God holds on to His own, so that in the end God was vindicated, and Satan's attempt to destroy Job's faith, as it would with that of any other believer, was unsuccessful. As he did with Job, Satan continually accuses believers before God (12:10; cf. Zech. 3:1).

No nation has experienced more of Satan's assaults than Israel. He has always had a special hatred for God's chosen people, "from whom is the Christ according to the flesh" (Rom. 9:5). First Chronicles 21 records one of his many attacks: "Satan stood up against Israel and moved David to number Israel.... God was displeased with this thing, so He struck Israel" (vv. 1, 7). The Lord's chastening took the form of a plague in which seventy thousand Israelites perished (v. 14). Throughout its history, Satan lured Israel and Judah into idolatry, immorality, and disobedience to God's law. As a result, God brought judgment on His people, sending them into captivity in Assyria and Babylon. In the future tribulation period Satan will once again attempt to destroy the chosen nation (12:1–6, 13–17).

From the beginning to the end of Jesus' earthly ministry, Satan fought with all his impotent fury against the Lord Jesus Christ. He tempted Christ for forty days at the beginning of His ministry, futilely seeking to turn Him aside from the work His Father sent Him to accomplish (Matt. 4:1–11). A long and relentless war was waged against Jesus by the Jewish leaders, whom He identified as belonging to the family of the devil (John 8:44). Satan never ceased from that effort, even attempting to use those close to Jesus against Him (Mark 8:32–33). Satan tried to destroy the faith of the apostolic leader, Peter, demanding from God the opportunity to test him severely (Luke 22:31–32) with the intent of destroying his faith (as he had tried unsuccessfully to do with Job). The test was allowed by God and was severe. It brought Peter to fear and denial of his Lord on three occasions (Luke 22:34, 54–61), but Peter repented (Luke 22:62) and was restored (John 21:15–23) to become the great preacher of the Day of Pentecost (Acts 2:14ff.). At the end of Jesus' ministry, "Satan entered into Judas who was called Iscariot, belonging to the number of the twelve" (Luke 22:3), who then betrayed Christ into the hands of His murderers.

The church has also been a special target of satanic assault. Shortly after its founding, Satan himself prompted Ananias and his wife Sapphira to corrupt the church by lying to the Holy Spirit (Acts 5:3). The couple's foolish, sinful, and hypocritical attempt to impress others with their spirituality ended when God put them to death before the whole congregation (Acts 5: 5–11). Satan also battled the apostle Paul, hindering him from visiting the Thessalonian church (1 Thess. 2:18) and tormenting him with "a thorn in the flesh, a messenger of Satan" (2 Cor. 12:7). Satan also attacks the church by bringing unbelievers into it, mixing in his tares among God's wheat (Matt. 13:38–39), blinding the minds of unbelievers so that they reject the gospel (2 Cor. 4:4; cf. Luke 8:12), and seeking to overwhelm believers with temptation, persecution, and discouragement (1 Pet. 5:8). God sovereignly allows and oversees all of Satan's assaults and fulfills His purposes in spite of them and through them. Satan is the servant of God.

In the future, Satan will serve God's purpose by being permitted to launch another deadly assault against the human race. That attack will come at the sounding of the fifth trumpet, during the time of God's judgment in the Great Tribulation (7:14). For millennia the heavens have declared God's glory (cf. Ps. 19:1–2), but in the future they will declare His wrath. The first four trumpet judgments will all involve either objects hurtling to earth out of the sky, or, in the case of the fourth trumpet, the heavenly bodies themselves will be affected (8:7–12).

While the destruction caused by the first four trumpet judgments will be catastrophic, the remaining three will be far worse. That was the sobering message given by "an eagle flying in midheaven" (8:13). He pronounced a threefold message of woe (one for each of the final three trumpets) on "those who dwell on the earth" (8:13)—a technical term in Revelation for unregenerate people (cf. 6:10; 11:10; 13:8, 12, 14; 14:6; 17:2,8)—because of the terrors the final three trumpet judgments would soon unleash. The eagle's message will give people one last opportunity to repent before the rising crescendo of divine judgment reaches its apex in the final three blasts of God's holy anger. Indeed, it appears that those who go through the fifth trumpet judgment without repenting may be confirmed in their unrepentant state (cf. 9:20–21; 16:9, 11).

Each of the first four trumpet judgments affect the physical universe in some way, but with the sounding of the fifth trumpet the focus will shift from the physical to the spiritual realm. The traumatic events associated with that fifth trumpet vision unfold in four scenes: the pit unlocked, the power unleashed, the appearance unveiled, and the prince unmasked.

THE PIT UNLOCKED

Then the fifth angel sounded, and I saw a star from heaven which had fallen to the earth; and the key of the bottomless pit was given to him. He opened the bottomless pit, and smoke went up out of the pit, like the smoke of a great furnace; and the sun and the air were darkened by the smoke of the pit. (9:1–2)

When the **fifth** elite presence angel **sounded** his trumpet, John **saw a star from heaven which had fallen to the earth.** In his visions, the apostle had already seen several heavenly bodies plunge to earth (cf. 6:13; 8:8, 10). Unlike them, however, this **star** was not an inanimate piece of celestial matter, but an angelic being (cf. Job 38:7). That he was said to have **fallen to the earth** suggests that this is a reference to Satan—the leader of all the fallen angels. Isaiah 14:12–15 describes his fall:

> How you have fallen from heaven, O star of the morning, son of the dawn! You have been cut down to the earth, you who have weakened the nations! But you said in your heart, "I will ascend to heaven; I will raise my throne above the stars of God, and I will sit on the mount of assembly in the recesses of the north. I will ascend above the heights of the clouds; I will make myself like the Most High." Nevertheless you will be thrust down to Sheol, to the recesses of the pit. (cf. Ezek. 28:12–16; Luke 10:18)

The fall of Satan described in 9:1 is not his original rebellion. Though he and the angels who fell with him (cf. 12:4) were banished from heaven, Satan retains access to God's presence, where he constantly accuses believers (12:10; Job 1:6). But during the Tribulation he and his demon hosts will unsuccessfully battle Michael and the holy angels. As a result of their defeat, they will be permanently cast down to the earth. Revelation 12:7–9 describes that battle scene:

> And there was war in heaven, Michael and his angels waging war with the dragon. The dragon and his angels waged war, and they were not strong enough, and there was no longer a place found for them in heaven. And the great dragon was thrown down, the serpent of old who is called the devil and Satan, who deceives the whole world; he was thrown down to the earth, and his angels were thrown down with him.

With his theater of operations now restricted to the earth, and his time running out (cf. 12:12), Satan will seek to marshal all of his demonic hosts—those already on earth, those cast to earth with him, and those incarcerated in the **bottomless pit** (literally "the pit of the abyss"). *Abussos* (**bottomless**) appears seven times in Revelation, always in reference to the abode of incarcerated demons (cf. 9:2, 11; 11:7; 17:8). Satan himself will be held prisoner there during the Millennium, chained and locked up with the other demonic prisoners (20:1, 3).

Scripture teaches that God has sovereignly chosen to incarcerate certain demons in that **pit** of punishment. Second Peter 2:4 says that "God did not spare angels when they sinned, but cast them into hell and committed them to pits of darkness, reserved for judgment." The phrase "cast them into hell" is a participle derived from the Greek noun *Tartarus*. Just as Jesus used a term for hell derived from the Jewish vernacular (*Gehenna;* cf. Matt. 5:22), so Peter chose a term from Greek mythology with which his readers would be familiar. Tartarus was the name used in Greek literature for the place where the worst sinners, those who had offended the gods personally, went after death and were punished. The place where God keeps demons imprisoned is actually different from the imaginary place of Greek mythology. Yet the use of the term *Tartarus* does seem to convey the idea that because of the heinousness of their sin, God has imprisoned certain fallen angels in such a place of severest torment and isolation. They remain in that place, awaiting their sentencing to final punishment in the eternal lake of fire (Rev. 20:10, 13–14).

The demons incarcerated in the abyss are undoubtedly the most wicked, vile, and perverted of all the fallen angels. Jude describes some of them as "angels who did not keep their own domain, but abandoned their proper abode," noting that God "has kept [them] in eternal bonds under darkness for the judgment of the great day, just as Sodom and Gomorrah and the cities around them, since they in the same way as these indulged in gross immorality and went after strange flesh, are exhibited as an example in undergoing the punishment of eternal fire" (Jude 6–7). That passage describes certain fallen angels who left the angelic domain to indulge in sexual sin with humans, just as the men of Sodom and Gomorrah attempted to engage in perverted sex with angels (Gen. 19:1, 4–5).

Peter reveals when this angelic sin occurred:

> For Christ also died for sins once for all, the just for the unjust, so that He might bring us to God, having been put to death in the flesh, but made alive in the spirit; in which also He went and made proclamation to the spirits now in prison, who once were disobedient, when the patience of God kept waiting in the days of Noah, during the construction of the ark, in which a few, that is, eight persons, were brought safely through the water. (1 Pet. 3:18–20)

The "spirits now in prison" in the abyss are those "who once were disobedient ... in the days of Noah." They are the demons who cohabited with human women in Satan's failed attempt to corrupt the human race and make it unredeemable (Gen. 6:1–4). That demons still fear being sent to the abyss is evident from the fact that some pled with Jesus not to send them there (Luke 8:31). That suggests that other demons have been incarcerated there since the events of Genesis 6. The demons released by Satan at the fifth trumpet may not include those who sinned in Noah's day (cf. Jude 6), since they are said to be in "eternal bonds" (Jude 6) until the final day when they are sent to the eternal lake of fire (20:10; Jude 7). Other demons imprisoned in the abyss may be the ones released. So the pit is the preliminary place of incarceration for demons from which some are to be released under this judgment.

After Satan received the key to the abyss from its keeper, the Lord Jesus Christ (1:18), **he opened the bottomless pit** and released its inmates. John Phillips comments,

> Picture what the world would be like if we were to open the doors of all the penitentiaries of earth and set free the world's most vicious and violent criminals, giving them full reign to practice their infamies upon mankind. Something worse than that lies in store for the world. Satan, cast out of heaven, is now permitted to summon to his aid the most diabolical fiends in the abyss to act as his agents in bringing mankind to the footstool of the Beast. (*Exploring Revelation*, rev. ed. [Chicago: Moody, 1987; reprint, Neptune, N.J.: Loizeaux, 1991], 125)

When the abyss opened, **smoke went up out of the pit like the smoke of a great furnace. Smoke** in Revelation may refer to holy things (8:4; 15:8), but is usually associated with judgment (9:17–18; 14:11;

18:9, 18; 19:3; cf. Gen. 19:28; Isa. 34:10; Joel 2:30; Nah. 2:13). Such a vast volume of smoke issued from the abyss that **the sun and the air were darkened by** it. The smoke polluting the sky symbolizes the corruption of hell belched forth from the abyss to pollute the world.

THE POWER UNLEASHED

Then out of the smoke came locusts upon the earth, and power was given them, as the scorpions of the earth have power. They were told not to hurt the grass of the earth, nor any green thing, nor any tree, but only the men who do not have the seal of God on their foreheads. And they were not permitted to kill anyone, but to torment for five months; and their torment was like the torment of a scorpion when it stings a man. And in those days men will seek death and will not find it; they will long to die, and death flees from them. (9:3–6)

Out of the vast, billowing, ominous cloud of **smoke** that darkened the sky and caused panic among earth's inhabitants John saw a new terror emerge. Vile demons, taking on a visible form resembling **locusts,** swarmed out of the abyss to plague **the earth.** The destructive power of locusts is noted in several Old Testament passages (Deut. 28:38; 2 Chron. 7:13; Ps. 105:34; Joel 2:25; Nah. 3:15); locust swarms consume all vegetation in their path. The scene is reminiscent of the locust plague in Egypt (Ex. 10:4–5, 12–20), and of the description of the locust plague in Joel 1:1–7; 2:1–5, but far worse. The imagery of the smoke is an apt depiction of a locust plague, since millions of the grasshopper-like insects swarm so thickly that they can darken the sky and blot out the sun, turning day into night. Locust swarms can be unimaginably huge (cf. Ps. 105:34); one swarm over the Red Sea in 1889 was reported to have covered 2,000 square miles. The destruction they can cause to crops and other vegetation is staggering (cf. 2 Chron. 7:13). John Phillips writes:

> The worst locust plague in modern times struck the Middle East in 1951–52 when in Iran, Iraq, Jordan, and Saudi Arabia every green and growing thing was devoured across hundreds of thousands of square miles. Locusts eat grain, leaf, and stalk, right down to the bare ground. When a swarm arises and flies on its way, the green field is left a desert; barrenness and desolation stretches as far as eye can see. (*Exploring Revelation,* 125–26)

But these were not ordinary locusts, but demons, who, like locusts, bring swarming destruction. Describing them in the form of

locusts symbolizes their uncountable numbers and massive destructive capabilities. The fact that three times in the passage (vv. 3, 5, 10) their **power** to inflict pain is compared to that of **scorpions** indicates they are not actual locusts, since locusts have no stinging tail as scorpions do. **Scorpions** are a species of arachnid, inhabiting warm, dry regions, and having an erect tail tipped with a venomous stinger. The stings of many species of scorpions are excruciatingly painful, and about two dozen species are capable of killing humans. The symptoms of a sting from one of the deadly species, including severe convulsions and paralysis, resemble those of demon-possessed individuals (cf. Mark 1:23–27; 9:20, 26). Combining in the description of the demons both locusts and scorpions emphasizes the deadliness of the demon invasion. But the devastating pain inflicted by these demons will be far worse than that of actual scorpions. In this judgment God brings demons into direct contact with the unrepentant people with whom they will spend forever in the lake of fire. The fact that these locust and scorpion-like creatures come from the pit and that their leader is the "angel of the abyss" (9:11) indicates that demons must be in view in this scene. Demons are also pictured as creatures from the animal kingdom in 16:13, where they appear as frogs. Sadly, even the horrifying experience of this demon infestation will not cause many to repent (cf. 9:20–21), if any.

Strict limitations were placed on the activities of this demonic host. This judgment, unlike the first four trumpet judgments, is not on the physical world. In fact, **they were told** (probably by God, who gave the angel the key to the pit in 9:1, and who controls everything for His purposes) that there were limits. God forbade the locust horde **to hurt the grass of the earth, nor any green thing, nor any tree** (cf. 8:7). That again shows that they were not actual insects, since real locusts devour plant life. The reference to **the grass of the earth** suggests that some time has passed since the first trumpet judgment scorched all the grass that was then in season (8:7). The damaged grass has grown again and is to remain untouched in this plague, indicating that enough time has elapsed for a partial recovery of the earth's environment.

The demons' business is not with vegetation, but **only** with **men** —not all people, but only those who **do not have the seal of God on their foreheads.** Believers will be preserved, just as God sheltered Israel from the effects of the Egyptian plagues (Ex. 8:22ff.; 9:4ff.; 10:23). Those who have the **seal of God** include not only the 144,000 Jewish evangelists (7:3–4; 14:1), but also the rest of the redeemed (cf. 22:4; 2 Tim. 2:19). This **seal** marks them as personally belonging to God and as such protected from the forces of hell. Jesus promised the faithful members of the Philadelphia church that "He who overcomes, I will make him a pillar in the temple of My God, and he will not go out from it anymore; and I will write on him the name of My God, and the name of the city of My God, the new Jerusalem, which comes down out of heaven from My God, and My new name" (3:12).

Ezekiel 9:4–6 illustrates the truth that God protects His people in the midst of judgment. God commanded an angel to go through Jerusalem and put a mark on the redeemed. Those who did not have that mark were subject to death when the city fell to the Babylonians.

> The Lord said to him, "Go through the midst of the city, even through the midst of Jerusalem, and put a mark on the foreheads of the men who sigh and groan over all the abominations which are being committed in its midst." But to the others He said in my hearing, "Go through the city after him and strike; do not let your eye have pity and do not spare. Utterly slay old men, young men, maidens, little children, and women, but do not touch any man on whom is the mark; and you shall start from My sanctuary." So they started with the elders who were before the temple.

Even what the demons can do to the unregenerate is limited. Although Satan has the power of death (Heb. 2:14), its exercise is subject to God's sovereign will and power, thus these demons **were not permitted to kill anyone.** After millennia of captivity, the vile demons would no doubt want to give full vent to all of their pent-up evil by slaughtering people. Certainly Satan would want to kill all the unregenerate to keep them from repenting. But God, in His mercy, will give people **torment for five months** (the normal life span of locusts, usually from May to September), during which they cannot die but will be given the opportunity to repent and embrace the gospel. **Torment** describes punishment in Revelation (11:10; 14:10–11; 18:7, 10, 15; 20:10; the only exception is 12:2; "pain" is the same Greek word elsewhere translated "torment"). That five-month period will be one of intense spiritual and physical suffering inflicted on unbelievers by the judgment of God through the demon horde. That fearful judgment is likened to the torment inflicted **by a scorpion when it stings a man.** Unbelievers will also hear the message of salvation in Jesus Christ preached by the 144,000 Jewish evangelists, the two witnesses, and other believers. The five months will be for many people the last opportunity to repent and believe, before they die or are permanently hardened in their unbelief (9:20–21; 16:9, 11).

So intense will be the torment inflicted on unbelievers that **in those days** (the five months of v. 5) **men will seek death and will not find it; they will long to die, and death flees from them.** All hope is gone; there will be no tomorrow. The earth people have loved and worshiped will have been utterly devastated, the land ravaged by earthquakes, fires, and volcanoes, the sea filled with the putrefying bodies of billions of dead creatures, much of the fresh water supply turned into bitter poison, the atmosphere polluted with gases and showers of heavenly debris. Then, worst of all, will come foul smoke from the pit of hell as the demons are released to spiritually and physically torment wicked people. The dream of a worldwide utopia under the leadership of Antichrist (the beast of 13:1ff.) will have died. Driven mad by the filth and vileness of the demon infestation, people will seek relief in death—only to find that death has taken a holiday. There will be no escape from the agony inflicted by the demons, no escape from divine judgment. All attempts at suicide, whether by gunshot, poison, drowning, or leaping from buildings, will fail.

The Appearance Unveiled

The appearance of the locusts was like horses prepared for battle; and on their heads appeared to be crowns like gold, and their faces were like the faces of men. They had hair like the hair of women, and their teeth were like the teeth of lions. They had breastplates like breastplates of iron; and the sound of their wings was like the sound of chariots, of many horses rushing to battle. They have tails like scorpions, and stings; and in their tails is their power to hurt men for five months. (9:7–10)

Having delineated the devastation the **locusts** (demons) will cause, John gives a more detailed description of their appearance in the vision. They are described as locusts because they bring massive, devastating, rapid judgment from God (cf. Ex. 10:4–5, 12–15; Deut. 28:38; 1 Kings 8:37; 2 Chron. 7:13; Pss. 78:46; 105:34; Joel 2:1ff.; Amos 7:1), but their exaggerated, terrifying features reveal them to be unlike any locust, scorpion, or any other creature ever before seen on earth. John can only give an approximation of what this formidable spiritual army looked like, as the repeated use of the terms **like** (used ten times in this passage) and **appeared to be** indicates. To describe the supernatural and unfamiliar demon horde, John chooses natural and familiar analogies.

The general **appearance of the locusts was like horses prepared for battle.** They were warlike, powerful, and defiant, like horses straining at the bit and pawing the ground in their eagerness to charge forward on their mission of death. Joel 2:4–5 describes a locust plague in similar terms. **On their heads** John saw what **appeared to be crowns like gold. The crowns** they wore are called *stephanoi*, the victors' crowns, indicating that the demon host will be invincible, unstoppable, and all-conquering. Men will have no weapon that can harm them and no cure for the terrible torment they inflict. That **their faces were like**

the faces of men indicates they are intelligent, rational beings, not actual insects. While Jeremiah 51:27 describes locusts as having bristles like hair, the description of their **hair** as being **like the hair of women** more likely emphasizes their seductiveness. The glory or beauty of a woman is her hair, which she may decorate to become more alluring. Like the Sirens of Greek mythology, these locustlike demons will lure people to their doom. Having **teeth like the teeth of lions** (cf. Joel 1:6), they will be far more fierce, powerful, and deadly than lions, ripping and tearing apart their victims. **Breastplates of iron,** designed to protect the vital organs and preserve the life of the soldier, here symbolize the demon horde's invulnerability; they will be impossible to resist or destroy. In a further metaphor drawn from the battlefield, John, like the prophet Joel (Joel 2:4–5), compares **the sound of their wings** to a moving army, noting that it **was like the sound of chariots, of many horses rushing to battle.** There will be no escaping their massive, worldwide onslaught; nowhere to run or hide. The threefold comparison of the demons to **scorpions** (cf. vv. 3, 5) stresses that their sole mission is **to hurt men.** The nature of this full-scale demonic torment that drives people to seek death and not find it, to pursue death and not catch it, is not described. However, a look at some biblical illustrations of demonic torment offers some good insights. The maniacs of Gadara were so tormented by demons that they were insane, living in tombs (Matt. 8:28). All about Galilee Jesus encountered tormented demoniacs (Matt. 4:23–24). A centurion's servant was tormented with paralysis (Matt. 8:6). A demon-possessed boy kept throwing himself into fires and water in acts of self-destruction (Mark 9:20–22). Such are the spiritual and physical torments demons can inflict. For **five months** they will do such to a whole world of ungodly sinners. The reiteration that the demons will be permitted to torment people for a limited time stresses God's sovereign power over the duration of their assault. Eventually, He will return them to the abyss with their evil master (20:1–3) and then send them to the lake of fire (20:10).

THE PRINCE UNMASKED

They have as king over them, the angel of the abyss; his name in Hebrew is Abaddon, and in the Greek he has the name Apollyon. The first woe is past; behold, two woes are still coming after these things. (9:11–12)

Unlike real locusts (cf. Prov. 30:27), the demons had a **king over them.** John gives his title as **the angel of the abyss.** Some identify this angel as Satan, but his domain is the heavenlies (Eph. 6:12), where he is the "prince of the power of the air" (Eph. 2:2). He is not associated with the abyss until he is cast into it (20:1–3). This angel is better viewed as a high-ranking demon in Satan's hierarchy. John notes that **his name in Hebrew is Abaddon, and in the Greek he has the name Apollyon.** John uses both names to emphasize his impact on both ungodly Jews and Gentiles. Both words mean "destroyer"—an apt name for the head of the devastating army of demons that rises from the abyss. **Abaddon** is used in the Old Testament to describe the place of eternal punishment (cf. Job 26:6; 28:22; 31:12; Ps. 88:11; Prov. 15:11; 27:20), thus further reinforcing this angel's connection with the abyss and hell. **Apollyon** comes from the Greek verb *apollumi,* which means "I destroy." These terms identify this leader as the king of the demonic death squad.

Having described **the first woe** (8:13; the fifth trumpet judgment), John cautions that God's wrath has not run its course. **Two woes** (the sixth and seventh trumpet judgments, including all the bowl judgments) **are still coming after these things,** so there will be nothing more than a brief sigh of relief before still more fearful judgments follow on those "who suppress the truth in unrighteousness" (Rom. 1:18).

Satanic Slaughter: The Sixth Trumpet (Revelation 9:13–21)

21

Then the sixth angel sounded, and I heard a voice from the four horns of the golden altar which is before God, one saying to the sixth angel who had the trumpet, "Release the four angels who are bound at the great river Euphrates." And the four angels, who had been prepared for the hour and day and month and year, were released, so that they would kill a third of mankind. The number of the armies of the horsemen was two hundred million; I heard the number of them. And this is how I saw in the vision the horses and those who sat on them: the riders had breastplates the color of fire and of hyacinth and of brimstone; and the heads of the horses are like the heads of lions; and out of their mouths proceed fire and smoke and brimstone. A third of mankind was killed by these three plagues, by the fire and the smoke and the brimstone which proceeded out of their mouths. For the power of the horses is in their mouths and in their tails; for their tails are like serpents and have heads, and with them they do harm. And the rest of mankind, who were not killed by these plagues, did not repent of the works of their hands, so as not to worship demons, and the idols of gold and of silver and of brass and of stone and of wood, which can neither see nor hear nor walk; and

they did not repent of their murders nor of their sorceries nor of their immorality nor of their thefts. (9:13–21)

Mankind lies between two powerful opposing spiritual spheres, each seeking to conform people to itself. No one is neutral in the cosmic battle; everyone is either part of the "domain of darkness" or of the "kingdom of [God's] beloved Son" (Col. 1:13). As they yield to one sphere or the other, people become the companions of God, or the companions of Satan; the companions of holy angels, or the companions of demons; the companions of saints, or the companions of sinners.

To doubt that reality is the gravest mistake any person can make, because making the wrong choice results in eternal disaster. God offers people the life-giving gospel of the Lord Jesus Christ; Satan and the forces of hell lure people to their destruction by dangling before them the "passing pleasures of sin" (Heb. 11:25). The loud voices of hell have always tried to drown out the preaching of the gospel.

There is coming a day when the siren call of hell will be so loud as to be all but irresistible. The people of that time will ignore the repeated, powerful preaching of the gospel and the warning conveyed by terrifying, devastating judgments from God. Having rejected all offers of grace and mercy, they will see death come upon mankind through the trumpet and bowl judgments, which will deliver death on a scale unprecedented in human history. Yet even then they will not repent; in fact, they will curse God (cf. 9:20–21; 16:9, 11). People at that time will have made the irrevocable choice to side with the forces of hell.

While there will be divine judgments throughout the seven-year Tribulation, they will escalate during the last three and one-half years— the time Jesus called "the great tribulation" (Matt. 24:21; cf. Rev. 7:14). As has been discussed in previous chapters, those judgments will unfold sequentially in three telescoping series: the seals, the trumpets, and the bowls. Out of the seventh seal comes the seven trumpet judgments, and out of the seventh trumpet comes the seven bowl judgments.

Like the fifth trumpet (9:1–12), the sounding of the sixth trumpet heralds another, more severe demonic attack on sinful mankind. This attack, unlike the previous one, brings death. It unfolds in three stages: the release of demons, the return of death, and the reaction of defiance.

THE RELEASE OF DEMONS

Then the sixth angel sounded, and I heard a voice from the four horns of the golden altar which is before God, one saying to the

sixth angel who had the trumpet, "Release the four angels who are bound at the great river Euphrates." (9:13–14)

In his turn, at the appointed moment, **the sixth angel sounded** his mighty trumpet. Immediately, John **heard a voice.** The Greek text literally reads "one voice," stressing that John heard a single, solitary voice. The voice is not identified, but it is possibly that of the Lamb, the Lord Jesus Christ. He was pictured earlier standing near the throne (5:6), when He took the seven-sealed scroll from the Father's hand (5:7) and broke its seals (6:1), thus unleashing the series of judgments of which the sixth trumpet is a part. Or this could be the voice of the angel whom John had seen standing near the golden altar of incense (8:3).

While identifying the source of the voice is not possible, its location is: it came **from the four horns** (small protrusions on each corner) **of the golden altar which is before God.** John had already seen this altar, the heavenly counterpart to the Old Testament altar of incense, twice before in his visions. In the tabernacle and temple, this altar was a place where incense was burnt, symbolizing the peoples' prayers for mercy rising to God. But in John's vision the golden altar became an altar of imprecatory intercession, as the martyred saints pleaded there with God for merciless vengeance on their murderers (6:9–11). Then in 8:5 it became an altar of judgment, as an angel took his "censer and filled it with the fire of the altar, and threw it to the earth." His action set the stage for the trumpet judgments, which followed shortly.

The original altar of incense is described in detail in Exodus 30:1–10.

> Moreover, you shall make an altar as a place for burning incense; you shall make it of acacia wood. Its length shall be a cubit, and its width a cubit, it shall be square, and its height shall be two cubits; its horns shall be of one piece with it. You shall overlay it with pure gold, its top and its sides all around, and its horns; and you shall make a gold molding all around for it. You shall make two gold rings for it under its molding; you shall make them on its two side walls—on opposite sides—and they shall be holders for poles with which to carry it. You shall make the poles of acacia wood and overlay them with gold. You shall put this altar in front of the veil that is near the ark of the testimony, in front of the mercy seat that is over the ark of the testimony, where I will meet with you. Aaron shall burn fragrant incense on it; he shall burn it every morning when he trims the lamps. When Aaron trims the lamps at twilight, he shall burn incense. There shall be perpetual incense before the Lord throughout your generations. You shall not offer any strange incense on this altar, or burnt offering or meal offering; and you shall not pour out a drink offering on it. Aaron shall make atonement on its horns once a year; he shall make atonement on it with the blood of the

sin offering of atonement once a year throughout your generations. It
is most holy to the Lord.

As noted in the discussion of 8:4–5 in chapter 18 of this volume, the
incense altar was located in front of the veil that separated the Holy of
Holies, where God's presence dwelt, from the Holy Place. No one but the
high priest could enter the Holy of Holies and he only on the Day of
Atonement. But the high priest was permitted to enter the Holy Place,
and was commanded to burn incense on the incense altar morning and
evening. While sacrifices were not normally offered on the incense altar,
the high priest was required to offer a sin offering on it once a year. That
illustrates the important biblical truth that atonement provides the basis
for prayer, worship, and communion with God. No one whose sins have
not been atoned for has access to God.

Shockingly, from the altar associated with mercy came words of
judgment. God is a merciful, gracious, compassionate God, yet His "Spirit
shall not strive with man forever" (Gen. 6:3). When this trumpet judgment
occurs, the time for mercy will have passed; the altar of mercy will become an altar of judgment. Sinful men will have finally and completely
rejected God's gracious offer of salvation. In the words of the writer of
Hebrews,

> Anyone who has set aside the Law of Moses dies without mercy on the
> testimony of two or three witnesses. How much severer punishment do
> you think he will deserve who has trampled under foot the Son of God,
> and has regarded as unclean the blood of the covenant by which he
> was sanctified, and has insulted the Spirit of grace? For we know Him
> who said, "Vengeance is Mine, I will repay." And again, "The Lord will
> judge His people." It is a terrifying thing to fall into the hands of the liv-
> ing God. (Heb. 10:28–31)

The voice coming from the surface of the altar between the four
protruding corners explicitly commanded **the sixth angel who had
the trumpet, "Release the four angels who are bound at the great
river Euphrates."** That the **four angels are bound** indicates that they
are demons (cf. 20:1ff.; 2 Pet. 2:4; Jude 6), since holy angels are nowhere
in Scripture said to be bound. Because holy angels always perfectly carry
out God's will, there is no need for Him to restrain them from opposing
His will. God's control over demonic forces is complete—they are bound
or loosed at His command. The perfect tense of the participle translated
bound implies that these four angels were bound in the past with continuing results; they were in a state or condition of bondage until God's
determined time came for them to be released to execute their function
as instruments of divine judgment.

The site of the four angels' imprisonment is familiar—**the great river Euphrates** (cf. Deut. 1:7; Josh. 1:4). Rising from sources near Mount Ararat in Turkey, the Euphrates flows more than seventeen-hundred miles before emptying into the Persian Gulf. It is the longest and most important river in the Middle East, and figures prominently in the Old Testament. It was one of the four rivers into which the river that flowed out of the Garden of Eden divided (Gen. 2:14). It was near the Euphrates that sin began, the first lie was told, the first murder was committed, and the tower of Babel (the origin of an entire complex of false religions that spread across the world) was built. The Euphrates was the eastern boundary of the Promised Land (Gen. 15:18; Ex. 23:31; Deut. 11:24), and Israel's influence extended to the Euphrates during the reigns of David (1 Chron. 18:3) and Solomon (2 Chron. 9:26). The region near the Euphrates was the central location of three world powers that oppressed Israel: Assyria, Babylon, and Medo-Persia. It was on the banks of the Euphrates that Israel endured seventy long, bitter, wearisome years of captivity (cf. Ps. 137:1–4). It is the river over which the enemies of God will cross to engage in the battle of Armageddon (16:12–16).

The use of the definite article suggests that these **four angels** form a specific group. Their precise identity is not revealed, but they may be the demons that controlled the four major world empires of Babylon, Medo-Persia, Greece, and Rome. Daniel 10 provides insight into the warfare between holy angels and the demons that influence individual nations. In verse 13 a holy angel told Daniel that "the prince of the kingdom of Persia was withstanding me for twenty-one days; then behold, Michael, one of the chief princes, came to help me, for I had been left there with the kings of Persia." Then in verse 20 he added, "Do you understand why I came to you? But I shall now return to fight against the prince of Persia; so I am going forth, and behold, the prince of Greece is about to come." Whoever they are, these four powerful fallen angels control a huge demonic army set to wage war against fallen mankind when God releases them to do so. Satanic forces, imagining they are doing the work of their leader the devil and aggressively thwarting the purposes of God, are actually God's servants doing exactly what He wants done.

THE RETURN OF DEATH

And the four angels, who had been prepared for the hour and day and month and year, were released, so that they would kill a third of mankind. The number of the armies of the horsemen was two hundred million; I heard the number of them. And this is how I saw in the vision the horses and those who sat on them: the

riders had breastplates the color of fire and of hyacinth and of brimstone; and the heads of the horses are like the heads of lions; and out of their mouths proceed fire and smoke and brimstone. A third of mankind was killed by these three plagues, by the fire and the smoke and the brimstone which proceeded out of their mouths. For the power of the horses is in their mouths and in their tails; for their tails are like serpents and have heads, and with them they do harm. (9:15–19)

Death, which had taken a holiday under the fifth trumpet (9:5–6), now returns with a vengeance. The **four angels** (the ones bound at the Euphrates River; v. 14) **who had been prepared** by God **for** this exact **hour and day and month and year** (cf. Matt. 24:36) **were released.** At the precise moment in the predetermined year, the month, and the very day and exact hour called for by God's sovereign plan, He will release these four high-ranking demons so that He can use them in His ongoing judgment of the world.

The shocking, terrifying purpose for the release of these demon leaders and their hordes was **so that they would kill a third of mankind** ("those who dwell on the earth"; 8:13). The judgment of the fourth seal killed one quarter of the earth's population (6:8); this additional **third** brings the death toll from these two judgments alone to more than half the earth's pretribulation population. That staggering total does not include those who perished in the other seal and trumpet judgments. The repeated emphasis throughout the trumpet judgments on one-third (cf. 8:7–12) demonstrates convincingly that these are controlled, precise divine judgments and not mere natural disasters.

The terrible slaughter will completely disrupt human society. The problem of disposing of the dead bodies alone will be inconceivable. The sickly stench of decaying corpses will permeate the world, and it will take an enormous effort on the part of the survivors to bury them in mass graves or burn them. How these demons inflict death is specifically revealed in v. 18.

To slaughter well over a billion people will require an unimaginably powerful force. John reported that **the number of the armies of the horsemen was** an astonishing **two hundred million.** This is likely an exact number, or more general specifications, such as those used in 5:11 and 7:9, would have been used. Then, as if anticipating that some skeptical readers would doubt that huge number, John emphatically insisted on the precision of the number, testifying **"I heard the number of them."** In addition to the demons who have roamed the earth throughout history, the "spiritual forces of wickedness in the heavenly places" (Eph. 6:12) recently cast to earth (cf. 9:1; 12:4), and the innumerable bound demons released from the abyss at the sounding of the fifth trumpet comes a new demon army two hundred million strong. The use of the plural **armies** may imply that the attacking force will be divided into four armies, each commanded by one of the formerly bound demons.

Some have suggested that this is the human army referred to in 16:12 and led by "the kings from the east," noting that the Red Chinese army reportedly numbered 200 million during the 1970s. But no reference is made to the size of the army led by the kings of the East. Further, that army arrives on the scene during the sixth bowl judgment, which takes place during the seventh trumpet, not the sixth. Though there may be at that time an existing standing army of **two hundred million,** the impossibility of marshaling, supplying, and transporting such a vast human force all over the globe also argues against this army being a human army. The figurative language used to describe this army's horses suggests that this is a supernatural rather than human force, as does the fact that it is commanded by the four newly released demons.

Before describing the horses, the actual agents of destruction, John briefly described **those who sat on them.** He noted that **the riders had breastplates the color of fire and of hyacinth and of brimstone.** The **color of fire** is red; that of **hyacinth,** dark blue or black like smoke; that of **brimstone,** a sulfurous yellow, describing the rock which, when ignited, produces a burning flame and suffocating gas. Those are the very colors and features of hell (cf. 14:10; 19:20; 20:10; 21:8), and they paint a terrifying picture of God's wrath poured out on the sinful world by these demons. These colors are reminiscent of the destruction of Sodom, Gomorrah, and the nearby cities (Gen. 19:24–28).

Horses are frequently associated with warfare in Scripture (e.g., Ex. 14:9ff.; Deut. 11:4; 20:1; Josh. 11:4; 1 Sam. 13:5; 2 Sam. 1:6; 8:4; Ps. 33:17; Prov. 21:31; Isa. 5:28; Jer. 6:23; Ezek. 23:23–24; 38:4, 15; Dan. 11:40; Hos. 1:7; Joel 2:4; Nah. 3:2–3), but it is clear that these are not actual horses. Using the descriptive language of his vision, John noted that **the heads of the horses** were **like the heads of lions.** Like **lions** these demon forces fiercely, relentlessly, determinedly stalk and slaughter their victims. John noted three ways that the demon horses killed their victims, all of which picture the violent, devastating fury of hell. They incinerated them with fire, and asphyxiated them with **smoke and brimstone.** John saw that the devastating result of this deadly demonic assault was to be that **a third of mankind was killed by these three plagues, by the fire and the smoke and the brimstone which proceeded out of their mouths.**

It may be noted that the word **plagues** will appear frequently in the remainder of Revelation (11:6; 15:1, 6, 8; 16:9, 21; 18:4, 8; 21:9; 22:18) as a term for the destructive final judgments. As if the description he has already given were not frightening enough, John sees more about the deadly power of the demons. He is made aware that not only is the **power of the horses in their mouths,** but also **in their tails.** Having likened the horses' heads to savage lions, John notes that **their tails are like** deadly, venomous **serpents and have heads, and with them they do harm.** The **horse's tails** were not actual **serpents,** because the horses were not actual horses. The horse was anointed with war force, the lion with vicious, deadly power, the serpent with deadly venom. These images describe the supernatural deadliness of this demon force in terms that are commonly understood in the natural realm. Unlike the scorpion stings inflicted during the previous demonic assault (9:5), the snakebites inflicted by this host will be fatal.

THE REACTION OF DEFIANCE

And the rest of mankind, who were not killed by these plagues, did not repent of the works of their hands, so as not to worship demons, and the idols of gold and of silver and of brass and of stone and of wood, which can neither see nor hear nor walk; and they did not repent of their murders nor of their sorceries nor of their immorality nor of their thefts. (9:20–21)

The death of one-third of the earth's remaining population will be the most catastrophic disaster to strike the earth since the Flood. Yet in an amazing display of hardness of heart, **the rest of mankind, who were not killed by these plagues, did not repent.** It is unimaginable that after years of suffering and death under the terrifying judgments from God, coupled with the powerful preaching of the gospel by the 144,000 Jewish evangelists (7:1–8), the two witnesses (11:1–14), an angel in the sky (14:6–7), and other believers (Matt. 24:14), the survivors will still refuse to repent. Like those who rejected Jesus despite seeing His miracles, hearing His powerful preaching, and the preaching of His resurrection, they will "fulfill the word of Isaiah the prophet which he spoke: 'Lord, who has believed our report? And to whom has the arm of the Lord been revealed?' For this reason they could not believe, for Isaiah said again, 'He has blinded their eyes and He hardened their heart, so that they would not see with their eyes and perceive with their heart, and be converted and I heal them'" (John 12:38–40). Having failed to heed the Bible's warning, "Today if you hear His voice, do not harden your hearts" (Heb. 4:7), they will perish (cf. Rev. 16:9, 11). Tragically, they will choose to worship the dragon and the beast (Antichrist) instead of the Lamb (cf. 13:4–8).

As he concludes his account of this amazing vision, John lists five sins representative of the defiance of those who refused to repent. First, they **did not repent of the works of their hands, so as not to worship demons, and the idols of gold and of silver and of brass and of stone and of wood, which can neither see nor hear nor walk** (cf. Deut. 4:28; Pss. 115:5–7; 135:16–17). Ever since the Fall, men have practiced idolatry, worshiping **the works of their hands.** That phrase is used throughout Scripture to refer to idols (cf. Deut. 27:15; 31:29; 2 Kings 19:18; 22:17; 2 Chron. 32:19; 34:25; Ps. 135:15; Isa. 2:8; 17:8; 37:19; Jer. 1:16; 25:6, 7, 14; 32:30; 44:8; Hos. 14:3; Mic. 5:13; Hag. 2:14; Acts 7:41). In ancient times (and even in some cultures today) people actually worshiped **idols of gold and of silver and of brass and of stone and of wood, which can neither see nor hear nor walk** (see God's scornful denunciations of such sinful folly in Ps. 115:1–8; Isa. 40:19–20; 44:8–20; Jer. 10:3–5; Dan. 5:23; cf. Rom. 1:18–32). But to worship any idol or false deity is in fact **to worship demons** (Deut. 32:17; Ps. 106:37). The Septuagint (the Greek translation of the Old Testament) rendering of Psalm 96:5 reads, "All the gods of the peoples are demons." The apostle Paul declared that "the things which the Gentiles sacrifice, they sacrifice to demons" (1 Cor. 10:20). When people worship idols, gods that do not exist, demons who do exist will impersonate those gods and hold those idolaters captive to their demonic power and deception. False religions are not void of the supernatural; they are full of it—because they are the best opportunities for demons to capture souls. They are the fortresses of 2 Corinthians 10:4–5 which must be assaulted with the truth if souls are to be delivered.

At that future point in world history, idolatry, mysticism, spiritism, satanism, and all other forms of false religion will become pandemic, as demons lead people into more wicked and vicious behavior. Unbridled, unrestrained, escalating wickedness will run amuck as never before in human history (cf. 1 Tim. 4:1; 2 Tim. 3:1–5, 13). As a result, in addition to idolatry, violent crimes like **murders** will be rampant. Bereft of any sense of morality, evil, unrepentant people will imitate the demon horde's murderous blood lust. Believers in the true God will no doubt be their prime targets, as they lash out seeking revenge for the disasters God has brought on them.

John describes a third sin his vision revealed will characterize that tragic time as **sorceries,** a Greek word from which the English words "pharmacy" and "pharmaceuticals" derive. Drugs were and still are believed to induce a higher religious state of communion with deities. (For a discussion of such practices, see *Ephesians*, MacArthur New Testament Commentary [Chicago: Moody, 1986], 229–34.) *Pharmakōn* can also refer to poisons, amulets, charms, séances, witchcraft, incantations, magic spells, contacting mediums, or any object that is tied to pagan idolatry to elicit lust or to seduce. People will dive deeper into the satanic trappings of false religion.

The fourth sin from which the unregenerate will refuse to turn away is **immorality.** *Porneia* (**immorality**) is the root word of the English word "pornography." It is a general term describing sexual sin of every variety, including fornication, adultery, rape, and homosexuality. Indescribable sexual perversions will be running rampant in that day.

Finally, people will refuse to repent of **thefts.** Like morality, honesty will be nonexistent, as people compete for the increasingly scarce supplies of food, clothing, water, shelter, and medicines.

Under the influence of the massive demon forces the world will descend into a morass of false religion, murder, sexual perversion, and crime unparalleled in human history. It is sobering to realize that the Lord will one day come "to execute judgment upon all, and to convict all the ungodly of all their ungodly deeds which they have done in an ungodly way, and of all the harsh things which ungodly sinners have spoken against Him" (Jude 15). In light of that coming judgment it is the responsibility of all believers to faithfully proclaim the gospel to unbelievers, thereby "snatching them out of the fire" (Jude 23).

When God Breaks His Silence
(Revelation 10:1–11)

22

I saw another strong angel coming down out of heaven, clothed with a cloud; and the rainbow was upon his head, and his face was like the sun, and his feet like pillars of fire; and he had in his hand a little book which was open. He placed his right foot on the sea and his left on the land; and he cried out with a loud voice, as when a lion roars; and when he had cried out, the seven peals of thunder uttered their voices. When the seven peals of thunder had spoken, I was about to write; and I heard a voice from heaven saying, "Seal up the things which the seven peals of thunder have spoken and do not write them." Then the angel whom I saw standing on the sea and on the land lifted up his right hand to heaven, and swore by Him who lives forever and ever, who created heaven and the things in it, and the earth and the things in it, and the sea and the things in it, that there will be delay no longer, but in the days of the voice of the seventh angel, when he is about to sound, then the mystery of God is finished, as He preached to His servants the prophets. And the voice which I heard from heaven, I heard again speaking with me, and saying, "Go, take the book which is open in the hand of the angel who stands on the sea and on the land." So I went to the angel, telling him to

give me the little book. And he said to me, "Take it and eat it; it will make your stomach bitter, but in your mouth it will be sweet as honey." I took the little book out of the angel's hand and ate it, and in my mouth it was sweet as honey; and when I had eaten it, my stomach was made bitter. And they said to me, "You must prophesy again concerning many peoples and nations and tongues and kings." (10:1–11)

A question that has troubled God's people throughout history is why God has allowed evil in the world. The wicked often appear to prosper. Sin seemingly runs wild and unchecked. Why, people ask, does God not stop all the carnage, corruption, and chaos in the world? Why does He allow His children to suffer? When will divine justice prevail and the righteous be delivered and the wicked punished?

In the midst of his trials Job complained that "the tents of the destroyers prosper, and those who provoke God are secure....Why do the wicked still live, continue on, also become very powerful?" (Job 12:6; 21:7). The psalmists frequently ask why God tolerates evil men. In Psalm 10:1–5 the psalmist asks God,

> Why do You stand afar off, O Lord?
> Why do You hide Yourself in times of trouble?
> In pride the wicked hotly pursue the afflicted;
> Let them be caught in the plots which they have devised.
> For the wicked boasts of his heart's desire,
> And the greedy man curses and spurns the Lord.
> The wicked, in the haughtiness of his countenance, does not seek Him.
> All his thoughts are, "There is no God."
> His ways prosper at all times;
> Your judgments are on high, out of his sight.

"How long, O God, will the adversary revile," lamented Asaph, "and the enemy spurn Your name forever? Why do You withdraw Your hand, even Your right hand?" (Ps. 74:10–11). In another Psalm Asaph pleaded, "O God, do not remain quiet; do not be silent and, O God, do not be still. For behold, Your enemies make an uproar, and those who hate You have exalted themselves" (Ps. 83:1–2). In Psalm 94:3–4 an anonymous psalmist complained to God: "How long shall the wicked, O Lord, how long shall the wicked exult? They pour forth words, they speak arrogantly; all who do wickedness vaunt themselves."

Echoing the cry of the psalmists, Jeremiah prayed,

> Righteous are You, O Lord, that I would plead my case with You;
> Indeed I would discuss matters of justice with You:
> Why has the way of the wicked prospered?

Why are all those who deal in treachery at ease?
You have planted them, they have also taken root;
They grow, they have even produced fruit.
You are near to their lips
But far from their mind.
But You know me, O Lord;
You see me;
And You examine my heart's attitude toward You.
Drag them off like sheep for the slaughter
And set them apart for a day of carnage! (Jer. 12:1–3)

"Your eyes are too pure to approve evil," affirmed Habakkuk, "and You can not look on wickedness with favor. Why," the confused prophet went on to ask, "do You look with favor on those who deal treacherously? Why are You silent when the wicked swallow up those more righteous than they?" (Hab. 1:13). The Tribulation martyrs in heaven cried out to God, "How long, O Lord, holy and true, will You refrain from judging and avenging our blood on those who dwell on the earth?" (Rev. 6:10).

All the pain, sorrow, suffering, and evil in the world cause the godly to long for God to intervene. A day is coming when He will break His silence, a day when all the purposes of God concerning men and the world will be consummated. At that time, the Lord Jesus Christ will return and establish His earthly kingdom. He will rule righteously, with "a rod of iron" (Ps. 2:9), and "the earth will be full of the knowledge of the Lord as the waters cover the sea" (Isa. 11:9). All the atheists, agnostics, and scoffers who mocked the thought that Christ would return (2 Pet. 3:3–4) will be silenced. The millennia of sin, lies, murders, thefts, wars, and the persecution and martyrdom of God's people will be over. Satan and his demon hosts will be bound and cast into the abyss for a thousand years (Rev. 20:1–3), unable any longer to tempt, torment, or accuse believers. The desert will become a blossoming garden (cf. Isa. 35:1; 51:3; Ezek. 36:34–35), people will live long lives (Isa. 65:20), and there will be peace between former enemies at all levels of society—and even in the animal kingdom (Isa. 11:6–8). The ravages of sin—broken hearts, broken relationships, broken marriages, broken families, broken dreams, broken people—will be healed. Sorrow, sadness, mourning, and pain will vanish like the morning mists before the noonday sun (cf. Rev. 7:17; 21:4).

The sounding of the seventh trumpet, which heralds the imminent return and reign of the Lord Jesus Christ, will usher in that long-anticipated day: "Then the seventh angel sounded; and there were loud voices in heaven, saying, 'The kingdom of the world has become the kingdom of our Lord and of His Christ; and He will reign forever and ever'" (11:15). The seventh trumpet will release the seven rapid-fire bowl judgments that immediately precede Christ's return to earth (16:1–21).

But before the seventh trumpet sounds there will be an interlude, which stretches from 10:1 to 11:14, allowing John (and present-day readers) to pause and assimilate the startling truths that have just been revealed to him. The interlude between the sixth and seventh trumpets parallels such interludes in the seal and bowl judgments. Between the sixth and seventh seals came the interlude of chapter 7; between the sixth and seventh bowls comes the brief interlude of 16:15. These interludes encourage God's people in the midst of the fury and horror of divine judgment, and remind them that God is still in sovereign control of all events. During the interludes God comforts His people with the knowledge that He has not forgotten them, and that they will ultimately be victorious.

That is especially true in the longest (in terms of the amount of material devoted to it) of the three interludes, this one between the sixth and seventh trumpets (10:1–11:14). Believers alive during that time will endure the unimaginable horrors of a demon-assaulted, sin-mad world. Like the believers of Malachi's day (cf. Mal. 3:16–17), they will fear being swept away by the divine judgments that are ravaging the earth. God will comfort and reassure them that He has not forgotten them and that He still controls events and protects His own.

Chapter 10 describes the opening events of this interlude preparing for the final trumpet blast. It does so by describing five unusual features: an unusual angel, an unusual act, an unusual answer, an unusual announcement, and an unusual assignment.

AN UNUSUAL ANGEL

I saw another strong angel coming down out of heaven, clothed with a cloud; and the rainbow was upon his head, and his face was like the sun, and his feet like pillars of fire; and he had in his hand a little book which was open. (10:1–2*a*)

As it does throughout Revelation (cf. 4:1; 7:1, 9; 15:5; 18:1; 19:1), *eidon* (**I saw**) marks the beginning of a new vision. Following his vision of the first six trumpets (8:6–9:21), John saw a vision of someone he had heretofore not seen. This **strong angel** is distinct from the seven angels who sound the seven trumpets. Noting the similarities between his description and that of Christ in 1:12–17, and that he, like Christ, descends in a cloud (cf. 1:7), some identify this angel as Jesus Christ. But several factors argue against that identification.

First, the use of *allos* (**another** of the same kind) identifies this angel as one exactly like the previously mentioned trumpet angels. If

Christ were being referred to here, the word *heteros* (another of a different kind) would be expected, since Christ is essentially different from angels. Christ could not be described as an angel exactly like the other angels, since they are created and He is the uncreated, eternal God.

Second, whenever Jesus Christ appears in Revelation John gives Him an unmistakable title. He is called "the faithful witness, the firstborn of the dead, and the ruler of the kings of the earth" (1:5), the son of man (1:13), the first and the last (1:17), the living One (1:18), the Son of God (2:18), "He who is holy, who is true" (3:7), "the Amen, the faithful and true Witness, the Beginning of the creation of God" (3:14), "the Lion that is from the tribe of Judah, the Root of David" (5:5), the Lamb (6:1, 16; 7:17; 8:1), Faithful and True (19:11), the Word of God (19:13), and "King of Kings, and Lord of Lords" (19:16). It is reasonable to assume that if Christ were the angel in view here He would be distinctly identified.

Third, other strong angels, who clearly cannot be identified with Christ, appear in Revelation (5:2; 18:21). Since other angels are so designated, there is no compelling reason to associate that title with Jesus Christ. Further, while the preincarnate Christ appeared in the Old Testament as the Angel of the Lord, the New Testament nowhere refers to Him as an angel.

Fourth, it is inconceivable that Jesus Christ, the Second Person of the Trinity, could make the oath that this angel makes in verses 5 and 6: "Then the angel whom I saw standing on the sea and on the land lifted up his right hand to heaven, and swore by Him who lives forever and ever, who created heaven and the things in it, and the earth and the things in it, and the sea and the things in it." Since He is God, the risen, glorified Lord Jesus Christ would swear by Himself (cf. Heb. 6:13).

Finally, this angel came **down out of heaven** to the earth. To identify him as Christ is to add another coming of Christ to the earth unforeseen elsewhere in Scripture, one that is not in accord with the biblical descriptions of the Second Coming (cf. Matt. 24:30; 25:31; 2 Thess. 1:7–8).

Other angels described in Scripture have the same splendor that this angel has. Ezekiel 28:11–15 describes Lucifer's glorious angelic appearance before his rebellion against God:

> Again the word of the Lord came to me saying,
> "Son of man, take up a lamentation over the king of Tyre and say to him, 'Thus says the Lord God,
> "You had the seal of perfection,
> Full of wisdom and perfect in beauty.
> You were in Eden, the garden of God;
> Every precious stone was your covering:
> The ruby, the topaz and the diamond;
> The beryl, the onyx and the jasper;

> The lapis lazuli, the turquoise and the emerald;
> And the gold, the workmanship of your settings and sockets,
> Was in you.
> On the day that you were created
> They were prepared.
> You were the anointed cherub who covers,
> And I placed you there.
> You were on the holy mountain of God;
> You walked in the midst of the stones of fire.
> You were blameless in your ways
> From the day you were created
> Until unrighteousness was found in you." ' "

Daniel saw a vision of an angel, whom he described as "a certain man dressed in linen, whose waist was girded with a belt of pure gold of Uphaz. His body also was like beryl, his face had the appearance of lightning, his eyes were like flaming torches, his arms and feet like the gleam of polished bronze, and the sound of his words like the sound of a tumult" (Dan. 10:5–6). (That the angel of Daniel's vision is not the preincarnate Christ is evident from the fact that he requires Michael's help to battle demons, v. 13.)

Having introduced this powerful angel, John describes his spectacular attire. He was **clothed with a cloud,** wearing the drapery of the sky over his mighty shoulders. That symbolizes his power, majesty, and glory, and the fact that he comes bringing judgment. Clouds are associated with the second coming of Christ in judgment in 1:7; 14:14–16; Matthew 24:30; Mark 13:26; 14:62; and Luke 21:27.

John also saw a **rainbow upon his head.** *Iris* (**rainbow**) was the Greek goddess who personified the rainbow, and served as a messenger of the gods. In classical Greek *iris* was used to describe any bright halo surrounding another object, such as the circle surrounding the eyes on a peacock's tail, or the iris of an eye (Marvin R. Vincent, *Word Studies in the New Testament* [Reprint; Grand Rapids: Eerdmans, 1946]; 2:477). Here it describes the brilliant, many-colored rainbow around the angel's head that reflects his glorious splendor. The same word was used in 4:3 to describe the rainbow that encircled the throne of God.

While the cloud symbolizes judgment, the rainbow represents God's covenant mercy in the midst of judgment (as it did in 4:3). After the Flood, God gave the rainbow as the sign of His promise never again to destroy the world by water (Gen. 9:12–16). The rainbow with which the angel is crowned will reassure God's people of His mercy in the midst of coming judgments. Malachi 3:16–4:2 presents this same duality of God's covenant promise of mercy to His people in the midst of judgment:

Then those who feared the Lord spoke to one another, and the Lord gave attention and heard it, and a book of remembrance was written before Him for those who fear the Lord and who esteem His name. "They will be Mine," says the Lord of hosts, "on the day that I prepare My own possession, and I will spare them as a man spares his own son who serves him." So you will again distinguish between the righteous and the wicked, between one who serves God and one who does not serve Him. "For behold, the day is coming, burning like a furnace; and all the arrogant and every evildoer will be chaff; and the day that is coming will set them ablaze," says the Lord of hosts, "so that it will leave them neither root nor branch. But for you who fear My name, the sun of righteousness will rise with healing in its wings; and you will go forth and skip about like calves from the stall."

Moving on to describe the angel's appearance, John notes first of all that **his face was like the sun** (cf. 18:1). His brilliant, radiant glory, far surpassing that of Moses (cf. Ex. 34:29–35), lit up the earth **like** the blazing noonday **sun** (cf. 18:1). Yet even that brilliance is but a pale reflection of the Shechinah glory of God, who "dwells in unapproachable light, whom no man has seen or can see" (1 Tim. 6:16), for, as He said to Moses, "You cannot see My face, for no man can see Me and live!" (Ex. 33:20). The same pure glory shone from the face of the exalted Lord Jesus in 1:16.

John next described the angel's **feet** and legs as being **like** firm, stable, immovable **pillars of fire.** That symbolizes his unbending holiness in stamping out his judgment on the earth, pictured here as **fire** that consumes the ungodly (cf. Mal. 4:1).

Some argue that the use of *biblaridion* (**little book**) in verse 2 distinguishes this book from the *biblion* ("book") of 5:1. But that reasoning overlooks the fact that *biblaridion* is the diminutive form of *biblion,* and that *biblion* is also used to refer to the **little book** in 10:8. Rather than distinguishing this book from the one in chapter 5, the diminutive form merely adds a further description of it in this vision. The book needed to be made smaller for the sake of the symbolism of this vision, since John was to eat it. The use of the perfect participle *hēneōgmenon* (**which was open**) emphasizes the idea of the scroll being open; having been opened, it is to remain open. That further identifies it with the now fully unrolled scroll of 5:1. The little book lying open in this unusual angel's hand unveils all the terrors of divine judgment yet to come.

AN UNUSUAL ACT

He placed his right foot on the sea and his left on the land; and he cried out with a loud voice, as when a lion roars; and when he

had cried out, the seven peals of thunder uttered their voices. (10:2b–3)

That the angel put one **foot on the sea** and the other **on the land** shows his massive size from the perspective of John's vision. Since no limitation is given in describing the **sea** and **land,** this action of the angel demonstrates God's sovereign authority to judge the entire earth (cf. 7:2; Ex. 20:4, 11; Ps. 69:34), which He will soon take back from the usurper, Satan. Paul wrote, "The earth is the Lord's, and all it contains" (1 Cor. 10:26). The angel's act also symbolically anticipates the coming judgments of the seventh trumpet and the seven bowls on the whole earth.

In keeping with his huge size, the angel **cried out with a loud voice, as when a lion roars.** His loud cry reflects the power, majesty, and authority of God. The Old Testament prophets also connect a loud, lionlike roaring voice with judgment. Jeremiah predicted that

> The Lord will roar from on high
> And utter His voice from His holy habitation;
> He will roar mightily against His fold.
> He will shout like those who tread the grapes,
> Against all the inhabitants of the earth. (Jer. 25:30)

Hosea wrote that "the Lord ... will roar like a lion; indeed He will roar" (Hos. 11:10), while in Joel's prophecy "the Lord roars from Zion and utters His voice from Jerusalem, and the heavens and the earth tremble" (Joel 3:16). Amos also depicts a loud judgment cry (Amos 1:2; 3:8). This does not mean that the voice of the angel was incoherent yelling. Rather, he was speaking clearly but with great volume to capture attention and cause fear. What the angel actually said is recorded in 10:6.

After the angel **cried out** an amazing thing happened: **the seven peals of thunder uttered their voices. Seven** speaks of completeness, finality, and perfection. **Thunder** is often a harbinger of judgment in Scripture (cf. 8:5; 11:19; 16:18; 1 Sam. 2:10; 2 Sam. 22:14; Ps. 18:13; John 12:28–30). Exodus 9:23 records that "Moses stretched out his staff toward the sky, and the Lord sent thunder and hail, and fire ran down to the earth. And the Lord rained hail on the land of Egypt." In 1 Samuel 7:10 "the Lord thundered with a great thunder on that day against the Philistines and confused them, so that they were routed before Israel." Isaiah wrote, "From the Lord of hosts you will be punished with thunder and earthquake and loud noise" (Isa. 29:6). These seven loud, shattering, powerful voices cry out for vengeance and judgment upon the sinful earth. The **thunder** was separate from the angel's voice and may have represented the voice of God (cf. 1 Sam. 7:10; Ps. 18:13). The text does not say what the **thunder** said, but hearing it certainly would have added to the terror of the scene of judgment (cf. 8:5; 11:19; 16:18).

AN UNUSUAL ANSWER

When the seven peals of thunder had spoken, I was about to write; and I heard a voice from heaven saying, "Seal up the things which the seven peals of thunder have spoken and do not write them." (10:4)

The **seven peals of thunder** did not merely make a loud noise, but communicated information that John **was about to write.** In obedience to God's commands, John had already written much of what he saw in his visions. In chapter 1 John relates that he "was in the Spirit on the Lord's day, and I heard behind me a loud voice like the sound of a trumpet, saying, 'Write in a book what you see, and send it to the seven churches: to Ephesus and to Smyrna and to Pergamum and to Thyatira and to Sardis and to Philadelphia and to Laodicea'" (1:10–11). Later in that chapter the risen, glorified Lord Jesus Christ commanded John, "Write the things which you have seen, and the things which are, and the things which will take place after these things" (1:19). John was also specifically commanded to write each of the letters to the seven churches (2:1, 8, 12, 18; 3:1, 7, 14). Later in Revelation, John would once again be commanded to write what he saw in his visions (14:13; 19:9; 21:5).

But before John could record the message of the seven peals of thunder he **heard a voice from heaven** (cf. v. 8; 11:12; 14:2, 13; 18:4) **saying, "Seal up the things which the seven peals of thunder have spoken and do not write them."** Whether the voice was that of the Father, Jesus Christ, or another angel is not revealed. The command, however, clearly originated with God—the very One who had commanded John to write (cf. 22:10). The reason John was forbidden to record the message of the seven peals of thunder is not revealed. It may be that the judgment they uttered is simply too terrifying to be revealed. Any speculation as to the specific content of their message is pointless; had God wanted it to be known, He would not have forbidden John to write it.

Daniel also was forbidden to record certain elements of his visions. In Daniel 8:26 he was commanded, "The vision of the evenings and mornings which has been told is true; but keep the vision secret, for it pertains to many days in the future." Later he was told, "Go your way, Daniel, for these words are concealed and sealed up until the end time" (Dan. 12:9). The apostle Paul was "caught up into Paradise and heard inexpressible words, which a man is not permitted to speak" (2 Cor. 12:4).

There are some truths that God has chosen not to reveal: "The secret things belong to the Lord our God, but the things revealed belong to us and to our sons forever, that we may observe all the words of this law" (Deut. 29:29); "God thunders with His voice wondrously, doing great things which we cannot comprehend" (Job 37:5). The words of the seven peals of thunder fall into that category. They are the only words in the book of Revelation that are sealed.

An Unusual Announcement

Then the angel whom I saw standing on the sea and on the land lifted up his right hand to heaven, and swore by Him who lives forever and ever, who created heaven and the things in it, and the earth and the things in it, and the sea and the things in it, that there will be delay no longer, but in the days of the voice of the seventh angel, when he is about to sound, then the mystery of God is finished, as He preached to His servants the prophets. (10:5–7)

In a solemn act, **the angel whom** John **saw standing on the sea and on the land** (v. 2) **lifted up his right hand** (the little book was in his left hand; v. 2) **to heaven** (where God dwells)—the standard gesture for taking a solemn vow (cf. Deut. 32:40; Dan. 12:7). To take such a vow is to affirm before God that one is going to speak the truth. That vow indicated that what the angel was about to say was of the utmost importance and truthfulness.

Some suggest that the angel's act violates the prohibition, given by the Lord Jesus Christ in Matthew 5:34–35, against taking oaths: "But I say to you, make no oath at all, either by heaven, for it is the throne of God, or by the earth, for it is the footstool of His feet, or by Jerusalem, for it is the city of the great King." But obviously a perfectly holy being could not do anything contrary to God's commands. The Bible does not forbid the taking of vows, but rather the evasive swearing of oaths with the intent to deceive (as the Scribes and Pharisees did; cf. Matt. 23:16–22). Scripture records the oaths of such godly people as Abraham (Gen. 21:25–31), Isaac (Gen. 26:26–31), David (1 Sam. 20:12–17), and the apostle Paul (Acts 18:18). Further, the Bible records that God Himself has taken oaths (e.g., Gen. 22:16–18; Luke 1:73; Acts 2:30; Heb. 6:13). (For a further discussion of the issue of taking vows, see *James*, MacArthur New Testament Commentary [Chicago: Moody, 1998], 263ff.)

The angel took his vow in the name of **Him who lives forever and ever, who created heaven and the things in it, and the earth**

and the things in it, and the sea and the things in it. That designation of God stresses His eternity (as in 1:18; 4:9, 10; 15:7) and His sovereign power in and over every single thing in His creation. It identifies God as the ultimate cause of all that is. Paul and Barnabas cried out to the crowd at Lystra that sought to deify them, "Men, why are you doing these things? We are also men of the same nature as you, and preach the gospel to you that you should turn from these vain things to a living God, who made the heaven and the earth and the sea and all that is in them" (Acts 14:15). To the pagan Greek philosophers on Mars Hill in Athens Paul declared:

> Men of Athens, I observe that you are very religious in all respects. For while I was passing through and examining the objects of your worship, I also found an altar with this inscription, "TO AN UNKNOWN GOD." Therefore what you worship in ignorance, this I proclaim to you. The God who made the world and all things in it, since He is Lord of heaven and earth, does not dwell in temples made with hands; neither is He served by human hands, as though He needed anything, since He Himself gives to all people life and breath and all things; and He made from one man every nation of mankind to live on all the face of the earth, having determined their appointed times and the boundaries of their habitation. (Acts 17:22–26)

In both instances, Paul identified God to pagan Gentiles as the source and first cause of the created universe. He thus answered the most compelling question in the human through the ages—the question of origins. This identification of God as Creator echoes the praise song of the twenty-four elders recorded in 4:11: "Worthy are You, our Lord and our God, to receive glory and honor and power; for You created all things, and because of Your will they existed, and were created." The comprehensive statement that God **created heaven and the things in it, and the earth and the things in it, and the sea and the things in it** reveals that the scope of God's creative power is all-encompassing (cf. Gen. 1:1; Ex. 20:11; Pss. 33:6; 102:25; 115:15; 124:8; 134:3; 146:5–6; Isa. 37:16; 42:5; Jer. 32:17; 51:15). His purpose for His creation will be fulfilled through judgment, renovation, destruction, and recreation.

The specific content of the angel's oath was **that there will be delay no longer,** answering the question of the martyrs, "How long?" (6:10), and the prayers of the saints in 8:3–5. The phrase **but in the days of the voice of the seventh angel, when he is about to sound** indicates that the judgment of the seventh trumpet is about to come and that it is not a single event, but covers **days**—indicating a period of time. This period includes the seven bowl judgments (16:1–21), which would appear to require some weeks or months to unfold. So the sounding of the seventh trumpet brings the final judgment depicted in the bowls of fury poured out on the earth. The time of God's patience is seen as having ended; the time for the final acts of judgment is seen as being at hand. The time anticipated in the disciples' questions recorded in Matthew 24:3 and Acts 1:6 has come. The prayers of all the saints of all the ages for the consummation of God's kingdom are about to be answered (cf. 6:9–11; Matt. 6:9–10). When the **seventh angel** sounds, "The kingdom of the world [will] become the kingdom of our Lord and of His Christ; and He will reign forever and ever" (11:15).

At that time **the mystery of God** will have been **finished, as He preached to His servants the prophets. Mystery** in Scripture refers to truths God has hidden and will reveal in His time. Paul wrote:

> Now to Him who is able to establish you according to my gospel and the preaching of Jesus Christ, according to the revelation of the mystery which has been kept secret for long ages past, but now is manifested, and by the Scriptures of the prophets, according to the commandment of the eternal God, has been made known to all the nations, leading to obedience of faith. (Rom. 16:25–26)

Mysteries hidden in the past that the New Testament reveals include the "mysteries of the kingdom" (Matt. 13:11), the mystery of Israel's blindness (Rom. 11:25), the mystery of the Rapture (1 Cor. 15:51), the "mystery of lawlessness" (2 Thess. 2:7), the "mystery of Christ" (Eph. 3:4) and of "Christ and the church" (Eph. 5:32), the mystery of Christ in the believer (Col. 1:26–27), and the mystery of the Incarnation (1 Tim. 3:16). Paul saw himself as a "steward" or guardian and dispenser of these great mysteries (1 Cor. 4:1), to "bring to light" these mysteries "which for ages [have] been hidden in God" (Eph. 3:9).

The **mystery of God** (cf. 1 Cor. 2:7; Col. 2:2) of which the angel spoke is that of "the summing up of all things in Christ, things in the heavens and things on the earth" (Eph. 1:10). It is the consummation of God's plan in bringing His glorious kingdom in Christ to fulfillment. It involves the salvation of the elect and their place in His glorious kingdom and all that goes with that. It includes the judgment of men and demons. The **mystery** previously hidden refers to all the unknown details that are revealed from this point to the end of Revelation, when the new heavens and new earth are created. God had **preached** that mystery (without all the details revealed in the New Testament) **to His servants the prophets** in the Old Testament, and men like Daniel, Ezekiel, Isaiah, Jeremiah, Joel, Amos, and Zechariah wrote of end-time events. Much of the detail, however, was hidden and not revealed until the New Testament (for example in Matt. 24, 25, and 2 Thess. 1:5–2:12), and more particularly in the previous chapters of Revelation. To believers living at that time in a world overrun by demons, murder, sexual immorality, drug abuse, thefts, and unparalleled natural disasters, the realization that God's glorious plan is on schedule, the promised kingdom is near, when "the earth will be filled with the knowledge of the glory of the Lord as the waters cover the sea" (Hab. 2:14), will bring great comfort and hope in the midst of judgment.

An Unusual Assignment

And the voice which I heard from heaven, I heard again speaking with me, and saying, "Go, take the book which is open in the hand of the angel who stands on the sea and on the land." So I went to the angel, telling him to give me the little book. And he said to me, "Take it and eat it; it will make your stomach bitter, but in your mouth it will be sweet as honey." I took the little book out of the angel's hand and ate it, and in my mouth it was sweet as honey; and when I had eaten it, my stomach was made bitter. And they said to me, "You must prophesy again concerning many peoples and nations and tongues and kings." (10:8–11)

The voice John had earlier **heard from heaven** (v. 4) forbidding him to record the words of the seven peals of thunder spoke to him again. As he had earlier (cf. 1:17; 4:1; 5:4–5; 7:13–14), John again became an active participant in this vision. He left the place of an observer to become an actor in the drama. The voice said to him, **"Go, take the book which is open in the hand of the angel who stands on the sea and on the land."** This third reference to the location of the angel emphasizes strongly the unusual authority he has over the earth. Then, in a graphic illustration of what a proper response on the part of believers to God's impending judgment should be, John was told, **"Take it and eat it; it will make your stomach bitter, but in your mouth it will be sweet as honey."** The angel knew what John's reaction to this truth would be. Obediently, like Ezekiel before him (Ezek. 2:9–3:3), John in the vision symbolically **took the little book out of the angel's hand and ate it.** As the angel had predicted, in John's **mouth it was sweet as honey;** but **when** he **had eaten it,** his **stomach was made bitter.**

The act of eating the scroll symbolized the absorbing and assimilating of God's Word (cf. Ps. 19:10; Jer. 15:16; Ezek. 3:1–3). When John took in the divine word concerning the remaining judgments as the Lord took possession of the universe, he found the words written on **the little book** both **sweet as honey** and **bitter. Sweet** because John, like all believers, wanted the Lord to act in judgment to take back the earth that is rightfully His and be exalted, honored, and glorified as He deserved. But the realization of the terrible doom awaiting unbelievers turned that initial sweet taste into bitterness.

All who love Jesus Christ can relate to John's ambivalence. Believers long for Christ to return in glory, for Satan to be destroyed, and the glorious kingdom of our Lord to be set up on earth, in which He will rule in universal sovereignty and glory while establishing in the world righteousness, truth, and peace. But they, like Paul (Rom. 9:1–3), mourn bitterly over the judgment of the ungodly.

In keeping with his bittersweet experience, John was told, **"You must prophesy again concerning many peoples and nations and tongues and kings." Again** indicates John was being commissioned a second time (cf. 1:19) to write the rest of the prophecies God was going to give him. What he was about to learn would be more devastating than anything yet revealed—and more glorious. He was to be faithful to his duty to record all the truth he had seen and would soon see. The prophecies John would receive would relate to everyone (summed up in the four people groups of 5:9 and 7:9) everywhere. So John is to warn of all the bitter judgments coming in the seventh trumpet and the seven bowls. As an exile on Patmos (1:9) he had no opportunity to preach to all nations, but he was to write the prophecies and distribute them, so as to warn all people of the bitterness of judgment to come, and of death and hell. Sinners everywhere may know because John recorded these prophecies that, while judgment is presently restrained, a future day is coming when the seventh angel will sound his trumpet and sin's dominion will be broken, the freedom of Satan and his demons will come to an end, godless men will be judged, and believers will be glorified. This chapter presents an interlude of hope tinged with bitterness that reminds all Christians of their evangelistic responsibilities to warn the world of that day.

Two Witnesses (Revelation 11:1–14)

23

Then there was given me a measuring rod like a staff; and some-one said, "Get up and measure the temple of God and the altar, and those who worship in it. Leave out the court which is outside the temple and do not measure it, for it has been given to the nations; and they will tread under foot the holy city for forty-two months. And I will grant authority to my two witnesses, and they will prophesy for twelve hundred and sixty days, clothed in sack-cloth." These are the two olive trees and the two lampstands that stand before the Lord of the earth. And if anyone wants to harm them, fire flows out of their mouth and devours their enemies; so if anyone wants to harm them, he must be killed in this way. These have the power to shut up the sky, so that rain will not fall during the days of their prophesying; and they have power over the waters to turn them into blood, and to strike the earth with every plague, as often as they desire. When they have finished their testimony, the beast that comes up out of the abyss will make war with them, and overcome them and kill them. And their dead bodies will lie in the street of the great city which mys-tically is called Sodom and Egypt, where also their Lord was cru-cified. Those from the peoples and tribes and tongues and nations will look at their dead bodies for three and a half days, and will not permit their dead bodies to be laid in a tomb. And those who dwell on the earth will rejoice over them and celebrate; and they will send gifts to one another, because these two prophets tormented those who dwell on the earth. But after the three and a half days, the breath of life from God came into them, and they stood on their feet; and great fear fell upon those who were watching them. And they heard a loud voice from heaven saying to them, "Come up here." Then they went up into heaven in the cloud, and their enemies watched them. And in that hour there was a great earthquake, and a tenth of the city fell; seven thousand people were killed in the earthquake, and the rest were terrified and gave glory to the God of heaven. The second woe is past; behold, the third woe is coming quickly. (11:1–14)

Throughout history God has faithfully sent His spokesmen to call sinners to repentance. During the long, dark years of Israel's rebellion, "the Lord warned Israel and Judah through all His prophets and every seer, saying, 'Turn from your evil ways and keep My commandments, My statutes according to all the law which I commanded your fathers, and which I sent to you through My servants the prophets'" (2 Kings 17:13). Tragically,

> however, they did not listen, but stiffened their neck like their fathers, who did not believe in the Lord their God. They rejected His statutes and His covenant which He made with their fathers and His warnings with which He warned them. And they followed vanity and became vain, and went after the nations which surrounded them, concerning which the Lord had commanded them not to do like them. (vv. 14–15)

> The Lord, the God of their fathers, sent word to them again and again by His messengers, because He had compassion on His people and on His dwelling place; but they continually mocked the messengers of God, despised His words and scoffed at His prophets, until the wrath of the Lord arose against His people, until there was no remedy. (2 Chron. 36:15–16)

> I sent you all My servants the prophets, again and again, saying, "Oh, do not do this abominable thing which I hate." But they did not listen or incline their ears to turn from their wickedness, so as not to burn sacrifices to other gods. Therefore My wrath and My anger were poured out and burned in the cities of Judah and in the streets of Jerusalem, so they have become a ruin and a desolation as it is this day. (Jer. 44:4–6)

Prophets such as Elijah, Elisha, Isaiah, Jeremiah, Jonah, and the others confronted both wayward Israel and sinful Gentile nations. Jeremiah's experience was typical of the reception that the prophets often received:

> The word that came to Jeremiah concerning all the people of Judah, in the fourth year of Jehoiakim the son of Josiah, king of Judah (that was the first year of Nebuchadnezzar king of Babylon), which Jeremiah the prophet spoke to all the people of Judah and to all the inhabitants of Jerusalem, saying, "From the thirteenth year of Josiah the son of Amon, king of Judah, even to this day, these twenty-three years the word of the Lord has come to me, and I have spoken to you again and again, but you have not listened. And the Lord has sent to you all His servants the prophets again and again, but you have not listened nor inclined your ear to hear, saying, 'Turn now everyone from his evil way and from the evil of your deeds, and dwell on the land which the Lord has given to you and your forefathers forever and ever; and do not go after other gods to serve them and to worship them, and do not provoke Me to anger with the work of your hands, and I will do you no harm.'" (Jer. 25:1–6)

Yet the picture has not been entirely bleak; God has always preserved a believing remnant. To the Romans Paul wrote, "Isaiah cries out concerning Israel, 'Though the number of the sons of Israel be like the sand of the sea, it is the remnant that will be saved'" (Rom. 9:27; cf. Rom. 11:4–5; Isa. 10:20–22; 11:11). God's salvation has come to the remnant of faithful Israel, as well as believing Gentiles, through the faithful preaching of the gospel. In Romans 10:13 Paul declares, "Whoever will call on the name of the Lord will be saved." Then the apostle asks rhetorically, "How then will they call on Him in whom they have not believed? How will they believe in Him whom they have not heard? And how will they hear without a preacher?" (v. 14).

In the New Testament, as in the Old, faithful preachers called for repentance and faith, offering all sinners the hope of forgiveness in Christ. Chief among those preachers was the Lord Jesus Christ Himself (Matt. 4:17; Mark 1:38). The ranks of New Testament preachers also included John the Baptist (Matt. 3:1–2), the Twelve (Matt. 10:5–7; Mark 6:7–12), Peter (Acts 2:14ff.; 3:12ff.), Stephen (Acts 7:1–56), Phillip (Acts 8:12, 35, 40), and the most prolific of them all, the apostle Paul (Acts 13:15ff.; 1 Tim. 2:7; 2 Tim. 1:11).

They in turn passed the truth of the gospel to a next generation of godly preachers, who passed it down to other preachers (cf. 2 Tim. 2:2), such as Timothy, Titus, and the prophets and apostles of the churches, as well as the early church elders and overseers. Along with the many unknown preachers through the ages there have been notable proclaimers of the gospel, such as Clement, Ignatius, Polycarp, Chrysostom, Irenaeus, Wycliff, Huss, Tyndale, Luther, Calvin, Zwingli, Latimer, Knox, Bunyan, Wesley, Whitefield, Maclaren, Edwards, Spurgeon, and a host of others down to the present day.

In the future, during Earth's darkest hour, God will raise up two exceptional and powerful preachers. They will fearlessly proclaim the gospel during the last three and one-half years of the seven-year Tribulation, the period that Jesus called "the great tribulation" (Matt. 24:21; cf. Rev. 7:14). During that time of horrific divine judgments on the earth, of rampaging hordes of demons terrorizing and slaughtering millions of people, and wickedness rampaging unrestrained, their gospel preaching, along with that of the 144,000 Jewish evangelists (7:1–10), the "angel flying in midheaven" (14:6), and the testimonies of other believers alive during that time, will be a final expression of God's grace offered to repentant and believing sinners.

In addition to preaching the gospel, these two preachers will proclaim God's judgment on the wicked world. Their ministry will likely stretch from the midpoint of the Tribulation until just before the sounding of the seventh trumpet. That trumpet will herald the pouring out of the rapid-fire bowl judgments, the battle of Armageddon, and the return of Christ. During that period, they will declare that the disasters befalling the world are the judgments of God. They will participate in fulfilling the words of the Lord Jesus Christ that the "gospel of the kingdom shall be preached in the whole world for a witness to all the nations, and then the end will come" (Matt. 24:14). They will also be used by God to bring salvation to Israel (cf. the discussion of v. 13 below).

But before introducing these two faithful witnesses, John records a fascinating incident in which he himself took part, an incident that sets the stage for the arrival of the two preachers.

THE TEMPLE MEASURED

Then there was given me a measuring rod like a staff; and someone said, "Get up and measure the temple of God and the altar, and those who worship in it. Leave out the court which is outside the temple and do not measure it, for it has been given to the nations; and they will tread under foot the holy city for forty-two months." (11:1–2)

Occasionally in Revelation the apostle John plays an active role in his visions (cf. 1:17; 4:1; 5:4–5; 7:13–14; 10:8–10). After his renewed commission to write the prophecies yet to come in Revelation (10:11), John again became involved in one of the very visions he was recording. He **was . . . given a measuring rod like a staff,** by either the same angel who spoke with him in 10:8 or the strong angel he spoke with in 10:9–11. *Kalamos* (**measuring rod**) refers to a reedlike plant that grew in the Jordan Valley to a height of fifteen to twenty feet. It had a stalk that was hollow and lightweight, yet rigid enough to be used as a walking **staff** (cf. Ezek. 29:6) or to be shaved down into a pen (3 John 13). The stalks, because they were long and lightweight, were ideal for use as measuring rods. In Ezekiel's vision, an angel used such a rod to measure the millennial temple (Ezek. 40:3–43:17).

John was told to **measure the temple of God,** including **the altar, and those who worship in it.** Obviously, this was not an effort to determine its physical dimensions, since none are given, but was conveying some important truth beyond architecture. It could have indicated, as on occasion in the Old Testament, that God sometimes marks things out for destruction (e.g., 2 Sam. 8:2; 2 Kings 21:13; Isa. 28:17; Lam. 2:8; Amos 7:7–9, 17). But John's measuring is better understood as signifying ownership, defining the parameters of God's possessions (cf. 21:15; Zech. 2:1–5). This measuring signified something good, since what was not measured was evil (v. 2). It is best to see it as God's measuring off Israel, symbolized by her temple, for salvation and for His special protection, preservation, and favor. The prophecies yet to be given to John will thus distinguish between God's favor toward Israel and His wrath on the pagan world.

That truth was no doubt very encouraging to John. At the time he wrote Revelation, Israel's future looked bleak. A quarter century earlier, the Romans had brutally suppressed the Jewish revolt of A.D. 66–70, slaughtering over one million Jews, devastating Jerusalem, and burning the temple. But in spite of that massive destruction, "God has not rejected His people whom He foreknew" (Rom. 11:2), and will preserve them until that future day when the believing remnant of the nation will be saved (Rom. 11:4–5, 26; cf. Zech. 12:10–13:1, 8–9).

Naos (**temple**) does not refer to the entire temple complex (cf. v. 2), but to the inner temple, made up of the Holy Place and the Holy of Holies. The **altar** is probably the brazen altar, located outside the inner sanctuary in the courtyard, since that is where **those who worship** in the temple would have gathered. The people were never permitted into the inner temple; only the priests could enter the Holy Place (where the incense altar stood; cf. Luke 1:8–10). The worshipers in John's vision depict a remnant of believing Jews alive during the Tribulation who are worshiping God.

The presence of the temple in this vision of the time of great tribulation brought with it the encouraging realization that the temple, destroyed by the Romans many years before John wrote, would be rebuilt in the future. The Bible mentions five temples. Solomon built the first, Zerubbabel built the second after the exile, Herod built the third (during the time of Christ), and the Lord Himself will build the fifth during the Millennium (Ezek. 40–48; Hag. 2:9; Zech. 6:12–13). The temple John saw in this vision was the fourth temple, which will be built in Jerusalem during the Tribulation (Matt. 24:15; 2 Thess. 2:4), and, along with it, the Jewish sacrificial system will be restored (cf. Dan. 9:27; 12:11).

The Tribulation temple will be built early in the first half of the Tribulation under the patronage and protection of Antichrist. Many orthodox Jews today dream of rebuilding their temple, but its site is now occupied (and in the minds of many Jews desecrated) by the Islamic shrine known as the Dome of the Rock. Because Muslims believe it to be the place from which Muhammad ascended to heaven, it is among the most sacred shrines in the Islamic world. For the Jews to wrest that site away from the Muslims and build their temple there would be unthinkable in today's political climate. But during the Tribulation, under the protection of Antichrist (cf. Dan. 9:24–27), they will be able to rebuild the temple.

The reinstitution of the temple worship will reawaken interest on the part of many Jews in the Messiah. Many will realize that "it is impossible for the blood of bulls and goats to take away sins" (Heb. 10:4). God will use that dissatisfaction to prepare their hearts for the day when He will

> pour out on the house of David and on the inhabitants of Jerusalem, the Spirit of grace and of supplication, so that they will look on Me whom they have pierced; and they will mourn for Him, as one mourns for an only son, and they will weep bitterly over Him like the bitter weeping over a firstborn. In that day there will be great mourning in Jerusalem, like the mourning of Hadadrimmon in the plain of Megiddo. The land will mourn, every family by itself; the family of the house of David by itself and their wives by themselves; the family of the house of Nathan by itself and their wives by themselves; the family of the house of Levi by itself and their wives by themselves; the family of the Shimeites by itself and their wives by themselves; all the families that remain, every family by itself and their wives by themselves. In that day a fountain will be opened for the house of David and for the inhabitants of Jerusalem, for sin and for impurity. (Zech. 12:10–13:1)

But the reawakening of interest in the true Messiah will provoke the insane jealousy of the false one. As more and more Jews return to the temple worship and begin seeking their Messiah, Antichrist will act. At the midpoint of the Tribulation, he will halt their worship, desecrate the temple (the abomination of desolation; Dan. 9:27; 12:11; Matt. 24:15), and set himself up as the only acceptable object of worship (13:15; 2 Thess. 2:4).

John's measuring of the temple symbolized the marking out of the believing Jewish remnant that God will spare from judgment. Zechariah wrote of that coming day:

> "It will come about in all the land,"
> Declares the Lord,
> "That two parts in it will be cut off and perish;
> But the third will be left in it.
> And I will bring the third part through the fire,
> Refine them as silver is refined,
> And test them as gold is tested.
> They will call on My name,
> And I will answer them;
> I will say, 'They are My people,'
> And they will say, 'The Lord is my God.'" (13:8–9)

> Behold, a day is coming for the Lord when the spoil taken from you will be divided among you. For I will gather all the nations against Jerusalem to battle, and the city will be captured, the houses plundered, the women ravished and half of the city exiled, but the rest of the people will not be cut off from the city. Then the Lord will go forth and fight against those nations, as when He fights on a day of battle. In that day His feet will stand on the Mount of Olives, which is in front of Jerusalem on the east; and the Mount of Olives will be split in its middle from east to west by a very large valley, so that half of the mountain will move toward the north and the other half toward the south. You will flee by the valley of My mountains, for the valley of the mountains will reach to Azel; yes, you will flee just as you fled before the earthquake in the days of Uzziah king of Judah. Then the Lord, my God, will come, and all the holy ones with Him! (14:1–5)

John's instructions on measuring the temple included a significant omission. He was commanded, **Leave out the court which is outside the temple and do not measure it.** The reference is to the court of the Gentiles, located outside the courtyard containing the brazen altar. It marked the boundary beyond which Gentiles were forbidden to go. In New Testament times, the Romans had given the Jews the right to execute any Gentile who went beyond the court of the Gentiles. For a Gentile to do so was to defile the temple. In fact, it was the false charge that Paul had brought Gentiles into the temple that sparked the riot that led to his arrest and imprisonment (Acts 21:28–29).

God redeems Gentiles, and will continue to do so during this age and the time of tribulation (5:9; 7:9). But He will reject those unbelieving

Gentiles who have united with Satan and the beast and oppressed His covenant people, Israel. The sharp distinction in this vision between Jews and Gentiles suggests that the church, having earlier been raptured (cf. 3:10), is not present during the Tribulation, because in the church, "there is no distinction between Greek and Jew, circumcised and uncircumcised" (Col. 3:11). In Ephesians, Paul writes that Christ

> is our peace, who made both groups into one and broke down the barrier of the dividing wall, by abolishing in His flesh the enmity, which is the Law of commandments contained in ordinances, so that in Himself He might make the two into one new man, thus establishing peace, and might reconcile them both in one body to God through the cross, by it having put to death the enmity (2:14–16).

By way of explanation, John was told not to measure the outer court because **"it has been given to the nations; and they will tread under foot the holy city for forty-two months."** The **forty-two months** (1,260 days; three and one-half years) correspond to the overtly evil career of Antichrist, which dominates the last half of the Tribulation (13:5). That period will be the culmination of the "times of the Gentiles" (Luke 21:24)—the thousands of years during which Gentile nations have in various ways occupied and oppressed the **holy city** of Jerusalem. Assyria, Babylon, Medo-Persia, Greece, Rome, the Turks, the British, and the Arabs have all ruled Jerusalem, and today Israel's self-rule is fragile and under incessant attack. But the devastating destruction and oppression by the rule of Antichrist and his demonic and human cohorts will surpass all other oppressors.

During this same forty-two-month period, God will shelter many Israelites in a place He has prepared for them in the wilderness (some speculate the rock city of Petra). Revelation 12:6 reads, "Then the woman [Israel] fled into the wilderness where she had a place prepared by God, so that there she would be nourished for one thousand two hundred and sixty days" (cf. v. 14). Many Jews will heed Jesus' warning to flee to safety:

> Therefore when you see the abomination of desolation which was spoken of through Daniel the prophet, standing in the holy place (let the reader understand), then those who are in Judea must flee to the mountains; whoever is on the housetop must not go down to get the things out that are in his house. Whoever is in the field must not turn back to get his cloak. But woe to those who are pregnant and to those who are nursing babies in those days! But pray that your flight will not be in the winter, or on a Sabbath. (Matt. 24:15–20)

The rest, however, who remain (some in Jerusalem; 11:13) will face terrible persecution from the forces of Antichrist. At that time, God will bring salvation to Israel, using the two powerful preachers who will appear in Jerusalem (v. 3), and will also suffer hostility and hatred (vv. 7–8).

At the end of the 1,260 days (forty-two months; three and one-half years), Christ will return (19:11–16), destroy Antichrist and his forces (19:17–21; 2 Thess. 2:8), judge the nations (Matt. 25:31–46), and establish His earthly millennial kingdom (20:1–10). Daniel 12:11–12 indicates that there will be a seventy-five-day gap between the victorious return of Christ and the beginning of the kingdom to take care of the features just mentioned.

So despite the maniacal efforts of Antichrist to destroy Israel, God will measure off Israel to save, preserve, and protect the nation. As Zechariah wrote, two-thirds of Israel will be purged in judgment and the remaining one-third will be saved and enter the glory of Messiah's earthly kingdom (Zech. 13:8–9). Instrumental in their conversion will be a unique, invincible two-man evangelistic team, which John introduces.

THE TWO MESSENGERS

And I will grant authority to my two witnesses, and they will prophesy for twelve hundred and sixty days, clothed in sackcloth." These are the two olive trees and the two lampstands that stand before the Lord of the earth. And if anyone wants to harm them, fire flows out of their mouth and devours their enemies; so if anyone wants to harm them, he must be killed in this way. These have the power to shut up the sky, so that rain will not fall during the days of their prophesying; and they have power over the waters to turn them into blood, and to strike the earth with every plague, as often as they desire. When they have finished their testimony, the beast that comes up out of the abyss will make war with them, and overcome them and kill them. And their dead bodies will lie in the street of the great city which mystically is called Sodom and Egypt, where also their Lord was crucified. Those from the peoples and tribes and tongues and nations will look at their dead bodies for three and a half days, and will not permit their dead bodies to be laid in a tomb. And those who dwell on the earth will rejoice over them and celebrate; and they will send gifts to one another, because these two prophets tormented those who dwell on the earth. But after the three and a half days, the breath of life from God came into them, and they stood on their feet; and great fear fell upon those who were watching them. And they heard a loud voice from heaven saying to them, "Come up here." Then they went up into heaven

in the cloud, and their enemies watched them. And in that hour there was a great earthquake, and a tenth of the city fell; seven thousand people were killed in the earthquake, and the rest were terrified and gave glory to the God of heaven. The second woe is past; behold, the third woe is coming quickly. (11:3–14)

The connection between this vision of the two preachers and the previous passage (vv. 1–2) should be clear. They are among God's unique witnesses who will proclaim His message of judgment during the final stages of the Gentile trampling on Jerusalem—and will preach the gospel so that the Jewish remnant can believe and enjoy God's protection. Seven features of the lives and ministry of these two remarkable and powerful preachers unfold in the text: their duty, attitude, identity, power, death, resurrection, and impact.

THEIR DUTY

And I will grant authority to my two witnesses, and they will prophesy for twelve hundred and sixty days, (11:3*a*)

Once again, the speaker who **will grant authority to** the **two witnesses** is not identified, but it could be only God the Father, or the Lord Jesus Christ. **Witnesses** is the plural form of *martus,* from which the English word *martyr* derives, since so many witnesses of Jesus Christ in the early church paid with their lives. Since it is always used in the New Testament to refer to persons, the two witnesses must be actual people, not movements, as some commentators have held. There are **two witnesses** because the Bible requires the testimony of two people to confirm a fact or verify truth (Deut. 17:6; 19:15; Matt. 18:16; John 8:17; 2 Cor. 13:1; 1 Tim. 5:19; Heb. 10:28).

It will be their responsibility to **prophesy.** Prophecy in the New Testament does not necessarily refer to predicting the future. Its primary meaning is "to speak forth," "to proclaim," or "to preach." (For a discussion of prophecy see *1 Corinthians,* The MacArthur New Testament Commentary [Chicago: Moody, 1984], 302ff.) The two witnesses will proclaim to the world that the disasters occurring during the last half of the Tribulation are the judgments of God. They will warn that God's final outpouring of judgment and eternal hell will follow. At the same time, they will preach the gospel, calling people to repentance and faith in the Lord Jesus Christ. The period of their ministry is **twelve hundred and sixty days,** the last three and one-half years of the Tribulation, when Antichrist's forces oppress the city of Jerusalem (v. 2), and many Jews are sheltered in the wilderness (12:6). The fact that they are actual preachers and not symbols of institutions or movements is indicated by the description of their clothing and behavior which follows.

THEIR ATTITUDE

clothed in sackcloth." (11:3*b*)

   Sackcloth was rough, heavy, coarse cloth worn in ancient times as a symbol of mourning, distress, grief, and humility. Jacob put on sackcloth when he thought Joseph had been killed (Gen. 37:34). David ordered the people to wear sackcloth after the murder of Abner (2 Sam. 3:31) and wore it himself during the plague God sent in response to his sin of numbering the people (1 Chron. 21:16). King Jehoram wore sackcloth during the siege of Samaria (2 Kings 6:30), as did King Hezekiah when Jerusalem was attacked (2 Kings 19:1). Job (Job 16:15), Isaiah (Isa. 20:2), and Daniel (Dan. 9:3) also wore sackcloth.
   The two witnesses will put on sackcloth as an object lesson to express their great sorrow for the wretched and unbelieving world, racked by God's judgments, overrun by demon hordes, and populated by wicked, sinful people who refuse to repent. They will also mourn because of the desecration of the temple, the oppression of Jerusalem, and the ascendancy of Antichrist.

THEIR IDENTITY

These are the two olive trees and the two lampstands that stand before the Lord of the earth. (11:4)

   The question of who the two witnesses will be has intrigued Bible scholars over the years, and numerous possibilities have been suggested. John identifies them merely as **the two olive trees and the two lampstands that stand before the Lord of the earth.** That enigmatic description is drawn from Zechariah 4:1–14:

> Then the angel who was speaking with me returned and roused me, as a man who is awakened from his sleep. He said to me, "What do you see?" And I said, "I see, and behold, a lampstand all of gold with its bowl on the top of it, and its seven lamps on it with seven spouts belonging to each of the lamps which are on the top of it; also two olive trees by it, one on the right side of the bowl and the other on its left side." Then I said to the angel who was speaking with me saying, "What are these,

my lord?" So the angel who was speaking with me answered and said to me, "Do you not know what these are?" And I said, "No, my lord." Then he answered and said to me, "This is the word of the Lord to Zerubbabel saying, 'Not by might nor by power, but by My Spirit,' says the Lord of hosts. 'What are you, O great mountain? Before Zerubbabel you will become a plain; and he will bring forth the top stone with shouts of "Grace, grace to it!"'" Also the word of the Lord came to me, saying, "The hands of Zerubbabel have laid the foundation of this house, and his hands will finish it. Then you will know that the Lord of hosts has sent me to you. For who has despised the day of small things? But these seven will be glad when they see the plumb line in the hand of Zerubbabel —these are the eyes of the Lord which range to and fro throughout the earth." Then I answered and said to him, "What are these two olive trees on the right of the lampstand and on its left?" And I answered the second time and said to him, "What are the two olive branches which are beside the two golden pipes, which empty the golden oil from themselves?" So he answered me, saying, "Do you not know what these are?" And I said, "No, my lord." Then he said, "These are the two anointed ones who are standing by the Lord of the whole earth."

Zechariah's vision had both a near and a far fulfillment. The historical fulfillment was the rebuilding of the post-exilic temple by Joshua the high priest (Zech. 3:1–10), the religious leader, and Zerubbabel, the political leader.

But Zechariah's prophecy also looks forward to the restoration of Israel in the Millennium (cf. Zech. 3:8–10). The **olive trees** and **lampstands** symbolize the light of revival, since olive oil was commonly used in lamps. The connecting of the lamps to the trees is intended to depict a constant, spontaneous, automatic supply of oil flowing from the olive trees into the lamps. That symbolizes the truth that God will not bring salvation blessing from human power, but by the power of the Holy Spirit (cf. Zech. 4:6). Like Joshua and Zerubbabel, the two witnesses will lead a spiritual revival of Israel culminating in the building of a temple. Their preaching will be instrumental in Israel's national conversion (Rev. 11:13; cf. Rom. 11:4–5, 26), and the temple associated with that conversion will be the millennial temple.

While it is impossible to be dogmatic about the specific identity of these two preachers, there are a number of reasons that suggest that they may be Moses and Elijah.

First, the miracles they will perform (destroying their enemies with fire, withholding rain, turning water into blood, and striking the earth with plagues) are similar to the judgments inflicted in the Old Testament by Moses and Elijah for the purpose of stimulating repentance. Elijah called down fire from heaven (2 Kings 1:10, 12) and pronounced a three-and-one-half-year drought on the land (1 Kings 17:1; James 5:17)—

the same length as the drought brought by the two witnesses (Rev. 11:6). Moses turned the waters of the Nile into blood (Ex. 7:17–21) and announced the other plagues on Egypt recorded in Exodus chapters 7–12.

Second, both the Old Testament and Jewish tradition expected Moses and Elijah to return in the future. Malachi 4:5 predicted the return of Elijah, and the Jews believed that God's promise to raise up a prophet like Moses (Deut. 18:15, 18) necessitated his return (cf. John 1:21; 6:14; 7:40). Jesus' statement in Matthew 11:14 that "if you are willing to accept it, John [the Baptist] himself is Elijah who was to come" does not necessarily preclude Elijah's future return. Since the Jews did not accept Jesus, John did not fulfill that prophecy. He came "in the spirit and power of Elijah, to turn the hearts of the fathers back to the children, and the disobedient to the attitude of the righteous, so as to make ready a people prepared for the Lord" (Luke 1:17).

Third, both Moses and Elijah (perhaps representing the Law and the Prophets) appeared with Christ at the Transfiguration, the preview of the Second Coming (Matt. 17:3).

Fourth, both left the earth in unusual ways. Elijah never died, but was transported to heaven in a fiery chariot (2 Kings 2:11–12), and God supernaturally buried Moses' body in a secret location (Deut. 34:5–6; Jude 9). The statement of Hebrews 9:27 that "it is appointed for men to die once and after this comes judgment" does not rule out Moses' return, since there are other rare exceptions to that general statement (such as Lazarus; John 11:14, 38–44).

Since the text does not specifically identify these two preachers, the view defended above, like all other views regarding their identity, must remain speculation.

THEIR POWER

And if anyone wants to harm them, fire flows out of their mouth and devours their enemies; so if anyone wants to harm them, he must be killed in this way. These have the power to shut up the sky, so that rain will not fall during the days of their prophesying; and they have power over the waters to turn them into blood, and to strike the earth with every plague, as often as they desire. (11:5–6)

Whether or not the two witnesses are Moses and Elijah, they will have miraculous power similar to those two Old Testament figures. If they are to have a singular impact on and capture the attention of the world during the terrifying events of the second half of the Tribulation, they will need to be capable of miraculous deeds.

Like Noah before the Flood and Moses before the plagues on Egypt, the two witnesses will fearlessly proclaim God's judgment, wrath, vengeance, and the need for repentance. Because of that, they will be universally hated (cf. vv. 9–10) and many will desire **to harm them** during the days of their preaching. When that harm is attempted, they will react with miraculous power—**fire** will **flow out of their mouth and devour their enemies.** There is no reason to assume that this is not real, literal fire, since God has in the past used fire to incinerate His enemies (Lev. 10:2; Num. 11:1; 16:35; Ps. 106:17–18). Those who wish **to harm** the two preachers **must be killed in this way** because God does not want their preaching stopped until their ministry is complete and will judge with death those who try to halt it.

In both the Old and the New Testaments, God often used miracles to authenticate His messengers. In the Tribulation time when the world is overrun by supernatural demonic activity, false religion, murder, sexual perversion, and rampant wickedness, the supernatural signs performed by the two witnesses will mark them as true prophets of God.

The extent of their great power will be revealed when they demonstrate **power to shut up the sky, so that rain will not fall during the days of their prophesying.** That will greatly intensify the torment people are experiencing. The third trumpet judgment resulted in the poisoning of one-third of the earth's fresh water supply (8:10–11). Added to that, the three-and-one-half-year drought lasting throughout the 1,260 days of their preaching (v. 3; cf. Luke 4:25; James 5:17) brought by the two witnesses will cause widespread devastation of crops and loss of human and animal life through thirst and starvation.

Further, like Moses the two witnesses will **have power over the waters to turn them into blood, and to strike the earth with every plague, as often as they desire.** The havoc these two miracle-working preachers will wreak all over the earth will cause them to be hated and feared. People will no doubt search desperately for a way to destroy them, but to no avail. They will be invulnerable and unstoppable for the duration of their ministry.

THEIR DEATH

When they have finished their testimony, the beast that comes up out of the abyss will make war with them, and overcome them and kill them. And their dead bodies will lie in the street of the great city which mystically is called Sodom and Egypt, where also their Lord was crucified. Those from the peoples and tribes and tongues and nations will look at their dead bodies for three and a

half days, and will not permit their dead bodies to be laid in a tomb. And those who dwell on the earth will rejoice over them and celebrate; and they will send gifts to one another, because these two prophets tormented those who dwell on the earth. (11:7–10)

Sinful men will try desperately and unsuccessfully to get rid of the two witnesses throughout their ministry in a kind of kamikaze effort that results in their own incineration. God, however, will protect them until **they have finished their testimony,** having achieved His purpose during the time He sovereignly determined for their ministry. At the end of that time, **the beast that comes up out of the abyss will make war with them.** This is the first of thirty-six references in Revelation to the **beast** and anticipates the more detailed information about him to come in chapters 13 and 17. He is introduced here with emphasis on his origin. He is said to come **up out of the abyss,** indicating that he is empowered by Satan. Since Satan is depicted as a dragon (12:3, 9), this figure is not Satan. The revelation about him in chapter 13 indicates that the **beast** is a world ruler (often called Antichrist) who imitates the true Christ, rules over the people of the world, and demands their worship (13:1–8). The **abyss** is the prison for certain demons (see the discussion of 9:1–2 in chapter 20 of this volume). Though he is a man, the **beast** is energized by the demonic presence and power coming from the **abyss.** To the great joy and relief of the sinful world, the **beast** (Antichrist) **will** finally **overcome** the two witnesses **and kill them** (cf. his other successful assaults in 12:17; 13:7).

After their deaths, **their dead bodies will** be contemptuously left to **lie** as rotting corpses **in the street of the great city** where they ministered and where they were killed. In the ancient world, exposing an enemy's dead body was the ultimate way of dishonoring and desecrating them. God forbade the Israelites to engage in that practice (Deut. 21:22–23).

The great city is Jerusalem, **mystically** (or better "spiritually") **called Sodom and Egypt** due to its wickedness. Tragically, the city of Jerusalem that was once God's city will be so overrun with evil that it will be like the wicked city of **Sodom** and the evil nation of **Egypt.** The description of Jerusalem as no better than **Sodom** and **Egypt** was to show that the once holy city had become no better than places which were known for their hatred of the true God and His Word. The footnote that the two witnesses will be killed in the city **where also their Lord was crucified** makes the identification of Jerusalem unmistakably clear. That the two witnesses will die in the same city as their Lord suggests that, as it was for Him, that city will be the focal point of their preaching. It also appears that Jerusalem will be the seat of Antichrist's rule (cf. 2 Thess. 2:3–4).

The use of the all-inclusive phrase **peoples and tribes and tongues and nations** (cf. 5:9; 7:9; 10:11) indicates that people around the world **will look at** the **dead bodies** of the two witnesses (on satellite television or some other form of visual media). In a morbid, ghoulish display of contempt and hatred, **for three and a half days** the world **will not permit their dead bodies to be laid in a tomb.** The unrepentant, sin-hardened masses will want to gloat along with their leader, the Antichrist, and glorify him for his victory over the two irritating preachers, who brought the drought and proclaimed the hated gospel.

The deaths of the two witnesses will touch off wild celebrations around the world. Incredibly, **those who dwell on the earth** (a technical term for unbelievers; cf. 6:10; 8:13; 13:8, 12, 14; 14:6; 17:2, 8) will **rejoice over them and celebrate; and they will send gifts to one another, because these two prophets tormented those who dwell on the earth.** Ironically, this is the only mention in Revelation of rejoicing. Sinners will be happy because those who declared to them God's judgments, **tormented** them with miracle power and messages condemning their sin and proclaiming God's impending judgment (vv. 5–7), and called for them to repent are dead. This emotional response graphically reflects the finality of their rejection.

THEIR RESURRECTION

But after the three and a half days, the breath of life from God came into them, and they stood on their feet; and great fear fell upon those who were watching them. And they heard a loud voice from heaven saying to them, "Come up here." Then they went up into heaven in the cloud, and their enemies watched them. (11:11–12)

The partying and gift giving of "Dead Witnesses Day" will be suddenly and dramatically halted by a most shocking event. **After the three and a half days** during which their bodies lay in disgrace on a Jerusalem street, **the breath of life from God** (cf. Gen. 2:7) **came into** the two witnesses, **and they stood on their feet.** Needless to say, **great fear fell upon those who were watching them.** Panic will seize the unregenerate world as their hated and reviled tormentors suddenly spring to life. If this is viewed on television, it will be replayed repeatedly. They no doubt expected the two resurrected witnesses to resume their ministry of preaching and working miracles, but God had other plans.

There came **a loud voice from heaven saying to them, "Come up here."** This is likely the voice of the Lord, who summoned John to heaven in 4:1. **Then** the two preachers **went up into heaven in the cloud,** as **their enemies watched them** in awe. This two-man Rapture will no doubt also be replayed endlessly for the entire world to see. It is reminiscent of the ascension of Elijah (2 Kings 2:11) and the mysterious death and burial of Moses (Deut. 34:5–6).

Some may wonder why the two witnesses were not permitted to preach after their resurrection. But signs and wonders do not make the gospel believable, because "if [unbelievers] do not listen to Moses and the Prophets, neither will they will not be persuaded if someone rises from the dead" (Luke 16:31). After hearing the teaching and observing the miraculous ministry of the Son of God, unbelievers rejected and killed Him.

Their ministry completed, the two ascended with the whole world watching up to God's glorious presence, where they no doubt heard Him say, "Well done, good and faithful slave[s] … enter into the joy of your master" (Matt. 25:21).

THEIR IMPACT

And in that hour there was a great earthquake, and a tenth of the city fell; seven thousand people were killed in the earthquake, and the rest were terrified and gave glory to the God of heaven. (11:13)

Punctuating the resurrection of the two witnesses, **in that hour there was a great earthquake, and a tenth of the city fell; seven thousand people were killed in the earthquake.** The term **people** in the Greek text is literally "names of men." That unusual phrase may indicate that the **seven thousand** who were killed were prominent people, perhaps leaders in Antichrist's world government.

As a result of the violent earthquake, and the astonishing resurrection of the two witnesses, **the rest were terrified and gave glory to the God of heaven. The rest** must refer to inhabitants of Jerusalem, Jews who will come to faith in Christ. Supporting that interpretation is the fact that giving **glory to the God of heaven** is a mark of genuine repentance in Revelation and elsewhere in Scripture (cf. 4:9; 14:7; 16:9; 19:7; Luke 17:18–19; Rom. 4:20). This passage, then, describes the reality of the salvation of Jews in Jerusalem, as God fulfills His pledge of blessing for Israel (Rom. 11:4–5, 26).

On that positive, hopeful note, the interlude ends. For the unbelieving world, however, it ends with the sobering warning that **the second woe is past; behold, the third woe is coming quickly.** The seventh trumpet (**the third woe;** cf. 9:12) will soon sound, bringing with it the final, violent bowl judgments and the return of Christ in glory to set up His kingdom. *Tachu* (**quickly**) means "soon" (cf. Rev. 2:16; 3:11; 22:7, 12, 20) and expresses the imminency of the last **woe,** which is the seven bowl judgments ushered in by the sounding of the seventh trumpet.

The Seventh Trumpet (Revelation 11:15–19)

24

Then the seventh angel sounded; and there were loud voices in heaven, saying, "The kingdom of the world has become the kingdom of our Lord and of His Christ; and He will reign forever and ever." And the twenty-four elders, who sit on their thrones before God, fell on their faces and worshiped God, saying, "We give You thanks, O Lord God, the Almighty, who are and who were, because You have taken Your great power and have begun to reign. And the nations were enraged, and Your wrath came, and the time came for the dead to be judged, and the time to reward Your bond-servants the prophets and the saints and those who fear Your name, the small and the great, and to destroy those who destroy the earth." And the temple of God which is in heaven was opened; and the ark of His covenant appeared in His temple, and there were flashes of lightning and sounds and peals of thunder and an earthquake and a great hailstorm. (11:15–19)

The sounding of the seventh trumpet marks a significant milestone in the book of Revelation. It sets in motion the final events leading up to the return of the Lord Jesus Christ and the establishment of His earthly millennial kingdom. Revelation 10:7 expresses the finality of the seventh trumpet: "In the days of the voice of the seventh angel, when he is about to sound, then the mystery of God is finished, as He preached to His servants the prophets." That mystery is the full revelation of the consummation of God's plan. It was prophesied by the Old Testament preachers, but its fullness was never revealed until the book of Revelation. That the seven bowl judgments, which represent the final outpouring of God's wrath, are included within the seventh trumpet is evident from 15:1: "Then I saw another sign in heaven, great and marvelous, seven angels who had seven plagues, which are the last, because in them the wrath of God is finished." Those "seven plagues" that finish God's wrath are the seven bowl judgments: "Then I heard a loud voice from the temple, saying to the seven angels, 'Go and pour out on the earth the seven bowls of the wrath of God'" (16:1). Since both the seventh trumpet and the seven bowls are said to finish God's wrath, the bowls must be part of the seventh trumpet judgment.

The last three of the seven trumpet judgments are so horrific that they are referred to as woes. In 8:13 John "heard an eagle flying in midheaven, saying with a loud voice, 'Woe, woe, woe to those who dwell on the earth, because of the remaining blasts of the trumpet of the three angels who are about to sound!'" After the sounding of the fifth trumpet John wrote, "The first woe is past; behold, two woes are still coming after these things" (9:12). Before the sounding of the seventh trumpet he added, "The second woe is past; behold, the third woe is coming quickly" (11:14).

The seventh trumpet sets in motion the final consummation of God's redemptive plan for the present universe. During its tenure will come the final fury of the Day of the Lord judgments (16:1–21), the final harvest of judgment on earth (11:18; 16:19), and the Lamb's defeat of the kings of the earth (17:12–18), culminating in the final, climactic triumph of Christ at Armageddon (19:11–21). The sounding of the seventh trumpet signals God's answer to the prayer, "Your kingdom come. Your will be done, on earth as it is in heaven" (Matt. 6:10). That answer sweeps through chapters 12–22 as God finishes His mighty work of reclaiming creation from the usurper, Satan.

It should be noted that although the seventh trumpet is the last in the sequence of the seven trumpet judgments, it is not to be equated with the "last trumpet" to which Paul refers in 1 Corinthians 15:52: "In a moment, in the twinkling of an eye, at the last trumpet; for the trumpet will sound, and the dead will be raised imperishable, and we will be changed" (cf. 1 Thess. 4:16). As indicated above, the seventh trumpet covers an extended period of time, thus distinguishing it from the instantaneous ("in a moment, in the twinkling of an eye") event of the "last trumpet."

Instead of calling for the moment of the Rapture of the church, as the "last trumpet" does, the seventh trumpet calls for prolonged waves of judgment on the ungodly. It does not parallel the trumpet of 1 Corinthians 15:52, but does parallel the trumpet of Joel 2:1–2: "Blow a trumpet in Zion, and sound an alarm on My holy mountain! Let all the inhabitants of the land tremble, for the day of the Lord is coming; surely it is near, a day of darkness and gloom, a day of clouds and thick darkness."

The seventh trumpet not only announces consuming judgment on unbelievers, but also the coronation of the Lord Jesus Christ. In the Old Testament trumpets were frequently sounded at the coronation of a king. During his attempted coup against his father David, "Absalom sent spies throughout all the tribes of Israel, saying, 'As soon as you hear the sound of the trumpet, then you shall say, "Absalom is king in Hebron"'" (2 Sam. 15:10). At the coronation of David's true successor, Solomon, "Zadok the priest . . . took the horn of oil from the tent and anointed Solomon. Then they blew the trumpet, and all the people said, 'Long live King Solomon!'" (1 Kings 1:39). Trumpets also sounded at the coronations of King Jehu (2 Kings 9:13) and King Joash (2 Kings 11:12, 14).

The sounding of the seventh trumpet also marks the end of the interlude that follows the sixth trumpet (10:1–11:14). As noted in previous chapters of this volume, each of the three series of judgments (the seals, trumpets, and bowls) contains an interlude between the sixth and seventh events. Between the sixth and seventh seals came the interlude of chapter 7; between the sixth and seventh bowls will come the brief interlude of 16:15. These respites serve to comfort and encourage believers amid the terrors of God's judgments, reassuring them that He has not forgotten them (cf. Mal. 3:16–4:2).

Although the seventh trumpet sounds in 11:15, the judgments associated with it are not described until chapter 15. Chapters 12–14 are a digression, taking readers back through the Tribulation to the point of the seventh trumpet by a different path. They describe the Tribulation not from God's perspective, but from Satan's. Chapters 4–11 focused on Christ's taking back what is rightfully His by means of the seal and trumpet judgments. Chapters 12–14 focus on the ultimate human usurper, the final Antichrist, whose career spans the same time period as the seal and trumpet judgments.

The scene as the seventh trumpet sounds unfolds in four stages: praise for sovereignty, paroxysms of rage, plan for judgment, and promise of communion.

Praise for Sovereignty

Then the seventh angel sounded; and there were loud voices in heaven, saying, "The kingdom of the world has become the kingdom

**of our Lord and of His Christ; and He will reign forever and ever."
And the twenty-four elders, who sit on their thrones before God, fell
on their faces and worshiped God, saying, "We give You thanks, O
Lord God, the Almighty, who are and who were, because You have
taken Your great power and have begun to reign.** (11:15–17)

Though its effects on earth were delayed (as with the seventh
seal; 8:2–5), there was an immediate response in heaven when **the seventh angel sounded** his trumpet. Expressing exhilaration at what was
about to take place, **there** came **loud voices in heaven saying, "The
kingdom of the world has become the kingdom of our Lord and
of His Christ; and He will reign forever and ever."** That dramatic
proclamation is obviously connected to the effects of the seventh trumpet. There is unrestrained joy that the power of Satan is to be forever broken, and Jesus Christ is to reign supreme as King of kings and Lord of
lords. With the defeat of the usurper, the question of sovereignty over the
world will be forever settled. What Jesus refused to take on Satan's terms
(cf. Luke 4:5–8) He will take on His own terms. Heaven rejoices that the
long rebellion of the world against God the Father and the Lord Jesus
Christ is about to end. The setting up of Christ's long-awaited kingdom is
the apex of redemptive history.

The use of the singular term **kingdom of the world** instead of
the plural "kingdoms" introduces an important truth. All of the world's
diverse national, political, social, cultural, linguistic, and religious groups
are in reality one kingdom under one king. That king is known in Scripture by many names and titles, including the accuser (Rev. 12:10), the
adversary (1 Pet. 5:8), Beelzebul (Matt. 12:24), Belial (2 Cor. 6:15), the
dragon (Rev. 12:3, 7, 9), the "evil one" (John 17:15), the god of this world
(2 Cor. 4:4), the prince of the power of the air (Eph. 2:2), the roaring lion
(1 Pet. 5:8), the ruler of the demons (Mark 3:22), the ruler of this world
(John 12:31), the serpent of old (Rev. 12:9; 20:2), the tempter (1 Thess.
3:5), and, most commonly, the devil (Matt. 4:1) and Satan (1 Tim. 5:15).
Though God scattered this kingdom at the tower of Babel (Gen. 11:1–9),
Satan still rules over the pieces of the once united kingdom. While God
ordains human governments for the well-being of man (Rom. 13:1),
those same governments refuse to submit to Him or acknowledge His
sovereignty (cf. Acts 4:26). They are essentially part of Satan's kingdom.

Jesus affirmed that Satan, though a usurper and not the rightful
king, is the present ruler of the world. In response to those who blasphemously accused Him of being in league with Satan, Jesus asked rhetorically, "If Satan casts out Satan, he is divided against himself; how then will
his kingdom stand?" (Matt. 12:26). Three times in John's gospel Jesus
called Satan "the ruler of this world" (John 12:31; 14:30; 16:11). As he did

at Babel, Satan will rule in the future over a united fallen mankind in one visible kingdom under Antichrist's (the Beast of 13:1–4) leadership.

Satan will not relinquish his kingdom without a struggle. In a desperate and doomed effort to maintain control of the world, God will allow him to overrun it with hordes of demons during the fifth and sixth trumpet judgments (9:1–19). But his efforts will not keep the true King from returning and establishing His earthly kingdom (cf. 19:11–21; 20:1–3, 10). Jesus Christ will return to sit on the throne of His father David (2 Sam. 7:12–16) and take over the whole world from the satanically controlled people who now possess it. This is really the theme of Revelation—the triumph of God over Satan as evil is purged from the world and Christ becomes its holy ruler.

The tense of the verb translated **has become** is what Greek grammarians refer to as a proleptic aorist. It describes a future event that is so certain that it can be spoken of as if it has already taken place. The perspective of the verb tense looks to a point after the action of the seventh trumpet will have run its course. Though this event is future from the point of chronological progress reached in the series, it is so certain that the verb form used views it as an already accomplished fact (cf. Luke 19:9). The timeless heaven rejoices as if the long-anticipated day when Christ will establish His kingdom had already arrived, although some time on earth must elapse before that actually happens. The phrase **the kingdom of our Lord and of His Christ** emphasizes two realities. *Kurios* (**Lord**) usually refers to Jesus throughout the New Testament, while in Revelation it more often refers to God the Father, thus emphasizing their equality of nature. This phrase also describes the kingdom in its broadest sense, looking forward to divine rule over the creation and the new creation. No differentiation is made between the earthly millennial kingdom and the eternal kingdom, as, for example, Paul does in 1 Corinthians 15:24–28. At the end of the thousand years, the millennial kingdom will merge with the eternal kingdom, in which Christ **will reign forever and ever.** Once the reign of Christ begins, it will change form, but never end or be interrupted.

The glorious truth that the Lord Jesus Christ will one day rule the earth permeates the Scriptures. In chapter 15 of Revelation John

> saw something [in heaven] like a sea of glass mixed with fire, and those who had been victorious over the beast and his image and the number of his name, standing on the sea of glass, holding harps of God. And they sang the song of Moses, the bond-servant of God, and the song of the Lamb, saying,
>
> "Great and marvelous are Your works,
> O Lord God, the Almighty;

> Righteous and true are Your ways,
> King of the nations!
> Who will not fear, O Lord, and glorify Your name?
> For You alone are holy;
> For all the nations will come and worship before You,
> For Your righteous acts have been revealed." (vv. 2–4)

That they sang the "song of Moses" (cf. Ex. 15:1–18) indicates that as far back as the Pentateuch Scripture anticipated the moment when the Lord Jesus Christ would become King of the world.

Psalm 2, a messianic passage whose imagery and language permeates this section of Revelation (cf. v. 18; 12:5; 14:1; 16:14; 17:18; 19:15, 19), also predicts the coming earthly reign of Christ:

> But as for Me, I have installed My King
> Upon Zion, My holy mountain.
> I will surely tell of the decree of the Lord:
> He said to Me, "You are My Son,
> Today I have begotten You.
> Ask of Me, and I will surely give the nations as Your inheritance,
> And the very ends of the earth as Your possession.
> You shall break them with a rod of iron,
> You shall shatter them like earthenware." (vv. 6–9)

The prophets also looked forward to that time when the Messiah would establish His earthly reign. Of that glorious day Isaiah wrote,

> Now it will come about that
> In the last days
> The mountain of the house of the Lord
> Will be established as the chief of the mountains,
> And will be raised above the hills;
> And all the nations will stream to it.
> And many peoples will come and say,
> "Come, let us go up to the mountain of the Lord,
> To the house of the God of Jacob;
> That He may teach us concerning His ways
> And that we may walk in His paths."
> For the law will go forth from Zion
> And the word of the Lord from Jerusalem. (Isa. 2:2–3)

Daniel wrote concerning that same day,

> "You [King Nebuchadnezzar] continued looking until a stone was cut out without hands, and it struck the statue on its feet of iron and clay and crushed them. Then the iron, the clay, the bronze, the silver and the

gold were crushed all at the same time and became like chaff from the summer threshing floors; and the wind carried them away so that not a trace of them was found. But the stone that struck the statue became a great mountain and filled the whole earth." (Dan. 2:34–35)

"In the days of those kings the God of heaven will set up a kingdom which will never be destroyed, and that kingdom will not be left for another people; it will crush and put an end to all these kingdoms, but it will itself endure forever. Inasmuch as you saw that a stone was cut out of the mountain without hands and that it crushed the iron, the bronze, the clay, the silver and the gold, the great God has made known to the king what will take place in the future; so the dream is true and its interpretation is trustworthy." (Dan. 2:44–45)

The vaunted empires of world history (the statue) will be shattered by the Messiah's kingdom (the stone cut out without hands); they will crumble to dust and blow away, but His kingdom will last forever. In another vision, recorded in Daniel chapter 7, Daniel

"kept looking in the night visions,
And behold, with the clouds of heaven
One like a Son of Man was coming,
And He came up to the Ancient of Days
And was presented before Him.
And to Him was given dominion,
Glory and a kingdom,
That all the peoples, nations and men of every language
Might serve Him.
His dominion is an everlasting dominion
Which will not pass away;
And His kingdom is one
Which will not be destroyed." (vv. 13–14)

"'But the saints of the Highest One will receive the kingdom and possess the kingdom forever, for all ages to come.' ... The Ancient of Days came and judgment was passed in favor of the saints of the Highest One, and the time arrived when the saints took possession of the kingdom." (vv. 18, 22)

Then the sovereignty, the dominion and the greatness of all the kingdoms under the whole heaven will be given to the people of the saints of the Highest One; His kingdom will be an everlasting kingdom, and all the dominions will serve and obey Him. (v. 27)

Looking forward to Messiah's kingdom Micah wrote,

> And it will come about in the last days
> That the mountain of the house of the Lord
> Will be established as the chief of the mountains.
> It will be raised above the hills,
> And the peoples will stream to it.
> Many nations will come and say,
> "Come and let us go up to the mountain of the Lord
> And to the house of the God of Jacob,
> That He may teach us about His ways
> And that we may walk in His paths."
> For from Zion will go forth the law,
> Even the word of the Lord from Jerusalem.
> And He will judge between many peoples
> And render decisions for mighty, distant nations.
> Then they will hammer their swords into plowshares
> And their spears into pruning hooks;
> Nation will not lift up sword against nation,
> And never again will they train for war. (Mic. 4:1–3)

Summing up a lengthy discussion of the Day of the Lord and the coming of Christ's earthly kingdom Zechariah wrote, "And the Lord will be king over all the earth; in that day the Lord will be the only one, and His name the only one" (Zech. 14:9).

When the angel Gabriel announced the birth of Jesus to Mary he told her that He would someday be the great King over the earth: "And behold, you will conceive in your womb and bear a son, and you shall name Him Jesus. He will be great and will be called the Son of the Most High; and the Lord God will give Him the throne of His father David; and He will reign over the house of Jacob forever, and His kingdom will have no end" (Luke 1:31–33).

The monumental moment in redemptive history anticipated in the Old Testament prophecies, in the announcement of Christ's birth, in the preview of Christ's second coming glory at the Transfiguration, in Christ's teaching and miracles, in the covenant promises to Israel, in the promise to believers that they will reign with Christ, in the promise to the twelve disciples that they would judge the twelve tribes of Israel, and in the promise of Jesus that He would return in glory will be imminent. And that will cause all heaven to praise God for the wonder of His sovereign plan that Christ should reign.

Zeroing in on one particular group in heaven offering praise, John notes that **the twenty-four elders, who sit on their thrones before God, fell on their faces** (cf. 5:8, 14; 7:11; 19:4) **and worshiped God.** As representatives of the glorified, raptured church (see the discussion in chapter 11 of this volume), these elders had been eagerly waiting for Christ to take back the earth from the usurper. Their joyous cry of praise is filled with gratitude: **"We give You thanks, O Lord God, the Almighty, who are and who were, because You have taken Your great power and have begun to reign"** and reflects their exhilaration that their prayers for the kingdom to come (cf. Matt. 6:10) have been answered.

The elders' praise focused on three of God's attributes. *Pantokratōr* (**Almighty**) describes God's sovereign, omnipotent, irresistible power. Nine of its ten New Testament uses are in Revelation (cf. 1:8; 4:8; 15:3; 16:7, 14; 19:6, 15; 21:22). It has the sense of God exercising His all-embracing, all-encompassing will by means of His irresistible power.

The phrase **who are and who were** expresses God's eternity. As the living God (cf. 7:2; Deut. 5:26; Josh. 3:10; 1 Sam. 17:26; 2 Kings 19:4, 16; Pss. 42:2; 84:2; Jer. 10:10; Matt. 16:16; 2 Cor. 3:3; Heb. 12:22), God had no beginning and will have no end. He was in that He has existed from eternity past; He is in that He exists now and for all eternity future. This way of expressing God's eternity was used three times previously in Revelation (1:4, 8; 4:8). Significantly, those three earlier occurrences add the phrase "who is to come." Since the present passage views Christ as already having come and established His kingdom, that phrase is not repeated here (cf. 16:5). Deceptively, the Antichrist is described in similar terms, as Satan attempts to concoct a poor imitation of the eternal King of the universe (17:8).

The elders also praised God for His sovereignty, **because** He had **taken** His **great power and . . . begun to reign.** The perfect tense of the verb translated **You have taken** signifies the permanence of God's sovereign rule. The words of Psalm 24:1, "The earth is the Lord's, and all it contains, the world, and those who dwell in it," are realized as Christ reigns in absolute power and authority over the earth.

All attempts to equate this glorious reign of Christ over the whole earth with any past event or with the church is utterly foreign and contradictory to the clear eschatological teaching of Scripture, including especially this passage. There is no way this text can be fulfilled except by the universal reign of Jesus Christ over the whole earth—as the prophets had for so long predicted.

PAROXYSMS OF RAGE

And the nations were enraged (11:18*a*)

The seventh trumpet vision reveals that, no longer afraid (cf. 6:15–17), **the** impenitent **nations were** defiant and **enraged** at the prospect of Christ's kingdom being established over the whole earth. The verb translated **were enraged** suggests a deep-seated, ongoing hostility.

This was not just a momentary emotional fit of temper but a settled burning resentment against God. Eventually, they will assemble armies to fight God (16:14, 16; 20:8–9). With no desire to repent of sin, angry resentment and hostility against heaven (16:11) will drive the nations to gather for their destruction at Armageddon (cf. Ps. 2:1, 5, 12; Acts 4:24–29).

The divine judgments people will experience during the Tribulation should cause them to turn from their sins and submit to God. Tragically, however, even under such frightening judgment and warnings of eternal hell, most of them will refuse to repent and will instead harden their hearts (cf. Rom. 2:1–10, which teaches that men refuse to repent in spite of God's goodness). They will be like Pharaoh, who kept hardening his heart (Ex. 8:15, 19, 32; 9:7, 34; 1 Sam. 6:6) until the point when God judicially fixed his heart in that hardened condition (Ex. 10:1; 11:10).

The unbelieving world will apparently reach that point at the final outpouring of God's wrath during the events of the seventh trumpet (cf. 16:9, 11). Their rage and hostility toward God will reach a fever pitch, and they will gather to fight against Him at the battle on the plain of Megiddo: "Spirits of demons, performing signs, [will] go out to the kings of the whole world, to gather them together for the war of the great day of God, the Almighty. . . . And they gathered them together to the place which in Hebrew is called Har-Magedon" (16:14, 16). They will by then be beyond the day of grace; there will be no salvation at Armageddon. The world's desperate, last-ditch effort to keep Christ from establishing His kingdom will, of course, fail, and they will be utterly destroyed:

> And I saw the beast and the kings of the earth and their armies assembled to make war against Him who sat on the horse and against His army. And the beast was seized, and with him the false prophet who performed the signs in his presence, by which he deceived those who had received the mark of the beast and those who worshiped his image; these two were thrown alive into the lake of fire which burns with brimstone. And the rest were killed with the sword which came from the mouth of Him who sat on the horse, and all the birds were filled with their flesh. (19:19–21)

Those unbelieving rejecters will have wasted their opportunity to repent at what they acknowledged as God's judgments (cf. 6:15–17). Instead, they will plunge into the depths of hostility and rejection and be punished in eternal hell.

PLAN FOR JUDGMENT

and Your wrath came, and the time came for the dead to be judged, and the time to reward Your bond-servants the prophets and the

saints and those who fear Your name, the small and the great, and to destroy those who destroy the earth. (11:18b)

The coming of God's **wrath**, like the coming of Christ's kingdom (v. 15), is so certain that it can be spoken of as if it had already happened. The verb translated **came** is another proleptic aorist (see the discussion of "has become" in v. 15 above), describing a future event as an already accomplished fact. Those who think that a loving God will not pour out His wrath on them cling to a false and dangerous hope.

That God will one day judge unbelievers is a constant theme of Scripture. Isaiah had much to say concerning that future day:

> Terror and pit and snare
> Confront you, O inhabitant of the earth.
> Then it will be that he who flees the report of disaster will fall
>   into the pit,
> And he who climbs out of the pit will be caught in the snare;
> For the windows above are opened, and the foundations of
>   the earth shake.
> The earth is broken asunder,
> The earth is split through,
> The earth is shaken violently.
> The earth reels to and fro like a drunkard
> And it totters like a shack,
> For its transgression is heavy upon it,
> And it will fall, never to rise again.
> So it will happen in that day,
> That the Lord will punish the host of heaven on high,
> And the kings of the earth on earth.
> They will be gathered together
> Like prisoners in the dungeon,
> And will be confined in prison;
> And after many days they will be punished.
> Then the moon will be abashed and the sun ashamed,
> For the Lord of hosts will reign on Mount Zion and in Jerusalem,
> And His glory will be before His elders. (24:17–23)
>
> Come, my people, enter into your rooms
> And close your doors behind you;
> Hide for a little while
> Until indignation runs its course.
> For behold, the Lord is about to come out from His place
> To punish the inhabitants of the earth for their iniquity;
> And the earth will reveal her bloodshed
> And will no longer cover her slain. (26:20–21)

> Behold, the name of the Lord comes from a remote place;
> Burning is His anger and dense is His smoke;
> His lips are filled with indignation
> And His tongue is like a consuming fire;
> His breath is like an overflowing torrent,
> Which reaches to the neck,
> To shake the nations back and forth in a sieve,
> And to put in the jaws of the peoples the bridle which leads to ruin.
> You will have songs as in the night when you keep the festival,
> And gladness of heart as when one marches to the sound of the flute,
> To go to the mountain of the Lord, to the Rock of Israel.
> And the Lord will cause His voice of authority to be heard,
> And the descending of His arm to be seen in fierce anger,
> And in the flame of a consuming fire
> In cloudburst, downpour and hailstones.
> For at the voice of the Lord Assyria will be terrified,
> When He strikes with the rod.
> And every blow of the rod of punishment,
> Which the Lord will lay on him,
> Will be with the music of tambourines and lyres;
> And in battles, brandishing weapons, He will fight them.
> For Topheth has long been ready,
> Indeed, it has been prepared for the king.
> He has made it deep and large,
> A pyre of fire with plenty of wood;
> The breath of the Lord, like a torrent of brimstone, sets it afire. (30:27–33)

Ezekiel 38–39 depicts the gathering of unbelievers to fight against Christ and His people, Israel, at the battle of Armageddon (It should be noted that another invasion, at the end of the Millennium, is also said to involve Gog and Magog; Rev. 20:8–10. The same names are used to indicate that this later invasion will be similar to the one during the Tribulation.):

> "You will come up against My people Israel like a cloud to cover the land. It will come about in the last days that I shall bring you against My land, in order that the nations may know Me when I shall be sanctified through you before their eyes, O Gog.
>
> 'Thus says the Lord God, "Are you the one of whom I spoke in former days through My servants the prophets of Israel, who prophesied in those days for many years that I would bring you against them? It will come about on that day, when Gog comes against the land of Israel," declares the Lord God, "that My fury will mount up in My anger. In My zeal and in My blazing wrath I declare that on that day there will surely be a great earthquake in the land of Israel. The fish of the sea, the birds of the heavens, the beasts of the field, all the creeping things that

creep on the earth, and all the men who are on the face of the earth will shake at My presence; the mountains also will be thrown down, the steep pathways will collapse and every wall will fall to the ground. I shall call for a sword against him on all My mountains," declares the Lord God. "Every man's sword will be against his brother. With pestilence and with blood I shall enter into judgment with him; and I shall rain on him and on his troops, and on the many peoples who are with him, a torrential rain, with hailstones, fire and brimstone. I shall magnify Myself, sanctify Myself, and make Myself known in the sight of many nations; and they will know that I am the Lord."'" (Ezek. 38:16–23)

The sounding of the seventh trumpet marks the fulfillment of the great judgment event that the prophets foresaw and saints of all ages have longed for (cf. Pss. 3:7; 7:6; 35:1–8; 44:26; 68:1–2). It will be the time when God pours out His wrath on His enemies.

Not only will the seventh trumpet signal the outpouring of God's wrath on earth, it will also indicate that **the time** has come **for the dead to be judged. Time** translates *kairos*, which refers to a season, era, occasion, or event. The establishing of Christ's kingdom will be a fitting time for the dead to be judged. The Great White Throne judgment (20:11–15) is not in view in this passage, as some argue, since that judgment explicitly involves only unbelievers. It is best to see the reference to judgment here as a general reference to all future judgments. The elders in their song make no attempt to separate the different phases of judgment as they are separated in the closing chapters of Revelation. They simply sing of future judgments as though they were one event, in the same way that other Scriptures do not distinguish future judgments from each other (cf. John 5:25, 28–29; Acts 17:31; 24:21).

The judgment will first of all be **the time** for God **to reward** His **bond-servants the prophets and the saints and those who fear His name, the small and the great.** Though the power to serve God in a way worthy of reward is a gift of God's grace, still all through the New Testament believers are encouraged to work in view of those promised rewards. In 22:12 Jesus declared, "Behold, I am coming quickly, and My reward is with Me, to render to every man according to what he has done." To the Corinthians Paul wrote, "Now he who plants and he who waters are one; but each will receive his own reward according to his own labor" (1 Cor. 3:8; cf. Matt. 5:12; 10:41–42; Mark 9:41; Col. 3:24; 2 John 8). The reward promised believers is that they will inherit the kingdom, in both its millennial (Matt. 25:34–40; Mark 10:29–31) and eternal (Rev. 21:7) phases. Believers are also promised crowns, including the crown of righteousness (2 Tim. 4:8), the crown of life (James 1:12; Rev. 2:10), and the crown of glory (1 Pet. 5:4).

The phrase **Your bond-servants the prophets** encompasses

all who have proclaimed God's truth throughout redemptive history, from Moses to the two witnesses (11:3–13). Scripture frequently designates prophets as the Lord's **servants** (e.g., 2 Kings 9:7; Ezra 9:11; Jer. 7:25; Ezek. 38:17; Dan. 9:6; Amos 3:7; Zech. 1:6). The time has come for them to receive "a prophet's reward" (Matt. 10:41). All those faithful men who stood for God in dark days and against opposition will then find their work revealed and rewarded.

Another group to be rewarded is **the saints,** further defined as **those who fear Your name** (cf. Pss. 34:9; 85:9; 103:11; 115:13; 147:11; Eccl. 8:12; Luke 1:50). **Saints** is a common biblical description for the redeemed in both the Old and New Testaments (e.g. 5:8; 8:3–4; Pss. 16:3; 34:9; Dan. 7:18; Matt. 27:52; Acts 9:13; 26:10; Rom. 1:7; 8:27; 12:13; 1 Cor. 6:1–2; 14:33; 16:1; 2 Cor. 1:1; 8:4; Eph. 1:15; 2:19; 6:18; Phil. 4:21–22; Col. 1:2, 4, 12; 1 Thess. 3:13; 2 Thess. 1:10; 1 Tim. 5:10; Philem. 5, 7; Heb. 6:10; Jude 3). All of God's saints, from **the small** to **the great** (an all-inclusive term; cf. 13:16; 19:5, 18; 20:12; Deut. 1:17; 2 Kings 23:2; Job 3:19; Ps. 115:13; Jer. 16:6; Acts 26:22), will receive rewards.

The judgment will also **destroy those who destroy the earth.** That is not a reference to those who pollute the environment, but to those who pollute the earth with their sin. That includes all unbelievers, especially in the context of Revelation the false economic and religious system called Babylon (cf. 19:2), Antichrist and his followers, and Satan himself, the ultimate destroyer. The apostle Paul wrote that the "mystery of lawlessness" (2 Thess. 2:7) is already at work in the church age, but during the Tribulation period it will reach its pinnacle of destructive activity, shredding the very fabric of society in every evil way.

Given stewardship and dominion over the earth (cf. Gen. 1:28), man instead fell into sin and throughout his history has continually corrupted the earth (cf. Rom. 8:19–21). When that corrupting reaches its apex, God will destroy the earth and create a new one (21:1; Isa. 65:17; 66:22; 2 Pet. 3:12–13).

PROMISE OF COMMUNION

And the temple of God which is in heaven was opened; and the ark of His covenant appeared in His temple, and there were flashes of lightning and sounds and peals of thunder and an earthquake and a great hailstorm. (11:19)

Bound up in the seventh trumpet is the promise to believers of unbroken fellowship with God forever. That fellowship is symbolized by the imagery of verse 19. The opening of **the temple of God which is in**

heaven (the place where His presence dwells; cf. chaps. 4, 5) revealed **the ark of His covenant.** The ark symbolizes that the **covenant** God has promised to men is now available in its fullness. In the midst of the fury of His judgment on unbelievers, God, as it were, throws open the Holy of Holies (where the ark was located; Ex. 26:33–34; 2 Chron. 5:7) and draws believers into His presence. That would have been unthinkable in the Old Testament temple, when only the high priest entered the Holy of Holies once a year (Heb. 9:7).

The **ark** symbolizes God's communion with the redeemed because it was there that blood sacrifices were offered to atone for men's sins (Lev. 16:2–16; Heb. 9:3–7). Also, it was from above the ark that God spoke to Moses (Num. 7:89). The ark of the covenant is called in Scripture the ark of testimony (Ex. 25:22), the ark of God (1 Sam. 3:3), and the ark of God's strength (Ps. 132:8). Inside it was "a golden jar holding the manna, and Aaron's rod which budded, and the tables of the covenant" (Heb. 9:4). All that symbolized that God would supply His people, was sovereign over His people, gave His law to His people, and entered into an eternal saving covenant with His people.

But along with the ark in the heavenly temple **there were flashes of lightning and sounds and peals of thunder and an earthquake and a great hailstorm.** Similar events are associated with God's majestic, glorious heavenly throne in 4:5. In 8:5 and 16:17–18 they are associated with judgment. Heaven is the source of vengeance on unbelievers, as well as covenant blessings for the redeemed.

The message of the seventh trumpet is that Jesus Christ is the sovereign King of kings and Lord of lords. He will one day take the rule of the earth away from the usurper, Satan, and from earth's petty human rulers. History is moving inexorably toward its culmination in Christ's earthly reign. When He returns, He will bring covenant blessings to the redeemed, but eternal judgment to those who reject Him.

In the light of that sobering truth, Peter exclaims, "What sort of people ought you to be in holy conduct and godliness" (2 Pet. 3:11)!

Bibliography

Allen, James. *What the Bible Teaches: Revelation*. Kilmarnock, Scotland: John Ritchie Ltd., 1997.

Barclay, William. *The Revelation of John*. Volume One. Philadelphia: Westminster, 1976.

_____. *The Revelation of John*. Volume Two. Philadelphia: Westminster, 1976.

Beasley-Murray, G. R. *The Book of Revelation*. The New Century Bible. London: Oliphants, 1974.

Beckwith, Isbon T. *The Apocalypse of John*. New York: Macmillan, 1919.

Carson, D. A.; Douglas J. Moo; and Leon Morris. *An Introduction to the New Testament*. Grand Rapids: Zondervan, 1992.

Cohen, Gary G. *Understanding Revelation*. Collingswood, N. J.: Christian Beacon Press, 1968.

Criswell, W. A. *Expository Sermons on Revelation*. Grand Rapids: Zondervan, 1969.

Erdman, Charles R. *The Revelation of John*. Reprint. Philadelphia: Westminster, 1966.

Guthrie, Donald. *New Testament Introduction*. Revised Edition. Downers Grove, Ill: InterVarsity, 1990.

Hailey, Homer. *Revelation: An Introduction and Commentary*. Grand Rapids: Baker, 1979.

Hemer, Colin J. *The Letters to the Seven Churches of Asia in Their Local Setting*. Sheffield: JSOT Press, 1986.

Lenski, R. C. H. *The Interpretation of St. John's Revelation*. Minneapolis: Augsburg, 1943.

Morris, Henry M. *The Revelation Record*. Wheaton, Ill.: Tyndale, 1983.

Morris, Leon. *The Revelation of St. John*. The Tyndale New Testament Commentaries. Grand Rapids: Eerdmans, 1969.

Mounce, Robert H. *The Book of Revelation*. The New International Commentary on the New Testament. Grand Rapids: Eerdmans, 1977.

Phillips, John. *Exploring Revelation*. Rev. ed. Chicago: Moody, 1987; reprint, Neptune, N.J.: Loizeaux, 1991.

Pfeiffer, Charles F., and Howard F. Vos. *The Wycliffe Historical Geography of Bible Lands*. Chicago: Moody, 1967.

Ramsay, W. M. *The Letters to the Seven Churches of Asia*. Albany, Oreg.: AGES Software. Reprint of the 1904 edition.

Ryrie, Charles C. *Revelation*. Rev. ed. Everyman's Bible Commentary. Chicago: Moody, 1996.

Seiss, Joseph A. *The Apocalypse*. Reprint. Grand Rapids: Kregel, 1987.

Swete, Henry Barclay. *Commentary on Revelation*. Reprint. Grand Rapids: Kregel, 1977.

Tenney, Merrill C. *Interpreting Revelation*. Grand Rapids: Eerdmans, 1957.

Thomas, Robert L. *Revelation 1–7: An Exegetical Commentary*. Chicago: Moody, 1992.

_____. *Revelation 8–22: An Exegetical Commentary*. Chicago: Moody, 1995.

Trench, Richard C. *Synonyms of the Greek New Testament*. Reprint. Grand Rapids: Eerdmans, 1983.

Vincent, Marvin R. *Word Studies in the Greek New Testament*. Reprint; Grand Rapids: Eerdmans, 1946.

Walvoord, John F. *The Revelation of Jesus Christ*. Chicago: Moody, 1966.

Yamauchi, Edwin M. *New Testament Cities in Western Asia Minor*. Grand Rapids: Baker, 1980.

Indexes

Index of Greek Words

Index of Scripture

Index of Subjects

Moody Press, a ministry of Moody Bible Institute,
is designed for education, evangelization, and edification.
If we may assist you in knowing more about Christ
and the Christian life, please write us without obligation:
Moody Press, c/o MLM, Chicago, Illinois 60610.